ᴄᴓMIGHTIER THAN

"Informative. . . . Reynolds is a rewarding researcher."
—Andrew Delbanco, *New York Times Book Review*

"Compact, clear, and packed with astonishing facts and provocative insights, this book will fascinate everyone from the general reader to the professional historian." —Debby Applegate,
Pulitzer Prize–winning author of
The Most Famous Man in America: The Biography of Henry Ward Beecher

"A valuable and engaging survey of [*Uncle Tom's Cabin's*] genesis and legacy, from its role in antebellum culture and politics to its echoes in milestone films and novels like *The Birth of a Nation, Gone with the Wind,* and *Roots.*" —*Salon*

"You can always count on David Reynolds to surprise and delight, and in his latest work, he does not disappoint. . . . Nothing less than an intellectual feast." —Jay Winik, author of *April 1865* and *The Great Upheaval*

"Clear and informative, *Mightier than the Sword* is a research-driven yet readable history." —Anne Trubek, *Cleveland Plain Dealer*

"Reynolds writes in a clear and readable fashion, and a book that could be didactic and cumbersome is instead easy to read and digest, in part because of the odd and quirky details the author uncovers."
—Marilyn Greenwald, *Pittsburgh Post-Gazette*

"A wonderful history of what may justly be considered America's national epic. . . . A sweeping narrative of the life of a book that continues to engage race, nation, democracy, and Christianity in a contentious drama."
—Joan D. Hedrick, Pulitzer Prize–winning author of
Harriet Beecher Stowe: A Life

"[Reynolds] deftly traces veins of popular culture to emphasize Stowe's continuing influence, thereby revising conventional interpretations."
—J. Kirkpatrick Flack, *East Hampton Star*

"While the author ably describes the influences and experiences that inspired Stowe to write the book, the story of its reception and impact is where Reynolds's work really astounds. American life after 1852, as Reynolds shows, takes place atop a cultural foundation laid by *Uncle Tom's Cabin*."
—Jeff McMillan, *California Literary Review*

"A provocative overview of the life and afterlife of one of American literature's most important texts. . . . A sharp work of cross-disciplinary criticism that gives new power to a diminished novel."
—*Kirkus Reviews*, starred review

"Reynolds is a virtuoso writer. . . . A fitting tribute to the 200th anniversary of Harriet Beecher Stowe's birth."
—*Publishers Weekly*

"All serious students of 19th-century American literature and culture will want to read [*Mightier than the Sword*]."
—*Library Journal*

DAVID S. REYNOLDS

MIGHTIER

❧ THAN THE ❧

SWORD

Uncle Tom's Cabin

and the

Battle for America

W. W. NORTON & COMPANY

New York • London

To my wife,
Suzanne Nalbantian Reynolds

For information about permission to reproduce selections from this book,
write to Permissions, W. W. Norton & Company, Inc.,
500 Fifth Avenue, New York, NY 10110

For information about special discounts for bulk purchases, please contact
W. W. Norton Special Sales at specialsales@wwnorton.com or 800-233-4830

Manufacturing by Courier Westford
Book design by Dana Sloan
Production manager: Anna Oler

Library of Congress Cataloging-in-Publication Data

Reynolds, David S., 1948–
Mightier than the sword : Uncle Tom's Cabin and
the battle for America / David S. Reynolds. — 1st ed.
p. cm.
Includes bibliographical references and index.
ISBN 978-0-393-08132-9 (hardcover)
1. Stowe, Harriet Beecher, 1811–1896. Uncle Tom's cabin.
2. Stowe, Harriet Beecher, 1811–1896—Influence.
3. Didactic fiction, American—History and criticism. I. Title.
PS2954.U6R39 2011
813'.3—dc22
2011000702

ISBN 978-0-393-34235-2 pbk.

W. W. Norton & Company, Inc.
500 Fifth Avenue, New York, N.Y. 10110
www.wwnorton.com

W. W. Norton & Company Ltd.
Castle House, 75/76 Wells Street, London W1T 3QT

1 2 3 4 5 6 7 8 9 0

CONTENTS

INTRODUCTION

O N JANUARY 1, 1863, Harriet Beecher Stowe attended a concert held at the Boston Music Hall in celebration of Abraham Lincoln's expected signing of the Emancipation Proclamation. Of the many galas held in the North that historic day, this one was especially impressive. Among the crowd of three thousand were Emerson, Longfellow, Whittier, Francis Parkman, and Oliver Wendell Holmes.

Two weeks earlier, Stowe had written her friend Charles Sumner, chair of the Senate Foreign Relations Committee, "Everybody I meet in New England says to me with anxious earnestness—*Will* the President stand firm to his Proclamation?" The answer came during intermission at the Music Hall event. A speaker announced that the news had come over the wires that the president had signed the Proclamation, freeing millions of slaves in states disloyal to the Union. The hall erupted with applause, shouts, and handkerchief-waving. Three cheers went up for Lincoln. Three more followed for William Lloyd Garrison, mingled with hisses from those still hostile to the controversial abolitionist.

When Stowe was spotted in the balcony, a new chant swept through the hall: "Harriet Beecher Stowe! Harriet Beecher Stowe! Harriet Beecher

Stowe!" Urged forward by those seated near her, her bonnet toppling off, she went to the railing, bowing and waving to the throng.

At that moment, the plain fifty-one-year-old Stowe, just five feet tall, was the most famous woman in America. Her wide-set eyes, which normally had a distant dreaminess, sparkled with emotion as tears flowed down her cheeks and her ample mouth broadened into a grin. Her aquiline nose gave her face a firm dignity that was softened by her gently sloped forehead and round cheeks framed by graying curls.

The crowd, convinced that she had helped make this moment possible, was responding to the torrent of energy unleashed by Stowe's anti-slavery best-seller *Uncle Tom's Cabin; or, Life among the Lowly,* published a decade earlier.

Did Lincoln feel this way about the novel, too? A month before the Boston event, Stowe had visited him in the White House to urge him to sign the Proclamation. His alleged greeting of her—"Is this the little woman who made this great war?"—is the most famous statement ever made about *Uncle Tom's Cabin.* Whether he actually said it is moot. In his era, many claimed that Stowe had brought on the Civil War.

Surprisingly, this crucial topic has never been discussed in detail. Although the novel is vaguely associated in most people's minds with the Civil War, several modern commentators have tried to argue that it had only a minimal influence on the political decisions leading to the war. One maintains that "its political effect" was "negligible." Another writes that "sentiment limited the degree to which [the novel] could effect radical political change." A third asks, "In what sense does a novel have the power to move a nation to battle?"

Such remarks ignore the tremendous authority of public opinion in America, which Tocqueville regarded as stronger than the government— an idea Lincoln echoed when he declared, "Our government rests in public opinion. Whoever can change public opinion can change the government." In his debates against Stephen Douglas, Lincoln emphasized, "Public sentiment is everything. . . . He who moulds public sentiment is greater than he who makes statutes."

No book in American history molded public opinion more power-fully than *Uncle Tom's Cabin*. Published in 1852, it set sales records for American fiction. An international sensation, it was soon translated into many languages. The Boston preacher Theodore Parker declared that it was "more an event than a book, and has excited more attention than any book since the invention of printing." Henry James noted that Stowe's novel was, "for an immense number of people, much less a book than a state of vision, of feeling and of consciousness in which they didn't sit and read and appraise and pass the time, but walked and talked and laughed and cried."

James was right. Sympathetic readers of *Uncle Tom's Cabin* were thrilled when the fugitive slave Eliza Harris carried her child across the ice floes of the Ohio River and when her husband George fought off slave catchers in a rocky pass. They cried over the death of the angelic little Eva and were horrified by the fatal lashing of Uncle Tom, the gentle, strong enslaved black man. They guffawed at the impish slave girl Topsy and shed thankful tears when she embraced Christianity. They sneered at the selfish hypochondriac Marie St. Clare and loathed the cruel slaveowner Simon Legree. They were fascinated by the brooding, Byronic Augustine St. Clare and were appalled by the stories of sexual exploitation involving enslaved women like Prue and Cassy.

Recent decades have witnessed a remarkable upsurge of interest in *Uncle Tom's Cabin*, but much remains to be said about the novel's place in history and what came together in Stowe's life and time to bring her to write it. The time is ripe for a thoroughgoing reassessment that gives the full measure of the novel's rich cultural background and its enormous impact.

This book shows that *Uncle Tom's Cabin* helped redefine American democracy on a more egalitarian basis. It helped rectify social injustice by affirming fairness and empowerment for marginalized or oppressed groups. The first three chapters reveal how the novel's unprecedented popularity can be explained by the fact that it absorbed images from virtually every realm of culture—religion, reform, temperance tracts,

antislavery writings, sensational pulp fiction, and popular performance—
and brought these elements together in memorable characters and two
compelling antislavery plotlines: the Northern one, involving the escape
of the fugitive slaves Eliza and George Harris with their son Harry, and
the Southern one, tracing the painful separation of Uncle Tom from his
family when he is sold into the Deep South.

Stowe's immersion in popular culture set the stage for her affecting
novel. Other writers of the day, such as Melville, Hawthorne, and Whitman, were also responsive to popular images but transformed them into
ambiguous symbols and characters. Stowe, in contrast, channeled them
into a realistic human narrative with a crystal-clear social point: slavery
was evil, and so were the political and economic institutions that supported it.

As chapter 4 will show, *Uncle Tom's Cabin* directly shaped the political
debates over slavery. Its dramatic portrait of the evils of slavery intensified the public sentiment behind the rise of Lincoln and the Republicans,
while it caused a reactionary surge of proslavery feeling in the South,
exacerbating the tensions that led to the Civil War. By the eve of the war,
as one Southerner of the day noted, the novel "had given birth to a horror
against slavery in the Northern mind which all the politicians could never
have created" and "did more than all else to array the North and South in
compact masses against each other."

As will be seen in chapters 5 and 6, the novel continued to provoke
controversy through Reconstruction and beyond. Its influence was greatly
amplified by tie-ins—popular plays and a host of merchandise known
as Tomitudes. Whether play or novel, *Uncle Tom's Cabin* was important
chiefly as an agent of emancipation. It gave impetus to revolutions in Russia, China, Brazil, Cuba, and elsewhere. In America, the novel remained
particularly inspiring for African-Americans and progressive whites. Most
recent commentators on the Uncle Tom plays and films have emphasized
their dissemination of racial stereotypes. Actually, though, Stowe's novel
and its offshoots gave off unconventional, even revolutionary racial messages that seemed truly dangerous to white supremacists of the Jim Crow

era, which lasted from the 1870s to the early 1960s. Most notably, the popular Southern author Thomas Dixon attended an Uncle Tom play in 1901 and was so infuriated by what he regarded as its endorsement of black power that he wrote bitterly of Stowe, "A little Yankee woman wrote a book. The single act of that woman's will caused the war, killed a million men, desolated and ruined the South, and changed the history of the world." Dixon responded to *Uncle Tom's Cabin* by penning virulently racist, anti-Stowe novels that became massive best-sellers. One, *The Clansman*, was the basis of D. W. Griffith's adeptly made yet thematically abhorrent film *The Birth of a Nation* (1915).

Even as the white supremacists were gaining a wide audience, *Uncle Tom's Cabin* and its spin-offs helped keep alive Stowe's progressive message. Stowe found ardent defenders among African-American leaders such as W. E. B. Du Bois and his fellow reformers in the NAACP. Over time, Stowe's vision gained ascendancy in America. During the civil rights movement—despite the condemnation of being an "Uncle Tom"—those who acted in the spirit of Stowe's firm-principled, nonviolent Uncle Tom, like Martin Luther King Jr., Rosa Parks, and thousands who participated in sit-ins and marches, proved the most successful in bringing about progressive change.

That an author could have so great an impact as Harriet Beecher Stowe seems unlikely, if not impossible—especially for a time when women had no political voice and in a nation about which the Scottish writer Sydney Smith had sniffed in 1820, "In the four quarters of the globe, who reads an American book? Or goes to an American play?"

Stowe herself had a simple explanation of her success: God wrote *Uncle Tom's Cabin*. After the novel became a best-seller and her brother Edward warned her not to become vain about its popularity, she told a friend, "Dear soul, he need not be troubled. He doesn't know that I did not write that book." Her friend exclaimed, "*What!* You did not write 'Uncle Tom'?" Stowe replied, "No. I only put down what I saw. . . . It all came before me in visions, one after another, and I put them down in words."

Stowe's claims about the divine authorship of *Uncle Tom's Cabin* may have satisfied her own pious yearnings, but they raise questions about the actual background and repercussions of the most influential book ever written by an American. The issues at the heart of *Uncle Tom's Cabin*—race, religion, gender, law, morality, democracy—are just as vital today as they were in Stowe's time. Exploring such questions gets to the very heart of the national experience.

⚬ MIGHTIER THAN THE SWORD ⚬

1

THE GOSPEL
ACCORDING TO STOWE

HARRIET BEECHER STOWE had written fiction before, but she had never claimed that it came from divine inspiration. *Uncle Tom's Cabin* was to be a special book for her and for America. Countless readers in the nineteenth century would have accepted Stowe's declaration of such holy stimulus. Not only did the novel spur the sale of Bibles throughout the world, but it was widely seen as a new Bible, with its ideal expression of religion for the era. It offered a religion of love to all—blacks and whites, the enslaved and the free, the poor and the rich, children as well as adults. This democratic redefinition of Christianity was groundbreaking in a time when most mainstream American churches either tolerated slavery or, in the South, actively supported it. *Uncle Tom's Cabin* proved that slavery violated the all-embracing gospel that Stowe announced to the world.

She arrived at this egalitarian religion after a long struggle against the Calvinistic doctrines of her New England heritage. She was part of a prominent religious family that did more to undermine Calvinist orthodoxy, with its grim view of God and the afterlife, than any other in America. Her father, Lyman Beecher, had felt a calling to the ministry.

Lyman Beecher

Born in New Haven in 1775 and educated at the Yale Divinity School, he was married in 1799 to the Guilford, Connecticut, native Roxana Foote, a bright, gentle woman talented in needlework, embroidery, and painting miniatures. The newlyweds relocated that year to East Hampton, New York, a rural town on eastern Long Island where Lyman served as a Presbyterian pastor for a decade before moving to the First Congregational Church in Litchfield, Connecticut, in 1810. Harriet Elizabeth Beecher was born there on June 14, 1811, the seventh of Lyman and Roxana's nine children—Catharine, William, Edward, Mary, the first Harriet (who died after one month), George, and then Harriet Elizabeth, followed by Henry Ward and Charles.

Lyman Beecher came to be recognized as one of New England's leading clergymen. An earnest preacher and social reformer, he was also an avid fisherman and had a mischievous, rollicking side. His conversations were peppered with colloquialisms and Yankee wit. Most religious people at the time frowned on light reading, but he loved Sir Walter Scott's novels and even had a weakness for Byron, whom he considered hell-bound yet upon whose death he wrote, "Oh, I'm sorry that Byron is dead. I did hope that he would live to do something for Christ. What a harp he might have swept!" Harriet later recalled her father coming home after evening services and unwinding merrily: "He was lively, sparkling, jocose, full of anecdote and incident, and loved to have us all about him, and to indulge in a good laugh." He played Scottish tunes on the fiddle and showed his children shuffle steps he had once learned at barn dances. Harriet, whose signature novel bubbled with humor even as it delivered serious messages, was the product of a home where being pious didn't mean you couldn't have fun.

Roxana was the moral guardian of the Litchfield home. She did not carp at her children or police their activities but had a purity and steadfast piety that served as a natural restraint on the often rambunctious household. Her untimely death from tuberculosis in 1816 did not diminish her saintly presence in the family. Harriet, though she did not remember her mother clearly, recalled her as a calm, healthy-minded woman who even after her death "had more influence in moulding her family, in deterring from evil and exciting to good, than the living presence of many mothers." Henry Ward Beecher later declared that although he was only three when his mother died, "no devout Catholic ever saw so much in the Virgin Mary as I have seen in my mother, who has been a presence to me ever since I can remember."

This association of motherhood with religion permeates Stowe's *Uncle Tom's Cabin*. The spiritually tormented slaveholder Augustine St. Clare is relieved by recollections of his pious mother. As he dies, he exclaims, "Mother!"—presumably on the verge of reuniting with her. Even the whip-wielding plantation owner Simon Legree, despite his wickedness, has his conscience pricked by memories of the mother who had prophetically warned him about the ill results of wayward living. Then there is the gallery of good mothers in the novel—Mary Bird, Rachel Halliday,

Chloe, and Eliza Harris—who are committed to both family and religion. The selfish Marie St. Clare helps define religion and motherhood by her failure in both areas.

When Lyman remarried a year after Roxana's death, the Beecher home gained another pious mother. The blue-eyed, auburn-haired Harriet Porter, whom Lyman had met while visiting Boston, never reached saintly status among Roxana's children, who respected her but found her cold and exacting. She and Lyman had four children: Frederick, Isabella, Thomas, and James. Her strictness may have contributed to the characterization of Ophelia in *Uncle Tom's Cabin* (though the main prototype for that scold of shiftlessness seems to have been the family fussbudget Aunt Esther Beecher, Lyman's spinster stepsister).

Lyman Beecher family c. 1859
Standing from the left: Thomas, William, Edward, Charles, Henry.
Seated from the left: Isabella, Catharine, Lyman, Mary, Harriet.
Superimposed in the foreground: James (left) and George (right).

The Beecher children were a varied mix of personalities. The oldest, Catharine, was a cheerful chatterbox and a rather lax student who once admitted to cheating on exams—not what we would expect of one destined to be a pioneer in women's education. Also anomalous was Henry, a tongue-tied, seemingly slow child who later became the century's most fluent preacher. Charles, full of pranks, received more than his share of spankings. George showed an intensity that did not bode well for his development into an introspective man who would die from a self-inflicted gunshot wound.

Harriet, a bookworm, had a creative spark early on. "Harriet is a great genius," her father boasted to his brother-in-law when she was eight. "I would give a hundred dollars if she was a boy & Henry a girl—She is as odd—as she is intelligent & studious." As a child, she displayed the dreamy, abstracted air she had throughout her life. Though only a mediocre student (mathematics was her weak subject), she had a driving curiosity and an inner fire. She loved going up to the garret of the Litchfield home and rummaging through barrels of sermons and books. She was bored by the musty theological tracts she found there but was delighted when she dug up entertaining fare such as *The Arabian Nights*, *The Tempest*, and *Don Quixote*, as well as historical works like *Magnalia Christi Americana*, the collection of New England sketches by the seventeenth-century Puritan minister Cotton Mather. "What wonderful stories those!" she said of Mather's book. "Stories, too, about my own country. Stories that made me feel the very ground I trod on to be consecrated by some special dealing of God's providence."

She felt that she had inherited a fiercely independent, militant spirit from her Puritan forebears. As she wrote, "The heroic element was strong in me, having come down by ordinary generation from a long line of Puritan ancestry, and just now it made me long to do something, I knew not what: to fight for my country, or to make some declaration on my own account"—a statement echoed later in her historical novels *Poganuc People*, whose heroine also is said to have a powerful "heroic element" that came from "a line of Puritan ancestry," and *The Minister's Wooing*, whose protagonist, Mary Scudder, possesses, in Stowe's words, "the true Puritan seed of heroism, never absent from the souls of true New England women."

It is telling that Stowe put herself squarely in the tradition of American Puritanism, which she associated with radical independence and rebellion against authority. Her stance invites us to reassess the notion, popular among recent cultural scholars, that Puritanism did not generate subversive agitation but instead melded with a benign faith in the glorious promise of America. Actually, Puritanism in the North fueled radical individualism and progressive movements against slavery, intemperance, and other social ills. Proslavery Southerners regularly branded New Englanders as law-defying Puritans who endorsed all kinds of disruptive "isms"—most dangerously, abolitionism. Many reformers in the North, for their part, felt energized by the Puritan spirit. Emerson in his lecture "New England Reformers" declared that the "fertile forms of antinomianism among the elder puritans seemed to have their match in the plenty of the new harvest of reform." A reform-minded Northern journalist went so far as to say, "Puritanism and nothing else can save this country. . . . The Puritan element, which demands religious freedom . . . is the nourisher of that civil liberty which releases the body from secular despotism."

No family manifested the Puritan zeal for reform more strongly than the Beechers, a family of social crusaders. Lyman Beecher was one of the founders of the so-called Benevolent Empire—the national network of reform groups dedicated to promoting temperance, missions, Sunday schools, tracts, and Bibles. Most of the thirteen children he sired by two wives were ardent social reformers. Several of them—notably Harriet, Henry Ward, Edward, and Isabella—were involved in a number of reform movements simultaneously.

Even as the Beechers applied their Puritan energy toward changing society, they reformed Puritanism itself by challenging some of its harshest creeds. They helped cause a sea change in religion, away from orthodox Calvinism toward the more hopeful gospel that has defined mainstream American Christianity ever since.

The Beechers, like all nineteenth-century-American Protestants, lived in the shadow of Jonathan Edwards, the eighteenth-century clergyman who had brought both emotional intensity and intellectual rigor to Puritan Calvinism. Lyman Beecher declared, "I have been steeped in Jonathan Edwards for more than forty years." Edwards had constructed an intricate defense of the Calvinist tenets of predestination (God determines our fate), total depravity (we are born in sin), and religious emotion. Edwards argued that God sent most humans to hell because He was furious at mankind as a result of Adam's disobedience in the Garden of Eden. Sinners fully deserved damnation. God devoted his immense strength to keeping hell's tortures alive for them for eternity. "The wrath of God burns against them," Edwards declared, "their damnation does not slumber; the pit is prepared, the fire is made ready, the furnace is now hot, ready to receive them; the flames do now rage and glow."

Yet God had sent His son Jesus Christ into the world to offer grace to a chosen few—the elect or the saints—who grasped their special status through the regenerative moment of conversion. The conversion experience was shattering, since it made the believer recognize the depth of his or her wickedness, and exhilarating, as it filled the believer with an overwhelming feeling of the beauty and majesty of God.

Everyone in the Beecher family had to come to terms with Edwards' theology. When Lyman Beecher was tried for heresy by the Presbyterian Church in the 1830s, he used Edwards and other orthodox Calvinists as his main avenue of defense. "When the theology of Edwards . . . goes down," he said, "I expect that the Bible itself and Christianity will go down."

Actually, however, Beecher accepted a modified version of Edwards' system introduced by the Yale theologian Nathaniel William Taylor, who insisted that good deeds played an important role in salvation. Beecher's long campaign against intemperance and other vices reflected both his premillennial effort to purify society for Christ's return to earth and his conviction that changing daily habits is a step toward salvation. Since Beecher was one of the first preachers to sermonize at length about such vices, he can be considered a major source of the nineteenth century's redefinition of sin as the result of bad behavior rather than of a totally depraved nature.

The Calvinist dilemma was crystallized in 1822, when Catharine's fiancé, Alexander Metcalf Fisher, died in a shipwreck off the coast of Ireland. A professor of mathematics and natural philosophy at Yale, Fisher was an intellectual prodigy and a churchgoer. But had he experienced conversion before his death? Lyman Beecher doubted it. Catharine, who had pored over his diary and found no evidence of a saving experience, was tormented by the idea that her beloved Alexander was in hell.

Could it be possible that a person as virtuous as Fisher would suffer hell's torments for eternity simply because he was not one of God's elect? Catharine was driven to deep contemplation, which led to her anti-Calvinist tract *Elements of Mental and Moral Philosophy*, in which she refuted predestination, her equally brilliant "Essay on Cause and Effect, in Connection with the Doctrines of Fatalism and Free Agency," and her later book *Common Sense Applied to Religion*. Her brother Edward also took on Calvinism in his theological tour de force *The Conflict of Ages*.

Meanwhile, Calvinism drove their brother Henry to depression. He later recalled, "There were days and weeks in which the pall of death over the universe could not have made it darker to my eyes than those on which I thought: 'If you are elected you will be saved, and if you were not elected you will be damned, and there is no hope for you. . . . It is all decreed. It is all fixed.'"

For Henry, relief came in the form of a vision of a loving God he had while he was a seminary student. "On one memorable day," he told his Brooklyn congregation, "whose almost every cloud I remember, whose high sun and glowing firmament and waving trees are vivid yet, there arose before me, as if an angel had descended, a revelation of Christ as being God, because he knew how to love a sinner." The important words here were "angel" and "love." Henry felt he was having direct contact with God in an experience he compared to an angelic visitation, and the comforting message was that Christ loved all sinners.

And so was born Henry Ward Beecher's brand of religious liberalism known as the Gospel of Love. Henry became for a time, as Debby Applegate has shown, "the most famous man in America," through his optimistic preaching. While Beecher had a large role in placing a compassionate Jesus at the heart of mainstream Christianity, his sister Harriet played an even larger one. A personal vision of the divine, which helped generate Henry's sanguine faith, was an even more important part of Harriet's religious development. Like him, she wanted to escape orthodox Calvinism. In her novel *The Minister's Wooing,* she portrayed early New England Calvinism as a severe religion that had conceived of God as a distant being, callous to good works and ready to cast most humans into the fiery pit. In a memorable scene in the novel, she portrayed Jonathan Edwards giving a hellfire sermon that made his congregation erupt with "shrieks and wailings" as Edwards calmly delivered his "refined poetry of torture." A fellow minister cried, "Oh! Mr. Edwards! Mr. Edwards! is God not a God of mercy?"

In the novel, she criticized Edwards' followers for denying humans access to God. She wrote, "There is a ladder to heaven, whose base God has placed in human affections, tender instincts, symbolic feelings, sacraments of love, through which the soul rises higher and higher, refining as she goes . . . and changes, as she rises, into the image of the divine." Calvinists, she lamented, "knocked out every round of the ladder but the highest, and then, pointing to its hopeless splendor, said to the world, 'Go up thither and be saved!' "

Harriet wanted to feel the consoling presence of a God with whom she could be intimate. Her two religious conversions—the first in the summer of 1825, when she was fourteen, and the second in 1843, when she was a homemaker in Cincinnati—instilled in her a sense of divine affection. The first one came after she heard her father give a sermon in Litchfield based on Jesus's assurance "Behold, I call you no longer servants, but friends." She later recalled, "Oh! How much I needed just such a friend, I thought to myself." She knew that to be converted she had to have a conviction of sin. In her excited state, she believed that Christ had given her that conviction. Later that day, she told her father of her conversion. His response was reassuring. He hugged her and asked, sobbing: "Is it so? Then has a new flower blossomed in the kingdom this day."

But was the conversion genuine? The question came up the next spring when she applied for membership in the First Church in Hartford, where she was then living while studying at her sister Catharine's Hartford Female Seminary. After hearing about her reported conversion, the church's pastor frowned and asked, "Harriet, do you feel that if the universe should be destroyed you could be happy with God alone?" Bewildered, she stammered, "Yes, sir." He fired another orthodox bullet: "You realize, I trust, in some measure at least, the deceitfulness of your heart, and that in punishment for your sins God might justly leave you to make yourself as miserable as you have made yourself sinful?"

Here was another Calvinist dilemma: You may think you're saved, but chances are you're not. No wonder Harriet went through psychological contortions. Her moods swung between confidence and melancholy. She worked for the religious conversion of the students at the Hartford Female Seminary, where in 1827 she began teaching part-time. She had studied there since her sister Catharine had founded the school in 1823, at the age of twenty-three. Harriet's message to the students was hopeful. Far from being distant and angry, God was a loving presence in everyday life. "Do not think of God as a strict severe Being," she told student Elizabeth Phoenix. "Think of him as a Being who means to make you perfect . . . who looks on all you say and do with interest— . . . and in every trivial incident which affects your mind he looks as on something of importance."

But it wasn't always easy for her to take her own advice. She often cried in bed until midnight. Sleep deprivation caused her to botch everyday tasks. She wrote to her brother Edward, "My whole life is one continued struggle: I do nothing right. I yield to temptation almost as soon as it assails me. My deepest feelings are very evanescent. I am beset behind and before, and my sins take away all my happiness."

Her bouts with depression brought her to the brink of skepticism.

If Jonathan Edwards and his followers had torn down the ladder to God, leading her to seek solace in a warmer kind of religion, they had also opened up intellectual investigation that could lead one outside the bounds of Christianity. In her novel *Oldtown Folks,* Harriet described the heretical potential of Edwards, who, she pointed out, applied "rationalistic methods" to religion and thus unleashed the "free discussion [that] led to all the shades of opinion of our modern days," including the nonconformist philosophy of Ralph Waldo Emerson and Theodore Parker.

This insight, which anticipated modern commentators who have traced a line from Edwards to Emerson and beyond, also echoed her father's argument that Edwards' theological reasoning carried the seeds of its own destruction. In an 1830 letter, Lyman praised Edwards' Christian commitment yet noted that his brilliance, unchained from his religious devotion, could have turned him into a forceful skeptic.

The Beechers were not ready to jettison traditional Christianity, as Emerson and Parker and later thinkers like Charles Saunders Peirce and William James did. Indeed, they wrestled with doubt. Harriet wrote her half-brother Thomas that life was full of "involuntary fear, perplexity, doubt, remorse, uncertainty, and endless conflict, flashes of truth, fragments of effort, yearnings of desire unutterable, untold."

Doubt and faith are interwoven in *Uncle Tom's Cabin.* The novel would not be as suggestive as it is if its religious affirmations were not counterbalanced by disturbing scenes that force us to ponder what Melville in *Moby-Dick* calls the "colorless, all-color of atheism from which we shrink." Several characters in *Uncle Tom's Cabin* have moments of anguished skepticism. The contemplative slaveowner Augustine St. Clare observes that slavery automatically obliterates definitions of right and wrong. And after the devastating loss of his daughter Eva, he verges on nihilism. "Who knows anything about anything?" he asks. He speculates that there may be "no more Eva,—no heaven,—no Christ,—nothing." The enslaved George Harris feels so maltreated that at one point he doubts God's existence and talks of suicide. Another slave, Cassy, wretched after years of sexual exploitation at the hands of Legree, declares, "There isn't any God,

I believe." Even the pious Uncle Tom momentarily wonders about God's presence when he is subjected to Legree's cruelty.

Push *Uncle Tom's Cabin* a bit more toward the dark side and we're in the doubt-riddled world of Melville, Hawthorne, and Dickinson. Hawthorne famously said of Melville that he had "pretty much made up his mind to be annihilated," adding that "he can neither believe, nor be comfortable in his unbelief; and he is too courageous and too honest not to try to do one or the other." Stowe also had times of metaphysical angst. When she read the writings of Madame de Staël, she wrote a friend that it would be dangerous for an American to try to follow that French Romantic author into introspective depths:

> In America feelings vehement and absorbing like hers become still more deep, morbid, and impassioned by the constant habits of self-government which the rigid forms of our society demand. They are repressed, and they burn inward till they burn the very soul, leaving only dust and ashes. It seems to me the intensity with which my mind has thought and felt on every subject presented to it has had this effect. It has withered and exhausted it, and though young I have no sympathy with the feelings of youth. All that is enthusiastic, all that is impassioned in admiration of nature, or writing, of character, in devotional thought and emotion, or in the emotions of affection, I have felt with vehement and absorbing intensity,—felt till my mind is exhausted, and seems to be sinking into deadness.

Her words—"dust and ashes," "withered and exhausted," "sinking into deadness"—suggest Bartleby-like inertia. For her, American individualism, coupled with Puritan self-examination, could breed a scalding introspection in which spiritual and human passions, repressed and pointed inward, burned the core of the soul.

Such individualism contributed to America's literary renaissance— optimistically in the self-reliance of Emerson and Thoreau and the self-singing of Whitman, darkly in Hawthorne's tortured characters, Melville's crazed isolatoes, and Dickinson's private, volcanic poetry. But Stowe was not prepared to follow the Transcendentalists into post-Christian self-reliance; nor was she interested in putting ambiguity itself at the heart of her writings, as Hawthorne, Melville, and Dickinson sometimes did.

Instead, she took advantage of an alternate characteristic of the American spirit: democracy and social equality. Walt Whitman noted that the great paradox of America was that it bred radical individualism and, at the same time, democratic union and love. Harriet used the latter impulses to change her relationship to those around her and to God.

She wanted to connect religion closely to common life and everyday language. After her first conversion, religion for her had become intrinsically *relational:* it was defined by intimacy with the Divine Friend and by emotional bonds between pious human beings. Without the dimension of friendliness, God seemed cold and tyrannical. Without shared religion, humans fell into depression and doubt. Her relational religion governed many of her private letters, in which she assumed the role of a lay preacher. As she wrote to her brother George in 1829, "I was made for a preacher—indeed I can barely keep my letters from turning into sermons. . . . It is as much my vocation to preach on paper as it is that of my brothers to preach viva voce."

This instinct to preach on paper, which would inspire her to write religious fiction, paralleled the innovations that other members of her family made in the pulpit. Her father and brothers, especially Henry, sped the transformation from strict doctrinal exposition to a more relaxed narrative style in popular American sermons. Henry became the nineteenth century's Prince of the Pulpit largely because of his storytelling capabilities. In Brooklyn's Plymouth Church, he delivered free-flowing sermons filled with secular illustrations that tugged the heartstrings and suggested the religious meaning of daily life. He filled them with stories from his family, nature, farming, and easily understood areas of common life. Harriet deeply admired her brother's innovative sermon style. Like Henry, she explored the world around her for illustrations of the divine. She found them in everyday people and incidents that she refashioned in stories and novels which, with their attention to homely detail, prefigured local-color realism even as they carried inspirational messages.

When in 1832 her father accepted the presidency of Lane Theological Seminary in Cincinnati, Ohio, and the pastorship of the city's Second Presbyterian Church, Harriet, her stepmother, several siblings, and an aunt went with him. The move west was a fresh start for Harriet and her writing. She turned away from the mannerisms of her earlier style. At twelve, while she was at Litchfield Female Academy, she had written an essay, "Can the Immortality of the Soul be Proved by the Light of Nature?," that imitated established theologians and philosophers. In stilted prose, she argued that only when Christ came into the world were humans relieved of their "secret, innate horror of annihilation." Two years later, at the Hartford Female Seminary, she wrote in her notebooks a draft of a Renaissance-type drama in blank verse, *Cleon,* about a once-profligate Athenian in Nero's time who became so dedicated to Christianity that he refused to silence his faith even when he was tortured.

In Cincinnati, Harriet made a dramatic leap to a freshly democratic voice for her short stories. Her springboard was the Semi-Colon Club, a Cincinnati literary group she and Catharine joined, whose members wrote papers and submitted them anonymously for amusement and discussion. In her early Semi-Colon pieces, Harriet lampooned the stiff, sober style she had formerly tried to emulate. Her first contribution to the group was a letter written in what she called the "outrageous style of parentheses and fogrification" of the eighteenth-century Anglican bishop Joseph Butler. Another piece, parodying Samuel Johnson, she said she wrote "because I have been stilting around in his style so long."

Her attack on pomposity led to an essay that became her first publication, "Modern Uses of Language," which appeared in March 1833 in the *Western Monthly Magazine,* edited by fellow Semi-Colon member James Hall. In the essay she argued that many highly regarded thinkers wrote in a vapid, opaque style that concealed their ideas. She mentioned several by name—among them Butler, Locke, Berkeley, Coleridge, and Dugald

Stewart—and claimed that obscure language is "generally employed in all philosophical, mathematical, metaphysical, and theological works."

Having satirized inflated writing, she showed how prose could be both unpretentious and religiously resonant in "A New England Sketch," based on the experiences of her Uncle Lot Benton of Guilford, Connecticut. When she presented the story to the Semi-Colon Club, James Hall encouraged her to submit it to a contest his magazine was running. The story not only won the prize of fifty dollars but was published in the magazine and later was widely reprinted, sometimes as "Uncle Tim" or "Uncle Lot."

Harriet begins the tale with "a little introductory breeze of patriotism," announcing that she is not going to write about England, France, Italy, or Greece but rather "my own land—my own New England." After describing a sleepy Connecticut village and its inhabitants, she follows a young minister, George Griswold, whose exemplary life and premature death bring about the religious regeneration of the story's two main characters: his crusty father, "Uncle Tim" Griswold, and a roguish friend, James Benton. Notably, it is not George's preaching that prompts the two conversions but rather the personal relationship he has with both men. His sermons, we're told, have "strong intellectual nerve, [with] the constant occurrence of argument and statement, which distinguished a New England discourse," but they only confuse his father, who declares, "George, that 'are doctrine is rather of a puzzler." His life, not his dense sermons, brings people to religion. The father embraces Christianity only when he realizes George is dying. James Benton, similarly, is won to religion after bonding emotionally with George, to whom he becomes so close that he puts aside his courtship of George's sister Grace. As George lies on his deathbed, "his face . . . that of an angel," he tells his loved ones that "man's best Friend" has given him wonderful news: "I shall see you again in heaven, and you shall see me again; and then your heart shall rejoice, and your joy no man taketh from you." After his death, his once-skeptical father cries, "I believe my heart's gone to heaven with him; and I think the Lord really *did* know what was best, after all." James, meanwhile, gives up his pursuit of Grace to devote his life to God by training for the ministry.

"A New England Sketch" introduces religious themes that would become central in *Uncle Tom's Cabin*. George Griswold is more religiously effective as a friend and family member than he is in the pulpit, just as the friendship between Uncle Tom and Eva forms the religious core of *Uncle Tom's Cabin*. As mentioned, Harriet had served as a lay preacher in her private letters to friends, and it is this kind of lay preaching, based on human emotion, that prompts the conversions of Tim and James—a foreshadowing of the way Tom and Eva convert those close to them. "A New England Sketch" also anticipates the novel by calling God "man's best Friend" and making heaven become a joyful reality when George dies.

The angelic and heavenly images that surround George Griswold reveal Harriet's debt to the visionary mode, an anti-Calvinist device present in American fiction since its eighteenth-century beginnings. Stowe's opposition to Calvinism is sometimes mentioned, but her crucial place in the growth of anti-Calvinist popular literature about angels and heaven has been overlooked.

Orthodox Calvinists had wanted to rid Christianity of residual elements of Catholicism—icons, saints, angelic intermediaries—that seemed to negate the absolute difference between the divine and the earthly. Jonathan Edwards had written that "all imaginary sights of God in Christ in heaven . . . and all impressions of future events, and immediate revelations of any secret facts whatsoever" were merely "external ideas" of the imagination. Especially reprehensible was "the pretended immediate converse, with God in Christ, and saints and angels of heaven."

If Calvinism had destroyed the ladder between the earthly and the divine, scores of American magazine-tale writers from the mid-eighteenth century onward tried to rebuild it by portraying benign angels and vistas of heaven. The earliest visionary stories, published in popular periodicals in the 1740s, were known as Oriental tales because they had Eastern settings and characters. Often based loosely on *The Arabian Nights*, one of Harriet's favorite books in childhood, many of these tales described a solitary hero having visions of otherworldly beings who uttered consoling truths or gave alluring information about the afterlife, including descriptions of hills, birds, streams, spices, and gems. Visionary devices were soon integrated into longer fiction. Enos Hitchcock's domestic novel *Memoirs of the Bloomsgrove Family* (1790) contains an episode in which a young man dreams of a "visionary ladder" connecting earth and heaven on which were ascending and descending "those benevolent agents who are supposed to be always attendant on good men." Above the ladder stands God, who speaks to the youth "in language of paternal affection." Other novelists of the period featured angelic characters and deathbed visions of friends. By the 1820s, the anti-Calvinist authors Catharine Maria Sedgwick and Lydia Maria Child absorbed visionary imagery into their novels' central action, planting the visionary ladder firmly in terrestrial experience. The heroine of Sedgwick's 1822 novel *A New-England Tale*, described as "an angel on earth," is told by one character, "You need not hide your wings—I know you—there is none but an angel would look on me with pity." Child's novel *The Rebels* (1825) portrays a girl who exerts "an angelic influence" until her death, when "she seemed like a celestial spirit, which, having performed its mission on earth, melts into a misty wreath, then disappears forever."

We cannot measure how much of the contemporary literature about visions and angelic characters Stowe read, but her letters and early fiction reveal an ongoing fascination with the visionary mode. Eva St. Clare, the child heroine of *Uncle Tom's Cabin*—who is compared to a "mythic and allegorical being" and seems like "some bright angel" when she helps a sinner—was the creation of a writer who yearned for contact with the spiritual world. Harriet's marriage to the widower Calvin Stowe in 1836 and the magazine pieces she wrote in the first dozen years of their marriage reflect this fascination, as does the visionary language she used to described her second, "true" conversion in 1843.

Calvin Ellis Stowe, a native of Natick, Massachusetts, had earned degrees at Bowdoin College and Andover Theological Seminary before being hired by Dartmouth as a professor of Greek. He went on to become one of the leading biblical scholars of the time. When in 1832 Lyman took his family west to head the Lane Theological Seminary, he invited Stowe to join the Lane faculty. Stowe accepted, making the move along with his young wife Eliza. During their first two years in Cincinnati, the Stowes became close to the Beechers, especially Harriet, who saw them often in meetings of the Semi-Colon Club.

Calvin Stowe was a curious combination of the brilliant professor, the rustic raconteur, and the visionary seer. Short and stocky (and eventually obese), the balding Stowe had a square-set jaw and muttonchop whiskers that gave him a frank, no-nonsense look. He knew seven languages yet loved to tell anecdotes in New England dialect. Like Harriet, he was a devout Christian who nevertheless was given to wide-ranging intellectual speculation that sometimes led him into mazes of skepticism. Also like her, he found relief in visionary experiences.

In an autobiographical essay Calvin read at the Semi-Colon Club in 1834, he described visions he had had since early childhood of aerial forms that passed through walls and floated in the air around him. They appeared often, especially when he was alone and in the dark. He recalled that when he was three, a tiny Indian man and a large Indian woman came nightly to his bedroom and quarreled over a bass violin, which they took turns playing. The Indians were followed over the succeeding months and years by other spirit visitors: a beautiful lady, a mulatto man, merry groups of six-inch-tall fairies, and, terrifyingly, a crowd of devils who hurled a dissipated man into the abyss of hell. As a child, he did not consider these visions abnormal. He found them entertaining, and he assumed everyone had them. Even as he grew older and became an intellectual powerhouse, the visions continued, although he recognized they were imaginary. In Calvin's telling, they actually grew stronger and more frequent as he aged. In old age, he had constant visions of a devil that only left when he read Bible passages aloud.

Today, Calvin Stowe's condition might be diagnosed as psychosis or paranoid schizophrenia and perhaps would generate a movie like *A Beautiful Mind*. In the nineteenth century, however, when visionary literature, religious prophets, spirit-rapping, and ghostly table-lifting were taken seriously—so much so that séances were held in the Lincoln White House and the century's leading philosopher, William James, founded an intellectual society for the study of the paranormal—such visions were not usually considered signs of insanity. Calvin could frankly present his story to the Semi-Colon Club without being dismissed as deranged.

How did Harriet react to his visions? There's evidence that they contributed to her own spiritual adventures. In *Oldtime Fireside Stories* she used Calvin as the model for her visionary hero Sam Lawson, who says, "I always lived in the shadowy edge of that line which divides spirit land from mortal life, and it was my delight to walk among its half lights and shadows." Although Harriet never reported seeing tiny fairies or oversized Indians, she had unusual paranormal experiences. Later in life, she became interested in spiritualism and was close to one of the movement's founders, Kate Fox. Harriet believed that the dead could communicate to the living through musical instruments, planchette writing, or mediums. She thought that much of popular spiritualism was spurious—"mountebank tricks with tables and chairs," and "harmless truisms" recited "in weary sameness," as she put it—and she never was as committed to the movement as were siblings Catharine, Charles, and especially Isabella (who received spiritual messages that she was the matriarch of the universe and ruled it along with Jesus Christ). But Harriet came to be convinced that she too could communicate with spirits. For example, she once had a long conversation with the deceased Charlotte Brontë, who gave her consoling news about the afterlife, including Brontë's report that "friends here, as during the earth-life, do know and love each other."

In the Cincinnati years, one of her main religious goals was to align visionary experiences with Christianity. Calvin Stowe was the perfect soul mate for her in this effort. On the one hand, he was a steadfast Christian. On the other, he shared the visionary spirit of the nineteenth century, which often soared to meta-Christian realms. He was pious yet unconventional. Harriet had come to know him well in the Semi-Colon Club and was especially close to his gentle, beautiful wife Eliza. "I fell in love

Calvin and Harriet Beecher Stowe

with her directly," Harriet said. When the twenty-five-year-old Eliza died of cholera in 1834, Harriet and Calvin were bonded by grief, friendship, and mutual respect that soon blossomed into love. They were married on January 6, 1836. Within a year, twin girls had arrived and were given the names Eliza Tyler Stowe and Harriet Beecher Stowe. They were followed over the next fourteen years by five more children, one of whom, Charles, died in early childhood.

These years brought fulfillment for Harriet in the forms of a growing family and steady literary productivity, but they also brought pain, tragedy, and periods of depression. Harriet had at least two miscarriages, and she and Calvin, both hypochondriacs, suffered from various real and imagined illnesses that drove each of them separately to long stays in a Vermont water-cure establishment. Calvin was a supportive husband who encouraged her to write, but his meager salary at Lane kept the family barely above poverty level. A main reason Harriet wrote magazine fiction was the money it brought in. But the forty dollars or so that she earned for a sporadic story could not save her from the grinding labor of motherhood and household duties. "I am but a mere drudge with few ideas beyond babies and housekeeping," she told her longtime confidante Georgiana May. Once, after "a dark, sloppy, rainy, muddy, disagreeable day" in the kitchen, she lamented to her husband, "I am sick of the smell of sour milk, and sour meat, and sour everything." Another time she wrote that she was "so loaded and burdened with cares as to drain me dry of all capacity of thought, feeling, memory, or emotion."

Death was a frequent visitor to her family and friends. Henry Ward Beecher and his wife Eunice in the 1840s had five children, three of whom died young. A number of Lane students died while Calvin taught there. When Sarah Beecher, the wife of Harriet's brother George, lost her mother in February 1843, Harriet's letters and magazine writings began to fill with visionary imagery of angels and heaven. She wrote in condolence to Sarah, "How lovely and attractive a place must that be to which all these chosen and selected spirits are constantly ascending. . . . Every such one makes Heaven more worth striving for." By June, Harriet's dreams of the afterlife were projected in a visionary tale she wrote for the *New-York Evangelist*. In the story, "Now We See through a Glass Darkly," a young wanderer meets a sweet-voiced man who guides him on a long journey that ends when the wanderer meets a glorious Being surrounded by thousands of angels singing, "Holy, holy, holy is the Lord of hosts."

Then came a crushing blow that brought forth more visionary outpourings. On July 1, 1843, Harriet's brother George took his shotgun into his backyard, supposedly to rid his garden of birds. He fired a shot but did not return to the house. He was later found dead, the top of his head blown off.

The Beecher family called the death an accident that occurred while George was cleaning his rifle, but biographer Joan Hedrick argues persuasively that George committed suicide as a result of depression after hopeless attempts at religious perfection. The tragedy sent waves of grief and religious meditation through the Beecher family. Harriet wrote, "The sudden death of George shook my whole soul like an earthquake; and as in an earthquake we know not where the ground may open next, so I felt an indistinct terror as if father, brothers, husband, any or all, might be just about to sink."

She overcame terror with visionary consolation. In a group letter to three of her surviving brothers, she said of George, "Even now he is with the glorified spirit of our mother in Heaven. . . . Oh that we could once lift the veil and look in!" She expanded on the point in a letter to Catharine and sister-in-law Sarah: "[George] is now a King and Priest unto God—'made like unto the angels.' . . . Our mothers too—*our* mother, Sarah and yours—they were both there to welcome him, and while we were full of dismay and anguish they were looking calmly and sweetly down, pitying our sorrows, yet seeing at the same time, that *all was right*, and that God's will was the best will—Nay there was joy among our friends, over one soul more born into eternal glory!"

These imaginings of relatives in heaven opened the way for her second conversion. Her initial exaltation after George's death gave way to a period when she felt "haunted and pursued by care that seemed to drink my life-blood." She prayed that by "some vision, some sudden and mighty influence, God would bring [about] . . . an entire IDENTITY of my will with God's."

Such a divine vision not only came; it stayed. Before long, she surrendered totally to Christ. She entered a new state that she described joyously to her brother Thomas, "The will of Christ seems to me the steady pulse of my being. . . . Skeptical doubt cannot exist. I seem to see the full blaze of the Shekinah." *Shekinah* refers to God's glorious presence revealed in a bright light, as in the burning bush Moses saw or the light that shone on the Bethlehem manger. Although Harriet thereafter was not always in a visionary state, she was able to summon it up when either she or her loved ones needed it.

She used her visionary capacities extensively in her magazine writings after the conversion. In her 1844 biblical tale "Old Testament Pictures" she refashioned the story of Jacob and the angel so that it became a lesson in how humans can intensely experience the divine. She described Jacob as one "always living on the borders of the invisible world, seeing glances of angel-wings from behind every tree, and hearing whispers of heavenly greeting in every breeze." After wrestling all night with a strange man, Jacob finds himself kneeling with uplifted hands "and gazing as into an opening heaven" directly at God. The moral is that "God the Omnipotent, the Creator, the Destroyer, is suffering himself to be detained in weak human hands, and controlled by the passionate earnestness of human desire. . . . He whose touch could annihilate, can yet be held by your infant hand—can be swayed by your prayer." She again emphasized the visionary power of prayer in the poem "Love and Fear," with lines like: "Through the light that dazzles, the fire that burns— / Through all the signs and wonders round thy throne, / We press, we burn with zeal unterrified, / To stand before Thee, face to face, alone."

By the late 1840s she believed that departed relatives were not waiting in a distant heaven but rather were always around their loved ones. They exuded goodwill and support in the homes of their relatives.

With her growing visionary inclinations, it is not surprising that she never complained about Calvin's continued sightings of phantoms, which now included the spirit of his deceased wife Eliza. One might think that Eliza's ghostly presence would make Harriet uneasy, but not so. She had loved Eliza, and every year she and Calvin commemorated Eliza's birthday. When *Uncle Tom's Cabin* brought in money, Harriet commissioned a portrait of the former wife that hung in a sitting room as a kind of family shrine. More than that, Harriet believed Calvin's report that Eliza's spirit communicated to him by plucking the strings of a guitar—so much so that in the late 1850s, after Harriet and Calvin's son Henry died and Calvin said he thought he heard Henry playing the guitar, Harriet soberly replied, "I cannot think that Henry strikes the guitar—that must be Eliza. Her spirit has ever seemed to cling to that mode of manifestation."

Actually, Calvin's problem, Harriet thought, was not that he saw too *many* spirits; rather, that he saw too *few*. Specifically, she wanted him to visualize Christ and heaven the way she did. She complained that he was too busy giving lectures, attending presbytery meetings, and reading books and newspapers to admit God fully into his life. His temper tantrums, his long absences from home, his mood swings, his failures as a breadwinner—all of these and more she accepted, for she loved him deeply. But she felt he needed a lesson in visionary ecstasy.

And so she gave him one. In a remarkable letter of May 1844, she chided him for his religious indifference and described her own visions of the divine world.

Calvin was visiting his native Natick at the time and had written despondent letters about religious doubts he was having. Harriet found them deeply troubling and wrote to him of her concern: "I am depressed by your letters. . . . The depth of your spiritual necessities is no exaggeration." Then she rhapsodized about her visionary capacities, explaining how she often lay half-awake in the morning and visualized Jesus sitting alone, "simple as a little child—yet majestic as a God," in a secret room in a dazzling palace, as successive generations of humans came to him:

> There hour after hour I see applicants—each admitted alone—old feeble men, lisping children,—illiterate poor slaves,—the despised—the forsaken—the guilty—the despairing all come—those whom the world has cast out and the church rejects come—and none are cast out—all when they enter, feel his might—his majesty—they bow the knee—they tremble—yet strange to hear when they speak it is with such deep outpourings of *love* as never came to the ears of an earthly majesty—Each one . . . says—*my* God,—*my* Saviour, *my* Friend—and He—is never weary—still that god-like immortal youth—that fullness of power, that fullness of peace rests in his glorious face—What wilt thou? he says to each suppliant—Ask—I am *Almighty*—nothing is too hard—What wilt thou?

Here Harriet gives a religious lesson to her husband through a detailed account of her "vision of how Jesus is working," replete with beauty, a sense of physical location, and a view of religion that is at once passionately personal and radically democratic (all are admitted, including slaves, criminals, the despised and rejected). The passage anticipates Whitman with its democratic expansiveness and Dickinson with its telescoping of time and space. Worlds move and generations come and go, as they do in Dickinson's poems about the afterlife (though Dickinson doesn't keep Christ firmly in place, as does Harriet). If Harriet's rhythmic lists of lowly types look forward to Whitman's democratic catalogues, her halting dashes and choppy phrases prefigure Dickinson's odd grammar, which bends and twists under the pressure of feeling or imagery.

Harriet ends this letter with a statement that seems outrageous if it is not put into context. "My dear husband," she advises, "you should go to Johnny Ross with your difficulties—You may be a very learned man and mighty in the scriptures and yet depend upon it he can tell you more than you yet know—How sublime from the mouth of a poor weak simple creature to hear that burst of triumph."

Johnny Ross, a Natick resident Calvin had once known, was a brutish, psychologically ill former alcoholic who had embraced religion in 1824. For Harriet to suggest that Calvin, one of the most sophisticated religious minds in America, consult a mentally challenged ex-drunkard would have been incredible if we didn't realize that by 1845 Harriet had turned completely from fruitless theological speculation to a faith in visionary experiences and childlike simplicity.

We should note that Ross, whom Harriet calls "a poor weak simple creature," had allegedly seen the infant Jesus twice, and that in her visionary letter to Calvin, Harriet described Jesus as "simple as a little child," one who welcomed the "lisping children" to heaven.

Children were essential to Harriet's religious vision because of their simplicity and sinlessness. In *Uncle Tom's Cabin*, Harriet created literature's quintessential sinless child in Little Eva, the angelic blonde who is a source of religious inspiration to others. The child was an important part of Harriet's rebellion against orthodox Calvinism. Calvinist leaders like Jonathan Edwards and Joseph Bellamy had preached the doctrine of infant damnation. In their view, a child was either elected or not elected by God to be a saint. Most people were sinners at birth and were doomed to eternal torment, no matter how young they were at the time of death.

Like other Beechers, Harriet rejected this bleak tenet. Her father had led the way by denouncing "the monstrous doctrine that infants are damned, and that hell is paved with their bones." He said he'd never met anyone who accepted the idea—he was probably being truthful, since this cornerstone of early Calvinist dogma had all but crumbled by his time. Even stronger attacks on infant damnation came from Catharine, Edward, and Charles in their religious writings. Henry Ward waved away the "stale yeast" of Augustinian Calvinism, whose idea of inborn sin he said was "so gross and so undiscriminating" as to be nonsensical.

Harriet's idealization of the child gained impetus from Romanticism and perfectionism. For Romantic authors from Wordsworth onward, the child came into the world fresh from God, enveloped in spirituality and innocence. The American Romantic philosopher Bronson Alcott called infant damnation a debased doctrine and thought children entered the world with superior wisdom and insight that adults could learn from—a view he put into effect at the Temple School, where he asked religious questions of students and had disobedient children strike the teacher on the principle that such an unnatural act would bring alive their innate goodness.

Perfectionism, the belief that humans could be sinless, was rooted in the holiness movement spearheaded by John Wesley and spread in America by the popular Methodist Church. In different forms, it permeated many phenomena in nineteenth-century America: Transcendentalism, anarchism, Garrisonian abolitionism, the free love movement, and later on New Thought and Christian Science. Perfectionism fit in with postmillennialism, an optimistic Christian view that matched the expansive mood of the growing nation. Postmillennialism posited that Christ's second coming would happen *after* the world enjoyed a thousand-year period of universal harmony and justice. This notion, which inspired social reforms aimed at preparing America for the coming golden age, contrasted with the darker premillennial views of orthodox Puritans like

Increase and Cotton Mather, who thought that the Second Coming and the Last Judgment would occur *before* that age arrived.

Especially attractive to Harriet was the postmillennial perfectionism of Charles Grandison Finney. The era's leading evangelical Christian, Finney had led mass revivals in upstate New York and Manhattan before accepting a call in 1835 to become a theology professor at the recently founded Oberlin Collegiate Institute in Ohio, about two hundred miles northeast of Cincinnati. Establishing what came to be known as the Oberlin doctrines, he endorsed the perfectionist doctrine of total sanctification, which meant that all who chose Christ were capable of living without sin. In essence, they became perfect—a reflection of God. Finney considered infant damnation a useless relic of old-style Calvinism. His postmillennialism fostered his social reform efforts, including antislavery and the education of women and blacks along with white men.

Harriet desperately wanted to believe that perfection was possible, as Finney's Oberlin doctrines claimed. She wrote a magazine essay, "The Interior Life," that was her version of an Oberlin paper. Addressing those who doubted perfectionism because they felt burdened with care and sin, she said that the Christian lives in Christ and thus is by definition pure and perfect. Christianity is joyful, elastic, not given to moping or depression. For the sincere Christian, sinlessness is like fresh water flowing forever from a pure fountain.

But she didn't look only to the Oberlin doctrines to find out about humanity's potential for pure goodness. Like Wordsworth or Alcott, she looked to children. "Well," she wrote Calvin, "we have five little wee babies and four of them pray for us every night and I think Christ takes especial pleasure in the fresh dewy prayers of little children." Children, she thought, had much to teach adults.

She showed just how much in her story "Children," published in 1846 in the *New-York Evangelist* and widely reprinted. She portrays little children, both naughty and nice, in everyday scenes and then contrasts their innocence and purity with corrupted, worldly adults who too often mold their children wrongly, making them ugly versions of themselves instead of preserving their goodness. Deriving her theme from the Bible passage "A little child shall lead them," she re-creates the scene where Jesus, when asked about life's mysteries by his disciples, puts in their midst a small child "as a sign of him who would be the greatest in the kingdom of heaven." Sinless children are the religious instructors of misled adults:

Wouldst thou know, O parent, what is that faith which unlocks heaven? Go not to wrangling polemics, or creeds and forms of theology; but draw to thy bosom thy little one, and read in that clear and trusting eye, the lesson of eternal life. Be only to thy God as that child is to thee, and all is done! Blessed shalt thou be, indeed, when "*a little child shall lead thee.*"

In another story of the period, "The Nursery," Harriet reveals how young Christians can be strongly optimistic even in the face of excruciating pain. A Mr. Thompson takes his two sons to witness a boy who is dying of a bone disease. Though he has been bedridden for a year and can neither sleep regularly nor turn on his side, the boy is happy, for the ordeal has brought him closer to Christ. Mr. Thompson, Alcott-like, asks the boy leading questions: How can he bear the pain? Does he know he's dying? Isn't he bitter about life? The boy replies, "I am happier now than I used to be when I was well, [when] I had not so much pleasure in thinking about heaven." As for the pain, "I know that God would not send it, if it were not best for me; besides, Jesus Christ suffered more pain than I suffered."

This fusion of Christ's suffering with the purity of childhood was magnified for Harriet when she lost her beloved son Charley, who died of cholera in July 1849. Eighteen months old when he caught the disease that ravaged Cincinnati that summer, Charley had been for Harriet the epitome of the sinless child. Shortly after his death, Harriet wrote to the absent Calvin, "My Charley—my beautiful, loving, gladsome baby, so loving, so sweet, so full of life and hope and strength—now lies shrouded, pale and cold, in the room below. Never was he anything to me but a comfort. He has been my pride and joy. Many a heartache has he cured for me."

She was anguished yet inspired. She felt Charley had taught her "one more great lesson of humanity which must needs be learned to attain perfection." The lesson was that deep religious knowledge comes only through severe suffering. "Poor Charley's dying cries and sufferings rent my heart," she wrote. "—Even so let it be—for thro[ugh] the baptism of sorrow we come to a full knowledge of the sufferings of God—who has borne for us all that we bear."

Actually, the baptism of sorrow she associated with Charley was part of a long process that had emerged through the illnesses, worries, and deaths of the preceding two decades. It was during this time that she developed an intense fixation on Jesus Christ as the humble sufferer, the grand symbol of the burdens borne by the lowliest members of society.

Her magazine fiction of the 1840s made a democratic connection between Jesus and America's oppressed classes. "The Bible as Comforter" contrasts two scenes: the fancy parlor of a wealthy man who rarely opens his ornate Bible because he sees it as a fallible document, and the hovel of a starving widow who reads her worn Bible constantly because of the comfort it gives her and her three children. The Bible teaches her patient self-denial and expectation of a happy home in heaven. Best of all, it contains the story of Jesus, with whom indigent outcasts like the widow can identify. She reminds her children that Jesus was poor too.

Harriet featured the humble, suffering Jesus in biblical fiction that she wrote to make the Gospels come alive for contemporary readers. The Bible, she argued, was full of fascinating human stories yet lacked "freshness and reality" for many who read it often. What was needed, she wrote, was a "blending together . . . of truth and fiction" to make it more vivid.

And so she joined the rush toward fictionalization of the Bible that led to best-sellers like J. H. Ingraham's *The Prince of the House of David*, Lew Wallace's *Ben-Hur*, and L. C. Douglas's *The Robe*, ancestors of the film epics that eventually became holiday TV staples. Some of her maga-zinc stories showed how far she was willing to go to embellish the Bible with imaginary details. In "A Tradition of the Church at Laodicea" she described a wealthy family in ancient Greece who, though Christians, have a party in their lavish home. The family gives a huge feast in which they disobey the Bible's injunction to share food with the disadvantaged or ill. In the midst of their festivities appears a lowly carpenter who confronts them and addresses them. He is the humble Jesus, who has come to remind the rich to sympathize with the poor and the suffering. The only one at the party who responds to him is a little girl, who goes up to him and takes his hand. The story ends by warning the reader to ask "Should I be well pleased to meet my Saviour there?" before entering into any situation.

Especially important for Harriet was Jesus's extraordinary suffering at Calvary. She vividly dramatized the Passion in her story "Atonement—A Historical Reverie." She begins the piece in secular, everyday fashion, describing a city long ago whose normally busy streets are deserted; then she pans outside the city, where mobs are gathered to see Christ crucified. Jesus is pictured alone on the Cross, wondering where God is, forgiving his enemies, and then gaining atonement from the Father. Among the witnesses are his mother, along with the disciple John and Mary Magdalene. Then the story flashes forward through the centuries, noting how the Cross symbol swept throughout the world, appealing to people of every ethnicity and nation. To all, the Cross says, "It is my blood, shed for *many*, for the *remission of sins*." The tale ends on a deeply human note: "A thrilling voice speaks from this scene of anguish to every human bosom: This is *thy* Savior. *Thy* sin hath done this. . . . Christ so presented becomes to every human being a friend nearer than the mother that bore him."

Her fixation on Jesus on the Cross, a traditional Catholic symbol, shows her growing attraction to traditional Christianity. Such an attraction was not unusual among Americans weary of conflicting Protestant creeds in a time when, as one writer noted, "old faiths are every year dissolving, and new ones every year forming." At least 700,000 nineteenth-century American Protestants found solace in the security and tradition of the Catholic Church. What bothered Harriet—and probably many of the converts—was Protestantism's absence of ritual and its emphasis on the solitary believer in direct contact with God, without a rite or another person to smooth the meeting.

Eventually, she took steps toward Catholicism: she was consoled by a Catholic priest, Father James O'Donnell, after her son Frederick drowned in 1857; on trips abroad, she basked in the beauties of Rome ("Papal Rome is an enchantress!" she wrote) and the magnetic presence of Blessed Pope Pius IX, whom she saw in a church procession. She later followed her daughters in becoming an Episcopalian, the nearest to a Catholic that a Protestant could be. She portrayed Catholic characters sympathetically in *The Minister's Wooing* and *Agnes of Sorrento* and even had the protagonist of *Oldtown Folks* confess, "I wish to my heart I had been brought up Roman Catholic! but I have not,—I've been brought up a Calvinist."

In *Uncle Tom's Cabin,* she created an aestheticism that reflected Catholic ritual. Eva is surrounded by Catholic images. Tom looks at her "as the Italian sailor gazes on his image of the child Jesus." Religious icons populate Eva's room. Over her bed is "a beautiful sculptured angel, with drooping wings, holding out a crown of myrtle leaves." On her fireplace mantel stands "a beautifully wrought statuette of Jesus receiving little children," flanked by vases filled with flowers. The link between Eva and Catholicism is strengthened not only by her French New Orleans setting but also by the fact that her father—whose name recalls the Catholic St. Augustine of Hippo—links his departed mother with "the saints that were arrayed in fine linen" in Revelations and recalls her singing the "fine old majestic music of the Catholic church . . . with a voice more like an angel than a mortal woman." The novel features a number of emblems—the coin given to Tom by the young George Shelby, Eva's widely distributed locks of hair, and the hair strand Legree receives from his pious mother as a keepsake—that prove to have religious significance, almost like sacred relics. Eva's hair has special significance. She gives ringlets to both blacks and whites in her household much as a priest distributes bread and wine at communion service.

Given such Catholic-related imagery in *Uncle Tom's Cabin,* it is understandable that when an Italian translation of the novel was published in Rome, only slight revisions were needed to convert it into a straightforward Catholic novel. A contemporary newspaper reported: "The Pope having read 'Uncle Tom' and being delighted with it, determined to have it done into Italian for the edification of his subjects. Strange changes took place in the sleight of words, and by the time 'Uncle Tom' and the rest of the characters in the book learned to speak Italian fluently, the 'good people' became fervent Papists and the 'bad folks' deep-dyed Protestants, and finally *Legree* puts *Uncle Tom* to death, because the poor negro would not forsake his belief in the doctrine of the—Immaculate Conception of the Virgin Mary!"

Despite its Catholic leanings, *Uncle Tom's Cabin* at the same time reflects Harriet's anti-Catholic bias. The daughter of Lyman Beecher, that scourge of Catholicism, was not about to give a blanket endorsement to Catholicism. In addition to her father, there was her brother Edward, who wrote *The Papal Conspiracy Exposed,* and Catharine and Charles, who also attacked the so-called Scarlet Beast of Rome. Harriet joined the anti-Catholic chorus in her 1846 article "What Will the American People Do?" Noting the immigrant surge that was bringing millions of Europeans to America, she called Roman Catholics "insidious, all-pervading, persevering." She foresaw the end of democratic America in the Catholic invasion and feared the submissiveness of its adherents and clergy to follow whatever the church decreed.

She thought the Catholic Church stifled independent thinking by putting priestly intermediaries between the individual and the Bible. In her *Primary Geography* she said of "Roman Catholics or papists": "They believe that [the pope] cannot make mistakes about anything in religion, and that he has a right to tell them what to believe and what to do. . . . They believe in the Bible, but are not allowed to read it." In *Uncle Tom's Cabin* she posits not only that laypeople can read the Bible but that the most marginalized people understand its deepest truths. The novel transfers religious authority from churches and theology to an uneducated enslaved black and a little girl. Tom, "a sort of patriarch in religious matters," preaches constantly to both blacks and whites. He is "looked up to with great respect, as a sort of minister among them." Like most other slaves, he is illiterate, but he learns to read the Bible with the help of Eva, who herself serves as a lay preacher.

There was a convergence between anti-Catholic and antislavery sentiment in the antebellum period, manifested especially in the Know-Nothing Party, one of whose leaders typically declared, "American Republicanism is FREEDOM; Romanism is SLAVERY!" In this view, both slavery and Catholicism held people in servitude. After the passage of the infamous Fugitive Slave Law, which imposed a $1,000 fine and up to six months in prison on anyone who helped a runaway slave, Charles Beecher wrote that the law was "a stab at the freedom of conscience, and of private judgment," much like "popery." The only person who obeyed this evil law, he insisted, was one who "makes the Congress his pope, cardinals, and holy college of Jesuits, to act the part of infallible interpreter for him, of the Bible and of duty."

Several of Harriet's most meaningful experiences had been visions, and *Uncle Tom's Cabin* was no different, according to her story about the catalyst for the novel. In February 1851, she attended the communion service at the First Parish Church in Brunswick, Maine. She had taken the bread and wine, and her thoughts went to the Last Supper and the Passion. She then had a vision that was "blown into her mind as by the rushing of a mighty wind." She saw four figures: an old slave being whipped to death by two fellow slaves, who were goaded on by a brutal white man.

This was Calvary, but not the biblical one: it was the *American* Calvary of slavery. Here, as in the Christ story, the humble man was cruelly tortured despite his innocence. Inspired by the vision, Harriet fought back tears, rushed home, and reproduced her vision in words. She read it to her children, one of whom cried, "Oh, mamma! Slavery is the most cruel thing in the world."

Harriet emphasized the visionary source of *Uncle Tom's Cabin* several times, as when she told a friend, "It all came before me in visions, one after

another, and I put them down in words." At the time it was not unusual
to claim that God spoke through humans. Religious enthusiasm in the
Second Great Awakening generated a number of self-styled prophets,
including Abel Morgan Sargent, who announced he was Christ come
again and could raise the dead, and Jacob Osgood, who said God allowed
him to control the weather and insects.

Harriet Beecher Stowe

Even more relevant to Harriet were the trance writers of the 1850s, who claimed to write or speak under divine inspiration. Spiritualism, which allegedly made possible communication with the spirit world, had started in 1848 and soon became a mass movement. During the decade in which *Uncle Tom's Cabin* appeared, many poems, stories, essays, and paintings were created by people in a trance, supposedly under the guidance of the divine world. Among the best-known trance writers and speakers were Andrew Jackson Davis, Cora Hatch, William Fishbough, Anna Henderson, Charlotte Tuttle, and Hattie Huntley. Many of these mediums announced that they were God's mouthpieces. Although Walt Whitman, the most famous poet of the 1850s, was not a card-carrying spiritualist and probably did not, as was long thought, write *Leaves of Grass* after having a religious vision, his poems are full of spiritual images and trance-like gamboling among distant times, places, and peoples.

Just as Whitman identified with the outcasts of society, Stowe's vision of the whipped slave revealed a democratic capacity to sympathize with the marginalized and oppressed, captured by *Uncle Tom*'s eventual subtitle, *Life among the Lowly*. When in March 1850 she told Gamaliel Bailey, editor of *The National Era*, that she was writing a narrative about slavery, she said that she would write three or four numbers for him. As it turned out, her "visions, one after another," took the form of weekly installments of *Uncle Tom's Cabin* that were published over the course of ten months, starting in June 1851, capped in March 1852 by John Jewett's publication of the two-volume novel.

The novel flowed from Stowe's deepest religious convictions, bringing many of them together in this single work. Her main religious characters, Tom and Eva, embodied themes from previous religious visions. If in the long vision she had described to Calvin she saw Christ in heaven as a "little child" who was friendly to "poor illiterate slaves," in the novel she made a child and an enslaved black the centers of religious authority. Both of them are Christ-like figures whose deaths inspired others to become pious. This child and her black friend possess qualities Stowe had come to place at the heart of religion: visionary closeness to the divine world;

an imaginative, pictorial approach to religion and the Bible; the view of God as a divine friend; the existence of angels; simplicity and innocence as holy; and religious behavior that was fundamentally relational, defined by loving connections with other humans and with God.

Visionary ecstasy bonds Eva and Tom. As she reads the Bible with him at sunset near Lake Pontchartrain, she gazes into the distance and says that she sees the New Jerusalem. When Tom sings a Methodist hymn about "spirits bright . . . robed in spotless white," she tells him she has seen such spirits in dreams. Tom's song about heaven inspires Eva to point at the gleaming clouds and exclaim, "I'm going *there*, to the spirits bright, Tom; *I'm going, before long.*" As she nears death, she talks about her forthcoming reunion with her loving Maker and assures Tom and others that she will meet them in heaven. Tom faithfully watches over her to the end, explaining to Ophelia that he wants to be with Eva when she dies, for "when that ar blessed child goes into the kingdom, they'll open the door so wide, we'll all get a look in at the glory." He indeed witnesses her joyful final moments, when she smiles and murmurs, "O! love,—joy,—peace."

Describing Eva and her setting gave Harriet the chance to indulge in the aestheticism she thought New England Protestantism lacked. In earlier American fiction, as mentioned, authors used visionary devices for their Oriental tales filled with sensual images. Stowe has Eva's home carry "the mind back, as in a dream, to the reign of oriental romance in Spain." Built "in the Moorish fashion," the St. Clare home was "arranged to gratify a picturesque and voluptuous ideality," with "Moorish arches, slender pillars, and arabesque ornaments," surrounded by gardens filled with exotic flowers and fragrant fruit trees.

Tom and Eva express a religion of love that wins over others. Tom is so powerful a religious force that he brings about the conversion of Cassy, the bitter slave concubine, and Sambo and Quimbo, the slaves who have savagely whipped him at Legree's command. Eva's main converts are her once-cynical father, a jaded agnostic who dismisses churches because of their hypocrisy, and Topsy, the heathen slave girl. Augustine St. Clare comes to Christianity through his daughter's unwavering faith. Topsy, so degraded by slavery that she mocks religion and flaunts her wickedness, eventually embraces religion when she receives love from Eva, who convinces her that Jesus loves her too. Formerly wild, Topsy becomes a devout Christian who later serves as a missionary to Africa.

In this updated biblical setting, Eva is both a Virgin Mary figure and a female Christ, whose death redeems others. The repentant Cassy, who tends to the wounded Tom, is the novel's Mary Magdalene. Tom is the male Christ who willingly endures great suffering as an example of self-sacrificing love. The Passion resonates in the text. As Tom nears death, he reads about Jesus's last days. Soon, "a vision rose before him of One crowned with thorns, buffeted and bleeding." Like Jesus on the Cross, Tom has a moment of doubt, asking if God has forsaken him. Also like Jesus, he forgives his enemies and announces a gospel of love. The Christ connection was strengthened in early illustrated editions of *Uncle Tom's Cabin,* several of which pictured Jesus on the jacket and in Tom's death scene, as well as in some of the Tom plays, in which Tom was whipped with his outstretched arms tied to a cross-shaped post.

The novel brings the Bible to earth, making it accessible and relevant to contemporary life. Stowe imagines North America as a biblical landscape that reflects the geography of slavery. Canada represents Canaan or heaven, the Deep South becomes Sodom or hell, and the Ohio River the Jordan River across which slaves flee. Stowe grasped what modern historians have confirmed: for enslaved blacks, biblical images expressed yearnings for freedom. After Eliza crosses the Ohio to freedom, Sam, an enslaved black, tells his mistress, Mrs. Shelby, that Eliza is "clar 'cross Jordan—as a body may say—in the land o' Canaan." Sam says Eliza has fled "as 'markably as if da Lord took her over in a charrit of fire and two hosses." When he and the other Shelby slaves sing hymns, they emphasize biblical images that are coded calls for emancipation. Their hymns make "incessant mention of 'Jordan's banks,' and 'Canaan's fields,' and the 'New Jerusalem'" and include fantasies of release, such as, "O, I'm going to glory,—won't you come along with me? Don't you see the angels beck'ning, and a calling me away? Don't you see the golden city and the everlasting day?"

Harriet's religious ideas dovetailed with her ideas on race. She was influenced by educators such as Alexander Kinmont and Francis Lieber. She probably attended lectures on race that Kinmont gave in Cincinnati in 1837 and 1838. Kinmont held that different races have innate qualities. Caucasians, he claimed, tended to be aggressive, intellectual, scientific, and ambitious. Blacks, in contrast, were spiritual, imaginative, nonintellectual, and childlike. This romantic racialism assigned black people to what today seems like an inferior position but what in that era could be associated with Christian virtue. "The sweeter graces of the Christian religion," Kinmont said, "appear almost too tropical and tender plants to grow in the soil of the Caucasian mind," whereas they "grow naturally and beautifully" among blacks. Kinmont prophesied a glorious epoch when blacks would establish in Africa a "far nobler civilization" than any other, exhibiting "all the milder and gentler" Christian virtues.

For Stowe too, blacks exhibited religious qualities she thought many whites lacked. One of Harriet's goals was to show the wrongheadedness of whites' contempt for blacks, who, she wrote, are more naturally Christian than "the hard and dominant Anglo-Saxon race." She considered the new religious style to be a special skill of blacks, whose imaginative powers yield "hymns and expressions of a vivid and pictorial nature," far livelier than those of "the colder and more correct" whites. Like Kinmont, she imagined a splendid future civilization in Africa where Christian blacks, no longer despised and downtrodden, would form the "noblest" society on earth, exhibiting "the highest form of the peculiarly *Christian life*," based on simplicity and heartfelt surrender to God.

Today such comments sound like racial stereotyping, but in Stowe's day they were progressive. Most white Americans of the time considered blacks greatly inferior to whites. Let's not forget that twelve American presidents owned slaves, as did many congressmen and Supreme Court justices. The slaveholder Thomas Jefferson, author of the Declaration of

Independence, wrote that blacks were intrinsically dull, unimaginative, and oversexed. Even some of the most committed antislavery figures expressed racist views. The antislavery scientist Louis Agassiz claimed that "the brain of the Negro is that of the imperfect brain of a seven months' infant in the womb of the White." The antislavery statesman Cassius Clay reported that he had studied blacks and concluded, "We can make nothing out of them. God has made them for the sun and the banana!" Even Lincoln, despite his belief that blacks were human and slavery was wrong, declared, "I am not nor ever have been in favor of bringing about in any way, the social and political equality between the black and white races," because "there is a physical difference between [them]" that would forever prevent them from living equally in America. Lincoln often used the then-common word "nigger," as did Whitman, who, with all his devotion to democracy, predicted, "The nigger, like the Injun, will be eliminated: it is the law of races. . . . A superior grade of rats comes and then all the minor rats are cleared out"—a mournfully ironic echo of then-popular ethnographic theories that lay behind racial genocide.

Stowe did not accept such ideas. Instead, she directed her era's belief in racial difference toward what then was a radical notion: blacks had the capacity to outshine whites in what counted most—true religion and richly human expressiveness.

Religion in *Uncle Tom's Cabin* is emotional and simple but not mawkish or yielding. Recent critics who see Tom and Eva as symbols of a feeble, "feminized" liberal Protestantism neglect evidence to the contrary. Many nineteenth-century liberal Protestants emphasized not only feeling but grit. They believed that their own religion bred sturdiness, in contrast to orthodox Calvinism and Catholicism, which, they thought, thwarted human effort and created languor and listlessness. The Unitarian leader William Ellery Channing criticized orthodox doctrines for "degrading man into a chattel slave of Power" instead of instilling "the Courage of pure Love." Another prominent liberal, William Ware, wrote that Calvinism generated timidity and dependence, while those who rejected it were typically strong and self-reliant. Henry Ward Beecher denounced "that crawling, that prostration, that takes the very manhood out of man" and declared that "the object of religion is not to make dreamy speculators, but real, earnest, vigorous men."

Stowe brought these ideas alive in a gallery of Christian characters who combine feeling and extraordinary strength. Indeed, she arranged her narrative so that many of her Christian characters learn to mingle gentleness and toughness. Take the enslaved couple Eliza and George Harris. At the beginning of the novel, Eliza becomes strengthened by her quest for freedom for herself and her child. It makes "flesh and nerve impregnable, and string[s] the sinews like steel." George, bitter over his enslavement, is the soldierly rebel through much of the novel but turns mild when he settles down with Eliza and forms a Christian home. The Ohioans who help the Harrises escape—the motherly Mrs. Bird and the Quakers Ruth Stedman and Rachel and Simeon Halliday—are initially placid characters who toughen when they actively resist the Fugitive Slave Law of 1850. Several other characters—St. Clare, Topsy, Sambo, and Quimbo—at first are callously indifferent to religion but are humanized when they accept Christianity. Aunt Ophelia begins as a rigidly orthodox Christian who softens when she witnesses Topsy's conversion.

How about Eva? Those who argue she embodies a weakly sentimental religion overlook her remarkable resilience. Her illness and death show that optimistic, visionary faith can breed extraordinary strength. Her death is affecting not because she is weak and lachrymose but because she is strong and confident. The people around her weep, but she remains cheerful and positive in spite of her debility. She tells Tom, "I can understand why Jesus *wanted* to die for us," explaining that she would like to die if it could end the misery of millions of enslaved American blacks.

Uncle Tom's name has become a byword for sheepish submissiveness, but this misinterpretation was created by popular plays and doesn't square with the novel. True, Tom has a gentle, childlike nature. This makes him the ideal Christian, in Stowe's terms. At the same time, though, he is self-reliant and strong. He is introduced as "a large, broad-chested, powerfully made man," with "an expression of grave and steady good sense" and a "self-respecting and dignified" air. He heroically saves Eva from drowning when she falls off the riverboat, and he remains tough in the face of Legree's atheistic taunts and sadistic cruelty. He could escape torture by telling Legree where Cassy and Emmeline are hiding, but he boldly refuses to do so, just as he had earlier refused to flee with Eliza because to do so would put Shelby's other slaves in jeopardy of being sold. We are told that Tom "felt strong in God to meet death, rather than betray the helpless." Legree regards Tom as a brash troublemaker who is despicable precisely because he is tough: "Had not this man braved him,—steadily, powerfully, resistlessly,—ever since he bought him?"

Altogether, *Uncle Tom's Cabin* went a long way toward winning Christianity for the antislavery cause. This was no mean feat. By the early 1850s, proslavery thought had gained the upper hand in the religious argument over slavery. Defenders of the South found ample sanction for slavery in the Bible. They pointed out that the great patriarchs of the Old Testament had been slaveholders: they found biblical evidence, for instance, that Abraham owned more than three hundred slaves. They insisted that when Noah cursed his disobedient son Ham, he was consigning Ham and his allegedly black descendants to eternal slavery. Nowhere in the New Testament, they continued, was slavery condemned. Not only did Christians tolerate slavery, but the Apostle Paul ordered the fugitive slave Onesimus to return to his master, Philemon.

The major churches, North and South, compromised on slavery. Harriet had a character in one of her novels impugn American churches: "About half of them defend [slavery] from the Bible, in the most unblushing, disgusting manner. The other half acknowledge and lament it as an evil; but they are cowed and timid, and can do nothing." By showing in virtually every scene of *Uncle Tom's Cabin* that the Bible was antislavery in religious spirit, she launched a major challenge to churchly straddling.

At the same time, she forcefully challenged abolitionists like William Lloyd Garrison, who were so repelled by the alliance of the American church with slavery that they came close to rejecting religion altogether. Although Stowe had great respect for Garrison and shared his antislavery zeal, she was uneasy about his de-emphasis on religion. She reportedly once asked him, "Mr. Garrison, are you a Christian?" which prompted his equivocal reply, "And who is my neighbor?" In a letter she wrote him after *Uncle Tom's Cabin* was published, she praised his antislavery newspaper *The Liberator* for its bold advocacy of the "progressive element in our times" but added, "What I fear is that it will take from poor Uncle Tom his Bible and give him nothing in its place." *Uncle Tom's Cabin* did what Garrison and other activists failed to do: it moved millions by promoting abolitionist religion through vibrantly portrayed human experiences and shared emotions. Many reviewers singled out the novel's religious impact. One wrote that it "spread the gospel of Jesus Christ" and provided "a very perfect antidote to the infidelity which has been generated in other ranks of the Anti-slavery reform."

    Uncle Tom's Cabin also put religion to use in another way. The novel staked a claim to act as a redemptive influence on a popular culture that was hurtling toward a tawdriness and commercialism that Stowe wanted to stall.

2

TAMING
CULTURAL BEASTS

COUNTLESS READERS WERE inspired by *Uncle Tom's Cabin* to embrace Christianity, among them the dying German poet Heinrich Heine. He had long been tormented by religious doubt but regained his faith in the Bible after reading Stowe's novel. The novel, which stimulated the sale of Bibles globally, was also used as a Sunday school text. One appreciative father reported that his young daughter, dying of cholera, was consoled by the prospect that soon she would join Tom and Eva in heaven—an example of why there were so many adaptations of it as a children's book.

Uncle Tom's Cabin not only offered salvation to individuals; it also filtered the most subversive, sensational, or raucous cultural energies of the time through the cult of domesticity, which put the home and the family at the center of life. Women's rights, graphic reform writing, sensational novels, and zany minstrel-show humor gained broad moral appeal when Stowe recombined their images with domesticity and with antislavery commitment. In doing this, she helped popularize the American home as a center of virtue and took the innovative step of converting it into an arena of progressive politics.

To hostile critics, however, *Uncle Tom's Cabin* only *intensified* subversive cultural forces and spread them far and wide. Proslavery reviewers insisted that Stowe used religion as a veneer for dangerous reforms and cheap sensationalism. George Frederick Holmes, a leading Southern apologist, associated *Uncle Tom's Cabin* with the anarchic "isms" that he said flooded Northern society, in contrast to the stable, conservative South. "Mrs. Stowe," he wrote, "throws an ultra Christian hue over all her writings" but really was a vehicle for the ideas of "the Abolitionists, the Communists, the Lippardists, the Spirit Rappers, and the whole confraternity of social humbugs, [who] all claim to speak as the oracles of heaven, and as special messengers entrusted with the authority of Christ." She reveled in "scenes of license and impurity, and ideas of loathsome depravity and habitual prostitution," and owed her popularity to "the fashionable favour extended to the licentious novels of the French School, and the women's rights' Conventions, which have rendered the late years infamous, have unsexed in great measure the female mind, and shattered the temple of feminine delicacy and moral graces." Other proslavery commentators made similar charges. The novel was variously branded as "revolting and unjust"; full of "obscene reflections" and "vivid descriptions of sensuality"; "shamelessly profligate"; the product of a shrew who was "deficient in the delicacy and purity of a woman" and who "painted from her own libidinous imagination scenes which no modest woman could conceive of."

Some of the longest proslavery reviews of *Uncle Tom's Cabin* argued that it was written by a radical reformer who had abandoned the domestic sphere and made a shocking entrance into the political arena. "Mrs. Stowe," wrote one reviewer, "belongs to the school of Women's Rights . . . one which would place woman on a foot of political equality with men, and cause her to look beyond the office for which she was created—the high and holy office of maternity." In the words of other reviewers, she was a "termagant virago," a "foul-mouthed hag" who "deliberately step[ped] beyond the hallowed precincts—the enchanted circle [of the home]"; "the man Harriet," who had "unsexed herself"; she was "a perfect female Hercules" characteristic of "these days of Bloomerism and Women's Rights, when . . . [a woman] puts on her seven league boots, and takes long strides to keep with the glorious march of the masculine mind."

Such comments weren't just outpourings of proslavery venom. They point to tensions within *Uncle Tom's Cabin* between the subversive and the conventional—opposing tendencies in the culture at large and in Stowe's private experience. In its time (and, as shall be seen, in later decades as well) *Uncle Tom's Cabin* could seem seditious and menacing. The novel isn't nearly as conservative as Ann Douglas suggests in *The Feminization of American Culture*, which associates its heroines with "the timid exploits of innumerable pale and pious heroines" of popular sentimental literature. On women's issues, Stowe actually occupied a middle ground. She didn't renounce women's rights, as did her sister Catharine when she signed a petition against awarding women the vote, but she didn't go to the opposite extreme of championing feminism on the lecture trail, as did her half-sister Isabella Beecher Hooker, a notorious agitator. Stowe wanted to reach mainstream readers in *Uncle Tom's Cabin* while making forceful points about both slavery and women. She did so by packaging daring ideas and images in conventional wrapping.

The portrayal of women in *Uncle Tom's Cabin* can be best understood if we consider it against the background of a large variety of contemporary novels, many of which have been ignored in discussions of Stowe. A few novels of the period tentatively promoted women's rights, but they failed to make a dent in the literary marketplace. Sarah J. Hale's *The Lecturess; or, Woman's Sphere* (1839), for instance, is about a woman who tours about giving lectures in order "to raise woman to that equality with man which is her right by the divine right of nature, and of which oppression alone deprives her." Even though Hale reins in this subversive subject by marrying off her heroine and having her recant her opinions on her deathbed, the novel was far too unconventional for the nineteenth century, and there's no evidence that it had much of a sale. Laura Curtis Bullard's novel *Christine: or, Woman's Trials and Triumphs* (1855) met with a similar failure. Bullard's heroine gives lectures and founds a woman's work bureau. Although she too abandons the reform circuit and becomes domesticated, this conservative ending was not enough to make the novel tolerable for nineteenth-century readers.

Female lecturers of the day were commonly denounced for abandoning the domestic sphere. One alarmed father said that he'd rather see his beloved daughter dead than have her join the "female croakers" who gave lectures. Stowe knew this conservative attitude well. Her sister Catharine, believing that woman's place was in the home or in the classroom as a teacher, came out strongly against women lecturers like the abolitionist Angeline Grimke, who, she said, compromised her feminine nature by venturing onto the lecture platform. Harriet herself shied away from speaking publicly. When she toured the British Isles in 1853, where many large functions were held in her honor, she didn't give speeches; nor did the crowds who came out to see her expect her to do so. She had her husband Calvin or her brother Charles talk while she sat silently by.

Where Stowe gave a voice to women was in her fiction through her voluble heroines. Many of the conversations in *Uncle Tom's Cabin* are dominated by women, most of whom express views that challenge corrupt male-dominated institutions, especially slavery. Emily Shelby, who has "a clear, energetic, practical mind, and a force of character every way superior to her husband," speaks out so strongly against slavery that her slaveholding husband remarks that she is "getting to be an abolitionist, quite." Mary Bird is another woman who outspeaks her husband, a senator who has voted in support of the proslavery Fugitive Slave Law. She lectures him on the wickedness of the law and actually wins him over when runaway slaves arrive at their door. Also talkative is the reform-minded Vermont spinster Ophelia, whom some reviewers associated with so-called strong-minded women or bluestockings.

Many of the enslaved black women in the novel are equally expressive. Cassy, Legree's enslaved mistress, stands out. She wields an uncanny power over her despotic master and is able to manipulate him through language. Also, she tells Uncle Tom the long history of her sufferings at the hands of male slaveowners—an extended narration that Stowe transposed, almost word for word, into her play *The Christian Slave*, a monologue all the more remarkable because Stowe wrote it expressly for Mary Webb, a Philadelphia actress whose mother was an escaped slave. Delivering the play with success in Massachusetts and London, Webb impersonated both the female and male characters, black and white; her rendering of Cassy, Uncle Tom, and Topsy won special praise. This unprecedented performance was at once cross-racial and cross-gender.

But what's most unusual about Stowe's orating women is that they didn't strike most readers of the time as unconventional. For sympathetic readers, Stowe and her characters epitomized true womanhood. One reviewer, remarking that "every word" of *Uncle Tom's Cabin* "issues glistening and warm from the mind of woman's love and sympathy," maintained that no other work offered "so many and such sudden and irresistible appeals to the reader's heart, which . . . only a wife and mother could make." Even the outspoken Mary Bird seemed like a true woman who remained within her proper sphere. A journalist raved that she exhibited "that refinement of taste, that delicacy of moral sensibility, and that exquisitely elevated and unworldly character, which is the glory of their sex," and therefore is "a woman after our own heart," an "example [to be] universally followed."

It wasn't just the woman orator that Stowe retooled. She took zestful, often rebellious characters from popular culture—the adventure feminist (the tough, active heroine who could assume male roles), the feminist criminal (the willful lawbreaker), the fallen woman (wronged by males and driven to prostitution), and the sensual woman (who defies true womanhood by reveling in sexual pleasure)—and folded them into the era's most virtuous heroine, the moral exemplar. Stowe was the first novelist to couple the kind of feisty, unconventional heroines that often appeared in yellow-covered pulp novels with the upright moral exemplar featured in more conventional best-sellers like Susan Warner's *The Wide, Wide World* (1850).

This coupling produced the multilayered heroines of *Uncle Tom's Cabin*. Eliza Harris became the century's best-known adventure feminist because of her brave flight across the icy Ohio; but she is also a devoted wife, mother, and Christian. Even the most degraded females in the novel—Cassy, Prue, and the naughty slave girl Topsy—attract our sympathy because they have an innate goodness that can flower as Christian virtue, as when Topsy tearfully embraces religion at Eva's bidding or when Cassy is moved by Tom's religious words.

Most extraordinary of all is what Stowe does with the stereotype of the feminist criminal, who in pulp novels subverted virtue, flouted convention, and even committed murder (one thinks especially of the scheming procuresses and man-killers of George Lippard's 1845 best-seller *The Quaker City*). Stowe gives us a range of women characters—Eliza, Mrs. Shelby, Mrs. Bird, and Rachel Halliday—who are, strictly speaking, feminist criminals, since they actively violate the Fugitive Slave Law, the much-touted bill the distinguished statesmen Henry Clay and Daniel Webster had fashioned to hold together the nation. But because the heroines in *Uncle Tom's Cabin* who break this law are also loving, domestic types, they do not come across as dangerous or subversive. The same applies to Little Eva. Eva actually has something in common with the religiously inspired antislavery lawbreaker John Brown, whom Stowe came to admire greatly when he exploded onto the national scene several years later. Although Eva's gentle approach is light-years distant from Brown's use of weapons (which Stowe eventually recognized as a viable response to slavery), Eva is similar to Brown in that she defies convention by loving enslaved blacks so much that she is willing to sacrifice her life for their freedom. As she approaches death, her joy is strengthened by the fact that she has persuaded her father, St. Clare, to free his slaves. But even though she opposes the laws of the land, Eva remains the good-hearted, angelic moral exemplar throughout. Any qualms that most nineteenth-century readers might have felt over her unorthodox status as a Southern girl opposed to slavery were drowned in tearful sympathy for her.

Stowe's strategy with other phenomena of her time—reform movements, sensational literature, and minstrel humor—was similar to her treatment of gender: she redirected potentially destabilizing cultural energies through domestic feelings that resonated powerfully for multitudes of readers.

The postmillennial dream of reforming America to prepare it for an imminent golden age fostered many reforms, among them temperance, utopian socialism, and moral reform (as the battle against prostitution, lewd behavior, and pornography was then called). At first, many writers and speakers of the period promoted such reforms in conventional writings that emphasized the remedies for, rather than the wages of, vice. But reform literature increasingly leaned toward the lurid and sensational. The rise of penny newspapers, featuring juicy reports of murder, suicide, accidents, and so forth, as well as the flamboyant showmanship of P. T. Barnum's exhibitions of freaks and oddities, whetted the public's appetite for the outlandish and the bizarre. Reformers hoping to attract the attention of curiosity-seekers showed a growing tendency to dwell on grisly or erotic results of vice. As a result, many reformers drifted beyond the boundaries of propriety and left themselves open to charges of crass sensationalism. In the 1830s the moral reformer John R. McDowall presented details about the prevalence of pornography and prostitution in New York City in such graphic detail that his newspaper was lambasted as an "infamous bawdy chronicle," "the most foul and loathsome journal that ever suffused the face of modesty ... a brothel companion." That decade also saw the rise of best-selling anti-Catholic works, most notably Maria Monk's *Awful Disclosures of the Hotel Dieu Nunnery of Montreal,* alleging that whoredom, infanticide, and murder were commonplace behind convent walls. The arrival of the Washingtonian movement in 1840 ushered in a new liveliness and vigor to temperance rhetoric, as reformed drunkards described the horrors of alcoholism. Some temperance lecturers were accused of sensation-mongering; even a prominent orator like John B. Gough, despite his sincere commitment to temperance, was variously called a "theatrical performer," a "mountebank," a "humbug," and the like because of his habit of acting out the terrors of delirium tremens on the lecture platform.

In popular fiction, there was a trend toward sensationalism that sometimes reached gloomy depths, as in George B. Cheever's *Deacon Giles Distillery*, in which demons produce barrels of liquor, or *The Confessions of a Rumseller*, in which a drunkard kills his daughter and drives his wife insane, or Timothy Shay Arthur's best-seller *Ten Nights in a Bar-room*, with its horrific portrayal of the collapse of a respectable community into complete moral degradation after the establishment of a saloon and a distillery.

The major writers of the American Renaissance felt the influence of the dark-reform mode, which used a reform pretext to explore irrational, sometimes criminal behavior. Poe, who battled alcohol dependence and periodically joined temperance groups, used dark-temperance imagery extensively in tales like "The Cask of Amontillado" and "The Black Cat," in which alcohol fuels homicidal madness. Whitman's Washingtonian novel *Franklin Evans* enjoyed a strong sale because of its melodramatic narrative of murder and savagery caused by tippling. Melville integrated dark-temperance scenes into *Moby-Dick,* as when the bartender in the Spouter-Inn served sailors "poison . . . deliriums and death" in "abominable" tumblers, or when the harpoon-maker Perth is described as a gloomy man whose once-happy family had been destroyed by "the Bottle Conjurer." "Upon the opening of that fatal cork," Melville writes, "forth flew the fiend, and shrivelled up his home."

The quintessential example of dark-reform literature was George Lippard's *The Quaker City; or, The Monks of Monk Hall* (1845), America's best-selling novel before the publication of *Uncle Tom's Cabin*. Based on a famous case in which a man was acquitted after murdering his sister's seducer, *The Quaker City* is ostensibly devoted to exposing vices such as rape, intemperance, and upper-class hypocrisy. But it dwells at such great length on the eroticism and perversity associated with such ills that it was denounced as "the most immoral work of the age" and became "more read, and more attacked, than any work of American fiction ever published."

In the novel, Lippard can't describe a drunkard without registering his surrealistic inebriated visions, or a woman on the verge of being seduced without dwelling on her "snowy globes," or a lascivious clergyman with-

George Lippard's The Quaker City; or, The Monks of Monk Hall *(1845),*
the best-selling American novel before Uncle Tom's Cabin

out noting his lip-smacking sexual hunger, or a monstrous pimp without
mentioning his sadistic love of blood. One of Lippard's critics complained
that his fiction was "founded on the principle that human nature must be
reformed, by an exhibition of its lowest degradations and by the delinea-
tions of its vilest passions. This is a ruinous doctrine."

The Beechers, as a reform-minded family bent on changing society,
found themselves confronted with such sensationalism in popular culture. Catharine Beecher's response to such writing was firm: she completely avoided descriptions of vice that might be considered excessive.
She thought that reform and religion could be promoted by fiction only
with the utmost caution, since, as she wrote, "works of imagination . . . are
often the channel for conveying the most widespread and pernicious
poisons." Women, Catharine argued, must be especially careful not to
embark on public reform projects other than conservative ones like edu-

cation or domestic reform. When Catharine impugned Angelina Grimke for speaking out publicly on slavery, she insisted that abolitionism generated only "denunciation, recriminations, and angry passions," whereas "woman is to win everything by peace and love." Her sibling Edward was also notably restrained in his accounts of vice.

Brother Henry was passionate in his attacks on vice but did not go beyond accepted limits. He denounced sensational novels as "monster-galleries" that exhibited "loathsome women and unutterably vile men, huddled together in motley groups, and over all their monstrous deeds,—their lies, their plots, their crimes, their dreadful pleasures, their glorying conversation." As a moral reformer, he showed warning signs of the libido that later made him the central figure in the century's most famous adultery scandal. In a reform lecture on "The Strange Woman," he described the magnetic attraction of brothels for young men, lingering on the temptations of these dens of iniquity. The typical house of prostitution, surrounded by lush gardens, seemed irresistible: "In every window are sights of pleasure; from every opening, issue sounds of joy—the lute, the harp, bounding feet, and echoing laughter. Nymphs have descried this Pilgrim of temptation;—they smile and beckon." Inevitably, he said, a man tempted by prostitutes finds himself in a hellish vortex of shame and sin.

In 1848 Beecher caused a sensation when he auctioned in his Brooklyn church the enslaved teenagers Mary and Emily Edmonson, who were threatened with being sold in the Deep South. Dwelling on the girls' physical charms and spiritual virtues, he invited his listeners to imagine to what use the sisters were destined. He implored his congregation to donate sufficient funds to save the girls from the sexual slave trade; the plate was passed, with his audience contributing everything from cash and coins to watches. More than enough was raised to purchase freedom for the sisters, whom Harriet and Calvin later lodged in their home before sending them to be educated at Oberlin.

Henry Ward Beecher, in short, knew how to be titillating without venturing into the openly erotic. There was good reason why he was able

Henry Ward Beecher

to convince a jury of his innocence (despite his probable guilt) when in the 1870s he was brought to trial for having an affair with the wife of a parishioner. He was a superb salesman of morality and was one of the most influential reformers in America.

Stowe became even more influential than her brother by finding her own middle ground between the sensational and the conventional in her reform writings. Unlike Catharine, she did not shy away from entering the public debate over major reforms. At the same time, she never plunged into the debate as vigorously as did half-sister Isabella, who created a scandal on the lecture platform as a women's rights advocate and a violent critic of establishmentarian hypocrites—including half-brother Henry during his adultery trial. Unlike Isabella, Stowe not only believed in her brother's innocence but avoided giving reform speeches.

The great popularity of *Uncle Tom's Cabin* can be attributed largely to the fact that it advocated controversial, sometimes subversive reforms without straying into the merely sensational or the openly transgressive. The proslavery reviewers who called the novel lewd or licentious failed to recognize that it dealt with popular reforms in a way that was new for American fiction: it was bold in promoting reform, but it never crossed the line into the kind of commercialized sensation-mongering that characterized some reform writing. To the contrary, its message of uplift and reform redirected it toward middle-class mores and heartfelt religion.

Stowe's sensitivity to her era's reform movements and popular culture has not been sufficiently recognized. Her father had been a pioneer in delivering sermons on reform issues, and she was a path-blazer in integrating reform into popular fiction and essays. During the Cincinnati years she tested out various ways of integrating such topics in magazine writings whose themes look forward to *Uncle Tom's Cabin*.

Like her father, she was strongly attracted to the cause of temperance. Lyman Beecher recognized the very real dangers of alcohol abuse. He had grown up in a time when the consumption of alcohol was rising quickly. The amount of absolute alcohol consumed annually by the average American increased steadily to more than seven gallons by the mid-1820s (over three times today's per capita consumption). In 1820, Americans spent $12 million on alcohol, an amount that exceeded total expenditures by the U.S. government. People of all backgrounds drank. "Everybody asked everybody to drink," Thomas Low Nichols wrote of his youth. "There were drunken lawyers, drunken doctors, drunken members of Congress, drunkards of all classes." Abraham Lincoln, a temperance advocate, said liquor was "like the Egyptian angel of death, commissioned to slay, if not the first, the fairest born in every family."

Lyman Beecher in 1814 took a stand against drinking among clergymen. He successfully called for an end to alcohol being served at ministers' ordinations. Eleven years later he delivered a series of firm but restrained temperance addresses. He did not wallow in the vicious behavior that resulted from alcohol abuse. He was more interested in possible solutions to the drinking problem than in horrifying examples of drunkenness. Only one of his six lectures focused on "The Evils of Intemperance," whereas three explored a ban on liquor sales. In 1826, a year after he gave the lectures, the American Temperance Society was founded, marking a shift toward total abstinence and the temperance pledge. Within a decade, membership in the society reached 1.5 million.

Stowe and several of her siblings were swept up in the temperance cause. Stowe was so devoted to it that she lambasted fiction that contained drinking scenes. One of her objections to Charles Dickens' writings was "the strong flavor of brandy and water, and spirituous drink of all sorts, which everywhere pervades them." She added, "If this age be *par excellence* a temperance age, we think that the writings of Dickens are as much *par excellence* anti-temperance tracts."

Like others in the temperance movement, Stowe wrote fiction promoting the reform. Her temperance tales, ranging from a conventional story on avoiding drink to dark sketches of alcoholism's ravages, had a variety of tones that were also registered in *Uncle Tom's Cabin*. In her 1842 tale "The Coral Ring: The Temperance Pledge," the heroine, Florence Elmore, saves a friend, George Elliot, from a possible drinking problem through a game by which he promises to follow her orders once she gives him a cross-shaped ring. When Florence spots him at a party on the verge of sipping wine, she rushes to him and warns him not to drink the vile substance. He obeys her and vows to take the pledge of total abstinence. This tame story is a throwback to temperance fiction of the 1820s, most of which stressed virtue rather than vice.

Still, Stowe knew how to dramatize the miserable results of intemperance. In "The Drunkard Reclaimed," she depicts an initially happy couple, Edward and Augusta Howard, whose marriage is destroyed by alcohol. At first, the lighthearted newlyweds laugh at a relative who urges them to take the temperance pledge. Augusta sniffs, "This tiresome temperance business! One never hears the end of it, nowadays. Temperance papers—temperance tracts—temperance hotels—temperance this, that, and the other thing, even down to temperance pocket-handkerchiefs for little boys! Really, the world is getting intemperately temperate." Soon, though, Edward and Augusta start going to parties where alcohol is served. He develops a drinking habit that leads to his abandoning his family. He moves to a faraway city, and Augusta follows him. He becomes a brutal drunkard and she a miserable woman: "There was the mother, faded and care-worn, whose dark and melancholy eyes, pale cheeks and compressed lips, told of years of anxiety and endurance. There was the father, with haggard face, unsteady step, and that callous, reckless air, that betrayed long familiarity with degradation and crime." Edward is finally helped by a friend who convinces him to become a teetotaler.

Two of Stowe's other dark-temperance stories, "Somebody's Father" and "Woman, Behold Thy Son!," present vignettes of drunken misery. In the former tale, a busload of people mocks a red-faced inebriated man who is groveling in the street; the jeers cease when a woman passenger points out the tragic probability that this ruined man has left behind a sad family. "Woman, Behold Thy Son!" traces the backsliding of a young man who takes the temperance pledge but then begins drinking wine at parties, which leads to his drunkenness and finally suicide.

In *Uncle Tom's Cabin*, Stowe skillfully blends dark and conventional temperance images. She advances the temperance cause indirectly in scenes in which evil schemes are hatched in an atmosphere of drinking. In the conversation that leads to the sale of Uncle Tom and little Harry, Arthur Shelby and the slave-trader Dan Haley drink wine—an ominous sign for readers familiar with temperance writings. Later on, when Haley meets Loker and Marks in a tavern to plot the capture of the fleeing Eliza, the three are drinking heavily. Haley orders "plenty of the *real stuff*." Loker guzzles "a big tumbler full of raw spirits" followed by "half a glass of raw brandy." Marks drinks a mint julep and then mixes "a tumbler of punch to his own taste." In the scene where the Harris family is being hunted down, their pursuers are described as "eight or ten [men], hot with brandy, swearing and foaming like so many wolves."

Later in the novel, the temperance theme takes on an even darker tone. Augustine St. Clare is killed when he tries to break up a brawl between drunken men in a café. The enslaved woman Prue, after years of sexual exploitation, becomes a wretched alcoholic who declares that she would rather spend eternity in hell than remain alive in the hands of slaveholders. Another sex slave, Cassy, drinks to drown her despair and encourages others to do likewise. When her friend Emmeline rejects brandy as "hateful," Cassy says, "I hated it, too; and now I can't live without it."

The nefarious Simon Legree overindulges in drink. His mother had tried to guide him toward virtue and clean living, but he rejected her: "He drank and swore, was wilder and more brutal than ever." Before she died, she sent him an envelope containing a lock of her hair. He opened the envelope while "carousing among drunken companions" and burned the hair, after which he tried "to drink, and revel, swear away the memory" of her, which was impossible, for her ghost haunted him. He continued his drinking, which led to his murderous cruelty, and he recognized alcohol's power for degradation. Shortly before torturing Tom, Legree plies his lackeys Sambo and Quimbo with liquor and carouses with them. The three are in a state of "furious intoxication . . . singing, whooping, upsetting chairs, and making all manner of ludicrous and horrid grimaces at each other."

Alternatively, the novel portrays the benefits of not drinking by the presence of many virtuous characters who have no interest in alcohol. The kindly people who help the fugitives—the Birds, the Hallidays, the Van Trompes, and Phineas Fletcher—are portrayed as upright, temperate folk whose strongest drink is tea. The novel's main voice for temperance is Tom. When St. Clare warns Tom not to drink too often, Tom replies emphatically, "I never drink." Marie St. Clare says of Tom, "I know he'll get drunk," but her husband assures her that Tom is "a pious and sober article." Not only does Tom avoid liquor, but he pleads with St. Clare to follow his example. Concerned about St. Clare's regular frequenting of places where drink is consumed, Tom worries about his master's spiritual condition. Tom warns St. Clare that he risks the "*loss of all—all*—body and soul." Tom gives biblical sanction for his hatred of alcohol, declaring, "The good Book says, 'it biteth like a serpent and stingeth like an adder.' " Tom's temperance plea is effective, for St. Clare vows to stay away from liquor. Later on, Tom also brings about redemptive change in other drinkers such as Cassy, Sambo, and Quimbo.

Having Tom inspire both whites and blacks to embrace temperance was a daring move on Stowe's part. In antebellum temperance reform, segregation was overwhelmingly the rule. For instance, in 1850 one of the largest national organizations, the Sons of Temperance, passed a rule against admitting black people, provoking the ire of Henry Ward Beecher. He publicly announced his resignation from the group, whose racist regulation he found "morally offensive to the last degree." Harriet went beyond her brother's protest and made an affirmation of the moral efficacy of black Americans. She created a black hero who brought about the regeneration of a dissipated white man.

The temperance message of *Uncle Tom's Cabin* was so compelling that after the novel appeared, an Edinburgh book publisher, Constable & Co., reportedly offered Stowe a $10,000 advance to write a novel devoted solely to temperance. Although she did not write the book, she had struck a chord among reform-minded Americans who made an analogy between chattel slavery and enslavement to alcohol. In July 1854 she traveled from Andover, where she and Calvin then lived, to Maine, where she attended a temperance and antislavery picnic held in her honor and accepted a post as the corresponding secretary of the Maine Ladies' Temperance and Anti-Slavery Association.

When Stowe realized that slavery was growing despite her challenge of it in *Uncle Tom's Cabin,* her bitterness was reflected in her intensified use of temperance themes in her next antislavery novel, *Dred.* She believed she could turn more people against slavery if she linked it to the more widespread issue of alcoholism. The novel's villain, Tom Gordon, matches Simon Legree's cruelty and outdoes his penchant for liquor. The debauched Gordon, devoid of morality and decency, brutalizes slaves and takes sexual advantage of enslaved women. And there is no Uncle Tom to sober him up.

Another movement that influenced Stowe was moral reform, which in that era focused on the fight against illicit sex, especially prostitution. For her, moral reform was closely connected to antislavery feeling. As a child, she reportedly heard about the sexual abuse of slave women through an oft-repeated story about her mother's sister, Mary Foote. In 1803, Mary was married to a planter from Jamaica, John James Hubbard, and moved there with him. Mary was overcome "with constant horror and loathing" witnessing slavery there. According to family legend, she was appalled to learn that her husband had sired several of his slaves. Despite the shame of leaving her husband, she was so distraught that she returned to America. In 1850, just before writing *Uncle Tom's Cabin,* Stowe used her aunt's feelings to describe her own about the Fugitive Slave Law: "I feel as Aunt Mary said—I feel as if I could be willing to sink with it were all this sin and misery to sink in the sea." The words also made it into the novel. St. Clare says he has often thought that "if the whole country would sink, and hide all this injustice and misery from the light, I would willingly sink with it."

From all sides, Stowe received testimony of the sexual exploitation of enslaved women. One of her housekeepers in Cincinnati, Eliza Buck, was a fugitive slave who had for years been the kept woman of her Kentucky master, who was the father of her children. Eliza had been a "very handsome mulatto girl," in Stowe's words, with "refined and agreeable" manners, who had been raised in "a good [white] family" in Virginia before being sold first to Louisiana and then Kentucky, where her master repeatedly took sexual advantage of her.

Eliza Buck was sadly representative of enslaved women, as Stowe well knew. It was commonly reported that female slaves were more valuable than males because of their capacity to be breeders or mistresses. While marriage between slaves was forbidden in most Southern states, procreation was viewed as a crucial role of enslaved women. The sexual partners of these women were often masters or male slaves chosen by their masters. Besides providing sexual gratification for slaveowners, this system guaranteed a steady increase in plantation workers. Thomas Jefferson, who may have fathered at least one child by his slave mistress Sally Hemings, had written, "I consider a woman who brings a child every two years as more profitable than the best man on the farm." A historian of the African diaspora found that planters in the American South expected their labor force to double every fifteen years because of breeding. Some children of breeders were kept at their home plantation, but many were sold away, causing unspeakable heartbreak for their mothers.

Enslaved women were not only raped by their owners, but also frequently sold into prostitution. Light-skinned enslaved women were very profitable in the "Fancy Trade," a prostitution network featuring so-called bright or brown-skinned girls that was centered in New Orleans and also prospered in cities such as Lexington, St. Louis, and Charleston. Antislavery minister Theodore Parker noted, "Girls, the children of mulattoes, are sold at a great price, *as food for private licentiousness, or public furniture in houses of ill-fame.*" William Lloyd Garrison branded slaveowners as "monsters who have . . . given over to prostitution and ravishment, with all possible impunity, a million and half of helpless females." The black abolitionist David Nelson declared, "Of the grown females belonging to more than two millions of our race, nearly every one is either a prostitute or an adulteress, and every grown male is either a fornicator or an adulterer." Abolitionist Wendell Phillips called the South "one vast brothel." Although the statistics on the sexual abuse of enslaved blacks cannot be known with certainty, there's no doubt that the scope of the problem was enormous.

How was Stowe to deal with this explosive issue? On the one hand, she was painfully aware of the sexual exploitation of enslaved women. But she was still like her housekeeper Eliza Buck, who, when describing her relationship with her Kentucky master, "always maintained a delicacy and reserve." Unlike some moral reformers, whose gloating over the details of tabooed behavior made them objects of derision or censure, Stowe had a genuinely puritanical distaste for any violations of her era's sexual standards, which discouraged sex outside of marriage. She and Calvin appear to have had an active sex life (their surest form of birth control were long periods of separation, as when her ten-month stay at a Vermont water-cure establishment was soon followed by his fourteen-month visit there). But she was shaken to the core by reports of illicit sex. The sensational cheap literature of the day was full of accounts of sexual misdeeds on the part of clergymen and other outwardly respectable types.

Stowe was truly horrified when she heard about such extramarital sexual escapades. When in 1844 her brother Henry told her of a number of ministers who had frequented brothels, she was revolted. Henry's "frightful list" of fallen clergymen, she said, "pursued me like a nightmare." Pitying the wives of such men, she wrote Calvin, "I can conceive now of misery which in one night would change the hair to grey and shrivel the whole frame to premature decrepitude!" She imagined the anguish she would feel if her husband committed adultery: "As I am gifted with a most horribly vivid imagination in a moment I imagined—nay saw as in a vision all the distress and despair that would follow a fall on your part till I felt weak and sick." She quickly assured Calvin that she knew he was faithful, but she said she had learned how devilishly strong the male sex drive could be: "What terrible temptations lie in the way of your sex—till now I never realised it." (Imagine her reaction had she known of Calvin's private confession to his father-in-law: "I try to be spiritually-minded, and find in myself a most exquisite relish, and deadly longing for all kinds of sensual gratification.") She had a "horrible presentiment" that one or more of her clergymen brothers would someday fall, though she was confident that Henry would not be one of them. As she wrote, "Henry the other night speaking of these shocking disclosures in the church said 'Well I thank my God that I can stand up as *strait as a poplar* in the judgement day for any sin of that kind.'"

Henry's statement, complete with its pre-Freudian image of a straight-standing tree, oozes with irony, given his later trial for sex with a married parishioner. But the irony exists only in retrospect, since Henry's failings surfaced—and probably only occurred—years later. At the time he made the statement, in the 1840s, he and Harriet shared an authentic disgust for religious figures who compromised conventional morality. Sensational novels and newspapers were full of hypocritical characters—not just the reverend rake but many other immoral types as well—that fascinated the public and helped generate the complexities in works by Melville, Hawthorne, and other major writers.

For Henry and Harriet, however, such hypocrites held little attraction. Henry focused on risqué foreign writers whose works, in an age before the international copyright, were freely pirated in America. He insisted that "dangerous" European writers, who created a "lively relish for exquisitely artful licentiousness, and . . . vulgarity," were widely read in "an age which translates and floods the community with French novels (inspired by Venus and Bacchus,) and which reprints in popular forms, Byron, and Bulwer[-Lytton], and Moore, and Fielding." Harriet was also appalled by the foreign literary invasion. When she read a translation of the French novelist Eugène Sue's *The Mysteries of Paris,* which probed the urban underworld, she felt trapped in a hothouse of amorality. "They are powerful," she wrote of Sue's novels, "but *stiflingly* devoid of moral principle— . . . tho full of luscious blossom and fruit [they] make you stagger and pant for the air—not the first discernment of any boundaries between right and wrong in them." Eugène Sue was just one of many foreign writers whose morality Harriet held suspect. Among the others were some of the same as her brother's choices (Byron—"many of the best constituted minds . . . have been fatally and irreparably injured by him"—and Bulwer-Lytton, whom she blamed for creating "a great rage for pickpockets, highwaymen, murderers," as well as Dickens, who struck her as irreligious).

Even worse, in Stowe's eyes, were many popular American writers. Imitating foreign ones, they wrote about the "mysteries and miseries" of cities such as New York, Philadelphia, Boston, New Orleans, San Francisco, and even Lowell and Nashua. Although these novels never went beyond what today would be considered soft-core pornography, they were shocking for their time, since they often pictured upper-class licentiousness and depravity. The 1840s also saw the rise of "flash" newspapers with names like *The Libertine, The New York Sporting Whip,* and the *Sunday Flash,* whose racy contents appealed mainly to young urban men known as "swells" or "sports." Then there were the mammoth weeklies and story papers that ran serial fiction, much of it with a Dickensian interest in low-life criminality.

Stowe knew such literature, and she was appalled by it. In an article on popular culture, she generalized about the American scene:

Any one who has kept the run of what is called the *trash* literature of the day, must have noticed, that since the appearance of Dickens, it has run very much in a foul and muddy current, full of the slang and filth of low and degraded society. The elegant peculiarities of "flash" literature, and the choice *bons mots* of the "swell" mob, have figured largely in our mammoth sheets, in imitations and reproductions, which had no resemblance to the original, except their constant familiarity of representation of what is lowest and most disgusting in society.

She made these pronouncements in the 1840s, when the nation witnessed an explosion of racy pamphlet fiction, which comprised almost two-thirds of American novels published during that decade. In this working-class fiction—frequently cheap paperbacks with gaudy covers, screaming titles, and melodramatic illustrations—we find many languorous accounts of women in total or partial dishabille. The master of the voyeur style, George Lippard, created an atmosphere of lust around even the most apparently virtuous heroines, such as the innocent Mary Arlington in *The Quaker City,* whom he describes asleep with "her youthful bosom . . . heaving up from the folds of her night-robe" as she lies "in all the ripening view of maidenhood." Leslie Fiedler calls fiction like Lip-

Illustration from George Thompson's Venus in Boston *(1849),
typical of the era's erotic pulp fiction*

pard's "the male novel," an apt term for these largely male-authored works
which typically have omniscient narrators who look upon women characters with a distinctly male gaze.

While Stowe attacked sensational literature as "low and degraded,"
how was she to portray in fiction the foulest reality in America: the use of
enslaved women as prostitutes and breeders? She does so in *Uncle Tom's
Cabin,* where she mixes the frank treatment of illicit sex, characteristic
of sensational fiction, with the values of piety and domesticity prevalent
in conventional writings. Many of the enslaved women in the novel are
directly or indirectly associated with the Southern sex trade. In the opening scene, the light-skinned Eliza Harris is ogled by Dan Haley, who
notes how she could bring a good sum if sold in New Orleans because
of her beauty. Eliza manages to avoid this fate, but George Harris's sister
Emily does not. Prue, the pathetic drunkard and petty thief, has been used
as a breeding machine. Emmeline, the fifteen-year-old quadroon girl, is
bought at auction by Legree with the apparent aim of taking advantage

of her. Cassy herself has an awful history of sexual exploitation. She had been bought by a man she came to love, but he fell into debt and sold her and their two children to a cousin who forced her to be his mistress.

In describing these women, Stowe suggests their sexual attractiveness without being tawdry. Eliza wears a "dress of the neatest possible fit" that "set off to advantage her finely moulded shape." Emmeline has soft, dark eyes with long lashes; her mother asks her to comb back her beautiful curls so that she will not tempt lustful buyers—a plan that backfires when the auctioneer demands the curls, explaining that they "may make a hundred dollars difference in the sale of her." Cassy was called by one man "the most beautiful woman in Louisiana."

Because of such veiled eroticism, some critics were quick to class *Uncle Tom's Cabin* with the sensational pulp fiction of the period. One wrote, "The gross misrepresentation of facts in 'Uncle Tom's Cabin' is not a greater violation of fair dealing than the vivid descriptions of sensuality are of female delicacy." Another maintained that Stowe "has found it easier, as most persons have, to make a picture of bad passions and a vicious atmosphere, than one of virtue and purity."

A fairer appraisal came from a correspondent to *The New York Times* who argued that Stowe's novel in fact was *not* like sensational fiction. Far from contributing to "the swarming issues of a filth-seeking press," he wrote, Stowe dealt with controversial topics in a manner that was "decorous" and "widely wholesome." Indeed, the erotic atmosphere of *Uncle Tom's Cabin* is very different from that of the era's sensational literature. There are no "snowy globes," "rose-tipped hillocks," or "seaweed-flanked" clams in the novel. Women's charms are described with relative restraint and from a different vantage point than in sensational fiction. The male gaze is still there, but the men who gaze are proslavery types the reader loathes. The venal Haley, the money-grubbing slave auctioneer, Cassy's deceitful lover, the brutal Legree—these are the ones who size up women's bodies for purposes of profit or pleasure. Stowe always distances illicit sex acts by time or space. They occur in a threatened future (Eliza, Emmeline), in the past (Prue), or offstage (Cassy).

As for the enslaved women themselves, they are distant from the women characters in sensational novels, who range from the sexually voracious, as in George Thompson's novels, to the erotically burgeoning, as in Lippard and others. Most of the enslaved women victimized by rape or sexual harassment in *Uncle Tom's Cabin* are surrounded by images of religion or family—and usually both. Emily Harris had been "a pious, good girl,—a member of the Baptist church" before being sold in the Deep South, and at the end she reappears as the good Madame de Thoux. Susan and Emmeline are a loving, Christian mother-daughter pair. Cassy, brought up in luxury, had attended a convent school, and after hellish experiences with slaveowners, she regains a family on discovering that Eliza is her long-lost daughter. Stowe's association of such conventional values with characters who have experienced or are threatened by illicit sex has a twofold effect: it points up the basic goodness of these enslaved women, and it makes their sexual exploitation by proslavery men all the more repugnant.

Stowe also makes a strong statement about sex in her portrayal of Uncle Tom. Tom's faithfulness to his family stood in sharp contrast to the widespread view of black males as lustful brutes. It was commonly thought that blacks lacked domestic feelings and were indifferent about their sexual partners. A Southern reviewer mocked Tom's fidelity, claiming that the typical enslaved man had no scruples about taking a new wife on each plantation. "The negro, in fact, is proverbially a Lothario," the reviewer wrote. "He is seldom faithful to his vows. He loves to rove." Many white Americans felt similarly. Thomas Jefferson had stated that black men "are more ardent after their female [than whites], but love seems with them to be more an eager desire, than a tender delicate mixture of sentiment and sensation. Their griefs are transient." Even an abolitionist like Theodore Parker could declare, "Lust is [black men's] strongest passion: and hence, rape is an offence of too frequent occurrence. Fidelity to the marriage relation they do not understand and do not expect, neither in their native country nor in a state of bondage." The black male as a sexual powerhouse appeared in antebellum pornography as a titillating figure, as in George Thompson's *City Crimes* (1849), in which a wealthy young woman refuses to sleep with her white fiancé but has a torrid affair with her black servant, explaining that "the fiery and insatiate cravings of my passions" could be satisfied only by "my superb African." In time, the image of the oversexed African-American became highly politicized, as the black rapist was represented as a major threat to Southern white women in Thomas Dixon's anti-Stowe novels, D. W. Griffith's film *The Birth of a Nation*, and the writings of Jim Crow–era historians like William Archibald Dunning.

Forcefully challenging such racism, *Uncle Tom's Cabin* makes marital fidelity between blacks the driving force of its two main plots: the escape of Eliza and George Harris, and the separation of Tom from his family. Both narratives explore domestic attachments among black people with sensitivity and nuance. In fact, it would not be until the appearance of Alex Haley's *Roots* in the 1970s that the portrayal of domestic affection among African-Americans would resonate as powerfully for both black and white readers as was the case with Stowe's novel.

While Stowe provided domestic alternatives to the sexual explicitness of sensational writers, she shared their interest in adventure, the Gothic, and working-class themes—though, again, she brought moderation and moral purpose to such themes. Omitted from modern analyses of *Uncle Tom's Cabin* is its seminal role in the development of adventure narratives, an ongoing phenomenon in American popular culture. As later chapters will show, adventure played a central role in the Tom plays and films. For now, it's sufficient to note that the novel matches the adventurous excitement of the sensational novels of the day. In the words of one reviewer, "The literary taste of our day . . . demands excitement. Nothing can be spiced too high. Incident, incident . . . crowds the pages of those novels which are now all the vogue. . . . For such tastes, Mrs. Stowe has catered well." Another declared that "Mrs. Stowe has been so successful" because of her emphasis on "the exciting, the startling and the terrible."

There were two main types of popular adventure fiction in that era: moral adventure, such as James Fenimore Cooper's novels, which feature a hero who remains virtuous in the midst of danger or trial; and dark adventure, which dwells on the violence and irrationality displayed by people in extreme situations. *Uncle Tom's Cabin* offers a unique combination of moral and dark adventure. In every scene in which adventure or sensationalism is prominent, morality and perversity are simultaneously present, and morality emerges victorious. Eliza evades her heartless pursuers and makes it across the ice floes, despite the odds against her. George Harris and his helpers fend off the drunken slave-catchers in the dramatic rocky-pass scene. Tom saves Eva from drowning in the Mississippi, providing an ethical alternative to the nefarious activities among slave-traders on the riverboat. On Legree's plantation, Tom is a shining, Christ-like presence in an atmosphere of wild revelry and bloody torture.

Stowe's depiction of Legree and his surroundings draws from Gothic images common in sensational novels. Aptly, Legree reads sensational fiction. We see him poring over "one of those collections of stories of bloody murder, ghostly legends, and supernatural visitations, which, coarsely got up and illustrated, have a strange fascination for one who once engages to read them." Legree himself is like a character in popular sensational works. In particular, he resembles Devil-Bug, the villainous keeper of Monk Hall in Lippard's *The Quaker City*. Both Legree and Devil-Bug are sadists who love to see the blood of their victims flow. Both inhabit dismal structures that have chambers of horror: Monk Hall has its skeleton-littered cellar where Devil-Bug tortures people, and Legree's home its garret, where he once imprisoned a slave woman who died. Both characters are haunted by the ghosts of their victims: Devil-Bug by a man he murdered and Legree by the dead slave woman and the mother he spurned. Devil-Bug laughs when he hears shrieking victims falling "down—down" through the trapdoors of Monk Hall, and Legree has a dream of falling into an abyss "down, down, down, amid a confused noise of shrieks, and groans, and shouts of demon laughter." Both are ostensibly powerful but in fact are outwitted by vindictive madwomen: Devil-Bug by Long-haired Bess, Legree by Cassy. Both villains get their due at the hands of black people. In a kind of metaphorical slave revolt, Musquito and Glow-worm crush

Devil-Bug to death with a boulder. Legree encounters a more benign yet ultimately more damaging revolt—a Christian one that presumably consigns him to hell while his black victims are headed toward eternal bliss. Thus, Stowe puts her religious stamp on the portrait of the villain.

An element of popular sensational literature that held special appeal for Stowe was its egalitarianism. Her subtitle, *Life Among the Lowly,* highlights her concern for the marginalized. Besides vivifying the plight of blacks, the novel contains passages defending oppressed white workers. Stowe had long-standing working-class sympathies. While growing up in Litchfield, she loved to spend time in the kitchen with her family's servants. When she moved to Cincinnati in the 1830s, she entered a radically democratic environment. Cincinnati, whose population grew from 750 in 1800, when it was just being settled, to over 100,000 by mid-century, was a mushrooming city settled by people of all classes and backgrounds. Tocqueville, who visited Cincinnati around the time Stowe moved there, found that "social ranks are intermingled," representing "democracy without limit or moderation." A settler in the religion attested that "every person felt that he or she was the social equal of every other person." Perhaps stimulated by this intensely democratic environment, Stowe became close to a variety of servants, black and white, who at different times worked in her home.

Much of Stowe's interest in popular literature lay in its democratic themes. Though disappointed over Dickens' neglect of religion, she praised him for bringing "the whole class of the oppressed, the neglected, and forgotten, the sinning and suffering, within the pale of sympathy and interest." She included humble characters in her early short stories, often adding a Christian twist. In "The Bible as Comforter" she contrasts an irreligious wealthy man with a starving seamstress who finds solace in religion. The seamstress, a common symbol of lower-class oppression in that era, reappears in another of her stories, in which a poor woman and her daughters toil tirelessly to produce garments that are unappreciated by the rich ladies who buy them. Charity to the poor is recommended in "The Tea Rose," whose heroine donates beautiful things to the indigent; in "So Many Calls," in which the impoverished Jesus appears to a rich man and persuades him to give to charity groups; and in "Christmas; or, The Good Fairy," in which a rich girl learns to give to "the lowly . . . the outcast, and distressed" in celebration of Jesus, "the brother and friend of the poor."

These rather conventional expressions of working-class themes gave way to a new militancy in *Uncle Tom's Cabin,* which offers a broad vision of whites and blacks degraded by capitalist forces. In the novel, the capitalist marketplace, the driving force behind slavery, is presented as harshly deterministic. It crushes ethics, poisons the law, and shatters families. Even good-hearted Americans become victims of the capitalist system of slavery. Arthur Shelby is a kindly man who is close to his slaves, but he is forced to sell Tom and Harry to avoid financial ruin. This tragic situation, resulting from capitalist speculation, generates all subsequent situations in the novel. On the positive side, Harry is taken by his mother into a Northern community of people, mainly Quakers, who are driven by the values of democratic love, not greed. Negatively, Tom is cast more deeply into slavery, which is governed by money. Religion, talent, physical strength, comeliness—slavery converts them all into marketable commodities. Haley demands a high price for Tom because of his good features. Not only does he embody "all the moral and Christian virtues bound in black morocco, complete!" but he's "broad-chested, strong as a horse," with uncommon "calculatin faculties" and "a strong talent for business." Virtually every chapter in the novel contains examples of middle-class virtues becoming grist for the moneymaking mill of slavery.

Stowe doesn't allow her readers to bask in the misconception that they are free of guilt. To the contrary, she points out that people like Haley are the product of an economic system that most Americans support. At one point, she directly challenges the reader. Slave-traders like Haley are "universally despised," she notes,

> But who, sir, makes the trader? Who is most to blame? The enlightened, cultivated, intelligent man, who supports the system of which the trader is the inevitable result, or the poor trader himself? You make the public senti-

ment that calls for his trade, that debauches and depraves him, till he feels no shame in it; and in what are you better than he?

Stowe's economic critique extends beyond enslaved blacks to poor whites. Some reviewers unfairly attacked her for exaggerating the suffering of slaves while ignoring the "wage slaves" in Northern and European cities. Actually, her working-class perspective gave rise to powerful passages in the novel where she extended her critique of capitalism to a prediction of a worldwide workers' revolution.

She wrote at a time when the world bristled with revolutionary prophecies. During the second half of 1851, just when the weekly installments of *Uncle Tom's Cabin* were appearing in *The National Era,* America was excitedly preparing for the imminent arrival of Louis Kossuth, the exiled Hungarian rebel who had been prominent in the European revolutions of 1848. Fleeing authorities in his native land, he was coming to America to win money and support for another Hungarian revolution in the wake of the one that Russia had thwarted. The press raved over Kossuth, whose struggle against European oppressors was compared to the American Revolution. *The National Era,* while it was publishing sections of *Uncle Tom's Cabin,* joined the Kossuth chorus: "The cause of Hungary was the cause of self-government, of popular rights, of Democracy, of mankind; and Kossuth was the life and leader of that cause. No Revolutionist has acted from nobler aims, with purer motives, upon more comprehensive and sagacious views."

Stowe shared the enthusiasm for the revolutions abroad that Kossuth had helped foster. She had St. Clare announce that "there is a mustering among the masses, the world over; and there is a *dies irae* [day of wrath] coming on, sooner or later. The same thing is working in Europe, in England, and in this country." It's possible that in writing these revolutionary words, Stowe felt the influence not only of Kossuth but also of Karl Marx. We don't know for sure whether she read Karl Marx and Friedrich Engel's *The Communist Manifesto* (1848). But it's worth noting that although an

English translation of *The Communist Manifesto* did not appear until 1872, the German edition of this landmark work was reprinted in 1850 in America, where it was widely distributed. Since Calvin Stowe was a foreign-language expert who sometimes read aloud to his wife from German books, translating them into English as he went, it's possible that *The Communist Manifesto* came to Stowe's attention.

At any rate, it's likely that she read English translations of selections from Marx that appeared in Horace Greeley's *New-York Tribune,* the era's leading reform newspaper. Chapter 19 of *Uncle Tom's Cabin,* which contains St. Clare's revolutionary pronouncements, appeared in the November 20, 1851, issue of *The National Era.* Since Stowe was churning out chapters at a furious pace each month to meet Gamaliel Bailey's deadlines, it's safe to say that she wrote this chapter between late October and mid-November. During these weeks, sections of Marx and Engels' book *Germany: Revolution and Counter-Revolution* appeared in the *Tribune.* In the chapters solely written by Marx, he traced the 1848 revolutions from the early rumblings of working-class discontent to the violent revolts in the German states, Austria, Italy, France, and elsewhere. In Marx's telling, "the working people, one and all, arose at once against a government detested by all," presaging an "impending struggle between the class of capitalists and the class of laborers."

Although we don't have evidence that Stowe read Marx's passages in the *Tribune* as she was writing her chapter, St. Clare's words about a world-wide revolution seem to echo Marx, especially when he uses Austria and Italy as examples of a forthcoming time "*when the boilers* [*will*] *burst.*" St. Clare's cynicism about churches also has Marxist overtones. In one of the chapters in the *Tribune,* Marx noted that the European religious establishment, Protestant and Catholic, "formed an essential part of the bureaucratic establishment of the Government in helping to suppress the discontent of the masses." A main source of St. Clare's skepticism is his disillusion with American churches, which he saw as complicit with slaveholding and other forms of oppression. "Religion!" he exclaims to his wife. "Is what you hear at church religion? Is that which can bend and turn, and descend and ascend, to fit every crooked phase of selfish, worldly society, religion? Is that religion which is less scrupulous, less generous, less just, less considerate for man, than even my own ungodly, worldly, blinded nature? No!"

Given such passages in *Uncle Tom's Cabin*, it's understandable that some readers saw the novel as a call for revolution. A reviewer in 1853 remarked that future years would bring "the eruption of the vast volcano that must dash all the thrones of Europe to the dust" in a "fearful struggle" largely influenced by "the notions of freedom . . . imbibed from the perusal of a romance by an American woman." Another reviewer agreed that Stowe's novel would "produce a very distinct and decided effect upon affairs in Europe," where people would "give to the book a political significance which feeds the flame that smoulders in the breast of the oppressed millions."

As will be seen, *Uncle Tom's Cabin* indeed influenced revolutionaries, a number of whom were also inspired by Marx and Engels. But the novel itself cannot be called Marxist. Although it demonizes capitalism, speaks of working-class revolution, and holds established churches responsible for oppression, as do Marx's writings, it doesn't endorse dialectical materialism. Karl Marx was a German atheist; Harriet Beecher Stowe was an American Christian. She can have St. Clare say that church religion is no better than "my own ungodly, worldly, blinded nature," but the novel creates ample religious space outside of the church, a space that St. Clare eventually occupies along with other characters in the novel. Immediately after his words about a mustering of the masses, St. Clare says, "My mother used to tell me of a millennium that was coming, when Christ should reign, and all men should be free and happy. And she taught me, when I was a boy, to pray, 'Thy kingdom come.' Sometimes I think all this sighing, and groaning, and stirring among the dry bones foretells what she used to tell me was coming!"

This is straightforward Christian millennialism. Eva's redemptive

George Lippard

death and Tom's preaching lead him to meditate soberly on religious matters. When he exclaims "Mother!" as he dies, we presume he has joined
the religious fold.

Actually, Stowe's revolutionary thinking is closer to George Lippard's
than to Karl Marx's. Lippard had always taken a strong working-class
perspective in his fiction, and in 1850, just before Stowe wrote *Uncle Tom's
Cabin,* he founded the Brotherhood of the Union, a radical labor group
that rapidly spread to twenty of America's thirty states. The Brotherhood
and its principles were reported prominently in newspapers. The Brotherhood's main goal, Lippard wrote, was to "protect the men who work,
against those usurpers of capital who degrade labor." Lippard endorsed a
revolutionary Christian socialism based on the Bible and the Declaration
of Independence. Just as Stowe saw the humble Jesus as the representative
with whom the poor could identify, so Lippard based his Gospel of Labor
on the example of the man he called the Carpenter of Nazareth.

Lippard and Stowe shared a vision of America as the place God had
chosen to restore social equality. Both writers lamented the distance they
saw between the ideals of the founding fathers and social inequities in
nineteenth-century America. Lippard wrote fictionalized "legends" of the

American Revolution that gained a large readership with their imaginative descriptions of national figures and symbols, such as Washington and the Liberty Bell.

What was especially unusual about the reform envisioned by Lippard and Stowe was that it embraced white workers as well as black people, enslaved and free. Northern labor reformers generally focused on white labor, not chattel slavery in the South. Like other labor reformers, Lippard also emphasized the oppression of poor whites; but he did not exclude enslaved blacks from his agenda. He wrote that "white and black slavery, cloaked under various names, blasphemes the memory of the Revolution, and turns the Declaration of Independence into a lie." America, he insisted, was chosen "for the regeneration of the oppressed of all nations and races."

Uncle Tom's Cabin similarly recognized the oppression of white and black workers. Like Lippard, Stowe considered ways in which capitalist oppression threatened all laborers, regardless of race. Besides predicting a revolution by white workers in Europe, St. Clare brings up slave insurrection. He mentions the Haitian Revolution of 1791, when enslaved blacks began a guerrilla war that drove French colonizers from Saint-Domingue, which became the independent nation of Haiti in 1804. Stowe's racial views, by which blacks were gentle and whites aggressive, prevented her from appreciating fully the Haitian Revolution. Ophelia castigates "that abominable, contemptible Hayti," and the enslaved George Harris, when thinking about a place to establish a separate African nation, declares, "Not in Hayti; for in Hayti they had nothing to start with. . . . The race that formed the character of the Haytiens was a worn-out, effeminate one; and, of course, the subject race will be centuries in rising to anything."

George himself comes closest to being the kind of black person Stowe thinks is capable of leading a slave insurrection, partially because he is biracial. Stowe emphasizes that "George was, by his father's side, of white descent. . . . From one of the proudest families in Kentucky he had inherited a set of fine European features, and a high, indomitable spirit, from his mother he had received only a slight mulatto tinge, amply compensated

by its accompanying rich, dark eye." His high energy, which Stowe suggests comes from his Caucasian side, accounts for the fact that he comes
closer than any of the other blacks in the novel to rebelling forcefully
against whites. When Loker and his men pursue him in the rocky pass, he
brandishes a pistol and threatens to kill anyone who approaches him.

In the scene, Stowe uses both the European revolutions and the spirit
of '76 to make her point about such revolutionary action. In his own
"declaration of independence," George warns the slave-catchers, "We'll
fight for our liberty till we die." Besides echoing Thomas Jefferson and
Patrick Henry, George possesses the populist spirit of Kossuth. With biting irony, Stowe notes how Americans welcome Kossuth, a fugitive from
his homeland, while branding fugitive slaves like George Harris and his
family as criminals:

> When despairing Hungarian fugitives make their way, against all the
> search-warrants and authorities of their lawful government, to America,
> press and political cabinet ring with applause and welcome. When despair-
> ing African fugitives do the same thing,—it is—what *is* it?

When George Harris takes up his pistol, the novel comes close to
justifying violence by blacks, but it backs off from endorsing slave insurrection. George Harris is not Nat Turner. He is trying to gain freedom
and wants to protect his family from slave-catchers. Although he shoots
the charging Tom Loker, he's relieved that Loker is not killed, and he
helps carry the wounded man to a woman who tends to him.

In time, when Stowe grew increasingly bitter about the growth of
slavery in the United States, she created a fictional character, Dred, who
inherited violent passions from his father, the insurrectionist Denmark
Vesey. She also became a strong supporter of the era's most notorious
promoter of slave rebellions, John Brown. But when she wrote *Uncle Tom's
Cabin,* she would have been treading on dangerous ground if she openly
praised slave rebellions, which had terrible connotations for most Ameri-

cans. And so, she used the novel to advocate black rebelliousness subtly and within the accepted norms of her time.

One of her shrewdest methods of doing so was by revising techniques from one of the most popular entertainment forms of her era, minstrelsy. Minstrel performers were whites who smeared their faces with burnt cork and spoke in an exaggerated version of what was considered the dialect of the "plantation darkey" (Jim Crow) or the "northern dandy negro" (Zip Coon). Minstrel shows, which took off in the 1840s, regaled thousands with weird dances, funny songs, and inflated speeches full of butchered grammar and improbable images.

Those interested in tracing the minstrel roots of *Uncle Tom's Cabin* have struggled with the fact that Stowe, who shared her family's disapproval of the theater, may never have attended any of the numerous minstrel shows that appeared in Cincinnati in the 1840s. Still, *Uncle Tom's Cabin* makes clear that Stowe had full awareness of the minstrel phenomenon, which was more widespread than has been recognized.

Actually, she didn't have to go to a theater to know about minstrelsy. She could have picked up its themes and lingo from one of the most popular humorous writings of the day, the "burlesque lectures" by "Professor Julius Caesar Hannibal," the creation of William H. Levison. Born in New York in 1829 and raised in New Jersey, Levison was a failed businessman who took a strong interest in minstrelsy when he saw a show by T. D. Rice, the pioneering blackface performer whose impersonation of the odd, jumping Jim Crow sparked the minstrel craze. Levison himself became a stage comedian before turning to humorous journalism. By the late 1840s he was writing for a popular humor magazine, the *New York Picayune,* and soon became its editor. He took the original step of transposing minstrelsy to the page. In effect, he was a writer in blackface. From 1849 onward, he published a long series of lectures by Julius Caesar Hannibal, a Northern black man who pretends to be a college professor but who in fact is an ignoramus thoroughly unfamiliar with standard English. In ungainly dialect, Hannibal lectures on all kinds of topics—

politics, fads, science, religion, women, nature—and addresses his crowds variously as "Fellow Citizens," "Blubd Bruddren an Sistern," "My Deah Woolly Heds," and so on. Hannibal's addresses instantly caught on with the *Picayune*'s readers and were reprinted in other periodicals. They were later collected in a book titled *Black Diamonds*.

Melville picked up on Levison's style, as indicated by the sermon given to the sharks by Fleece, the ship's cook in *Moby-Dick*. Levison's Hannibal gives lectures *about* animals (including, notably, "De Whale"); Melville's Fleece lectures *to* the sharks. He addresses the ferocious creatures, Hannibal-like, as "Belubed fellow-critters" and gets frustrated when they ignore his advice to stop devouring the dead whale attached to the ship—a symbol of what Melville calls life's "universal cannibalism," by which all living creatures prey on each other.

Just as Melville enriched minstrel writing in the Fleece scene, so Stowe gave her own version of it in *Uncle Tom's Cabin*. She knew that few readers—even ones who strongly opposed slavery—could stomach a sympathetic account of slave insurrection, and so she cloaked this explosive issue in minstrel comedy. Two of Arthur Shelby's enslaved blacks, Sam and Andy, team up with Mrs. Shelby to frustrate Haley's efforts to capture Eliza. If Sam and Andy seem like laughable minstrel "darkeys," Mrs. Shelby is the pious wife, similar to mother figures in domestic novels. But in collaborating to help Eliza violate the Fugitive Slave Law, these conventional-appearing characters undermine the authority of the white males—Shelby, Haley, Loker, and Marks—who are trying to enforce the law.

This portrait of a group rebellion, in which two blacks are in partnership with a white woman, ventured toward dangerous territory, but Stowe made it palatable by using the accepted techniques of minstrelsy. Sam is in many ways like Levison's Julius Caesar Hannibal. Proud of his knowledge, he "speechifies" to fellow blacks, whom he comically addresses as "my feller citizens and ladies of de other sex in general." Hannibal, in a lecture on "Polly-tishuns" had described the politician as one who would "pint wich ebber way de wind ob pop'lar 'pinion blow him." Stowe, similarly, compares Sam to a politician ready to bend in different directions. Sam at first sides with Mr. Shelby and then supports Mrs. Shelby, a shift explained by the fact that his head "contained a great deal of a particular species much in demand among politicians of all complexions and countries, and vulgarly denominated 'knowing which side your bread is buttered on.'" Like the politicians Hannibal describes, Sam seemingly adjusts his principles according to the exigencies of the moment. And like Hannibal himself, Sam uses malapropisms and convoluted logic when he orates like an "electioneering politician" to his befuddled listeners.

Such behavior can make Sam and Andy seem like deplorable examples of nineteenth-century racist caricature—"bumbling, giggling, outsized adolescents," as one critic calls them. But some have recently noted deeper dimensions in these characters. We can understand them most clearly by contrasting them with the popular Julius Caesar Hannibal, whose lectures reflect the typical racial attitudes of the era, which saw blacks as subhuman, irresponsible, stupid, and lustful. Levison has Hannibal note that "colored folks" have flat noses like the monkey, which in turn is said to be "de connectin link" between blacks and the Fiji Mermaid at Barnum's Museum. Hannibal also tells of a friend, Brudder Cato Puggs, who mistook an orangutan for his grandmother. In a speech on phrenology, the pseudoscience that read character traits in skull bumps, Hannibal maintains that the largest bumps on a black person's head are those of "don't-care-a-d—nativeness" and "Amativeness," or the sex drive, which "plays de debil wid de fair sex" and sometimes "swells to such an 'xtent dat it oberwellms do wole brain." And in the front of the brain, where the intellect should be, black people have "all bone," which "'counts fully for de nigger's hed bein' hard 'nuff to butt down de stone fence."

Many antebellum Americans guffawed at such racist passages, just as they did at the protruding lips, woolly wigs, and oversized feet of performers on the minstrel stage. And many laughed along with Stowe's Sam and Andy, who with their antics and clumsy language could come off as minstrel clowns. But they are *not* minstrel clowns. They are enslaved blacks who, along with an antislavery woman, use their wits to outsmart white males intent on enforcing an unjust, proslavery law. Besides stalling Haley through tricks like upsetting his horse, they delay him further with intentionally garbled words about which route Eliza may have taken. To make this potentially offensive scene more acceptable, Stowe has Sam seem comically wishy-washy, but his actions on behalf of the fleeing Eliza in fact support his boast that he is devoted to principles he would die to defend.

Stowe's refashioning of minstrelsy controls her portraits of three other black characters in the novel: Eliza's son Harry, St. Clare's slave girl Topsy, and Uncle Tom. Little Harry is surrounded by minstrel images. His master, Shelby, greets him with "Hulloa, Jim Crow.... Come here, Jim Crow," and orders him to perform for the slave-trader Haley. Harry sings a "wild, grotesque" song and makes "many comic evolutions of the hands, feet, and whole body," including imitations of a rheumatic old man and a psalm-singing churchman. Haley is so pleased that he offers to buy the boy.

Behind the apparent fun, however, are pathos and imminent tragedy. The comic performer here is an enslaved child whose innocence makes his prospect of being sold truly alarming. His capers delight white spectators, as on the minstrel stage, but they are the prelude to a threatened separation of Harry from his mother Eliza, a hidden witness to the scene. Our sympathies flow to Eliza when she prepares to save her son, and they turn into cheering support as, with the help of Sam, Andy, and Mrs. Shelby, she uses wile and courage to elude pursuers and carry him to freedom.

Stowe also improves upon minstrelsy in her memorable portrait of the enslaved girl Topsy. At first glance, Topsy seems to have walked straight off the minstrel stage and into the novel. She's "a noted character" in the St. Clare household because "her talent for every species of drollery, grimace, and mimicry,—for dancing, tumbling, climbing, singing, whistling, imitating every sound that hit her fancy,—seemed inexhaustible." It's understandable that when the Topsy character was later developed in Tom shows, minstrel acts, and films, she became a stock figure of wild silliness, the ancestor of slapstick comedians.

In the novel itself, she possesses minstrel-like qualities along with far richer qualities. Her defiant naughtiness typifies minstrelsy, as does the racial stereotyping associated with her ignorance. But Topsy is a vehicle for Stowe's message that enslaved blacks, even when they were thoroughly dehumanized, are capable of profound human feeling that can obliterate racial barriers. When Topsy announces that she "never was born" but "just grow'd," we laugh, but on another level we feel the same kind of pity that we feel for Frederick Douglass, who reports in his *Narrative* that as a child he, like many other enslaved blacks, was barred from knowing basic facts such as his birthday or the identity of his father. Our pity grows when Topsy courts punishment by stealing small household items. She expects to be whipped. "I spects it's good for me," she says. She jokes about Ophelia's feeble lashings, which she says "wouldn't kill a skeeter," and adds, "Oughter see how old Mas'r made the flesh fly; old Mas'r know'd how!" This is humorous but at the same time horrible. Repeated torture has inured this child to the horror of the slaveholders' whip.

Topsy's brash wickedness comes not only from years of degradation as a slave but also from the Calvinistic instruction she has received from Ophelia. Announcing, "I'se so wicked!," Topsy gives a mini-sermon in which she declares that all people, white or black, are also sinners. "Miss Feely says so," she declares. "I's so awful wicked there can't nobody do nothin' for me." Through Topsy's comic assertion, Stowe makes another stab at Calvinism, aimed this time at its doctrine of total depravity. Calvinists claimed that it was a religious duty to confront one's inborn evil tendencies. Jonathan Edwards, for example, said he was overwhelmed by his "sinfulness and vileness," which seemed like "an infinite deluge, or infinite mountains overhead." When Topsy declares that she's the "wickedest critter in the world," she's repeating what she learned from Ophelia, whose religious orthodoxy the novel mocks.

The bond that develops between Topsy and Ophelia not only dispels this grim Calvinist dogma but also challenges racial prejudice. Stowe showed that whites and blacks could join through sincere affection. Eva's declaration that she loves Topsy and wants her to be good may seem saccharine today, but in that era it was a radical crossing of the racial divide, one made possible through a full recognition of shared emotions.

A similar use of sentiment to make a racial statement comes through in Uncle Tom, who also has associations with minstrelsy. The cultural historian Eric Lott suggests that Tom can be placed among romantically racialized black figures featured in some minstrel songs, including "Old Uncle Ned, Old Black Joe, and so on," each of whom, he writes, represents the "gentle, childlike, self-sacrificing, essentially *aesthetic*" enslaved black man. True, gentleness and self-sacrifice were among the qualities minstrel blacks shared with Uncle Tom. But the soft old Tom whom Lott speaks of actually developed over time in plays and minstrel shows that appeared *after* the novel was published (in this connection, it is telling that one of the songs Lott refers to, the nostalgic "Old Black Joe," appeared eight years after the publication of *Uncle Tom's Cabin*).

In the novel, as noted in chapter 1, Tom is both gentle and tough. As such, he possesses contrasting qualities, as did several black characters in *earlier* minstrel shows. One of the first known minstrel songs, Dan Emmet's "The Fine Old Color'd Gentleman" (1843), emphasizes the combined mildness and strength in its title character, Sambo:

> O Sambo was a gentleman,
> One of de oldest kind.
> His temper was very mild
> When he was let alone,
> But when you get him dander up
> He spunk to de backbone.

The Sambo of this song is like Uncle Tom, but Tom's character is far deeper than Sambo's. In Tom, mildness and toughness have Christ-like resonance. While Sambo is mild when he's "let alone," Tom's mildness, in contrast, *is* his strength. Instead of fighting, he willingly endures the whip because of his firm adherence to religious and moral principle. In the

Christian terms of the novel, his perseverance in virtue constitutes both his goodness and his power.

The minstrel songs by the era's leading writer of them, Stephen Foster, have special connections to *Uncle Tom's Cabin*. Foster transformed minstrel music by emphasizing that blacks possessed the same feelings and motivations that whites did. Foster compositions such as "Oh! Susanna," "Nelly Was a Lady," "Camptown Races," "Old Uncle Ned," "Old Folks at Home," and "My Old Kentucky Home" dramatized a range of emotions among blacks.

The latter three songs are particularly notable in relation to Tom. "Old Uncle Ned" (1848) describes an overworked slave whose death elicits great sorrow in the whites close to him:

> *When Old Ned die Massa take it mighty hard,*
> *De tears run down like de rain;*
> *Old Missus turn pale and she gets berry sad,*
> *Cayse she nebber see Old Ned again.*

The sadness of "Massa" and "Missus" after Ned's passing affirms the same kind of racial bonding through emotion that runs through *Uncle Tom's Cabin*, from the closeness of blacks and whites on the Shelby plantation through Tom's friendship with St. Clare and Eva to the scene where George Shelby grieves over Tom's death. The song portrays slaves' labor and suffering sympathetically ("Den lay down de shubble and de hoe, / . . . No more hard work for Old Ned"), as does *Uncle Tom's Cabin*. Another similarity is the happy afterlife both the song and the novel envisage for the deceased slaves: Ned has "gone whar de good Niggas go," just as Tom is headed to heaven.

Another of Foster's songs, "Old Folks at Home" (1851), ushered into minstrelsy the kind of poignant nostalgia that Uncle Tom sometimes displays after he is parted from his family. The opening lines epitomize the song's somber tone:

Way down upon de Swanee ribber,
Far, far away,
Dere's wha my heart is turning ebber,
Dere's wha de old folks stay.

All up and down de whole creation,
Sadly I roam,
Still longing for de old plantation,
And for de old folks at home.

Although the geography here differs from that in *Uncle Tom's Cabin*—the Suwannee River is in the Deep South, whereas Tom's heart is in Kentucky, far to the north—a spirit of aching grief links the novel and the song. The anguish resulting from Tom's separation from Chloe and his children echoes the pain expressed by the song, which conveys a great sense of loss: "All de world am sad and dreary, / Ebry where I roam." The song, with its evocative gloom, was sung in many Tom plays, including Stowe's *The Christian Slave*. Over time, however, the song contributed to misrepresentations of the novel, especially in later plays, where the plantation was idealized as a lost utopia, the symbol of an idyllic Old South—very distant from the novel, where Tom eventually rises above his memories of home and decides that "Heaven is better than Kintuck."

Another Foster song even more relevant to *Uncle Tom's Cabin* is "My Old Kentucky Home," which originated in a composition Foster scribbled in his sketchbook called "Poor Uncle Tom, Good Night" (1852). This early version, which was not published, was written in response to the novel, whose spirit it tried to capture. The first verse, which opens with "De sun shines bright in de old Kentucky home" and portrays the blissful side of plantation life, mirrors the happy early time of Tom in his cabin with his family and friends. The song quickly descends into gloom: "By'm by Hard Times comes a knockin at de door / Den poor Uncle Tom good night." The suffering slave is said to have only "A few more days for to tote de weary load" and "A few more days for to totter on de road" before he dies. As in the novel, death brings the promise of heaven, a far better place than Kentucky:

> *Oh good night, good night, good night*
> *Poor Uncle Tom*
> *Grieve not for your old Kentucky home*
> *You'r bound for a better land*
> *Old Uncle Tom*

The song roughly follows the arc of Tom's life, from initial joy through death followed by heavenly relief. But fidelity to the novel diminishes in the song's final version, "My Old Kentucky Home, Good Night!" It may be that Foster, a Democrat, did not want to alienate others in his party and thus changed the song from a sympathetic portrait of an enslaved black to a paean to Kentucky. In revising the song, Foster discarded black dialect and even Tom, whom he replaced with a woman. His chorus became:

> *Weep no more, my lady,*
> *Oh! weep no more today!*
> *We will sing one song*
> *For the old Kentucky Home,*
> *For the old Kentucky Home, far away.*

This chorus completely changed the song's meaning. Instead of Tom anticipating heaven and putting aside memories of Kentucky, an unnamed "my lady"—presumably a white slaveholder—fondly recalls her old Kentucky plantation, where enslaved blacks had played and worked. Since "My Old Kentucky Home" was often used as song in Tom shows, it helped change the popular image of *Uncle Tom's Cabin*, which in some circles came to be identified with the plantation myth and, later on, the Lost Cause.

As for Tom, what he longs for is his wife Chloe and the children they are raising—not for the plantation itself or Kentucky. Indeed, *Uncle Tom's*

Cabin was the first novel that depicted the full range of emotions among enslaved blacks. Minstrelsy, as we have seen, was one source of this journey into the emotional life of black people. But minstrelsy took on wholly new progressive dimensions when filtered through Harriet Beecher Stowe's capacious imagination. The same is true of other popular phenomena she observed, including religion, sentimental-domestic fiction, temperance, moral reform, and sensationalism. Stowe embraced all these aspects of American life, investing them with fresh meaning.

3

ANTISLAVERY PASSION

HARRIET BEECHER STOWE was constantly questioned about the roots of history's most influential antislavery novel. Its factual basis was important for the efforts of both abolitionist and proslavery groups.

Indeed, the question has intrigued readers ever since the novel first appeared. Stowe addressed the issue in *The Key to "Uncle Tom's Cabin"* (1853), in which she presented shocking stories about slavery from newspapers, slave narratives, and personal testimony. But the *Key* tells only part of the story. It would have been dangerous for her to reveal all of her sources. She was cagey, for instance, about the background of Eliza Harris's escape across the frozen Ohio River. She didn't say she had gotten the story from the Rev. John Rankin, a Ripley, Ohio, clergyman who had aided a runaway woman who appeared at his door after making the daring crossing of the ice. Since Rankin performed such rescues for many years, to reveal his identity might have put him in peril of arrest under the Fugitive Slave Law.

Stowe's interest in protecting friends was not the only reason for the confusion about sources. A more basic one is that there *is* no single source for any of the major characters or chapters in *Uncle Tom's Cabin*. We've seen that all kinds of cultural phenomena—visionary fiction, biblical narratives, pro- and anti-Catholicism, gender issues, temperance, moral reform, minstrelsy—contributed to the novel, whose every character radiates multiple meanings. To isolate individual sources strips the novel of suggestiveness and diminishes what may be called its distributive power: its capacity for generating varied responses in different contexts.

Antislavery passion connected the multiplicity of elements of *Uncle Tom's Cabin,* with passion being the key word. Stowe's contemporaries responded to the novel in profoundly emotional ways. A reviewer noted, "We have never read a story of more power. . . . The human being who can read it through with dry eyes, is commended to Barnum." An Ohio newspaper wrote, "He who can read this thrilling narrative without a heaving heart, a moistened eye, and a tear-bedewed cheek, can boast of sensibilities less susceptible than ours." The seasoned antislavery editor Horace Greeley was so moved by the novel that when he read it during a train ride he had to go to a hotel room to collect himself.

There was good reason why *Uncle Tom's Cabin* moved readers more powerfully than any other antislavery work. It sprang from the deepest emotions of a sensitive, reform-minded woman. The period between Harriet's birth (1811) and her return east from Cincinnati in 1850 was bookended by powerful slavery-related experiences.

As mentioned earlier, the first was the story she heard in childhood of her Aunt Mary's shattering discovery of her husband's slave children in Jamaica. The next hit even harder: the death by cholera of Stowe's beloved son Charley in 1849. She wrote a friend, "It was at *his* dying bed, and at *his* grave, that I learnt what a poor slave mother may feel when her child is torn away from her." Her sorrow over Charley's passing helped generate the pathos of scenes in *Uncle Tom's Cabin* such as Eva's death and the account of Mary Bird sorting through her deceased son's clothing, which prompted this: "Oh, mother that reads this, has there never been in your house a drawer, or a closet, the opening of which has been to you like the opening of a little grave?" Throughout the novel, the loss of children by death or separation forms an emotional bond between whites and blacks.

This interracial bonding through shared grief was highly unusual for the era. Most white women didn't think about enslaved black mothers when they lost a child, as Stowe did when Charley died. Nor did they connect the Passion with slave torture, as she did in her communion-service vision of an enslaved man being whipped.

How did this radically democratic sympathy for black people arise? What were the phases by which Stowe evolved into the author of so moving and comprehensive an indictment of slavery as *Uncle Tom's Cabin*?

Stowe describes her creative process in the opening paragraph of *The Key to "Uncle Tom's Cabin"*: "This work, more, perhaps, than any other work of fiction that ever was written, has been a collection and arrangement of real incidents, of actions really performed, of words and expressions really uttered, grouped together with reference to a general result, in the same manner that the mosaic artist groups his fragments of various stones into one general picture. His is a mosaic of gems—this is a mosaic of facts." A mosaic of facts arranged with reference to a general result—this is perhaps the most truthful statement Stowe ever made about the real-life ingredients of *Uncle Tom's Cabin*. Not just the novel as a whole but individual characters and incidents are composites of facts Stowe absorbed from the intensifying controversy about slavery.

There were two main sources of Stowe's hatred of slavery: her familiarity with the abolitionist movement in various forms and her contact with fugitives from slavery whom she knew, heard of, or read about. As was true with religion and temperance reform, she responded ambivalently to her father's attitudes toward slavery and abolition. Although Lyman Beecher considered slavery morally wrong and advocated the emancipation and education of blacks, he was on the conservative end of the antislavery movement, which was not a high priority for him in the midst of his other concerns. Rum, Sabbath-breaking, Catholicism, gambling—these were among the main targets of his reformist zeal. He was a member of the American Colonization Society, whose goal was to ship free blacks or emancipated slaves to the African colony of Liberia or elsewhere. Although colonization did not have dramatic results—only about thirteen thousand black people returned to Africa between 1817 and 1865—it won the support of some of the leading lights of the era, including Abraham Lincoln, Andrew Jackson, Henry Clay, and Daniel Webster.

For Lyman Beecher and others, colonization offered a moderate solution to the slavery problem. Beecher believed that slavery could be abolished gradually. He disapproved of antislavery activities that might alienate the South and thus threaten the American Union. For this reason, he rejected the views of his Boston parishioner William Lloyd Garrison. In 1829, Garrison turned from colonization to a more radical brand of antislavery reform, one that called for immediate emancipation or, barring that, the separation of the North from the South. At first, Garrison regarded Lyman Beecher as Boston's finest preacher and as the city's most effective promoter of the reforms Garrison espoused, including the battles against gambling and drinking. But Garrison came to view such issues as secondary to slavery, which he saw as a uniquely heinous institution that violated America's egalitarian ideals. By the mid-1830s, Garrison harshly criticized Beecher, whose temporizing over slavery was an impetus behind the Garrisonians' becoming "come-outers," or reformers who abandoned organized religion and political parties. The church, the government, and American law were, in Garrison's view, tainted by the South's corrupt institution. Garrison used acidic rhetoric to assault slavery. "No union with slaveholders!" was his rallying cry. He branded the Constitution, which condoned slavery, as "a covenant with death and an agreement with hell."

Beecher viewed Garrison and his cohorts in the American Anti-Slavery Society as extremists. When Garrison declared that America must repent for its sins by immediately freeing all enslaved blacks, Beecher replied, "Oh, Garrison, you can't reason that way! Great economic and political questions can't be solved so simply. You must take into account what is expedient as well as what is right." Beecher founded the Society for the Elevation of Colored People, a conservative counterpart to Garrison's Anti-Slavery Society. He shrank from Garrison's earth-rattling

William Lloyd Garrison

denunciations of the South. In 1835, Beecher wrote his son William that he hoped "the abolitionists as a body will become more calm and less denunciatory," adding that they were "made up of vinegar, aqua fortis, and oil of vitriol, with brimstone, saltpetre, and charcoal, to explode and scatter the corrosive matter."

This antipathy toward the Garrisonians, common throughout the North, was shared by several members of the Beecher family. Catharine sharply censured what she considered the excessive harshness of Garrison's statements. So did Henry, who called Garrison well-intended but lacking in "conciliation, good-natured benevolence, even a certain popular mirthfulness." Henry declared, "Anti-slavery under [Garrison] was all teeth and claw. . . . It fought. It gained not one step by kindness. . . . It bombarded everything it met, and stormed every place which it won."

Harriet was also suspicious of Garrisonian abolitionism. She recalled that "there was a class of professed abolitionists in Cincinnati . . . but they were unfashionable persons and few in numbers" and "were regarded as a species of moral mono-maniacs who . . . had lost all sight of proportion and good judgment."

Still, she was strongly influenced by the city's antislavery leaders, particularly Theodore Dwight Weld and James G. Birney, who disagreed with Garrison. They had espoused abolitionism under the influence of the postmillennial Christian perfectionist Charles Grandison Finney, whose religious ideas, as we saw in chapter 1, also shaped Harriet's. Finney himself saw slavery as un-Christian but, like Lyman Beecher, minimized it in his reform efforts. However, some of his converts—notably Weld, Birney, and the wealthy New York dry-goods merchants Arthur and Lewis Tappan—made abolishing slavery their main focus. Weld, the son of an upstate New York clergyman, had in 1826 experienced a religious conversion at a Finney revival in Utica. Intent upon reforming America in preparation for the millennium, Weld devoted himself to temperance and then abolitionism. Weld's brand of abolitionism called for immediate emancipation but avoided the abrasiveness and anticlericalism that characterized Garrison.

Weld had known Lyman Beecher in the East and moved west to enroll in the Lane Theological Seminary when Beecher was its president. Beecher could not have known that the young seminarian would turn Lane into a powder keg that exploded over the issue of slavery. Weld had been giving antislavery lectures throughout Ohio and elsewhere, and he won many of his fellow students at Lane to the abolitionist cause. His antislavery proselytizing came to the attention of Lane's trustees, who in 1834 imposed a gag order on campus discussions of slavery. This ruling, made while Lyman was on a trip to New England, goaded Weld to organize a student debate over colonization versus immediate emancipation. After eighteen days of discussion, the student body voted unanimously in favor of the latter. In protest against the seminary's stodgy trustees, forty students, led by Weld, dropped out of Lane in October 1834 and enrolled at Oberlin Collegiate Institute, two hundred miles to the northeast.

Weld continued lecturing widely against slavery until, in 1836, fatigue, depression, and a severe throat irritation put a stop to his speaking career. He soon married the feminist-abolitionist Angelina Grimke, whose outspokenness on the lecture platform outraged Catharine Beecher because it seemed unfeminine. In 1839, Weld wrote the landmark volume *Ameri-*

can Slavery as It Is, a compendium of reports and newspaper clippings, many of Southern origin, that was one of antebellum America's most searing indictments of slavery. It was a useful resource for Harriet Beecher Stowe, who later said that "she kept that book in her work basket by day, and slept with it under her pillow at night, till its facts crystallized into Uncle Tom."

Many painful facts in Weld's book—references to slaves being whipped, scalded, torn from their families, and so forth—could have fueled Stowe's rage and provided information for *Uncle Tom's Cabin.* But Stowe was not a wholehearted admirer of Weld, whose book drew an unrelieved picture of slavery in language that sometimes bristled with sarcasm. She recoiled from the bitterness of Weld's attacks on the South. "With all credit to my good brother Theodore," she wrote, "I must say that prudence is not his forte, and that there was a plentiful lack of that useful article in all those worthy reformers. . . . It seems to me that it is not necessary always to present a disagreeable subject in the most disagreeable way possible, and needlessly to shock prejudices."

She appreciated the more moderate tone of Weld's friend and follower James G. Birney. Born in Kentucky to a wealthy slaveholding family, Birney in 1818 moved to Huntsville, Alabama. He owned slaves, whom he liberated after becoming convinced of the wickedness of slavery. He at first endorsed colonization but then came to doubt its efficacy. Finneyite abolitionism, with its platform of immediate emancipation, shaped his views, especially when Weld, during a tour of the South, visited him and discussed slavery with him. Apparently Birney met Harriet when he came north in 1830 and called upon Catharine to ask her to recommend teachers for the Huntsville Female Seminary, with which he was associated at the time.

Uncomfortable about living in a slave state, Birney relocated to Ohio, where he and another abolitionist, Gamaliel Bailey, founded *The Philanthropist.* Promising a "mild" and "moderate" discussion of slavery, the paper began operation in Cincinnati in January 1836 but soon found itself at the center of an uproar. Public meetings led by some of the city's leading citizens passed resolutions stating that Birney's newspaper was inflammatory and must be suppressed. On July 12, anti-abolitionists forced their way into Birney's newspaper rooms and destroyed the printing press. The attack was a warm-up for an uprising on the night of July 30, when a throng of more than 4,000 surrounded Birney's newspaper building, broke into it, and heaved the press out the window, smashing it and throwing the pieces into the river. Equipped with tar and feathers, the mob went to the homes of Birney and two other abolitionists, who had already left town. A racist rampage followed, as the mob sacked a number of houses inhabited by blacks in the city.

The Beechers, as respectful acquaintances of Birney, kept a close eye on the escalating efforts to suppress *The Philanthropist*. Henry published articles in his own paper, the *Cincinnati Journal,* charging Birney's opponents with a gross violation of freedom of the press. Harriet, pregnant with twins and living temporarily with her siblings and her father, wrote her husband, who was abroad, "I can easily see how such proceedings may make many converts to abolitionism, for already my sympathies are strongly enlisted for Mr. Birney." She wrote an informal satire on the mob leaders and endorsed Henry's editorial forays against the proslavery faction.

The situation became so volatile that Henry armed himself when he went into the city. Harriet was being brought toward a more active response to slavery because of such incidents. She wrote that she expected "there would actually be war to the knife," a prospect that held no fear for her, since, in her words, "we were all too full of patriotism not to have sent every brother we had rather than not to have had the principles of freedom and order defended." On hearing of the planned action against Birney's office, she wrote, "I hope that he will stand his ground and assert his rights." She expected that Birney would defend the building with "armed men." She even seemed ready to take up arms herself. She wrote, "If I were a man I would go, for one, and take good care of at least one window."

Although the fracas over *The Philanthropist* subsided, suppression of antislavery activism had become a major national issue. In 1835, Garrison was dragged by a rope through the Boston streets by an anti-abolitionist mob; he was saved by the city's mayor, who put him in jail for his protection. In the South, the distribution of abolitionist literature was widely interfered with. In Congress, antislavery petitions were tabled, leading to the infamous gag orders that infuriated congressmen like John Quincy Adams.

Suppression of abolitionism led to murderous violence in the case of Elijah P. Lovejoy, the Alton, Illinois, antislavery editor who was killed in November 1837. The Beechers had a special affinity with Lovejoy, for Harriet's clergyman brother Edward, then president of Illinois College, was Lovejoy's close friend and religious counselor. After Lovejoy's antislavery newspaper in St. Louis had been attacked three times by mobs, Edward encouraged him to establish a paper in Alton, across the river and twenty-five miles to the north. Edward went with Lovejoy to the Alton warehouse where the editor's printing press was stored, and he encouraged Lovejoy and his followers to arm themselves, which they did.

Fortunately for Edward, he was not at the warehouse when on November 7 it was stormed by furious proslavery citizens who shot and killed Lovejoy. After Lovejoy's death, Edward defended the antislavery martyr in a book about the Alton riots—a bold defense at a time when Lovejoy was widely charged with having been a seditious abolitionist who brought violence on himself through his provocative behavior. The South, naturally, anathematized Lovejoy, and so did the South's fiercest opponents, the Garrisonians, who, as nonviolent resisters, criticized Lovejoy for taking up arms.

For Edward, the use of weapons was justified. He wrote that Lovejoy "died in the defense of justice, and of the law, and of right: and with the instrument of justice in his hands." Lovejoy, he emphasized, had not died in vain:

Though dead he still speaketh; and a united world can never silence his voice. Ten thousand presses, had he employed them all, could never have

done what the simple tale of his death will do. Up and down the mighty
streams of the west his voice will go: it will penetrate the remotest corner
of our land: it will be heard to the extremities of the civilized world.

This assessment was shared by some other forward-looking people,
including Lincoln, who called the murder of Lovejoy "the most important
single event that ever happened in the new world."

Although we don't know how Stowe reacted to the Lovejoy incident,
we can surmise that her brother's praise of the Alton freedom fighter
became one of the many tributary streams that fed into her portrait of
the rebellious slave George Harris and her later enthusiasm for the insurrectionist John Brown. Just as Edward compared Lovejoy to "the heroes
of Bunker Hill, of Yorktown, of New Orleans," so Harriet portrayed the
pistol-wielding Harris as the embodiment of the spirit of '76.

Despite her growing regard for firm-principled reformers, Harriet
showed little interest initially in getting directly involved in abolitionism.
Actually, she seemed dissatisfied with the various strategies of antislavery
advocates. It was dangerous, after all, to proclaim oneself an abolitionist
during that tumultuous decade. Catharine, evidently responding to antislavery remarks by Harriet, reported that she "sometimes talks quite *Abolitiony* at me & I suppose quite anti to the other side." "Abolitiony" or not,
Harriet traded ripostes on extreme antislavery types with family members. From England, Calvin wrote, "Ultra Abolitionism here has the same
nasty Radicalism, the same dogmatic narrowness, that it has in America."
When Harriet visited her brother William in Putnam, Ohio, she wrote
Calvin that the people there were "about half abolitionists" and "as ultra
as to their measures as anything that has been attempted." She was still
undecided as to how slavery could best be combated. She declared there
was a need for "an *intermediate* society" but was puzzled as to how any
action against slavery could be effective. She wrote, "No one can have this
system of slavery brought before him without an irrepressible desire to *do*
something, and what is there to be done?"

Fifteen years after posing this question, she resoundingly answered it by writing *Uncle Tom's Cabin.* All the quarrels over abolition and colo-nization had left her confused about organized movements against slav-ery. *Uncle Tom's Cabin* presented a new way of dealing with slavery: it summoned readers into the consciousness of human beings involved in slavery, especially enslaved blacks themselves. For its era, the novel was a remarkable testament to a white woman's capacity to enter into the sub-jectivity of black people—not just to recognize their humanity, which was rare enough, but to sense the total range of their emotions.

Where did she develop this sympathy for blacks? It would seem she did not inherit it from her father. Although Lyman Beecher saw blacks as human and educable, he had difficulty rising above the racial views of the time. He cast a suspicious eye on the openness to African-Americans that people like Theodore Dwight Weld demonstrated. Weld and his cohorts worked closely with blacks in segregationist Cincinnati, which had around eight hundred black people in 1834, less than half of what there had been only five years earlier. The exit of blacks was due to discriminatory regula-tions, such as one passed in 1829 requiring blacks to pay a bond if they wanted to stay in the city. The Weldians not only established educational centers for blacks—a lyceum, a reading school, and Sabbath schools—but grew close to many, staying at their homes and attending their weddings, funerals, and picnics. Lyman Beecher disapproved of this level of involve-ment and warned Weld, "If you want to teach in colored schools, I can fill your pockets with money; but if you will visit colored families, and walk with them in the streets, you will be overwhelmed."

Although Harriet never completely shed her racial prejudice, she showed a capacity for bonding with blacks from a young age. The fact that most of the black people she fraternized with were servants of her family does not diminish the fact that she brought a special democracy to the mistress-servant relationship. She loved spending time in the kitchen with servants like the African-Americans Zillah ("the smartest black woman I ever knew," she recalled) and Candace, who comforted the sob-bing Harriet after her mother died.

We've seen that the fugitive slave Eliza Buck, one of her servants in

Cincinnati, was an example for her of the sexual abuse of enslaved women. Eliza Buck seems to have a particular bearing on the portrait of Cassy, whose checkered life includes a period when she has a master whom she loves and regards as her husband. Likewise, Eliza Buck, as Stowe wrote, "always called [her master] her husband, and spoke of him with the same apparent feeling with which any woman regards her husband." Eliza also anticipated Cassy's role as a caregiver for the wounded Tom, for she told Stowe of often stealing out at night on her Louisiana plantation and "ministering to poor slaves, who had been mangled and lacerated by the whip."

Stowe's closeness to her Cincinnati servants also informed her descriptions of Uncle Tom, Chloe, and Eliza Harris. After the Civil War, replying to inquiries about the origins of Tom, she declared that while her novel was "not the biography of any one man," her "first conception of Uncle Tom came to me while I was living in Cincinnati." According to the story, a free black woman who worked for her as a cook often told her about her enslaved husband, who managed his master's farm in Kentucky and was "such a Christian she could not get him to run away." As with Tom, this man's master sent him on errands to Ohio, where a slave could proclaim his freedom, but the man did not do so because he "had given his word as a Christian to his master that he would not take advantage of the law." Tom's wife Chloe seems to bear similarities to the liberated slave known as Aunt Frankie, a skilled housekeeper who helped Stowe in Cincinnati. Stowe wrote that anyone who saw Aunt Frankie's "honest, bluff, black face, her long, strong arms, her chest as big and stout as a barrel, and her hilarious hearty laugh" would instantly "appreciate the beauty of black people." Chloe exhibits the same domestic capabilities and warmhearted cheer as Aunt Frankie.

Yet another character source among Stowe's servants was an enslaved young woman who had escaped from a cruel Kentucky master who came to Ohio in pursuit of her. Stowe and her family took action to prevent her capture in a way that directly anticipated Eliza Harris's passage north through Ohio in *Uncle Tom's Cabin*. As Harriet explained the situation, her husband and her brother Henry "performed for the fugitive that office which the senator [John Bird] is presented as performing for Eliza." They drove the runaway a dozen miles along a dark, solitary road to the home of the rugged John Van Zandt (renamed John Van Trompe in the novel), who took over protection of the girl and made sure she evaded her pursuers.

Like other characters in the novel, however, Eliza Harris cannot be pinned to a single source. The main prototype for this character, actually, was a slave woman who in 1838 fled across ice shards on the Ohio River and found her way to Canada with the help of abolitionists. Stowe got the story from Reverend John Rankin, who lived on a hill overlooking the river in Ripley, about sixty miles southeast of Cincinnati. A Tennessee-born minister who had moved to Ripley in 1822, Rankin played an important role in Ohio abolitionism. When Henry Ward Beecher was asked after the Civil War, "Who abolished slavery?" he is said to have replied, "The Rev. John Rankin and his sons did it"—the kind of abundant praise often lavished on Rankin, who was known locally as the Father of Abolition and the Martin Luther of the movement. From his Presbyterian pulpit in Ripley, he preached the equality of all humans, regardless of race, and disobedience to wicked laws, especially those that supported slavery. With his young abolitionist friend Theodore Dwight Weld he founded the Ohio State Anti-Slavery Society. He and his nine sons were among the most active conductors on the western branch of the Underground Railroad. They helped hundreds of fugitives escape north.

This abolitionist family welcomed a mulatto woman and her child one night in February 1838. The woman had been held in slavery by a Dover, Kentucky, farmer, Thomas Davis, who did not treat her harshly but had financial difficulties. Realizing that either she or her two-year-old boy was about to be sold, she took the child into her arms and trekked to the Ohio River, ten miles north. According to some accounts, an Englishman or Scotsman who lived near the river took her in until her pursuers with their dogs were heard approaching. Seizing a wooden plank, she ventured onto the ice, which was breaking up in places. Plunging on, she found herself sometimes sinking into the frigid water. She pushed her child forward onto the ice floes and used the plank to hoist herself out of the water. When she reached the Ohio side, she encountered a man on the riverbank. He was Chancey Shaw, who patrolled the bank looking for fugitive slaves whom he caught with the intention of returning them to their masters for reward money. But the courageous woman and her whimpering son aroused his pity. He told her she had earned her freedom and directed her up the hill to the Rankin house.

She entered the Rankins' door, which was kept unlocked for such emergencies, and huddled near the fire. The family went into action. She and her son were given dry clothing and food, and three of Rankin's sons lifted her onto a horse and escorted her to Red Oak, four miles away. There the Reverend James Gilliland took over, forwarding her and her son north until she arrived at the Newport, Indiana, home of the Quakers Catherine and Levi Coffin, who were apparently the models for Rachel and Simeon Halliday in *Uncle Tom's Cabin*. The Coffins named her Eliza Harris and took steps to ensure that she made it across Lake Erie to Canada. Three years later, in the summer of 1841, Eliza returned to Ripley, asking the Rankins to help her rescue her grown daughters and their children, who were still enslaved by Thomas Davis. In a daring rescue, the Rankins retrieved Eliza's family and managed to send them all to Canada.

So dramatic an episode, it would seem, required little fictional embellishment. But Stowe did embellish it. She added the Kentucky tavern scene to make her dark-temperance point about the alcohol-fueled wickedness of the slave-chasers Haley, Loker, and Marks. Whereas the real-life Eliza made her way to Canada and years later returned for her family, Stowe has Eliza reunite quickly with her husband George in Ohio. This reunion, along with the invented shoot-out in the rocky pass, enhanced the episode's romance and adventure. To show the inhumanity of the Fugitive Slave Law, Stowe added the scene in which Senator Bird, a supporter of the law, follows his natural impulses instead of legal duty by aiding the runaway woman. Bird's real-life counterpart appears to have been Reverend Charles Upham, Stowe's neighbor in Maine who endorsed the

Fugitive Slave Law but then violated it one day when a pitiable runaway slave appeared at his door.

Stowe also revised the Eliza Harris episode by emphasizing the positive role of women. While the extant reports feature males such as Chancey Shaw, John Rankin and his sons, and Levi Coffin, Stowe's version has three women—Emily Shelby, Mary Bird, and Rachel Halliday—assume major roles. These women combine boldness and tenderness in ways that invest middle-class domesticity with protofeminist force. Eliza herself is reshaped to make a number of points about women, religion, and ethics. In the accounts of the real Eliza, she is usually described as a stout, plain girl, and little mention is made of her religious views. Since Stowe wanted to expose the South's exploitation of enslaved women, she presented Eliza as a lovely, deeply Christian quadroon who later faces the constant threat of being recaptured and sold into sexual slavery.

Eliza's beauty and piety are evidently derived from a young enslaved woman Harriet Beecher saw during her one trip into slave territory: her brief, memorable journey to Kentucky in the summer of 1833, three years before her marriage. Accompanying her vivacious friend Mary Dutton, a fellow teacher at the Western Female Institute, Harriet took the sixty-mile steamboat trip from Cincinnati to Maysville, Kentucky, and then continued six miles overland to the town of Washington, Kentucky. They stayed at the home of one of their students, Elizabeth Marshall Key, and took day trips to surrounding towns and plantations. Stowe later recalled spotting in a Kentucky church "a beautiful quadroon girl who sat in one of the slips of the church, and appeared to have charge of some young children." Inquiring about the girl after the church service, she learned that "she was as good and amiable as she was beautiful; that she was a pious girl, and a member of the church." She was shocked when she learned that the girl "was owned by Mr. So-and-so," a fact that "struck a chill to [her] heart."

The Kentucky trip apparently yielded other material that was incorporated into *Uncle Tom's Cabin*. Besides seeing the beautiful quadroon girl in church, Beecher stopped over at a plantation that may have been in her mind when describing the Shelby estate in the opening chapters of *Uncle Tom's Cabin*. As Mary Dutton remembered, during the plantation visit Beecher sat quietly, abstracted in thought and seemingly oblivious of everything around her. But when Mary later read *Uncle Tom's Cabin*, she recognized "scene after scene of that visit portrayed with the most minute fidelity," including moments when "the negroes did funny things and cut up capers."

Mary Dutton's suggestion that the Shelby chapters were reproductions of the actual Kentucky plantation is in line with the way Stowe explained her composition process to the newspaper editor Gamaliel Bailey: "My vocation is simply that of *painter*, and my object will be to hold up in the most lifelike and graphic manner possible Slavery, its reverses, changes, and the negro character, which I have had ample opportunity for studying. There is no arguing with *pictures*, and everybody is impressed by them, whether they mean to be or not."

This statement reflects antebellum America's optimistic faith in mimesis—also visible in the public's enthusiasm for the new medium of photography, introduced in 1839 by Louis Daguerre, and for American art, such as the Hudson River School of landscapes and folksy genre paintings, which had near-photographic realism. In this sense, Stowe was close in spirit to Walt Whitman, who once described his head as a "little house" filled with "many pictures" and who said that in his poems "every thing is literally photographed. Nothing is poeticised."

But as we know, every medium, even photography, reflects the subjectivity of the artist. Whitman's ostensibly realistic pictures of everyday people and places catalogued in his poems are creatively constructed, as are the underlying materials in *Uncle Tom's Cabin*. The Shelby chapters are refashioned to suit the novel's antislavery thrust, and they carry all the inflections of religion, reform, and popular culture discussed earlier in this book.

As for Stowe's statement to Bailey about "the negro character, which I have had ample opportunity for studying," that too is a claim that needs to be qualified. We've seen that her personal contact with black people was, in general, limited to her association with family servants and her Kentucky trip, while her ideas about race were shaped by the romantic racialism of contemporaries like Alexander Kinmont. Another main source of information about the experiences of American blacks was one of the most powerful literary genres of the era: the slave narrative.

Few issues remain as nebulous as the relationship between *Uncle Tom's Cabin* and these works. The subject has a long history. Shortly after *Uncle Tom's Cabin* appeared, the black abolitionist Martin Delany claimed that Uncle Tom's character was so heavily indebted to Josiah Henson's narrative that Henson should receive a share of the book's proceeds. Delany also saw other narratives at work in the novel, including those of Frederick Douglass, Henry Bibb, and Lewis Clarke.

Blacks who considered themselves prototypes of characters in the novel took pride in their association with the world-famous best-seller. Henson promoted himself as "the real Uncle Tom"; his home in Dawn, Canada West, is still called Uncle Tom's Cabin Historic Site. When Henson was interviewed late in life about his connection with the novel, he directly linked his entire experience with specific characters. The aged Lewis Clarke, also, was more than willing to talk about having been the model of George Harris. And there were press battles about who had been the real slaveowner behind Simon Legree.

Harriet Beecher Stowe grew exasperated with all the boasts and guesswork. She eventually informed the *Brooklyn Magazine,* "None of the characters in Uncle Tom's Cabin are portraits." She explained, "I knew of several colored men who showed the piety and honesty of Uncle Tom—but none of them had a history like that I have created for him. Some of the events in the life of Lewis Clark [*sic*] are somewhat like some in the story of George Harris. I read his history while writing the story merely to see that I was keeping within the limits of probability."

She was not equivocating. She was merely acknowledging what the surviving evidence tells us: she collated antislavery material from many sources—including her previously mentioned black servants and their accounts—and certain slave narratives were prominent among them. Not only the autobiographies of ex-slaves but also Richard Hildreth's vivid novel *The Slave; or, Memoirs of Archy Moore* (1836) must be considered as repositories of material used in *Uncle Tom's Cabin*. Although Stowe never mentioned having read Hildreth's novel, it's hard to believe she didn't, given its prominence in antislavery circles and certain similarities between it and *Uncle Tom's Cabin*. And she did know the autobiographical narratives of Douglass (1845), Clarke (1846), William Wells Brown (1847), Henry Bibb (1849), and Henson (1849).

There are elements of each of these works that anticipate *Uncle Tom's Cabin*—a fact that has led some critics to select one work and identify it as the real source of the novel. But in considering these writings, we should keep in mind Stowe's insistence that no individual source yielded any character. Each of her main characters can be evaluated in light of several compelling slave narratives that appeared in the period leading up to *Uncle Tom's Cabin*, so that we can agree with Martin Delany, who wrote, "I am of the opinion that Mrs. Stowe has draughted largely on all the best fugitive slave narratives."

Take Uncle Tom. We saw that one inspiration for this character was the pious husband of a cook Stowe employed in Cincinnati. But there certainly are other sources for him. Stowe noted in the *Key* that she "had received more confirmations of that character, and from a great variety of sources, than of any other character in the book." One source, which Stowe definitely knew, was Josiah Henson's autobiography, but certain aspects of Uncle Tom suggest that two other blacks Stowe never mentioned—Thomas, the hero of Richard Hildreth's *Memoirs of Archy Moore*, and especially Thomas Magruder, an ex-slave in Indiana—were in the mix as well.

Stowe reported that while writing her novel she read Henson's narrative, for which she later penned a laudatory preface. Henson in old age recalled that ever since *Uncle Tom's Cabin* appeared, "I have been called 'Uncle Tom' and I am proud of that title." He felt that he "had not lived in vain," since he was an inspiration behind the novel he called "the begin-

Josiah Henson

ning of the glorious end, . . . a wedge that finally rent asunder that gigantic fabric [of slavery] with a fearful crash."

Since it's plausible that Henson was at least partly behind Stowe's conception of Uncle Tom, it's worth considering his life and character. Born in Maryland in 1789, Henson was an athletic youth who experienced a religious conversion at eighteen. He attended a sermon that inspired him with its "glad tidings of the Gospel to the poor, the persecuted, and the distressed, its deliverance to the captive." His Methodist faith buoyed him despite much maltreatment, the worst of which was a savage beating by an overseer, Bryce Litton, who, along with two black assistants, assaulted Henson with wooden stakes. The attack broke Henson's shoulders and arms, leaving him so maimed that he couldn't raise his hands above his shoulders for the rest of his life. He became a lay preacher among his fellow slaves. He also earned the confidence of his master, Isaac Riley, who, after suffering financial losses due to a dissolute lifestyle, entrusted him to lead a group of some twenty slaves over a thousand miles west to the farm of Riley's brother Amos in Kentucky. Henson led the group through Ohio, where antislavery people urged him to proclaim himself free, but his Christian honor prevented him from breaking his oath. Later, however, the financially strapped Isaac Riley instructed Amos to sell Henson in the Deep South, even though in the interim he had promised Henson his freedom. After a heartbreaking goodbye to his wife and children, Henson was taken by Amos by boat toward New Orleans. Incensed at his deception at the hands of the Riley brothers, he decided to escape north, and did so in 1830.

Henson's story casts light on a perennial question about Uncle Tom: Does Christianity produce sheepish passivity? In Henson's narrative and Stowe's response to it, the answer is no. Even Henson's most self-abnegating moment—when he refuses to claim freedom in Ohio due to Christian honor—is presented as a sign of strength, not weakness. Henson reports that he was not tempted to run away because of "my own strength of character, the feeling of integrity, the sentiment of high honor." It was only after realizing that the Rileys had deceived him that he decided to flee. Stowe found Henson courageous in both his initial refusal to escape and his later decision to do so. In the first instance, she wrote, "his Christian principle was invulnerable," and in the second he exhibited "a degree of prudence, courage, and address, which can scarcely find a parallel in any history." Both Henson and Uncle Tom, then, remained firm while maintaining their Christian honor.

At one point, when Henson is enraged at the prospect of being sold in New Orleans, he picks up an ax and thinks of killing the sleeping Amos Riley and three other whites. But he holds himself back, asking how a Christian could justify such violence. This Christian forbearance makes him more like Uncle Tom than another character in antislavery literature whom one historian has rashly labeled the "real source" of Stowe's hero: Thomas of Richard Hildreth's novel *Memoirs of Archy Moore*. Like Henson and Uncle Tom, Thomas is a pious slave whose Christianity impels him to be obedient. He is a preacher among his fellow slaves, and, as Hildreth writes, "he never tasted whiskey . . . and preferred being whipped to telling a lie." For a time, Thomas's religion engenders submissiveness: Hildreth tells us, "His religious teachers had thoroughly inculcated into a soul, naturally proud and high-spirited, that creed of passive obedience and patient long-suffering" by which "it was his duty to submit in humble silence" to "whatever cruelties or indignities" were inflicted on him. This sounds like Uncle Tom, but what follows does not. Thomas abandons Christianity when his wife is killed by her master, whom Thomas shoots in revenge. In his case, maltreatment leads to rebellion and bitter isolation. Anticipating Stowe's Dred more than Uncle Tom, Thomas adopts life as a maroon in the swamps and eventually returns to the African religion of his ancestors.

A more tantalizing possible source for Uncle Tom is Thomas Magruder. Magruder was over a hundred years old when he died in 1857, and his obituary in *The Saturday Evening Post* was headlined "DEATH OF THE ORIGINAL UNCLE TOM." Magruder, his wife Sarah, and their children Moses and Louisa were slaves of a Kentuckian, Thomas Noble. After Noble's death, they became the property of Noble's daughter, who freed them in 1831 and sent them to Indianapolis to work for her brother Noah Noble, later the governor of Indiana. Noah Noble built for the Magruders a cabin on Market and Noble Streets that came to be known locally as Uncle Tom's Cabin long before Stowe's novel appeared. When Henry Ward Beecher lived in Indianapolis in the early 1840s, he befriended Noble and took an interest in Old Magruder and his family. Beecher, who lived on Market and New Jersey Streets—just two blocks away from Magruder— became a frequent visitor to the Magruder home. WPA researchers as well as local newspapers reported that Harriet Beecher Stowe, while visiting Henry in the city, dropped in several times on Magruder, taking notes about his experiences. While Stowe left no direct evidence of having visited Magruder, it's certainly possible that she did. We know that she went to Indianapolis in July 1843, shortly after her brother George's suicide, and stayed a month there with Henry, taking the opportunity to see another brother, Charles, who also lived in Indianapolis. If Stowe did meet Magruder, she encountered a man whose spirit anticipated Uncle Tom's. Magruder was a devout Methodist. "If there ever was a Christian in the world," his obituary read, "we believe 'Uncle Tom' [Magruder] was one. Indeed he had no distinguishing mark but his Christian virtues." Also intriguing is the fact that the Magruders took into their home an ex-slave named Peter, so that under their care were Peter and their children Moses and Louisa—a family arrangement similar to that in *Uncle Tom's Cabin*, where Tom and Chloe have two sons, Pete and Mose, and a daughter. Another striking parallel is that in time Louisa bore a daughter, Martha, who also lived in the cabin and was nicknamed Topsy.

Uncle Tom's Cabin also appears to owe much to an 1846 volume that contained two autobiographies by escaped slaves from Kentucky, Milton Clarke and his brother Lewis Garrard Clarke. Milton's narrative contains a scene that blends slave torture, domesticity, and religion in a way strikingly similar to Uncle Tom's death scene. An astonishing moment as Tom approaches death is when he forgives his torturer, Legree. In assigning Tom this Christ-like quality, Stowe may have been inspired by a scene in Milton Clarke's narrative that shows a Christian slave, Sam, dying under similar circumstances. Like Tom, Sam is torn from his family and whipped to death for a trivial offense. His master strings up his hands and, with two assistants, gives Sam such a brutal flogging that the slave dies soon thereafter. Just before his death, Sam murmurs, "Mother, tell master he has killed me at last, for nothing; but tell him if God will forgive him, I will." Did this scene inspire Stowe's ur-vision of the whipped slave while she was sitting in the Brunswick church?

We can't know for sure, as there's no record of her having read Milton Clarke's narrative. But she probably *did* read it, since it was part of the dual-narrative book that also contained the autobiography of Milton's brother Lewis, who had an important role in Stowe's portrayal of the fugitive slave George Harris. Lewis Garrard Clarke was a light-skinned Kentucky quadroon who had escaped from slavery in 1842. Stowe quotes extensively from his narrative in the *Key*, where she spells out several connections between him and George. Like Lewis, George is extremely

Lewis Garrard Clarke

light-skinned, with "European" facial figures. Markedly, he has a sister sold in New Orleans as a sex slave; she escapes this fate when she is purchased by a wealthy Frenchman who frees her and marries her.

Did Stowe meet Lewis Clarke before writing her novel? Clarke insisted that she had interviewed him at length during a trip she took to New England to visit family in the 1840s. In the *Key,* Stowe hints that she became acquainted with him: "Soon after [Clarke's] escape from slavery, he was received into the family of the sister-in-law of the author, and there educated. . . . The author has frequently heard him spoken of in the highest terms by all who knew him." There is no testing Clarke's claim that Stowe got much information from him. He loved to brag about his alleged links to *Uncle Tom's Cabin,* as when he declared: "If [Stowe] had not gotten acquainted with me, she never could have written that book in her life, for she would not have been able to get the information."

While Stowe hated this kind of exaggeration and would have been able to devise a plot without Clarke's narrative, she admitted that her novel contained some incidents similar to those in Clarke's narrative, which she consulted for information about slavery from a mulatto's perspective. Born in 1811, Clarke was the son of an enslaved woman and a Scotsman who was a friend of Clarke's Kentucky master, John Benton. As a boy, Clarke was put in the custody of Benton's sister, Betsey, a tyrannical woman who beat him sadistically. Besides enduring physical torture, Clarke was painfully torn from his mother and siblings, who lived on a plantation thirty miles away. Worse, he and his family members were sold separately at a slave auction. An especially pitiable victim of the auction was Clarke's sister Delia, who, he writes, "was so unfortunate as to be uncommonly handsome, and . . . was considered a great prize for the guilty passions of slaveholders." The auctioneer got a high price for her by promoting her as "a pious good girl, member of the Baptist church." Only the lucky chain of events that led to her liberation and subsequent marriage to a wealthy Frenchman named Coval saved her from concubinage. Clarke himself was sold to a Kentucky landowner, Thomas Kennedy Jr., whose plantation was four miles from Paint Lick in Garrard County. It was from this plantation that Clarke fled north.

There's a legend in Garrard County that Paint Lick—"the town of P—, in Kentucky" referred to in the novel's first sentence—was the town Stowe visited during her 1833 trip to Kentucky and that the Kennedy plantation was the Shelby place in *Uncle Tom's Cabin*. But this story goes against Stowe's own account of her meeting with Clarke, and the evidence suggests that the Mason County village of Washington, not Paint Lick, was the place she visited with Mary Dutton. When Clarke later in life described to reporters real-life counterparts to Uncle Tom characters he had known on his Kentucky plantation, he was largely fabricating an imaginary scenario in which he occupied center stage.

But there was nothing imaginary about Stowe's debt to Clarke's life. There is good reason she showcased his narrative in her chapter on George Harris in the *Key*, where she links Clarke and his sister Delia to George and his sister, a Baptist girl who was sold for sex but later reappears as the Frenchwoman Madame de Thoux. She also reprints other graphic passages from Clarke, including scenes of torture and the forced separation of families. She took note of Clarke's rapture upon his arrival in Canada, echoed in the Harrises' joyful arrival there. Doubtless Stowe was struck by other elements of Clarke's narrative, such as its horrific descriptions of mothers who killed their children to save them from slavery—passages that must have contributed to similar accounts of child murder in both *Uncle Tom's Cabin* and *Dred*. Also, her temperance theme may have been reinforced if not stimulated by Clarke's report that masters "are nearly *all* hard drinkers—many of them drunkards."

Still, Clarke was not the only person who provided a basis for George Harris. Another was Frederick Douglass, who, as explained in the *Key*, was a prime example for Stowe of the slave's capacity for self-education, as manifested in Douglass's memorable passages about his joy of learning to read.

As for George's sister, she could have been modeled not only on Clarke's sister but also on a number of other enslaved women described in slave narratives as having been sold for sexual purposes. Especially pertinent is William Wells Brown's narrative, which focuses on two women sold as sex slaves: a St. Louis quadroon, Cynthia, a white-skinned, blue-eyed woman of "almost unparalleled beauty" who has four children by a slaveowner who eventually sells her in the New Orleans market; and Brown's sister Elizabeth, who along with four other women was chained and sent south to be auctioned off in the Fancy Trade.

Simon Legree is perhaps the hardest major character in *Uncle Tom's Cabin* to pin to a single real-life figure. Stowe's brother Charles had spent time in the Deep South before returning north in 1844. He told her that on the steamboat coming back from New Orleans, he met an overseer who brandished a callused fist and declared, "I got that from knockin' down niggers." This hardened overseer is one of several possible sources for Legree. Others include the planter Robert McAlpin, the sugar producer Meredith Calhoun, and Bryce Litton, the overseer who broke Josiah Henson's shoulders. Of the three, Calhoun seems the least like Legree, for he was said to have been a kind master, though he had a Legree-like habit of getting drunk with two of his black lackeys. Litton is a better Legree candidate, for he also had two black henchmen, who helped him assault Henson. Robert McAlpin resembles Legree even more strongly. His Cloutierville, Louisiana, plantation, ten miles from the Red River, reportedly was similar to Legree's. Also, McAlpin had a special reputation for cruelty. A man who knew him well said, "His chief delight was to torture his own Negroes, even unto death. And he done it [*sic*] as often as his hellish spirit prompted him to do it." When McAlpin died after a drunken binge in 1852, a cabin on his property became a traveling exhibit as Uncle Tom's Cabin and his property was incongruously renamed Little Eva Plantation.

Masters like Legree appeared in several slave narratives. Henry Bibb's autobiography includes a number of masters who torture their slaves, including one who whips Bibb until he passes out, his screams having been silenced by a handkerchief rammed down his throat. William Wells Brown's narrative contains graphic scenes of slave torture, including one about an obedient slave who receives a hundred lashes from a master who wants to humble him, and another about a man whose visits to his wife on another plantation are punished by his being suspended by his hands and savagely whipped. In what seems to be a direct anticipation of Legree, Brown emphasizes the special cruelty of men from Northern backgrounds. Friend Haskell, Brown's overseer on a Missouri farm, was, as Brown writes, "a regular Yankee from New England. The Yankees are noted for making the most cruel overseers." The hotelkeeper John Colburn, to whom Brown was hired out, "was from one of the free states; but a more inveterate hater of the negro I do not believe ever walked on God's green earth."

This point about racial prejudice in the North is represented in *Uncle Tom's Cabin* not only in the portrayal of the New England–reared Legree but also in the description of the quintessential New Englander, Aunt Ophelia. We saw in chapter 1 that Ophelia's fussiness and strictness reflected similar qualities in Harriet's Aunt Esther Beecher and her stepmother Harriet Porter Beecher. Ophelia's other notable quality, her prejudice against blacks, made an important statement about the pervasiveness of racism in antebellum America. In discussing Ophelia in the *Key*, Stowe notes that "although slavery has been abolished in the New England states, it has left behind the most baneful feature of the system— . . . the prejudice of caste and color." She gives examples of racial discrimination against even distinguished blacks, such as Frederick Douglass, who was refused a sleeping berth on a passenger ship, and Dr. James W. C. Pennington, who had to walk to work because he was not allowed on buses.

Many commentators bore witness to such Northern discrimination. Tocqueville observed, "Race prejudice seems stronger in those states that have abolished slavery than in those where it still exists, and nowhere is it more intolerant than in those states where slavery was never known." William J. Watkins, a free Northern black journalist and speaker, similarly maintained that "prejudice at the North is much more than that at the South," and William Lloyd Garrison declared, "The prejudices of the North are stronger than those of the South."

The depiction of Ophelia's racism is especially striking because it suggests that white Northerners recoiled from direct contact with black people with whom they presumably sympathized. St. Clare, noting Ophelia's physical revulsion toward Topsy, says, "I have often noticed, in my travels north, how much stronger [prejudice] was with you than with us. You loathe [blacks] as you would a snake or a toad, yet you are indignant at their wrongs." Ophelia finally overcomes her racism when she and Topsy are bonded by their grief over the death of Eva.

Uncle Tom's Cabin can be distinguished from slave narratives because of its efforts to present Southerners as favorably as possible. Among the main characters, the only cruel slaveholders described at length are Legree and Marie St. Clare, and they are viewed as products of the degraded slave system, as are slave-traders like Haley and the slave-chasers Marks and Loker. Also, *Uncle Tom's Cabin* leaves bloody torture offstage. Instead of witnessing gushing blood and torn flesh caused by whips, as in the slave narratives, we see the aftermath of punishment: Topsy's reference to bygone "whippins," Prue's reported death by flogging, and Tom lying wounded in a shed after his flogging. The torture imagery is still very powerful, but we are spared the firsthand views of bloodletting, shrieks, and perverse sadism that assault us in the narratives.

Moreover, Stowe postpones accounts of slave torture until the second half of the novel. This contrasts with many of the slave narratives, in which torture scenes greet us early on. One thinks, for example, of the first chapter of Douglass's narrative, with its scene of Aunt Hester tied up and whipped until "her warm red blood (amid heart-rending shrieks from her, and horrid oaths from him) came dripping to the floor," or Josiah Henson's earliest memory, which was his blood-soaked father coming home, his back lacerated and an ear cut off, after being whipped for protesting against a "brutal assault" on his wife by his master. In *Uncle Tom's Cabin,* the whipping scenes are preceded by many chapters indicating that the slave system, not its participants, are evil. Arthur Shelby is kindly, as are his wife and son. It is only the economics of slavery that forces him to sell Tom and Harry, despite his reluctance to do so. Haley, Loker, and Marks are presented as products of a wicked institution for which the North, the novel tells us, is just as guilty as the South. Augustine St. Clare, though a slaveowner, is a thoughtful, humane man who curses slavery and whose plan to free his slaves is foiled only by his accidental death.

The novel's relatively benign treatment of Southerners was deliberate. Because Stowe wanted the South to change its mind about slavery, she avoided the kind of wholesale demonization of slaveholders she feared might alienate all Southerners. She actually had two Southern characters, Emily Shelby and St. Clare, speak *against* slavery. By doing so, she felt she could challenge the South's peculiar institution from within by having some slaveowners say that slavery was evil.

But if she thought the South would in any way take her novel as a peace offering, she was sorely mistaken. In fact, her efforts to be compassionate made her seem far *more* dangerous than virulent abolitionists like Garrison, whose rancorous tone and calls for disunion made him easily dismissable in the South and unpopular even in the North.

Besides, her concessions to the South were more apparent than real.

She was not like Whitman, who in an effort to keep his nation from splitting apart announced himself the "poet of slaves and of the masters of slaves" and wrote lines about blacks working contentedly in cotton fields. Nor was she like Hawthorne, who in his indifference over slavery penned a campaign biography of his dough-faced friend Franklin Pierce, who as president worked to appease the South.

The anti-Southern message of the slave narratives had stirred Stowe's deepest emotions as a reformer, a Christian, and a parent. At the core of all slave narratives was the disruption slavery imposed on families. Typical was Henson's experience of constantly witnessing slave sales: "Husbands and wives, parents and children were separated forever. Affection, which was as strong in the African as in the European, was disregarded." Or, as Clarke wrote, "Generally, there is but little more scruple about separating families than there is with a man who keeps sheep in selling off lambs in the fall." Having read about family separations in the narratives and witnessed them among her black servants in Cincinnati, Stowe could sympathize utterly with slave families torn asunder when she declared that her son Charley's death taught her "what a poor slave mother may feel when her child is torn away from her."

In 1850, Stowe was confronted with a cacophony of voices surrounding the slavery issue. In the North, the Fugitive Slave Law galvanized antislavery feeling, speeding the disintegration of the Second American Party System and causing the collapse of the Whig Party. Yet the antislavery movement was deeply divided. The Garrisonians savagely attacked the Union and its political and religious institutions. Finneyite abolitionists like Arthur and Lewis Tappan endorsed Christian persuasion as the surest path to abolition. The Transcendentalists Emerson and Thoreau called for self-reliant individual protest against the government. Free-soil politicians like John P. Hale and William Henry Seward advocated keeping slavery where it was and halting its westward spread. The colonization movement had expanded beyond whites and included some blacks who saw emigration as the best method of escaping racial prejudice and rampant discrimination in America.

Meanwhile, millions of enslaved blacks suffered incessant physical and psychological pain. Some managed to escape north on the Underground Railroad, but many more who tried to flee were captured and taken back to their masters.

Stowe surveyed the confusing spectacle and decided that the institution of slavery could be gotten rid of only if the nation faced up to its sins. Politics had failed to wipe out slavery. So had speeches, sermons, and all other forms of persuasion. Even fiction had failed when it took an openly subversive stance, as in the case of Hildreth's *Archy Moore*.

What was needed was a novel that appealed to what a great leader would soon call "the better angels of our nature." *Uncle Tom's Cabin* gave America iconic angels, in the form of a white girl and an enslaved black who died for the redemption of others. It unsparingly exposed the toll that slavery took upon blacks and whites, who were bonded by a common humanity. It put aside reformist wrangles, political squabbles, and sectional tensions. We're all in this together, it announced. The responsibility for slavery lies with Northerners as well as Southerners. There's a way to escape this evil: by *feeling right* as human beings, guided by the spirit of a loving, democratic Christianity.

Although feeling right didn't end slavery—it took a bloody civil war to do that—it opened the way for a widespread acceptance in the North of antislavery arguments that had long been ignored or dismissed. Written in protest against a nefarious law, *Uncle Tom's Cabin* accomplished what Lincoln said was more important than making statutes: it molded public opinion. And it did so with a vigor unmatched by any other American novel.

4

IGNITING THE WAR

To UNDERSTAND THE NOVEL'S effect on the Civil War, it's useful to work backward from Lincoln's victory in the presidential race of 1860. Without the election of an antislavery Republican, it's probable that the war would not have begun when it did, for the secession of the eleven Southern states, which triggered the war, would not have occurred. But what lay behind Lincoln's victory? Many people of the time charged Harriet Beecher Stowe with having created the dramatic shifts in popular attitudes toward slavery that lay behind the Civil War. The claim has substance. *Uncle Tom's Cabin* shaped the political scene by making the North, formerly largely hostile to the antislavery reform, far more open to it than it had been. The novel and its dissemination in plays, essays, reviews, and tie-in merchandise directly paved the way for the public's openness to an antislavery candidate like Lincoln. Simultaneously, it stiffened the South's resolve to defend slavery and demonize the North.

In writing a novel directly aimed at the Fugitive Slave Law, Stowe was challenging the long-revered Whig senators Daniel Webster of Massachusetts and Henry Clay of Kentucky, who endorsed the law as a part of the Compromise of 1850. By imposing harsh penalties on Northerners who abetted blacks attempting to escape from slavery, the law helped preserve the Union by confirming the clause in the Constitution that mandated the return of any "Person held to Service or Labour in One State" who escaped "into another."

Stowe was the leading popularizer of higher law—held by those who looked beyond the Constitution or the Fugitive Slave Law to the law of natural justice, supported by God and morality—which its advocates considered more sacred than any human statute. Frederick Douglass wrote of *Uncle Tom's Cabin*, "We doubt if abler arguments have ever been presented in favor of the *'Higher Law'* than may be found here [in] Mrs. Stowe's truly great work." Another reviewer described "the tears which [*Uncle Tom's Cabin*] has drawn from millions of eyes, the sense of a 'higher law,' which it has stamped upon a million hearts."

By the same token, Southerners denounced the novel as the epitome of Northerners' defiance of the Constitution. The *Southern Literary Messenger* branded the novel as "this new missionary of the higher law" and declared that "this portentous book of sin" enforced "the doctrines and practices of the higher-law agitators at the North." A proslavery Democratic newspaper likewise associated Stowe with "all the enemies of the Constitution; all the disciples of the higher law" in the North.

Both the eulogists and critics of *Uncle Tom's Cabin* were right about its support of the higher law. Stowe viewed the history of American slavery as an unfolding drama with defenders of the higher law as heroes and its opponents as villains. Chief among the latter, in her eyes, was Daniel Webster. She was among several prominent Northerners who were appalled when Webster capitulated to the proslavery side by putting his famous eloquence at the service of the Fugitive Slave Law. The poet Whittier wrote of Webster: "So fallen! So lost! the light / Which he once wore! The glory / From his gray hair gone / Forevermore!" Longfellow added his poetic lament: "Fallen, fallen, fallen, from his high estate." For Emerson, Webster's apostasy revealed that "no forms, neither constitutions, nor laws, nor covenants, nor churches, nor Bibles, are of any use in themselves. The Devil nestles comfortably into them all."

Harriet Beecher Stowe wrote that when Webster endorsed the fugitive bill he "moved over to the side of evil! It was as if a great constellation had changed sides in the heavens, drawing after it a third part of the stars." Many Americans, she noted, temporarily heeded "the serpent voice with which he scoffed at the idea that there was a law of God higher than any law or constitution of the United States." But then came a majestic rebound. "Back came the healthy blood," she wrote, "the re-awakened pulses of moral feeling . . . and there were found voices on all sides to speak for the right, and hearts to respond." *Uncle Tom's Cabin* led this major cultural rebound.

Stowe had deep personal connections to advocates of the higher law. Before her novel appeared, one of the strongest pronouncements against the Fugitive Slave Law was an 1851 sermon by her brother Charles, *The Duty of Disobedience to Wicked Laws,* which equated breaking the law with godliness. Stowe also had a personal history with William Henry Seward, the New York senator who in his famous reply to Daniel Webster publicized the controversial phrase by declaring that in considering slavery Americans must follow "a higher law than the Constitution."

In the 1840s Seward had served as a lawyer in a nationally visible legal case along with another future Lincoln appointee, Salmon P. Chase, whom Stowe had known since her early Cincinnati days. The case, which came before the Supreme Court in 1846, originated in Ohio close to where Stowe lived and involved her friend John Van Zandt, the model for John Van Trompe in *Uncle Tom's Cabin.*

Van Zandt was the farmer and conductor on the Underground Railroad to whom Calvin Stowe and Henry Ward Beecher had conveyed one of the Stowes' servants, a fugitive slave. Van Zandt had formerly lived in Kentucky and, after liberating his slaves, had settled in Hamilton County, Ohio.

In the spring of 1843, another attempt by Van Zandt to help fugitive slaves landed him in court. The incident occurred in the Walnut Hills neighborhood where Harriet and Calvin Stowe lived. On April 24, Van Zandt had driven his wagon a dozen miles down the Montgomery Turnpike from his farm to Cincinnati, where he sold his spring vegetables at a market. He stayed the night with friends in nearby Walnut Hills and started toward home early the next morning. Around 3 a.m., near Lane Seminary, he encountered a family of nine blacks who, he learned, had two days earlier fled the Boone County, Kentucky, farm of their master, Wharton Jones. The runaways begged Van Zandt to take them thirty or forty miles north. Ever obliging to fugitives, Van Zandt agreed to do so. He hid with eight of the blacks in his covered wagon and had the ninth, Andrew, drive the team. The wagon had not gone fifteen miles before it was stopped by two slave-catchers, Hefferman and Hargrove, who had been surveilling Van Zandt. Though the slave-catchers missed seizing Andrew, who fled into nearby woods, they captured the remaining blacks, who were sent back to their Kentucky master. Van Zandt was taken into custody and soon appeared before the Ohio circuit court, which charged him with violating the Fugitive Slave Law of 1793.

Van Zandt asked the Ohio antislavery lawyer Salmon Chase to defend him in court. The tall, muscular Chase, known as the Attorney General of Fugitive Slaves because of his famous defenses of runaways, accepted the case pro bono. After his eloquent pleas on behalf of Van Zandt failed to persuade the court, Chase appealed all the way to the Supreme Court, where he was joined on the defense team by the slight, red-haired New Yorker Seward.

Before the Supreme Court, Chase and Seward turned the Van Zandt case into a lesson on the higher law. Chase pitted the principles of liberty and justice against the 1793 law regarding fugitives. "No legislature," he declared, "can make right wrong, or wrong right. No legislature can make light, darkness; or darkness, light. No legislature can make men, things, or things, men." Even the highest court in the land, Chase asserted, cannot "disregard the fundamental principles of rectitude and justice." In words that Stowe quoted approvingly many years later, Chase added that on questions "which partake largely of a moral and political nature, the judgment, even of this Court, cannot be regarded as altogether final. The decision, to be made here, must, necessarily, be rejudged at the tribunal

Salmon P. Chase

William Henry Seward

of public opinion—the opinion, not of the American People only, but of the Civilized World."

As it turned out, Chase was right, though not in the way he antici-pated. His appeal to higher law failed to persuade the Supreme Court, which decided against Van Zandt, stating that it must "stand by the Con-stitution and the laws." Van Zandt was penalized with a fine of $1,700, far more than he could afford. Soon, as Stowe wrote, "he died broken-hearted." After his death, the fine was passed on to his heirs.

But the case was not lost, for both Chase and Van Zandt had a deter-mined friend who would put all fugitive slave enactments on trial before the tribunal of the entire world. *Uncle Tom's Cabin*, William Seward declared, became "Van Zandt's best monument."

Van Zandt's and that of many others, too, including Josiah Henson, Lewis Clarke, and Eliza Harris. Stowe expertly wove together these and other real-life stories with popular cultural threads—from visionary and biblical fiction through moral reform and minstrelsy—she had gathered during her long literary apprenticeship. By bringing together all of these strands, Stowe directed the whole range of America's favorite pop-culture images toward an assault on slavery. In doing so, she created a uniquely influential higher-law document, one that far superseded her earlier efforts in antislavery fiction.

Not that those efforts had been in vain. Between 1845 and 1851, she published three antislavery short stories, each of which in some way anticipated *Uncle Tom's Cabin.* Her 1845 tale "Immediate Emancipation" portrays a kindly slaveowner who voluntarily frees his slave Sam, who has fled north and is living with Quakers. On hearing that Sam desires freedom, the master issues manumission papers. The moral is that a man unfortunate enough to be a slaveholder "may be enlightened, generous, humane, and capable of the most disinterested regard for the welfare of the slave"—a message that prefigures the positive portrayal of St. Clare in *Uncle Tom's Cabin.*

The Fugitive Slave Law of 1850 brought new urgency to Stowe's anti-slavery writing, as seen in two stories she published shortly after the law was passed, "The American Altar of 1850" and "The Freeman's Dream." In the former, a fugitive slave living in blissful domesticity in the North is cruelly torn from his wife and children when two slave-catchers arrest him and send him south, where he is sold at auction. In "The Freeman's Dream," a Northern man who refuses to assist a family of runaway slaves dreams of being swept heavenward to face Jesus, who condemns him for not having aided the suffering blacks. Stowe makes the higher-law message clear: "Of late, there seem to be many in this nation, who seem to think that there is no standard of right and wrong higher than an act of Congress, or an interpretation of the Constitution."

Uncle Tom's Cabin intensified the attack on the Fugitive Slave Law and broadened the critique of many other proslavery laws as well. The novel's opening chapter emphasizes the deleterious effects of proslavery laws. Anyone who "witnesses the good-humored indulgence of some masters and mistresses, and the affection and loyalty of some slaves," Stowe writes, might be tempted to idealize slave life, "but over and above the scene there broods a portentous shadow—the shadow of *law*." Enslaved blacks can fall at any moment into "hopeless misery and toil, so long as the law considers all these human beings, with beating hearts and living affections, only so many *things* belonging to a master."

The novel's two main plots—the flight of Eliza and George Harris to Canada and the transporting of Uncle Tom to the Deep South—affirm the higher law. The Northern narrative directly flouts the Fugitive Slave Law. The heroes of this triumphant episode are the runaways and the kindly whites who assist them, including the Birds, John Van Trompe, the Hallidays, and Simeon Fletcher. The villains are those who enforce the law—the slave-chasers Haley, Loker, and Marks. The narrative is full of references to the law it opposes. The short, frail Mary Bird becomes a powerhouse of subversive energy when she castigates her politician husband for having voted in the Senate for what she calls "a shameful, wicked, abominable law." John Bird, in turn, willingly puts aside his legal obligation and upholds the higher law when he takes pity on the fugitives and conveys them to Van Trompe, who in turn forwards them to the Hallidays. Even as the Harrises make their way north, they remain in the malevolent grasp of the law. In the rocky pass scene, one of the slave-chasers tells George, "We have the law on our side, and the power," which prompts George's reply, "We don't own your laws; we don't own your country . . . We'll fight for our liberty till we die."

What is most remarkable about this narrative is that it stimulates the reader's enthusiastic approval of lawbreaking. The Harrises' flight appeals to the higher law of godly justice, morality, and patriotism. All these higher ideals glow like a halo around the fugitives and their abettors—a religious aura captured in contemporary illustrations, such as an engraving by Hammat Billings in a gift-book edition that depicted Eliza wearing flowing, Madonna-like clothing while her son Harry wears a halo-like round hat.

Also at work is a more basic form of persuasion—the appeal to human emotion. If the novel begins by lamenting that proslavery law treats humans as "things," the Harris narrative dramatizes in scene after scene the humanity of enslaved blacks and the compassion of antislavery whites. Proslavery law forbade slave marriages, but George and Eliza, who were

married in a ceremony held in the Shelbys' parlor, display a mutual tenderness and devotion that make them husband and wife, no matter what
the law may say. Their escape, then, is motivated by true love and the goal
of creating a permanent home—pious objectives on their own. Stowe
invites us to pity this threatened family and engages the reader emotionally with mirth (over the clowning of Sam and Andy), fear (that the
Harrises will be caught), admiration (for everyone who aids the fugitives),
and loathing (toward the crude, drunken men who pursue the runaways).
Both the heroes and villains of the drama are products of the slave system.
This atmosphere of cruel inhumanity can breed either resistance, among
its humane foes, or compliance, among its heartless enforcers.

The same whirl of emotions surrounds the Southern plot, which tears
Uncle Tom from his family and takes him through various scenes that
culminate in his death at the hands of Simon Legree. If the Northern
narrative exposes the injustice of the Fugitive Slave Law, the Southern
one highlights the cruelty of proslavery laws that make possible the sale of
enslaved men and women as chattel. This domestic slave trade is condoned,
Stowe tells us sarcastically, by "American legislators ... our great men" who
declaim loudly "against the *foreign* slave-trade." Congress had abolished
the international slave trade in 1808, leading to widespread complacency
among Southern politicians. As Stowe writes, "Trading Negroes from
Africa, dear reader, is so horrid! But trading them in Kentucky,—that's
quite another thing!" For Stowe, the selling and buying of black men and
women in the South was "the vital force of the institution of slavery" and
"the great trade of the country." This business, she wrote, was "at this very
moment, riving thousands of hearts, shattering thousands of families, and
driving a helpless and sensitive race to frenzy and despair."

Stowe constructed her Southern narrative strategically to accentuate
the horrific aspects of the domestic slave trade. A historian of the domestic slave trade estimates that between 1790 and 1860 approximately one
million African-Americans were transported from the Upper South to
the Deep South, about two-thirds of them as a result of sale. Many were
sold repeatedly.

Tom's being sold three times, then, was by no means beyond probability. His owners—Shelby, St. Clare, and Legree—typify a range of Southern masters, from the kind to the sadistic. Economics and chance cause Tom's suffering, while law and proslavery religion sanction it. Tragedy also befalls several other slaves Tom encounters on his Southern journey. In the chapter titled "Select Incident of a Lawful Trade," Tom witnesses the melancholy spectacle of the enslaved Lucy, who commits suicide by leaping off a riverboat after hearing that her child has been sold and that she will not be rejoining her husband. This scene yields the caustic observation by the narrator that the law and the church form a devilish league in support of slavery. Tom, we are told, sees Lucy's fate as "something unutterably horrible and cruel" because he is just a "poor, ignorant black soul" who doesn't take "enlarged views." Then comes this dart: "If he had only been instructed by certain ministers of Christianity, he might have thought better of it, and seen in it an every-day incident of a lawful trade, a trade which is the vital support of an institution which an American divine tells us has '*no evils such as are inseparable from any other relations in social and domestic life.*'"

The "American divine" alluded to here was Reverend Joel Parker, a celebrated Philadelphia clergyman and former president of the Union Theological Seminary. Parker was infuriated by Stowe's criticism, especially since she identified him by name in a footnote. After *Uncle Tom's Cabin* appeared, he sent angry letters to her and Calvin demanding "a full and public retraction" of this "calumny." She responded by explaining that the words she had quoted in her novel were from several previous newspaper reports of remarks Parker had made in an 1846 debate on slavery. Since he had never protested against those reports, why was he bothered now? She added, accurately, that the newspaper paraphrases in fact caught the spirit of Parker's original words: "What are the evils that are inseparable from slavery? *There is not one, that is not equally inseparable from depraved human nature in other lawful relations*"—exactly the kind of churchly waffling that made Stowe's blood boil. Parker hired an attorney and filed a lawsuit. The affair was played up in the press, with the correspondence between Parker,

Stowe, and Henry Ward Beecher reprinted in newspapers on both sides of the slavery divide. Stowe did not recant but promised to omit Parker's name from future editions of the novel. She did so, and the lawsuit died of inanition.

The Parker affair proved to be a minor squall in the storm of responses, positive and negative, that greeted *Uncle Tom's Cabin*. Interest in the novel grew steadily while the successive chapters came out serially in Gamaliel Bailey's *National Era* between the summer of 1850 and the following spring. Reading the weekly installments aloud became a family affair. On March 20, 1852, the Boston publisher John P. Jewett issued a then-substantial 5,000 copies of the two-volume novel. This first printing was available in three formats: a paper-covered edition priced at $1.00, a $1.50 cloth edition, and a fancier "full gilt" version at $2.00. These prices, equivalent to a range of $24 to $48 today, were well above those of the city-mysteries novels of the day (which usually appeared as cheap pamphlets) and were in line with those of more respectable volumes—illustrated Bibles, collections of Fireside poetry, and domestic novels—designed for a middle-class readership. Such volumes were typically printed on the flatbed-and-platen press that had been introduced in 1830 by Jacob and Seth Adams. The Adams press combined efficiency and high quality, making possible attractive books with handsome print and fine engravings. At extra expense, Jewett made a stereotype, a metal plate with set-up type that facilitated multiple printings.

Uncle Tom's Cabin was irresistibly attractive to nineteenth-century readers in whatever format it appeared. It had just the right blend of engaging storytelling and popular culture to make its higher-law, antislavery message palatable to many readers. Within a month of its publication another 15,000 copies were demanded, and by May 22 Jewett announced that 50,000 had been printed, which amounted to fifty tons of books distributed nationally in small boxes or packages that were shipped mainly by train or steamboat. The number of printed copies had doubled by the end of June. According to reports, even with three Adams presses running

Title page of the first edition of Uncle Tom's Cabin
by Harriet Beecher Stowe, published by John P. Jewett

twenty-four hours a day, three paper mills supplying paper, and a hundred booksellers selling work, Jewett could not keep up with the demand.

The production and distribution of the novel was considered a massive achievement, facilitated by recent technological advances. One journalist crowed, "What could have been done towards transporting so large a number of packages in so short a time, only a few years hence?" Another wrote of the novel, "Such a phenomenon as its present popularity could have happened only in the present wondrous age. It required all the aid of our new machinery to produce the phenomenon; our steam-presses, steam-ships, steam-carriages, iron roads; electric telegraphs." The same writer noted, "Never since books were first printed has the success of Uncle Tom been equaled; the history of literature contains nothing parallel to it, nor approaching it; it is, in fact, the first real success in bookmaking, for all other successes in literature were failures when compared with the success of Uncle Tom."

Within a year of its publication, *Uncle Tom's Cabin* had sold some 310,000 copies in America, about three times the number of either of the two previous record-setting American novels, George Lippard's *The Quaker City* (1845) and Susan Warner's *The Wide, Wide World* (1851). Its sale in England was three times higher yet. One million copies of *Uncle Tom's Cabin* sold in the United Kingdom during the first year; worldwide, the number was over two million. In that year, translated editions appeared in French, German, Spanish, Italian, Danish, Swedish, Flemish, Polish, and Magyar, soon to be joined by versions in Portuguese, Welsh, Russian, Arabic, and other languages.

Reading the novel aloud was a favorite pastime of families and literary groups. The *Literary World* declared, "Uncle Tom has probably ten readers to every purchaser, and in a calculation of the readers we must stretch our powers of arithmetic to a degree far beyond to what they have been tasked by the number of purchasers." Garrison's *Liberator* hailed the "victorious Uncle Tom, with his millions of copies, and ten millions of readers."

Foreign sales exceeded American mainly because of the absence of an international copyright. Publishers abroad could issue American works with no obligation to pay the author; the same held true with the American publication of foreign writings. In August 1852, a pirated British edition of *Uncle Tom's Cabin* was sold in penny parts that were soon collected in a "railway edition," priced attractively at a shilling (approximately twenty-five cents at the time), that sold nearly 100,000 copies within a month, initiating what was called "a new era in cheap literature."

It's possible, as one American observer claimed, that Stowe lost about $200,000 in foreign royalties as result of piracy—a notion, Stowe wrote, that filled her "with horror!" But three British publishers—Thomas Bosworth, Clarke & Co., and Richard Bentley—generously offered her an interest in the sale of their editions. Meanwhile, she made approximately $30,000 from the first American edition of *Uncle Tom's Cabin*. That amount could have been far higher had she and Calvin accepted John Jewett's original proposal to divide the book's proceeds with him in return for their investment in its production, an offer they refused because of their pinched finances; instead, they accepted 10 percent on sales, with Jewett taking care of publication and publicity. Still, $30,000 was a healthy sum in a day when the average American worker earned far less than $1,000 annually for a ten-to-twelve-hour-a-day job. Three decades later, in the 1880s, Stowe's royalties, having dipped during the Civil War, grew again to an average of $2,400 yearly.

The novel soared to popularity on gusts of long reviews and controversies that enhanced its visibility. Never before had an American novel bred as much discussion as *Uncle Tom's Cabin*. City-mysteries novels, from Lippard's *The Quaker City* through Thompson's *City Crimes*, sold well but were considered too vulgar to be taken seriously by most reviewers. Domestic novels like *The Wide, Wide World* were promoted in newspaper ads but received little sustained critical attention. Two of the greatest American novels, Hawthorne's *The Scarlet Letter* (1850) and Melville's *Moby-Dick* (1851), did not attract the widespread recognition they deserved. Hawthorne's novel elicited reviews that ranged from the admiring to the bemused in elite journals like the *North American Review*, the *Church Review*, and *Brownson's Quarterly Review*. *Moby-Dick* drew some brief, politely positive responses along with a number of thrashings that relegated Melville to literary oblivion.

The reception of *Uncle Tom's Cabin* was unique for its time, even with its sharply divided responses. In the North, the novel aroused antislavery feeling among many who had previously disliked abolitionists or cared little about enslaved blacks. Frederick Douglass emphasized that Stowe's novel won over the indifferent. "The touching, but too truthful tale of *Uncle Tom's Cabin*," he wrote, "has rekindled the slumbering embers of anti-slavery zeal into active flame. Its recitals have baptized with holy fire myriads who before cared nothing for the bleeding slave." Booker T. Washington noted that "the value of *Uncle Tom's Cabin* to the cause of Abolition can never be justly estimated," explaining that it "so stirred the hearts of the northern people that a large part of them were ready either to vote or, in the last extremity, to fight for the suppression of slavery."

A year and a half after *Uncle Tom's Cabin* was published, Stowe wrote a friend, "The effects of the book so far have been, I think, these: 1st. to soften and moderate the bitterness of feeling in *extreme abolitionists*. 2nd. to convert to abolitionist views many whom the same bitterness had repelled. 3rd. to inspire the free colored people with self-respect, hope, and confidence. 4th. to inspire universally through the country a kindlier feeling toward the negro race."

There's evidence that she had an impact in all of these areas. Her claim of having strongly affected abolitionists is confirmed by William Lloyd Garrison's response to her novel, which moved him profoundly. In reading it, he wrote, "We confess to the frequent moistening of our eyes, and the making of our heart grow liquid as water, and trembling every nerve within us, in the perusal of incidents and scenes so vividly depicted in her pages." He declared that the novel's effect must be "prodigious, and therefore eminently serviceable to the tremendous conflict now waged for the immediate and entire suppression of slavery on the American soil."

Equally receptive to *Uncle Tom's Cabin* were three antislavery groups hostile to Garrison: Tappanites, colonizationists, and free-soil politicians. Lewis and Arthur Tappan, who had in 1840 broken with Garrison because of his radicalism, also readily embraced Stowe's novel. At an 1853 meeting of the Tappans' American and Foreign Anti-Slavery Society, *Uncle Tom's Cabin* received enthusiastic praise: "In the recent work of HARRIET BEECHER STOWE, we have a portraiture of American slavery that is read by tens of thousands, causing many of them to weep and pray, and resolve that they will strive, while life shall last, for its overthrow and annihilation."

Stowe was overjoyed by the embrace of *Uncle Tom's Cabin* by widely different antislavery groups. She later confessed, "The fact that the wildest and extremest abolitionists united with the coldest conservatives . . . to welcome and advance the book is a thing that I have never ceased to wonder at."

This coming together of once-distinct antislavery groups was strengthened by Stowe's triumphant tour of Great Britain in the spring and summer of 1853. Stowe went there simply to arouse a general feeling against slavery—a notion she expressed when she noted the "many factions" of antislavery reform, each of them intent on "sending to England and Scotland to enlist our friends there in their various controversies," while she and Calvin "maintained a strict neutrality as to all their personal feuds, bitternesses, seeking to unite [the antislavery cause] when it was possible." The original invitation had come to her in December 1852 from Reverend Ralph Wardlaw, who represented antislavery groups in Glasgow. Hoping to sway world opinion on behalf of the slave, Stowe gratefully accepted Wardlaw's offer of an all-expenses-paid visit to the British Isles in support of the antislavery cause. As it turned out, her tour took her not only to Scotland and England but to the Continent as well.

Along with Calvin, her brother Charles, and other family members, she left Boston on March 30, 1853, and, after a stopover on the Irish coast, soon arrived in Liverpool, where a public dinner was given in her honor. From there, the party journeyed to Glasgow and other places in Scotland before going south through English towns until it reached London. She had told Charles Sumner that she would "decidedly reject empty parade and useless flattery" in Europe, explaining, "I have a purpose there." She certainly fulfilled her purpose of spreading the antislavery gospel, but there was no way she could escape parade and flattery. Great Britain was in the grip of Tom Mania, and everywhere she went she was feted, cheered, and praised. In London, she met many notables, including the Duchess of Sutherland, the Earl of Shaftesbury, Prime Minister Viscount Palmerston, and Mr. and Mrs. Charles Dickens (on a second trip, in 1856, she met Queen Victoria and Prince Albert). In keeping with the customs of the day, Stowe sat quietly during the celebrations, allowing Calvin or

Charles to speak for her. After the exhausted Calvin returned to America at the end of May, Stowe and the others went on to the Continent, where they visited France, Switzerland, and Germany before stopping again in England and then going home at the end of August.

Many American and European newspapers printed ongoing reports of Stowe's trip. Especially well publicized were monetary contributions and an antislavery petition, known as the Stafford House Address, that was accompanied by over 500,000 signatures collected in twenty-six volumes. The money, gathered from penny offerings throughout Great Britain, amounted to a total of $20,000, donated to Stowe with no strings attached; she devoted the bulk of it to the antislavery cause. The Stafford House Address, a plea by "many thousands of women of Great Britain and Ireland to their sisters, the women of the United States of America," urged American women to use whatever influence they had to combat slavery, which was described as an un-Christian and immoral institution.

The tour's effect extended internationally. "Even our diplomacy stands aghast at the rushing, swelling, flood of Uncle Tomism which is now sweeping the Continent," intoned the *New-York Tribune*. "Uncle Tom shines in every *feuilleton,* rests on every center-table, and faces the footlights of every stage."

Sweeping the force along was a powerful cultural phenomenon known as "Uncle Tomitudes": representations of characters or scenes from the novel in virtually every popular medium then available. The Tomitudes, which anticipated twentieth-century mass merchandising, often carried an antislavery message.

Engravings and paintings based on the novel quickly became popular. Nine months after the novel appeared, *The Liberator* noted that "artists of all grades now find it not only a congenial, but a remunerative work to represent the creations of Mrs. Stowe's genius in pictures and statues." Especially popular were illustrations of Eva and Tom seated together in St. Clare's garden reading the Bible, a scene that communicated a spirit of racial bonding and shared religion.

The proliferation of pictures of black people was itself a political statement. The Jewett edition of 1852 featured illustrations of enslaved blacks with their families or with whites—precursors of the "engravings of various degrees, merit and price [of] Uncle Toms, Evas, and Topsys without number" that, according to *The Liberator,* were sold widely after the novel appeared. More dramatically, dioramas, or tremendous paintings slowly unrolled before audiences, were among the fads of the day. In 1855 came a grand diorama by J. N. Stills that was unwound before audiences to the accompaniment of a lecture and piano music; the proceeds of the show went to antislavery reform.

The *Uncle Tom* tie-ins were remarkable for their sheer variety. American toy producers came out with card games. One, played like Go Fish, had twenty cards with Tom-related images: Uncle Tom's cabin, his Bible, Eva's flowers, Ophelia's basket, and so on. Another involved "the continual separation and reunion of families," the aim being to create five groups, each of which had four picture cards.

Europe saw an explosion of Tomitudes. A European dice game, with instructions in English, French, and German, came with two dice and nine cards that pictured vignettes from the novel, including the Tom-Eva scene, the deaths of St. Clare and Tom, and moments like "Haley fastens Uncle Tom on the wagon for the market 'down South' " and "The human merchandise knows another soul owner." There also appeared jigsaw puzzles, including a 52-piece one that depicted eighteen scenes from the novel and a 34-piece one showing eleven. Tom-related chinaware and trinkets abounded. Images from Stowe's novel appeared on candlesticks, snuffboxes, spoons, earthenware plates, biscuit tins, mantelpiece screens, handkerchiefs, German needlework wall hangings, Limoges spill vases, and Staffordshire items that included mugs, pitchers, jars, and figurine sets.

Although a few of these tie-ins perpetuated the racial stereotypes of blackface minstrelsy, many offered sympathetic, realistic representations of enslaved blacks. The card game about family reunions included some cards, including Tom and George, that avoided stereotypes. Many Tomitudes portrayed blacks positively. In particular, the china, needle-

Section of a mantelpiece screen

European card game

Spill vase with Uncle Tom and Little Eva

Uncle Tom's Cabin *jigsaw puzzle*

work, and decorative screens were notable for their lack of racism. One mantelpiece screen is forthright in its depiction of slavery's cruel side; it includes a picture of the half-naked, chained sister of George Harris being whipped and another of Lucy leaping into the river, with the ironic caption "The soul driver experiences a mercantile drawback."

Overall, the Tomitudes shied away neither from the novel's harsh scenes, including the pursuit and punishment of slaves, nor from its progressive moments, such as Eva's interracial bonding with Tom and Topsy. In time, Tom-related dolls offered especially resonant suggestions about race. One very popular doll in the early twentieth century, for example, was a two-ended affair with Eva and Topsy connected vertically at the waist and a long skirt in the middle that dropped over one of the heads when the doll was flipped. Turning the doll over, a child could change it from Eva to Topsy by draping the black girl's skirt over the white girl's face.

The possibilities for political interpretations of the Tomitudes are endless. Suffice it to say that references to *Uncle Tom's Cabin* before the Civil War were ubiquitous. In London, one could buy Uncle Tom's Shrinkable Woolen Stockings, Uncle Tom's Improved Flageolets, and Uncle Tom's Pure Unadulterated Coffee. Pastry shops, restaurants, dry goods shops, and creameries were named "Uncle Tom's Cabin." In Paris, where five newspapers serialized the novel, restaurants offered menu items named after Tom characters, and licorice was sold as Uncle Tom's Candy.

The most influential tie-ins were songs and plays based on the novel. Often the two were intermingled; popular Tom songs became integrated into plays, or the plays introduced songs that became independently popular. The ambiguities of minstrelsy were reflected in the extraordinary range and flexibility within the performance culture that quickly arose around *Uncle Tom's Cabin*.

The two plays that proved by far the most popular dramatizations of the novel were versions by George H. Aiken and H. J. Conway. Many more people saw plays based on *Uncle Tom's Cabin* than read the novel. It's vital, therefore, to take a look at these two main dramatized versions, which dominated theaters in the 1850s, remained popular during the Civil War, and then exploded onto the world scene in the decades after the war. (Because of the copyright situation at the time, Stowe made nothing from the plays, which in a later era would have brought her millions. The Uncle Tom play that she wrote in 1853, a dramatic monologue called *The Christian Slave*, was performed only a handful of times in New England and London.)

Aiken's play has a special place in the history of the American theater. It introduced single-feature entertainment. Previously, an evening's bill was divided between a play and other performances, such as farces, song-and-dance routines, melodramas, or minstrel skits. Since Aiken's play contained all of these elements and more, they needed no embellishment. As theater manager George C. Howard, who both produced and acted in the Aiken play, boasted, "I was the first, I may say, to introduce one play entertainments." Before him, he said, "no evening at the theater was thought complete, without an after piece, or a little ballet-dancing." The Tom play also introduced the matinee, first used in the 1850s to accommodate women and children who wanted to attend the show during the day.

The first serious full-length representation of Stowe's novel, Aiken's play appeared countless times in numerous venues to the end of the nineteenth century and well into the twentieth, becoming the longest-running play in American history. Like the novel on which it was based, it tugged on the heartstrings while making dramatic appeals to conscience and the higher law.

George Aiken got involved in the *Uncle Tom* project through George C. Howard. Howard spent the 1840s moving between Philadelphia, Boston, and Providence, directing and acting in reform plays. He married the actress Caroline E. Fox, and they had a daughter, Cordelia, a charming child with a gift for acting who seemed a perfect fit for Stowe's Eva. George had Caroline contact her twenty-two-year-old Providence cousin George Aiken about creating an Uncle Tom vehicle for Cordelia and others in the Howard family. Aiken quickly wrote a four-act play based on *Uncle Tom's Cabin*, which the Howards put on with great success at the Troy Museum in upstate New York.

Aiken slightly revised Stowe's story without losing its adventure, pathos, or antislavery spirit. He dispensed with some characters, including the Birds, and added others, notably the funny con man Gumption Cute and the stiff Deacon Abraham Perry, who woos the fussy Ophelia. In the early days, the play was very much a family affair: Cordelia Howard as Eva became the Shirley Temple of her day; her grandmother played Ophelia; her father was St. Clare; her mother played Topsy (a role that made her famous and that impressed Stowe when she saw the play in Boston); Caroline's brother, Charles Fox, doubled as Phineas Fletcher

George Howard, the actor and theater manager prominent in early productions of George Aiken's play Uncle Tom's Cabin

and Gumption Cute; and George Aiken played both George Harris and George Shelby.

After the play enjoyed a long run in Troy that began in September 1852, Howard took it to Albany, where it opened in January 1853. In mid-July it moved to New York City's National Theatre, managed by the rotund impresario Frank C. Purdy. The National, located in a rundown district of warehouses and saloons, had long featured blood-and-thunder melodramas and silly farces that appealed to raucous audiences. Like most New York theaters, it was a popular gathering place for prostitutes trolling for customers.

Purdy saw in *Uncle Tom's Cabin* an opportunity to fill his theater while bolstering its respectability. Theaters had a terrible reputation in that prudish time, when, in polite circles, underpants were referred to as "inexpressibles," a pregnant woman was said to be "in a delicate condition," frilly stockings hid piano legs, nude sculptures were sometimes cloaked in gauze, and theaters themselves were often euphemistically called "museums" to hide the fact that they ran plays. Since George Aiken's play retained the piety and the sharp hero-villain distinctions of Stowe's novel, it offered an ideal opportunity for Purdy to burnish the image of his theater. When Harriet Beecher Stowe was approached by the singer Asa Hutchinson about writing an Uncle Tom play, she rejected the idea as "wholly impracticable" and "dangerous," saying that even a thoroughly moral play would "make the public hungry for less exalted fare, and soon there would be five bad plays to one good"—though soon enough she wrote her own version, the dramatic monologue *The Christian Slave*.

Purdy's handling of Aiken's play was a step toward making theatergoing respectable. Attracted by Aiken's pious message, women and even clergymen flocked to see *Uncle Tom's Cabin* at the National, which Purdy was soon promoting as "The Moral Temple of New-York"—an image he reinforced in the theater's lobby, whose walls were lined with religious passages from the play. The air of propriety was sufficient to make possible Saturday shows, formerly avoided because performance of a play on the eve of the Sabbath was considered sacrilegious.

Aiken's script shows why his play appealed to churchgoing types who had formerly dismissed the theater as devilish. Aiken amplified the religiosity of Stowe's novel. In his play, the optimistic Christianity of Tom, Eliza, and Eva are heightened by inspiring songs and stage sets. Eva's death becomes even more of a comforting visionary experience than it is in the novel. Its celestial aura is enhanced by no less than four religious songs: Tom's hymn about "bright angels" in the "New Jerusalem"; Eva's song about "spirits bright... robed in spotless white"; a tune called "Eva to Her Father," in which the little girl asks St. Clare to free his slaves after she dies; and "St. Clare to Little Eva in Heaven," with St. Clare begging her to "smile upon me from above; / Open those bright gates of pearl."

The latter two compositions, written by George Howard for the play, became popular on their own, joining many songs and poems about Eva which were so common that a music journal commented, "Every music publisher must have his 'Little Eva' song just now, and all the minor composers are ... busy on this theme." By putting special emphasis on Eva's redemptive death, Howard and Aiken made good use of the irresistible charm and attractiveness of little Cordelia Howard, who was billed as "The Youthful Wonder" or "The Child of Nature." The religious impact of Eva's death gained celestial glory in the concluding tableau of Aiken's expanded six-act version, showing the heaven-bound Eva, on a dove, looking down on Tom and St. Clare.

Besides religion, a key to the success of Aiken's play was its sensationalist scenes: Eliza's escape across the ice, George's gunfight in the rocky pass, and Legree's whipping of Tom. Aiken also added comic touches, mainly through the characters of Topsy, Gumption Cute, Phineas Fletcher, and Marks. Of them, Marks is the most surprising choice for comic use, since in the novel he is little more than a self-seeking slave-catcher. In the Aiken play, he introduces himself by saying, "I am a lawyer, and my name is Marks," which prompts Phineas's retort, "A land shark, eh? ... The law is a kind of necessary evil; it breeds lawyers just as an old stump does fungus." The comic repartee that follows made Marks a hilarious figure for nineteenth-century audiences—so much so that Marks became a featured figure of humor in Tom shows later in the century. Phineas himself gained comic stature with outlandish colloquialisms like "Chaw me up into the tobaccy ends!" and "Chaw me into sassage meat, if that ain't a perpendicular fine gal!"

Topsy, expertly played by Caroline Howard, was also a comic hit, well on the way to her eventual status as one of the main figures of wild fun in nineteenth-century America. Mrs. Howard got big laughs with all the standard Topsy lines—"Never was born," "Spect I grow'd," "I'se so wicked," and so on—and brought down the house with a song and dance in which she did physical contortions while screeching a song by her husband in which Topsy flaunts her wickedness and spouts nonsense lines like "Ching a ring a ring ricked" and "Ching a ring a smash goes the breakdown."

Gumption Cute today seems like an extraneous character in the Uncle Tom narrative. But one can see why Aiken added him, as he is a humorous poseur and a shape-shifting con man of the sort popular in antebellum America. Melville, whose novel *The Confidence-Man* appeared in 1857, was hardly the only author fascinated by the confidence man figure, who appeared regularly in novels about so-called city-mysteries in the 1840s and 1850s. Cute is a harmless trickster notable for the failures of his cons. He fails as a teacher, a spirit-rapper, a wildcat banker, an overseer on a cotton plantation, and a filibusterer on an anti-Spanish campaign in Cuba. He talks comically about becoming a Barnumesque showman and exhibiting Topsy as a "woolly gal," just as Barnum had exhibited a Woolly Horse. Besides giving Aiken a chance to lampoon Barnum (who is said to be from "down South," a dig at the Conway play then showing at Barnum's Museum), Cute rang many pop-culture bells—spiritualism, wildcatting, speculation, filibustering—for nineteenth-century audiences who took an interest in such topics. Cute's clumsy efforts to inherit Ophelia's money by pretending to be her relative as he discourages the advances of her suitor, Deacon Abraham, adds another rib-tickling scene to the play.

Religion, thrills, comedy: the crowd-pleasing elements were all there in Aiken's play, which skillfully integrated Stowe's popular culture devices and enhanced them through music, dance, and tableaux (scenes in which actors stood frozen and silent in expressive positions against colorfully painted backdrops). There were a total of seven tableaux in the expanded six-act play. Some of the play's backdrops moved like dioramas. Purdy bragged that his painting of the Mississippi by moonlight, which rolled by on a 10,000-square-foot canvas, was large enough "to rig out more than half of the nation's Navy!"

The varied spectacles in the Aiken play had a central thread: the wickedness of the institution of slavery and the laws supporting it. Without the abolitionist theme, the special effects would have created another forgettable melodrama of the type that crowded American stages—a froth of danger, fun, and sap. But true to the spirit of Stowe's novel, Aiken didn't let the audience forget that the play dealt with the era's most pressing issue, slavery, with its victims as heroes and its enforcers as villains.

The play appealed to audiences of all backgrounds and ages. Horace Greeley, William Lloyd Garrison, the young Mark Twain, and the even younger Henry James were among those who were deeply stirred by the play, which set attendance records, both in the short run and over the long term. At the National, it ran to packed houses for 365 days straight, initiating what came to be known as the long run, before it moved on to many other cities. Since it was quickly imitated and revised in different cities and contexts, it's impossible to guess how many people saw it. In its many variations, it became the most-watched play ever written by an American.

Its main competitor, the H. J. Conway version of *Uncle Tom's Cabin*, opened in November 1852 at the Boston Museum and played for two hundred nights there. The next fall, P. T. Barnum brought the play to his American Museum on Broadway in New York, where it ran in competition with the Aiken version, which was at the National Theatre. Like many other adaptations, Conway's *Uncle Tom's Cabin* took liberties with Stowe's plot. Conway killed off Legree and liberated Tom, who was reunited with his wife and children and settled happily in a cabin in the

North. Conway added minstrel characters, including "Ginger, a Banjo Player" and "Pompey, with a Plantation Jig." The production was high on spectacle. Ads for the play promised thrilling scenes like "The Accident. THE ALARM! THE RESCUE!" and "*THE ATTACK! THE DEFENSE! THE RESULT!*"

Some saw the Conway play as a melodramatic entertainment. The *New-York Tribune,* for instance, dismissed it as "a mere burlesque negro performance" by white actors in blackface. Still, it contained enough digs at slavery to please many antislavery papers and displease proslavery ones.

Actually, the play combined brief racial caricatures along with biting comments on slavery and the institutions that supported it. In portraying Sam, for instance, Conway exaggerates both the minstrel-like humor and the antislavery rebelliousness of Stowe's character. In the play's opening scene, Sam seems like the carefree minstrel buffoon. Leading other slaves in singing praise to their master, George Shelby, Sam announces, "Yes, niggers, lay down de shubble and de hoe and take down de fiddle and de bow. Dis afternoon we gone for de dance, I'll eat de pigeon wing," after which he and his fellows yell, "Hurrah for Massa George!" But Sam soon proves to be more devoted to the higher law than to his master. In helping Eliza escape, he declares, "Tant easy to fool dis massa, but my conscience tell me I must." He goes so far as to have a Nat Turner–like fantasy of murdering the slave-chaser Tom Loker, when he says, "My conscience tells me to cut dat massa's troat wouldn't be no sin."

Besides depicting Sam's subversive energy, Conway portrays George Harris with the same ennobling qualities he has in the novel. Conway's George, like Stowe's, is devoted to his wife, cynically bitter about being enslaved, and as determined to fight for his freedom as the nation's founders did for theirs. Through George, Conway delivers the point that made Stowe's portrayal of blacks so unusual for its day. George tells Mr. Wilson: "Don't I stand before you every way just as much a man as you are? Look at my face, look at my hands, look at my body (*draws himself up*). Why am I not a man as much as any body?" This affirmation of African-American manhood is close in spirit to Walt Whitman's humanized portraits of blacks in *Leaves of Grass* and even closer to ex-slave Sojourner Truth's proclamation at an 1851 women's rights convention, "Ain't I a woman?"

At times, Conway pushes as far into subversive territory as does Stowe in her most daring moments. Conway turns St. Clare's skeptical commentary on slavery into the relativist pronouncement that politicians and clergymen "may warp and bend language and ethics to a degree that shall astonish the world at their ingenuity, but after all, neither they nor the world believe in it one particle the more. [Slavery] comes from the devil!"

Conway introduces a new character, Penetrate Partyside, who is at once foppish and acerbic. Partyside, a Connecticut Yankee who is traveling through the South recording observations for a book he is writing about human nature, brings humor and a love interest to the plot, for he marries Ophelia (here called Aunty Vermont) and engages in funny fisticuffs with proslavery characters. But Partyside is also a trenchant critic of slavery. He uses black humor as social critique in the way that characters in Lippard's *The Quaker City* do. He even uses Lippard's favorite word to describe a skewed world: *queer*. When on a riverboat he sees a group of slaves, he writes in his notebook: "Mem. Niggers chained like dogs generally; because they are going to be sold according to law particularly. Queer!" He enlarges upon this higher-law sentiment with a direct stab at the nation: "Penetrate, put that down in your remarks on the wisdom, mercy, and justice of the laws of the United States, the home of the free and the land of the brave!"

In light of this sharply antislavery theme, the play's happy ending seems like an apt reward for Tom, whose strength and goodness are emphasized throughout. Conway makes it clear that the evil Legree is headed straight to hell; as he dies, he yells, "The demons drag me! Down, down." Tom, meanwhile, is sent not to the afterlife but to the North, where Partyside and Aunty Vermont have bought a cabin for him and his family, who have been set free by the kindly George Shelby. The ending, then, is a proclamation of the triumph of Tom's goodness.

Perhaps the greatest significance of the *Uncle Tom's Cabin* play—mainly the Aiken and Conway versions, but also others that sprang up in the 1850s—was the response among working-class types who, in many cases, had never even heard of Stowe's novel. Small wonder that many antislavery figures saw the play as an important force for social change. Abolitionists were overjoyed by its impact. One might think that the Garrisonians would have found fault with the most popular version, Aiken's, since George Harris brandishes weapons against his would-be captors and Legree is killed—violations of Garrison's pacifist principles. Aiken wisely makes Legree's death accidental, and he emphasizes Tom's nonresistance, which was in tune with Garrisonian thought. At any rate, paeans to the play appeared in Garrison's *Liberator*. The ultrapacifist abolitionist Parker Pillsbury wrote a letter insisting that the Aiken play had made theater, once reviled, a holier place than the church in America. "Now, the Theatre is openly . . . before and better than the Church," he wrote. "Now we have got the Theater *versus* the Church, on the question of slavery. The Theatre says it's of the Devil. The Church claims that it is of God. Let us wait patiently for the verdict. The question is before a jury of the civilized world."

The jury of the civilized world is the one that Salmon Chase had futilely appealed to in the Van Zandt case and that Harriet Beecher Stowe reached in her novel. The play of *Uncle Tom's Cabin* intensified the appeal. By 1853, six versions were appearing on the London boards and four in Paris. In America, adaptations of the Aiken and Howard plays sprouted throughout the North.

Everywhere, the play made converts to the antislavery cause. Nothing pleased abolitionists more than the fact that people who had formerly been opposed or indifferent to abolition were persuaded by the play to take a more positive attitude toward it. The converts included everyone from clergymen to average workers.

Among the latter, the most surprising were the so-called b'hoys, or Bowery Boys—the vernacular name for urban street types who were often butchers, firemen, newsboys, and other workers distinguished by their red shirts, heavy boots, and boisterousness. By the 1850s, "the b'hoys" had become an inclusive, flexible term, often used interchangeably with "rowdies," "roughs," or "shirt-sleeves," to describe average workers throughout the nation—an expansiveness poeticized in 1855 by Walt Whitman, who in seeking a quintessentially democratic American persona for *Leaves of Grass* called himself "one of the roughs," a type quickly recognized by early reviewers, who variously called him "Walt Whitman the b'hoy poet," "the 'representative man' of 'the roughs,' " and "the 'Bowery Bhoy' in literature."

The approval of an antislavery drama by young workers was especially striking because the b'hoys, always itching for a "muss," were previously known for anti-abolitionist and anti-black violence. How shocking, then, to see the b'hoys and their ilk cheering for fugitive slaves, hissing at a cruel slaveowner, and weeping over the death of an enslaved black man. This reversal in working-class attitudes was noted by many who attended the Aiken play. Garrison wrote in *The Liberator:* "If the shrewdest abolitionist among us had prepared a drama with a view to make the strongest anti-slavery impression, he could scarcely have done the work better. O, it was a sight worth seeing, those ragged, coatless men and boys in the pit (the very *material* of which mobs are made) cheering the strongest and sublimest anti-slavery sentiments! The whole audience was at times melted to tears, and I own that I was no exception."

The workers' response was visible not just in New York, where versions of the play appeared in several theaters, but in all the other Northern cities where the play toured. For instance, a Philadelphia journalist commented, "One may infer a hopeful change in public sentiment, when they see three thousand persons unconsciously accepting anti-slavery truth; hundreds of boys—incipient rowdies, growing up to become the mobocracy of another generation, but preparing unwittingly to '*mob on the right side.*' "The day was coming, he predicted, when "abolitionists may have to intercede to save slaveholders and slave-hunters from the fury of the mob, so long directed against us."

Indeed, many workers who had exulted in the recapture of fugitive slaves in the early 1850s had experienced a shift in attitude by the middle of the decade. An observant British professor, Nassau William Senior, attributed the shift to the popularity of Uncle Tom plays. At first, Senior noted, the Fugitive Slave Law, though opposed by some Northerners, was actually popular among most people because of widespread racial prejudice, which quelled sympathy for fugitive slaves. For the first two years after the law was passed "the lower classes in New York and Boston enjoyed the excitement of a negro hunt as much as our rustics enjoy following a fox hunt." But then came *Uncle Tom's Cabin*. For workers, the plays were even more influential than the novel. Senior noted that night after night audiences screamed and cried at scenes that had a strong antislavery message. Senior wrote, "The sovereign people was converted; public sympathy turned in favour of the slave."

And so, Senior pointed out, when in 1854 the runaway slave Anthony Burns was seized in Boston, outrage swept the city. Federal troops were needed to escort Burns to the ship that was to carry him south, and the city was draped in mourning. Nearly 50,000 people lined the streets, assailing the grim procession with shouts of "Kidnapper! Slave Catcher! Shame! Shame!" Senior concluded laconically, "The attempt will not be repeated. As far as the Northern States are concerned, 'Uncle Tom' has repealed the Fugitive Slave Law."

The slaveholding South Carolina planter John Ball Jr. agreed. He too claimed that the Uncle Tom plays had nullified the law. "Perhaps a slaveholder might have succeeded in catching his 'property,' as late as a year ago," he grumbled in September 1854, "but that he certainly could not do so since 'Uncle Tom' Purdy" and his troupe caught the popular fancy.

Just as remarkable as the enthusiastic response of young workers was that of religious people who had previously disdained the theater. Noting that among those who attended the Aiken play were "persons seldom seen within the walls of the theater," a correspondent for *The National Era* wrote that, along with the b'hoys, the play was "frequented by persons of the highest respectability, not excepting clergyman." Even prostitutes, for whom theaters were a prime place of operation, were often diverted from their work by several of the play's characters, especially the repentant sex slave Cassy—and those who stuck with their job had difficulty finding customers among the entranced playgoers. Fittingly, the Aiken play also made possible another virtually unheard-of phenomenon: an audience that was racially diverse. Before the play had had a year's run, several theaters granted admission to African-Americans, who were assigned their own section.

The popularity of the play, as was true of the novel, resulted from its appeal to primal emotions. Yells, cheers, laughter, and boos permeated the performances. Handkerchiefs were ubiquitous. Few plays elicited as many tears as *Uncle Tom's Cabin*. Antislavery passion overwhelmed audiences. "Men, women, and children, had their eyes suffused regarding the miseries of humanity," a journalist noted. "The touch of nature was a true Abolitionist: it abolished the prejudice of colour and caste."

As the play stimulated antislavery feeling among various social classes, Stowe's novel simultaneously stimulated the popularity of antislavery literature in the North. The American and Foreign Anti-Slavery Society reported, "The immense issues of 'Uncle Tom's Cabin,' and the extraordinary avidity with which it has been read, have called forth other antislavery publications, and given to literature of this description unwonted popularity and success." The most popular single work was Stowe's followup to her novel, *The Key to "Uncle Tom's Cabin"* (1853), which buttressed her scenes and characters with facts collected from many sources. Forty thousand copies of the *Key* were ordered in advance of publication, and 100,000 copies sold in a year.

Other popular Northern works that appeared in 1852–53 were William Jay's *Miscellaneous Writings on Slavery,* Joshua R. Giddings' *Speeches in Congress*, Charles Sumner's *White Slavery in the Barbary States,* Julia Griffiths' *Autographs for Freedom,* Lydia Maria Child's *Memoirs of Isaac Hopper,* and John Greenleaf Whittier's *A Sabbath Scene*. All told, these works together sold over half a million copies. Richard Hildreth's fictional slave narrative, *Memoirs of Archy Moore,* which had sold modestly when it had first appeared in 1836, became an international best-seller when it was reissued in 1852 as *The White Slave; or, Memoirs of a Fugitive.* The 1850s also brought several slave narratives, including Douglass's *My Bondage and My Freedom*, which reportedly sold 5,000 copies within two days and 20,000 over a few months; *Three Years in Europe* and *The American Fugitive in Europe* by William Wells Brown; *Father* [Josiah] *Henson's Story of His Own Life*, with an introduction by Stowe; and *Narrative of Sojourner Truth*, for which Stowe wrote a promotional blurb after Truth visited her in Hartford.

The major authors also offered literary representations of slavery. The tensions over slavery generated the ambiguities of Melville's 1853 short story "Benito Cereno," in which the wily slave Babo at first seems like a submissive Uncle Tom but turns out to be an extra-militant George Harris (or, rather, George Harris as Nat Turner). Other writers offered literary meditations on Stowe's central concern: the dilemma of fugitive slaves. Whitman, despite his sometime sympathy for the South, defended runaway slaves in his poem "Song of Myself," as did Thoreau in his speech "Slavery in Massachusetts," and Emerson in his thoughtful address of May 1854 on the Fugitive Slave Law. All three came out strongly not only for fugitives but also for the higher law, as Stowe had.

The least understood aspect of *Uncle Tom's Cabin* is its political impact. Actually, the novel demonstrably had a key role in the political reshuffling that lay behind the rise of the antislavery Republican Party. *Uncle Tom's Cabin* appeared at the moment when the Whig Party was crumbling as a result of internal divisions over slavery. As the novel's stature grew in antislavery circles, enhanced by the growing popularity of the Uncle Tom plays and other tie-ins, it gave strong impetus to antislavery politics in the North. Besides establishing a common ground between competing abolitionists, Stowe reached out to a number of leading politicians, including Charles Sumner, Cassius Clay, Salmon Chase, and Edward Everett Hale.

Her efforts paid off. On the eve of John Frémont's strong run for president on the antislavery Republican ticket of 1856, an observant journalist noted a growing shift among voters to the antislavery side, attributing it to Stowe's novel:

> Individuals composing the old political parties are beginning to look dispassionately and without prejudice upon the Anti-Slavery aspect of political affairs. Much of Anti-Slavery truth, heretofore discarded by them as fanatical, is now received and read by all. *Uncle Tom's Cabin,* thundering along the pathway of reform, is doing a magnificent work on the public mind. Wherever it goes, prejudice is disarmed, opposition is removed, and the hearts of all are touched with a new and strange feeling, to which they before were strangers.

Henry Wilson, one of the founders of the Republican Party, declared that "many votes cast for Fremont were but the rich fruitage of seed so widely broadcast by Harriet Beecher Stowe."

The novel was often mentioned in prominent political speeches. In an address to the House of Representatives, the Massachusetts congressman Orin Fowler commended the novel. Another antislavery politician, Joshua Giddings, also featured the novel in a speech before the House, declaring, "A lady with her pen, has done more for the cause of freedom, during the last year, than any savant, statesman, or politician of our land. The inimitable work, *Uncle Tom's Cabin,* is now carrying truth to the minds of millions, who, up to this time, have been deaf to the cries of the down-trodden." George W. Julian, the Indiana politician who became one of the founders of the Republican Party and later was a close advisor to Lincoln, affirmed that Stowe's novel had exposed the evils of slavery to untold millions.

The one region that firmly resisted the Uncle Tom epidemic was the American South. Most Southern states discouraged the sale of the novel, and some criminalized it. When the novel gained an underground popularity in some areas of the South, proslavery writers stiffened their attacks. "The wide dissemination of such dangerous volumes [as *Uncle Tom's*

Cabin]," a Richmond newspaper announced, could lead to "the ultimate overthrow of the framework of Southern society amid circumstances of tragic convulsion from which the imagination starts back with horror!" Owning the novel could result in prosecution and imprisonment. The Methodist minister Samuel Green, a free black in Maryland, was found guilty of possessing a copy of Stowe's novel and was sentenced to ten years in the state penitentiary; he served half his term and was freed only during the Civil War.

Just as Stowe's novel spread antislavery sentiment in the North, it gave rise to a whole new reactionary literature of the South, which exponentially bolstered proslavery sentiment there. Slavery was considered throughout most of the South as a natural, biblically sanctioned institution. Lengthy defenses of it were generally thought unnecessary. After all, Washington and Jefferson had owned slaves, and so had most other presidents, Supreme Court justices, and presidents pro tem of the Senate. The rise of Garrisonian abolitionism in the 1830s had put the South on the defensive, impelling politicians like the South Carolinians John C. Calhoun and James Henry Hammond to defend the institution. The proslavery argument had been steadily building since then; the reaction to *Uncle Tom's Cabin* gave it further stimulus.

A writer for the *Richmond Enquirer* noted in 1857 that not long ago few would have bothered to apologize for slavery but now long paeans to it appeared in all kinds of writings: novels, poems, articles, speeches, and tracts. The writer boasted, "We have, indeed, a Pro-Slavery literature," but then ruefully admitted that the South had "produced no romance quite equal to 'Uncle Tom's Cabin.'"

Slavery's defenders warned of the racial disruption the book might engender. Southerners feared that the novel could lead to slave rebellions. In *Abolitionism Unveiled*, Henry Field James predicted that the South would be devastated by blacks who acted in the spirit of Stowe's militant slave George Harris. With bitterness, James invited Stowe and her antislavery friends to go ahead and "thus display your intense *love* of the *negro* by the wholesale massacre of your kindred after the flesh; envelop our dwellings in flames; convert our cotton and sugar estates into a wilderness; erase our cities from the earth." The Northerners that James held responsible for this forthcoming cataclysm included abolitionists, free-soil politicians, and, especially, Harriet Beecher Stowe: "I would say to Mrs. Stowe, 'Come up and see here the fruits of 'Uncle Tom's Cabin.'... These are thy works, and they will surely follow thee.'"

Another book, Dr. A. Woodward's *A Review of Uncle Tom's Cabin; or, An Essay on Slavery,* similarly characterized Stowe's novel as an explosive device that threatened to rip apart the nation. Stunned by the novel's extraordinary popularity, Woodward insisted that if Stowe's "vile aspersions of southern character, and her loose, reckless and wicked misrepresentations of the institution of slavery" continued to spread, America would soon tumble into "revolutions, butcheries, and blood."

By the mid-1850s, *Uncle Tom's Cabin* had become such an alarming phenomenon to Southerners that it seemed necessary to challenge it in every genre, even in poetry. The most important poems were the book-length *The Patent Key to Uncle Tom's Cabin; or, Mrs. Stowe in England* (1853) by "A Lady in New-York" and the 1,500-line *The Hireling and the Slave* (1854) by the South Carolina politician and lawyer William J. Grayson. Both poems insisted that antislavery figures like Stowe ignore the fact that the hireling, or the poor white worker, is far worse off than the enslaved black. Several standard criticisms of Stowe—that she loved blacks unnaturally, hobnobbed traitorously with foreign aristocrats, ignored poor whites, and lied about slavery just to make money—took on ersatz cleverness when delivered in iambs and couplets. The "Lady" holds that enslaved blacks are joyful and white workers pitiable, while Stowe "gathers gold and silver pence, / For pleading long in slave's defence," and "pockets it—well satisfied—'Cost but a lie—I'm glad I tried!'"

The Southern novelists had the broadest appeal of Stowe's opponents. A Southern paper stated, "Thousands will peruse an interesting story, and thus gradually imbibe the author's views, that would not read ten lines of a mere argumentative volume on the same theme. The enemies of the Con-

Southern political cartoon titled "A Dream Caused by the perusal of Mrs. H. Beecher Stowe's popular work Uncle Tom's Cabin" *(c. 1853), which shows the hellish society the South feared could result from Stowe's novel. At the center, a black man dressed as a Quaker holds a flag "*WOMEN OF ENGLAND TO THE RESCUE.*" To the left of the center, near a cave marked "*UNDERGROUND RAILWAY,*" Harriet Beecher Stowe, surrounded by devils, holds a book titled* Uncle Tom's Cabin, I Love the Blacks. *On the right, a woman (probably Stowe again) rides in a parade of demons. In the distance, monsters hurl copies of* Uncle Tom's Cabin *into a bonfire.*

stitution must not be left, therefore, to monopolize so potent a weapon." At least twenty-nine anti-Tom novels were published before the Civil War. Taken together, they had an imposing cultural presence and added significantly to the mushrooming body of proslavery literature.

The first of the novels—released within a month of the publication of *Uncle Tom's Cabin* in book form—was W. L. G. Smith's *Life at the South; or, "Uncle Tom's Cabin" As It Is*. Other prominent anti-Tom novels were Mary Eastman's *Aunt Phillis's Cabin*, David Brown's *The Planter*, Robert Criswell's *"Uncle Tom's Cabin" Contrasted with Buckingham Hall*, Maria J.

McIntosh's *The Lofty and the Lowly,* and J. W. Randolph's *Uncle Robin in His Cabin in Virginia, and Tom in His One in Boston.*

Like the poem by A Lady, many of the anti-Tom novels tried to show that enslaved blacks in the South were far better off than free blacks in the North. In Smith's *Life at the South,* Tom, a slave who desires freedom despite the kindness of his master, flees to Canada only to become wretched because of harsh working and living conditions there. Poor and underfed, Tom moans, "Oh! what a fool I was to come away.... I alwars had my cabin full of good things; and my wife— ... alwars there to smile, talk, an' sing." By chance, Tom meets his slave wife Dinah and their master, who are visiting Buffalo, and returns with them to the South, where he is willingly re-enslaved.

This and many similar narratives in the anti-Tom novels directly challenged the jubilant triumph Stowe associated with defying the Fugitive Slave Law. If abolitionists truly wanted slaves to be happy, says a slaveholding character in David Brown's *The Planter,* they would urge blacks to *appreciate,* not *resist,* the law. The slaveholder goes on to explain, "When I think of [slaves'] happy condition, in contrast with the miserable and lifelong struggle for subsistence, of our free negroes at the North, I am hardly able to imagine a more cruel act than it would have been to emancipate them."

The anti-Tom novels made much of the racial prejudice that existed in the North, where, as Criswell writes in *Buckingham Hall,* "Negroes are subjected to the most humiliating of slaveries, universal tyranny of prejudice; they may be said, indeed, to be as they really are, *masterless slaves.*" The blacks in these novels who make it to the North find themselves in a nightmarish world of poverty, starvation, sexual assault, and, in some cases, murderous violence.

Fugitive slaves in anti-Tom novels do not find lasting protection or solace among Northern abolitionists. To the contrary, abolitionists are portrayed as hypocrites or con artists who pretend to help blacks but who in fact are racist, exploitative, and venal. Vidi's *Mr. Frank, the Underground*

Mail Agent portrays two abolitionists, Dixey and Barton, who entice slaves to escape and yet actually loathe blacks. Dixey says, "I could never bear the sight of a nigger." He adds that the very thought of "a woolly-headed, thick-lipped, flat-nosed, ivory-eyed [black person] on a warm day in July" is enough to make him "throw up." This novel contains a harrowing portrait of an enslaved woman who is lured North by abolitionists who consign her to "an infernal den" where she is locked up for months and forced to be the mistress of a wealthy merchant, "the husband of a lovely woman; the father of six children; a prominent member of Dr. Fairface's church, and a liberal patron of all modern reforms!"

Such attacks on hypocritical Northerners show how anti-Tom novels used themes and characters that for a decade had been popularized by city-mysteries novelists like George Lippard, George Thompson, and Ned Buntline. City-mysteries writers had described the Northern city as a horrifying place where the heartless "upper ten" (well-to-do hypocrites) maltreated or neglected the "lower million," the less fortunate members of society who often fell into indigence or vice. Many of these novels described wretchedness among the poor.

The anti-Tom novels converted this theme into a defense of slavery, arguing that the South's enslaved blacks were far better off than either poor whites or free blacks in the North. Northerners, Caroline Rush writes, pity slaves and yet ignore their own "poor wretches," especially "that most desolate and pitiable class of all the poor, the plain needle-woman," who illustrates "the slavery that exists at the North." A character in Randolph's *The Cabin and the Parlor* scolds a Northerner who calls slaveowners murderers when "it is just as fair for us to turn on you of the North, and declare you all equally assassins, because grasping, heartless men in your midst grind down poor operatives to the starving point, or murder them." Randolph portrays a slave who rejects the idea of running away because, as he says, "poor white folks hab a wus life dan de wus slave"—a statement supported by Randolph's description elsewhere in the novel of a Northern slum, crowded with ramshackle structures, inhabited by ten or a dozen families each, amidst decaying garbage and stagnant water pools, with the air ringing with curses yelled by "the lowest types of degraded humanity."

Such accounts of lower-class squalor and upper-class oppression in the North show the anti-Tom writers trying to win readers who had for years gobbled up city-mysteries novels, pulp fiction about the urban underworld. Both whites and blacks in Northern cities, the anti-Tom novels indicate, were worse off than Southern slaves, who had masters who cared for them. Caroline Lee Hentz has a character assert, "The negroes of the South are the happiest *labouring class* on the face of the globe." This idea is seconded in another anti-Tom work in which enslaved blacks are called the happiest people on earth since they are "provided with every desired comfort" and have "not a care beyond the present," with food and shelter gained by "comparatively nothing of labor."

Slaveowners are presented as good Christians who do an immense favor to blacks by exposing them to the blessings of Western civilization. Brown in *The Planter* writes, "Look now at what the institution of Southern slavery has done in this department of Christianizing the pagan portion of mankind." In their native environment, the argument ran, Africans were unredeemed barbarians. Now they had a wonderful opportunity to save their souls by becoming Christians. Mrs. Henry Rowe Schoolcraft in *The Black Gauntlet* has a white woman declare that "slavery is the school God has established for the conversion of barbarous nations," and that "were I an absolute Queen of these United States, my first missionary enterprise would be to send to Africa, to bring its heathen as *slaves* to the Christian land, and keep them in bondage until *compulsory* labor had tamed their beastliness, and civilization and Christianity had prepared them to return as missionaries of progress to their benighted black brethren."

Yet none of the anti-Tom novels came close to selling as well as *Uncle Tom's Cabin*. The main reason was that Stowe had preempted them on virtually every point. Racism in the North? She had memorably captured that in her ironic portrait of Ophelia. The miseries of white workers, often as great as those of enslaved blacks? She expressed this proto-Marxist idea compellingly through St. Clare, who spoke of a forthcoming working-class revolution. The kindness of many Southern slaveowners? She granted that. Colonization? Like some of the anti-Tom writers (and like many leading Americans from Jefferson through Andrew Jackson to Henry Clay and Lincoln), she proffered that as a possible solution to the race problem. The importance of Christianity and Western culture for blacks? This was an essential theme for her. Stowe was thus a frustrating writer for proslavery novelists to rebut, since she agreed with them on many points—except the central moral issue of slavery.

Uncle Tom's Cabin was also far more entertaining than any of the anti-Tom novels. Stowe's Northern plot, featuring ever-threatened runaways assisted by kindly people, was both more exciting and more agreeable than the cynical anti-abolitionist and anti-Northern narratives offered by the proslavery novels. Her Southern story had many diverting elements—Topsy's antics, Eva's heartrending death, Legree's torture of the noble Tom—that the bland Southern scenes in anti-Tom novels couldn't begin to compete with. More often than not, the anti-Tom novels were talky, contrived, and clumsy. Even the better-written ones, such as Hall's *Frank Freeman's Barber Shop* or Thomas Bangs Thorpe's *The Master's House*, lacked the pathos, thrills, humor, and allegorical contrasts that made *Uncle Tom's Cabin* a worldwide sensation. The anti-Tom authors often borrowed Stowe's devices—like the visionary mode (one slave says of his master, "I a'most seed shining angels, flyin' wid him to Heaven, when he died last night")—but Stowe used them so much more effectively that their efforts paled in comparison.

Always slanted, the anti-Tom novels sometimes strained credibility. For instance, anyone even faintly familiar with slave narratives, let alone newspapers, knew that slave auctions were often very painful for all involved. In Baynard Hall's novel, the auctions were "irresistibly merry." The blacks on sale were largely indifferent as to who purchased them, and rarely were slave families separated. Everyone present was excited and happy. This kind of misrepresentation impelled one outraged author, writing under the name of Nicholas Brimblecomb, to pen a Swiftian reply to the anti-Tom novels titled *Uncle Tom in Ruins! Triumphant Defence of Slavery!* Today, Brimblecomb's irony is readily apparent, though some of its passages would not have been out of place in a straightforward anti-Tom novel, as when abolitionists are called "vile" deceivers "guilty of the grossest falsehoods," such as "declaim[ing] about the forcible separation of husbands and wives, parents and children."

Southern authors, in short, had a problem: the large proslavery oeuvre contained not one work that caught the public's fancy as did Stowe's novel. In her own medium—imaginative literature—she seemed unassailable. Attacks against her even seemed to backfire, as when Julia Tyler's widely reprinted reply to the Stafford House Address was mocked in the *New-York Tribune* as a popgun blast against Gibraltar.

What was needed, some Southerners realized, was a shift of the discussion from fiction to fact, from invective to logic. Enter George Fitzhugh.

A Virginia lawyer and planter with a burning hatred of *Uncle Tom's Cabin*, Fitzhugh, more clearly than anyone else, saw the need for a detailed proslavery response to the North's antislavery publications, especially Stowe's novel. Devoted to formulating a defense of slavery grounded in the analysis of society and economics, he introduced the term "sociology" into the language in his 1854 book *Sociology for the South; or, The Failure of Free Society,* followed three years later by another book, *Cannibals All! or, Slaves without Masters.*

The South soon regarded him as its most convincing proponent for slavery. Before Fitzhugh, it had been customary for proslavery reviewers to associate Stowe with socialism, spiritualism, women's rights, and other Northern "isms" that Southerners saw as anarchic, radical, and distant from the stable society of the South. Fitzhugh retains this antiradical critique, as when he denounces Ophelia of *Uncle Tom's Cabin* as a strong-minded "she-man," or when he rattles off lists of allegedly wicked Northern movements: "Bloomer's and Women's Rights ... and Mormons, and anti-renters, and 'vote myself a farm' men, Millerites, and

Spirit Rappers . . . and Grahamites, and a thousand other superstitious and infidel Isms at the North."

But in general, Fitzhugh avoided clashing at length with Stowe or other abolitionists. Instead, he put one of the most controversial Northern "isms," socialism, to his own use. If Stowe had incorporated socialist ideas into her antislavery arguments, he did so in his proslavery one. Drawing from economists and social theorists—Charles Fourier, Pierre-Joseph Proudhon, Robert Owen, and others—he put the well-known sufferings of white workers to use in defense of slavery. With the rise of industrialism, Fitzhugh argued, it became readily apparent that members of the working class were universally oppressed and hopelessly wretched. In Northern cities, they were in the hands of heartless capitalists who had little or no regard for their well-being. In hard times, they often lacked adequate food or shelter. Most white workers were, in the subtitle of Fitzhugh's second book, slaves without masters. A socialist reorganization of society therefore made sense. And the Southern plantation, Fitzhugh maintained, was the ideal socialist group, for it supplied workers with masters who fed, sheltered, and instructed them. Proclaiming that "our negroes are confessedly better off than any free laboring population of the world," he wrote, "slavery is a form of communism, and as the Abolitionists and Socialists have resolved to adopt a new social system, we recommend it to their consideration."

But didn't slavery violate the founding fathers' doctrine of equality? Jefferson and the others were bamboozled by Locke and the Enlightenment into believing in human equality, Fitzhugh argued. Anyone could see that there are differences of capacity between people. All of history, he wrote, shows that "men are not born physically, morally, or intellectually equal." In the North's free society, inferior people sank into hopeless misery. In the South's slave society, the inferior class, blacks, had found its natural, desirable position.

Fitzhugh also dealt with Stowe's point in *Uncle Tom's Cabin* that many people held in slavery were largely of white descent. (George Harris, for instance, is so light-skinned that he passes as Hispanic.) "Almost the whole interest of Mrs. Stowe's Uncle Tom's Cabin," Fitzhugh wrote, "arises from the fact, that a man and woman, with fair complexion, are held as slaves." On this point, Fitzhugh said, we must refer to history and to racial theory. First, he wrote, "we must take high philosophical, biblical, and historical grounds, and soar beyond the little time and space around us to the earliest records of time, and the farthest verge of civilization." Since all ancient societies, including biblical ones, considered it normal to hold certain people—often white people—in slavery, why shouldn't the South enslave blacks even if they were light-skinned?

As for race, Fitzhugh pointed to current pseudoscientific theory, which supposedly proved the physical inferiority of Africans. Popular magazines often featured phrenological charts displaying the faces of various races, with the Caucasian, made to look refined and intelligent, placed on top and the African, made to appear brutish and ignorant, at the bottom. This racist pseudoscience gained strength in the 1850s when the new field of ethnology was explicated in books like Josiah C. Nott's *Types of Mankind* (1854) and *Indigenous Races of the Earth* (1857), which alleged the inferiority of people with even a small amount of African blood.

All of the sociology and science Fitzhugh offered in support of slavery had great political impact. In the South, Fitzhugh's ideas were distilled in two of the era's most famous proslavery speeches: the so-called Mud-Sill Speech of 1858 by South Carolina senator James Henry Hammond, who told the North that "your hireling class of manual laborers and 'operatives,' as you call them, are essentially slaves" and that the American South practiced slavery with special beneficence by providing for an inferior race; and the 1861 Cornerstone Speech by the vice president of the Confederacy, Alexander H. Stephens, who insisted that the South had "the highest civilization ever exhibited by man" because it was founded on "the great truth that the Negro is not equal to the white man, that slavery—subordination to the superior race—is his natural and normal condition."

Fitzhugh also influenced the future leader of the Republican Party, Abraham Lincoln. In a letter to Horace Greeley, Fitzhugh wrote, "Tis not possible that our two forms of society can long co-exist," a statement he expanded on in *Cannibals All!* and in a May 1856 article anonymously published in the *Richmond Enquirer,* where he wrote, "Two opposite and conflicting forms of society *cannot,* among civilised men, co-exist and endure. The one must give way, and cease to exist; the other become universal." In 1858 came the immortal expression of this notion in Lincoln's "House Divided" speech, as well as Seward's prediction of an "irrepressible conflict." Lincoln, who knew Fitzhugh's writings well, made clear that neither he nor Seward was "entitled to the enviable or unenviable distinction of having first expressed the idea," which, he said, "was expressed by the *Richmond Enquirer* in Virginia in 1856; quite two years before us." That was Fitzhugh's article.

By the time the impact of *Uncle Tom's Cabin* had filtered through the novel's early reception and reached Lincoln, it had helped set the way for the tremendous sparring over the meaning of America that emerged in the Lincoln-Douglas debates of 1858 and the presidential contest of 1860. Stowe saw differences between whites and blacks but fully recognized the humanity of black people and considered their enslavement a gross injustice, totally at odds with the nation's founding principles. Lincoln's ideas were similar to hers on these counts. Also similar was their impulse to reach out to the South—Stowe through including some favorable portraits of Southerners and Lincoln through his idea of malice toward none.

While the repercussions of *Uncle Tom's Cabin* spread, Stowe continued to promote her antislavery message. Having made sure that as many politicians as she knew had received copies of the novel, she used whatever influence she could muster in the political scene—a forbidden sphere for women then—to continue to challenge slavery. In early 1854, she was horrified by Stephen Douglas's proposed bill that threatened to open up the Kansas and Nebraska territories to slavery. She helped organize an antislavery rally in Boston, featuring such luminaries as Garrison, Wendell Phillips, Horace Greeley, and her brother Henry, which was intended to capitalize on what she called "the popular impressions, which have been produced by the reading and acting of *Uncle Tom's Cabin* and the literature following." She worked with her brother Edward to distribute a petition against the bill, signed by leading ministers, that she thought stalled it in Congress. In March, the *Tribune* published her "Appeal to the Women of the Free States of America on the Present Crisis in Our Country," exhorting women to pray, petition, and arrange events to stop a bill that she said would lead to the nationalization of slavery.

Her bold efforts didn't sit well with proslavery politicians. As one of Stowe's contemporaries wrote, *Uncle Tom's Cabin* "penetrated the walls of Congress, and made the politicians tremble. It startled statesmen, who scented danger near." Stephen A. Douglas of Illinois, already known as a straddler on slavery, castigated Stowe on the floor of the Senate, declaring that rapture over Stowe showed that "literature under the name of Uncle Tom's Cabin and other such works" was part of "the broad stream of abolition, treason, and insurrection" that was "holding us up to the hate and prejudice of the world." Similarly, Michigan senator Lewis Cass highlighted *Uncle Tom's Cabin* in his public declaration that "publications [that] originated in a distempered imagination, or something worse, giving the most exaggerated description of the sufferings of slavery, and thus exciting false impressions both at home and abroad, should be discountenanced by every American."

But Stowe didn't give up. Even after the Kansas-Nebraska Act passed, she spearheaded two more antislavery petitions in June and told Garrison that towns everywhere "ought to petition until the Senators shall be flooded." She also attended functions in 1856 for the antislavery Republican presidential candidate John Frémont, who captured much of the North, but no Southern states, with his antislavery arguments. She had little regard for the victor of that race, James Buchanan. Now living in Andover, Massachusetts, where Calvin taught at the theological seminary, she temporarily took into her home Mary and Emily Edmonson, the black girls whose freedom had been bought by her brother Henry's congregation in Brooklyn, and she subsequently paid for their tuition at Oberlin. She applied the money from the British penny offerings toward funding antislavery newspapers and lectures, education for free blacks, and the purchase of several enslaved blacks to secure their freedom.

In 1856, she penned another novel about the South, *Dred*, a title that, by uncanny coincidence, presaged the anti-black *Dred Scott* decision the next year. *Dred* turned into a meditation on slavery far more bitter than *Uncle Tom's Cabin*. The novel at first followed the dalliances of the belle Nina Gordon but shifted its focus to Dred, a fugitive slave hiding out in Southern swamps who prophesies a forthcoming violent judgment day for slaveholders. The sour turn in the novel reflects the darkening of Stowe's vision of the South after the May 1856 bloody, near-fatal bludgeoning of her friend Charles Sumner by the South Carolinian Preston Brooks on the Senate floor—an event mentioned in the second part of *Dred,* which is full of cynical commentary about the intransigence and bullying tactics of proslavery Southerners.

Dred shows up periodically like a black Robin Hood to rescue abolitionists or vent angry words against slaveholders. Although Dred dies before he can organize any sort of slave rebellion, as had his putative father, Denmark Vesey, the novel shows that Stowe, the creator of the gentle Uncle Tom, was now thinking of violence as a solution to the slavery problem. In this she resembled Thoreau, who had made a classic plea for nonresistance in his 1849 essay "Civil Disobedience" but who became the era's most ardent champion of the antislavery warrior John Brown.

The proslavery incursions into Kansas, combined with the Supreme Court's 1857 ruling in the *Dred Scott* case that blacks had no rights that white Americans needed to respect, led both Thoreau and Stowe to embrace Brown. After Brown's futile antislavery raid on Harpers Ferry, Virginia, in 1859, followed by his trial and execution, Thoreau, Emerson, and their fellow Transcendentalists, now believing that only bloodshed would end slavery, influenced Northern opinion by arguing publicly that Brown was a hero on a par with the leaders of the American Revolution. They compared his death by hanging to the martyrdom of Jesus.

Stowe's esteem for Brown matched theirs. She called Brown "a brave,

good man who calmly gave up his life to a noble effort for human freedom and died in a way that is better than the most successful selfish life."
She echoed the Transcendentalists when she wrote that "[Brown's] death
will be mightier for that cause than even his success. The cross is the way
to the throne." She even went beyond them by insisting that Brown was
"*the man who has done more than any man yet for the honor of the American
name.*"

Like Thoreau and Emerson (and unlike her brother Henry), she
embraced the whole John Brown, even his murderous violence in Kansas.
She took the Cromwellian view that in Kansas, as she wrote, "a race of
men, of whom John Brown was the immortal type . . . fought with fire
and sword and blood . . . [and] acted over again the courage, the perseverance, and the religious ardor of the Old Covenanters." In Kansas, Brown
proved himself "our first great commander, who fought single-handed for
his *country,* when traitors held Washington and used the United States
Army only as a means to crush and persecute her free citizens and help
on the slave conspiracy."

Some Southerners plausibly charged Stowe with having prepared the
way for the North's positive reception of Brown. For Thomas Dixon, the
author of pro-Southern best-sellers in the early twentieth century, Stowe
and John Brown were intertwined. Without *Uncle Tom's Cabin,* Dixon
wrote, there would have been no John Brown, and thus no Civil War. In
his 1921 historical novel *The Man in Gray,* Dixon insisted that Stowe had
spread flammable material far and wide, and Brown had lit it with the
torch of violence. In his novel, Dixon has Colonel Robert E. Lee, before
Harpers Ferry, say of *Uncle Tom's Cabin,*

It is purely an appeal to sentiment, to the emotions, to passion, if you will—
the passions of the mob and the men who lead mobs. And it's terrible. As
terrible as an army with banners. I heard the throb of drums through its
pages. It will work the South into a frenzy. It will make millions of Abolitionists in the North who could not be reached by the coarser methods of

abuse. It will prepare the soil for a revolution. If the right man appears at the right moment with a lighted torch—.

Remove the proslavery hyperbole, and we have a credible picture of what actually happened. The point was made concisely by a Virginia contemporary of Stowe who said of *Uncle Tom's Cabin:* "That book and old John Brown's raid may be said to have brought on the Civil War."

Despite her admiration for Brown, Stowe hadn't completely lost hope for a peaceful end to slavery. She was ecstatic over the Republican victory in the presidential race of 1860. Although she thought the Republicans didn't go far enough in opposing slavery, she hoped that their goal of halting its spread would eventually lead to its demise. She could hardly believe how far Northerners had come. It wasn't long ago, she wrote, that open expressions of antislavery feeling would have been considered "rank abolition heresies," whispered in the ear rather than aired in the street. But now Northern men, women, and children everywhere were debating slavery and its evils.

Not that Northerners had converted to radical abolitionism. Garrison and his ilk were still widely considered extremists. Racism was rife. Eleven anti-abolition riots erupted in Northern cities between the beginning of 1859 and the attack on Fort Sumter in April 1861. Lincoln, trying to establish himself as a moderate, opposed abolitionism and John Brown before the war. Stowe, in turn, was dubious because of Lincoln's support for the Fugitive Slave Law and his early determination to save the Union at any cost, whether or not slavery survived.

Nonetheless, Lincoln's opposition to slavery was universally known. He had made that point resoundingly in his debates with Stephen Douglas, in which he stated, "I confess myself as belonging to that class in the country that believes slavery to be a moral and political wrong." He was elected president in 1860 on an antislavery Republican ticket. Stowe knew that, on the deepest level, he and she were in accord.

Stowe's respect for Lincoln grew in the course of the war, which under his direction became increasingly aimed to emancipate the slaves instead of simply to preserve the Union. Her habit of involvement with antislavery politics led to her historic visit to the White House in early December 1862, a visit she made, as she wrote, "to satisfy myself that I may refer to the Emancipation Proclamation as a reality and a substance not to fizzle out at the little end of the hour." We cannot know whether Lincoln was swayed by his interview with her, but we do know that the meeting was a cordial one and was followed a few weeks later by his signing of the proclamation. Lincoln was now the brightest star in Stowe's constellation of American heroes.

By the end of the war, there was a symbolic blending of the ideals of Lincoln, Brown, and Stowe. Having resorted to total war in directing the Hammer and Anvil Campaign of Grant and Sherman, Lincoln declared in the Second Inaugural Address that "if God wills that [the war] continue . . . until every drop of blood drawn with the lash shall be paid by another drawn with the sword, as was said three thousand years ago, so still it must be said 'the judgments of the Lord are true and righteous altogether.' " Here Lincoln put divine justice first, like Brown and Stowe. His imagery recalled theirs too. He combined Brown-like God-directed retaliatory violence in his reference to the sword, Brown's weapon of choice, against an institution he associated with the lash, the same mode of torture that had generated *Uncle Tom's Cabin* when Stowe had her communion-service vision of a slave being whipped to death.

The Civil War was not only Lincoln's war; it was Stowe's and Brown's, too. Among the tributes made to Stowe at her seventy-first birthday party, held in Connecticut in 1882, was a poem about the war by Oliver Wendell Holmes that drove the point home:

> *All through the conflict, up and down*
> *Marched Uncle Tom and Old John Brown,*
> *One ghost, one form ideal;*
> *And which was false and which was true,*
> *And which was mightier of the two,*

The wisest sybil never knew,
For both alike were real.

Both were real, because both had stoked tremendous passions, North and South, that poured into Gettysburg, Chancellorsville, Chickamauga, and all the other bloody battles over the principles Uncle Tom and John Brown had died for.

After the war, Stowe felt that her novel had completed its job. In 1866, she wrote a British friend that she had "been reading Uncle Toms Cabin again—and when I read that book scarred and seared and burned into with the memories of an anguish and horror that can never be forgotten and think it is all over now!—all past!"

But the cultural work of *Uncle Tom's Cabin* was not finished. In many ways, it was just beginning. Over the following decades, its impact gathered new energy and changed American society in ways Stowe could not have foreseen.

5

TOM EVERYWHERE

WRITING *UNCLE TOM'S CABIN*, its *Key*, and *Dred* had been excruciating for Stowe. "I suffer excessively in writing these things," she confessed to a friend. "Many times in writing 'Uncle Tom's Cabin,' I thought my health would fail utterly." Exploring slavery yielded terrible thoughts: "This horror, this nightmare, abomination! Can it be in *my* country!"

The fame that accompanied the novel's publication was gratifying but dizzying. Never had an American author been as widely discussed, or cursed, as she. Though there's no evidence that she received death threats, there were chilling moments. One day at Andover, Calvin opened an envelope with a Southern postmark that contained a piece of cardboard on which was pinned an ear cut from the head of a slave, with a scribbled note saying that this was an effect of her defense of "D—n niggers."

We cannot wonder that she directed her literary energies away from reform to other themes. The almost thirty books she wrote after *Uncle Tom's Cabin* and *Dred* range from narratives about her New England roots (*The Minister's Wooing, Oldtown Folks, Sam Lawson's Oldtown Fireside Stories*) to fiction and nonfiction on international topics (*Agnes of Sorrento, Sunny Memories of Foreign Lands, Lady Byron Vindicated*), to local-color

realism (*The Pearl of Orr's Island, Poganuc People, Pink and White Tyranny*),
to biblical studies (*Footsteps of the Master, Bible Heroines*), and children's
stories (*Little Pussy Willow, Queer Little People, A Dog's Mission*).

Throughout the years she was buffeted by tragedies. In 1857 her
nineteen-year-old son Henry, a Dartmouth freshman, drowned in a
swimming accident in the Connecticut River. Another son, Fred, after
receiving a head wound at Gettysburg as a Union soldier, became an alcoholic and left for San Francisco in 1871 on a voyage from which he never
returned. Her daughter Georgiana struggled with morphine dependency
brought on by treatments for illnesses. Her brother Henry was brought
before the world as an accused adulterer in a highly publicized trial that
tormented her, even though she supported him entirely throughout. "This
has drawn on my life—my heart's blood," she wrote. "He is my life. . . . I
felt a blow at him more than at myself."

As she approached old age, she suffered the loss of several friends and
family members. "The longer I live," she told the novelist George Eliot,
"the deeper and sadder becomes my sense of the hopeless, essential, unutterable sorrowfulness of living this *present* life taken by itself."

Calvin remained supportive, but he was sometimes frustrated over
his failure to match her success. "If I could only do what you have done,"
he wrote to her. "I suffer & have nothing. Your birth pangs bring living,
immortal children, Uncle Tom & Dred—mine, long continued, agoniz-
ing, never ceasing, all end in abortions." He taught at the Andover Theological Seminary until 1863, when, at sixty-one, he retired. He was now
able to dedicate his time to biblical scholarship, which yielded his impressive work *Origin and History of the Books of the Bible* (1867). Obese and
bespectacled, he had long white hair that fell from his bald dome, with an
ample beard that made him look like a prophet—Harriet called him her
Rabbi, or simply Rab. (Mark Twain's young daughter Susy once saw him
and exclaimed, "Santa Claus has got loose!")

Despite many challenges, Harriet's spirit never sank for long. She was
buoyed by the international friendships she had gained and by the solidity
and traditions of the Episcopalian church, which she joined in the 1860s

Harriet Beecher Stowe, c. 1880

along with her daughters Georgiana and Eliza. She also retained her faith in a readily accessible afterlife, believing in what she called "a real, Scriptural spiritualism."

Although her writing shifted away from reform, she didn't abandon social and political issues. She sharply observed the complex status of newly liberated African-Americans after the Civil War. Exultant over the fall of slavery, she nonetheless foresaw the possibility of a new form of slavery emerging in the South. She expressed her fears in a magazine tale, "A Family Talk on Reconstruction," in which a married couple discusses the future of American blacks. The wife takes the rosy view that the Freedman's Bureau and Republicans in Congress would bring equal rights. Her husband disagrees. "The whites will oppose the negro in every effort to rise," he predicts; "they will debar him of every civil and social right . . . and then they will hound and hiss at him for being what they made him."

Tragically, history proved him right. Although African-Americans sporadically gained ground in the years just after the Civil War, the harsh Southern reaction to their advance led to disenfranchisement, segregation, and anti-black violence. Stowe, then, was right in prophesying a backlash. She was so wary of a Southern crackdown, in fact, that she at first thought that awarding blacks the vote might have to wait until whites were prepared for the change. She said that suddenly giving blacks the vote would cause "an immediate war of races." Only through education, she believed, could people of both races learn tolerance. Once education had dispelled racism, the path to political and social equality would be opened.

To this end, she wanted to establish a school where blacks and whites studied in the same building—a model of the kind of interracial education she hoped would spread throughout the nation. In 1867, she and Calvin purchased a place in the town of Mandarin, Florida. She chose Florida not only for its attractiveness as a winter home (and as a place where they hoped their son Fred could conquer his drinking habit) but also because it seemed the ideal location for her educational experiment. She saw that many freedmen were moving there, and she wanted to help them. "Florida is the state to which they have, more than anywhere else, been pouring. Emigration is positively and decidedly setting that way." The Episcopal church had developed an educational system for the British laboring class that she wanted to emulate in Mandarin, where she thought she'd be "doing Christ's work on earth" by helping "that poor people whose cause in words I have tried to plead." Whites needed to be educated too. "Teaching the whites is the only way of protecting the blacks," she explained. "The only way to protect black schools from mobs, was to set up schools for the white children, and civilize that class of whom mobs are generally composed." In late 1869 she opened a school that on Sundays served as a church where Calvin preached. It had a long room divided by folding doors, separating the blacks from the whites, for "to try to put them in one room would raise the rebellion at once." But even this gesture toward racial division did not satisfy whites in the area, since, in her words, they "despise Negroes and hate them." One night her experimental school was burned to the ground.

Although her forward-looking experiment in semi-integrated education proved short-lived, Stowe did not need to prove herself a hero to American blacks. Often when she traveled, as her son Charles reported, she was "greeted everywhere with intense enthusiasm by the colored people, who, whenever they knew of her coming, thronged the railways stations in order to glimpse her whom they venerated as above all women." When she died, in 1896, an association of ex-slaves, the John Brown League, gathered "to honor the woman who aided their liberation—Harriet Beecher Stowe . . . whose publication of 'Uncle Tom's Cabin' was the force which turned the scale in their favor." A black newspaper also hailed her by saying, "It is probable that no other American woman has done so much for this country."

Actually, the influence of Stowe's novel had grown exponentially since the Civil War and would continue to expand in the twentieth century, with its effects still widely felt today. If we trace the history of *Uncle Tom's Cabin* over this period, we see that its cultural power resulted not only from the novel but also from its many spin-offs—particularly plays, songs, and films—that swayed millions who never read the novel.

Shortly after *Uncle Tom's Cabin* first appeared, American reviewers predicted that the novel would fuel revolutions abroad. They were right. The novel's progressive themes resonated internationally. Although *Uncle Tom's Cabin* was banned in Russia until 1857 because of what was seen as its incendiary content, it was familiar in French and German translations to a number of leading Russian thinkers who spearheaded the movement to liberate the nation's 22 million serfs, peasants held in virtual slavery by the ruling elite. Ivan Turgenev, author of *A Sportsman's Sketches, Fathers and Sons*, and other influential progressive writings, spread word of *Uncle Tom's Cabin* after he read it in French in 1853. His cousin, the radical Nikolai Turgenev, read it and wrote that Russia experienced "similar horrors" to those described in *Uncle Tom's Cabin,* explaining that "many of the scenes described in the book seem like an exact depiction of equally frightful scenes in Russia." Another leading Russian radical, Alexander Herzen (known as the father of Russian socialism), similarly saw the novel as an allegorical attack on Russia's serf-based society.

The accession to power of the reform-minded Tsar Alexander II in 1855 eroded the conservative censorship of journalism and led to the public circulation of *Uncle Tom's Cabin*. Particularly significant was the promotion of the novel by two of Russia's most prominent progressive writers, Nikolai Chernyshevsky and Nikolai Nekrasov. Chernyshevsky, who also came to admire John Brown and Lincoln, was so enthusiastic about Stowe's novel that he sent free copies of it to subscribers to his widely read magazine *The Contemporary*. Nekrasov, who took over the magazine with another activist, Ivan Panaev, continued sending the novel to subscribers. In Moscow, the editor Mikhail Katkov published the novel as an appendix to his brilliant literary journal *The Russian Herald*. Meanwhile, the 1857 Russian translation of the novel was immensely popular throughout the nation. The excitement over *Uncle Tom's Cabin* thus helped raise the antislavery passions that led to Tsar Alexander II's abolition of serfdom in February 1861.

The ongoing appeal of Stowe's novel is indicated by the fact that sixty-seven separate editions were published in Russia between 1857 and 1917. During this time, it fed directly and by example into the proletarian spirit behind the Russian Revolution. Chernyshevsky drew upon it for his 1863 novel *What Is to Be Done?*, which was an even greater inspiration behind the Russian Revolution than Marx's *Capital*. In the book, Chernyshevsky had a character read *Uncle Tom's Cabin* to women workers in a dressmaking collective and refer to Stowe as a great woman who drew an ennobling portrait of the oppressed. It's not surprising that Stowe's novel would appeal to revolutionaries, since she had framed American slavery in the context of international labor unrest and had gone so far as to call the Civil War "nothing else" than "a war for the rights of the working classes of mankind, as against the usurpation of privileged aristocracies," part of a larger conflict that "has gone through all nations, dividing to the right and left the multitudes."

What *is* surprising is that her novel appealed equally to a Christian Socialist like Leo Tolstoy and a Marxist materialist like Nikolai Lenin. For Tolstoy, *Uncle Tom's Cabin* exemplified "the highest art"—greater even than Shakespeare—because it promoted "the brotherhood of God and man." For Lenin, *Uncle Tom's Cabin* was his favorite book in childhood, and he gave it a place of pride in his room. He mentioned it often, once declaring that it provided "a charge to last a lifetime."

Did *Uncle Tom's Cabin* save Lenin's life and thus make possible the October Revolution of 1917? This possibility is raised by the fact that in 1907 Lenin and his wife, threatened by the tsarist clampdown on rebels, escaped from the Finnish mainland by making their way across the breaking ice of the moderately frozen Örfjärden Sound to an island. From there they took a boat to Sweden, starting his long European exile. One historian has called it Lenin's "weird Uncle Tom's Cabin night"—the Bolshevik leader preserving his life by imitating Stowe's famous fugitive Eliza Harris. Whether or not Stowe's novel inspired Lenin's escape, it is telling that a Russian-born Harvard professor, Leo Wiener, who specialized in the origins of the Russian Revolution, wrote in 1917, "It may be asserted that *Uncle Tom's Cabin* was . . . the prime cause for the progressive ideas in both countries [i.e., the United States and Russia]." *Uncle Tom's Cabin* remained a top seller in the Soviet Union. Also popular was an often-performed Russian version of a Tom play, minus Stowe's religious themes.

Russia was not the only nation where social change was influenced by *Uncle Tom's Cabin*. In 1901 it became the first American novel to be translated into Chinese when it appeared under the title *The Black Slave Appeals to Heaven*. Its translators, Lin Shu and Wei Yi, said they issued the book "to cry out for the sake of our people because the prospect of enslavement is threatening our race"—a reference to the domination of China by foreign powers as well as the maltreatment of Chinese immigrants in America. One of the founders of the Communist Party in China, Chen Duxiu, in 1905 called theater "a big school for the world" and actors "teachers of the people," a notion reinforced two years later when Chinese students in Tokyo first staged Zeng Xiaogu's play *Heinu yutian lu* (*Black Slave's Cry to Heaven*), based on Shu and Yi's translation.

The adaptability of *Uncle Tom's Cabin* to persecuted peoples was exemplified by a Yiddish version that was performed at Glickman's Jewish Theater in Chicago in 1900. In this performance, Tom read from the Talmud, not the Bible, and Jewish actors in blackface sang "coon songs" to "Hebrew melodies." Coincidentally Topsy was played by an actress named Anna Frank. A Jewish attendee was quoted as saying, "The negro was enslaved in the south and hunted and tortured. Have not my people been enslaved and hunted and tortured? Who should be able to act Uncle Tom if not a Jew?"

There's evidence that a Portuguese translation of *Uncle Tom's Cabin* published in Paris and distributed by booksellers in Brazil fanned antislavery feelings. "Down in Brazil," as one commentator noted, "the emancipation of the slaves was mainly due to an editor who kept his paper red hot with abolition arguments. He did not have much success until he printed 'Uncle Tom's Cabin.' " Distribution of the novel in Cuba reportedly contributed to the 1886 abolition of slavery there, combining its powers with the abolitionist novel *Francisco* by the Cuban author Anselmo Suárez y Romero. The black Cuban champion of freedom José Martí, who spearheaded that nation's separation from Spain—which came after his death in the wake of the Ten Years' War and the Spanish-American War—considered *Uncle Tom's Cabin* the basic text of liberation for the Western hemisphere. In effect, it became just that. As Susan Gillman has found in her exploration of "broadly pan-American citations of Stowe," the novelist "has always been the first lady dominating this American-hemispheric-feminist tradition, invoked by critics in both Latin and North America since the mid-nineteenth century."

The international significance of *Uncle Tom's Cabin* impressed no less a writer than Henry James, who had fond recollections of reading the novel and seeing Tom plays in his youth. He was stunned by the universal attraction of *Uncle Tom's Cabin*. It was, he wrote, "as if a fish, a wonderful 'leaping' fish, had simply flown through the air. This feat accomplished, the surprising creature could actually fly anywhere, and one of the first things he did was thus to flutter down on every stage, literally without exception, in America and Europe." (He didn't mention the many other nations—India, Australia, and New Zealand, to name a few—the Tom plays reached.)

It's telling that James remarked on the numerous stage versions. He recognized that as striking as was the ongoing popularity of the novel in its many translations, the Tom shows had an even stronger impact than the book. By the 1870s, Uncle Tom plays were being shown across America, England, and the Continent. In the 1880s, between twenty and fifty Tom troupes toured America each year, and the next decade saw as many as five hundred companies traveling annually. Actors known as Tommers traveled far and wide in wagon trains, stopping everywhere to perform the play. "There were dozens of *Uncle Tom's Cabin* companies," recalled a playgoer, "and they came back year after year to every hamlet and village in the nation." One Tom troupe traveled nearly eleven thousand miles, starting out from Illinois and giving shows throughout the Midwest, Northwest, California, and Arizona.

For many towns, the arrival of the show was a big event, trumpeted by posters and enlivened by a Tom parade. Crowds gawked at the procession of Tom wagons, garish and gilt-edged, as the actors in costume—Tom, Eva, Topsy, Legree, and the rest—waved from their perches. After the parade came the show itself. When there was no theater in town, a tent sufficed as a performance space, or the town hall or a lecture room was appropriated for the evening.

The Tom shows were among the primitive beginnings of mass entertainment in America. Given the technological limitations of the era, it is remarkable how widely the Tom shows reached. Perhaps the greatest testament to the popularity of the shows is the fact that because of its widespread enactment there is no way of saying how many performances took place between 1852, when the play first appeared, and recent times, when Tom characters and themes have spread into film and TV. In 1912, Stowe's son Charles estimated that the Tom show had been put on 250,000 times, but modern scholars have found this number too low.

At any rate, even if we knew the number of Uncle Tom performances, we'd only have a partial idea of the play's significance, since most people saw the play more than once. The author J. Frank Davis wrote in 1925, "In America today are vast numbers of middle-aged men and women who remember that 'Uncle Tom' was the first theatrical performance they ever saw. Also the second, third, fourth . . . I was one of those. Until I was 13 years old I never saw a professional company of actors in anything but 'Tom'—but I had seen that production five or six times." All told, he confessed, in the period up through his early adulthood he had seen the play some twenty-five times (not even close, he said, to the sixty-three times claimed by a New York journalist he knew of).

For a sensitive playgoer like Henry James, such repeated viewings of the Uncle Tom play yielded an education in aesthetic discrimination. James recalled going to so many Tom plays as a child in New York that he became adept at discriminating between performances in which emotion seemed inauthentic or excessive and ones that had the ring of honesty and power. James had an especially fond memory of an actress in the Eliza role who stirred him every time he saw her. The Tom plays, he wrote of himself in the third person, were his "great initiation; he got his first glimpse of that possibility of a 'free play of mind' over a subject which was to throw him with force at a later stage of culture . . . into the critical arms of Matthew Arnold." The plays nurtured in James the aesthetic detachment, the impartial witnessing of contrasting emotions that lay behind his authorial flexibility and subtlety. They helped him see human feelings as performative and theatrical, sometimes skillfully so, sometimes not. They were thus part of the development of a literary artist who at the height of his powers reminded himself to heed "the ever-importunate murmur, Dramatize it, dramatize it!"

If the plays had aesthetic ramifications in James, they had distinctly political ones for many other Americans. On the one hand, the plays in which Stowe's liberation plot was emphasized often became vehicles for progressive politics. On the other hand, versions that minimized the liberation narrative and foregrounded the pleasures of plantation life fed into a romanticization of the Old South and the Lost Cause.

No popular genre offered a greater opportunity for empowering blacks during and after Reconstruction than did the Uncle Tom plays. There's a common misconception that many of the plays turned Stowe's black characters into a gallery of lackeys, buffoons, and smiling entertainers. True, among the countless stage adaptations of Stowe's story, a certain number did make a turn toward racism. But most did not, since the overwhelming majority adhered to the original Aiken play, which had generated political controversy before the Civil War and continued to do so through Reconstruction and beyond.

Over time, the Tom plays and films yielded new possibilities for the empowerment of African-Americans. The more vigorously Eliza charged across the ice, the stronger she appeared. When George in the rocky pass leveled a gun against his would-be captors, he became a striking symbol of black resistance to white power. Whenever Tom was portrayed as a muscular, middle-aged man, as he was in Stowe's novel, he could seem heroic in his refusal to obey Legree, and his passive resistance became a sign of power, not submissiveness.

The Tom plays empowered African-Americans in another way as well: they became the first major venue for large groups of black performers, and they opened the way for the assumption of leading roles by black actors. In this sense, the plays carried forward the progressive spirit of Stowe, who in 1853 wrote her dramatized version of *Uncle Tom's Cabin*, called *The Christian Slave*, expressly for Mary E. Webb, a mulatto who, in an amazing display of acting, performed all of the characters in the play before audiences in New England and London.

It took nearly two decades for Tom show managers to catch up to Stowe's idea of using African-American performers. Before then, all of the slave characters were played by whites in blackface—a continuation of the minstrel tradition. By the early 1870s, groups of blacks, many of them emancipated slaves, were called upon to perform musical and dance numbers in the plantation scenes of Tom shows. From that time forward the onstage presence of "genuine" black people was a major draw for playgoers lured by ads such as one in 1880 that strained punctuation in promising a "MULTITUDE OF COLORED FOLK—MEN, WOMEN, AND CHILDREN, BLACKS! MULATTOES!! QUADROONS!!! OCTOROONS!!!!"

Then came another innovation: the appearance of a black actor in the lead role. In 1878, a Richmond theater manager, Gustave Frohman, got the idea of having "a real Negro play Uncle Tom." He offered the role to the outstanding black performer Sam Lucas. Lucas, who was born in Ohio in 1840, was a multitalented musician, songwriter, and comedian who had sung and played guitar in Mississippi River boats during the Civil War before touring with several minstrel companies in the early 1870s. Two years after accepting Frohman's offer to play Tom, Lucas appeared with another company at Boston's Gaiety Theatre in which *all* of the lead slave roles were played by blacks. This pioneering example of African-Americans as the featured performers in a mainstream play was praised by Stowe herself, who in 1880 wrote a public letter, read aloud before several performances, congratulating the troupe and noting how far blacks had come since the days of slavery.

Stowe's paean to these actors adds substance to the increasing recognition of the positive contribution early black performers made to American culture. It was once thought that black performers were degraded by their allegedly happy-go-lucky routines, which bridged minstrelsy with the brainless "coon songs" that became the rage in the 1890s and beyond. But just as minstrels could carry subversive messages, so black performers after the Civil War found new avenues of self-expression and social advancement through showmanship, even when some of this material seems embarrassing in retrospect.

Sam Lucas is a case in point. On the one hand, when he toured with groups like the Georgia Minstrels and the Hyers Sisters Combination, he regularly sang minstrel songs that reflected the racial stereotypes of the day. But as a skilled songwriter, he often inserted into minstrel-like songs words that celebrated emancipation, as in his popular tune "De Day I Was Sot Free." Moreover, he joined the growing number of black singers who brought alive their distinct cultural heritage by regularly singing spirituals, the songs derived from slavery that came to be known as jubilee music (referring to emancipation).

Stowe and brother Henry instantly recognized the importance of spirituals, which would become a source of many types of popular entertainment, right up to today. The jubilee craze began when nine African-Americans—five women and four men—associated with Nashville's Fisk University went on a singing tour to raise funds for their struggling institution, founded in 1866 for the education of former slaves. Following the pattern of previous African-American minstrel groups, some twenty of which had appeared during the 1860s, the Fisk singers at first performed standard minstrel songs such as "Home Sweet Home" and "Old Folks at Home." But when they introduced spirituals in a concert in Cincinnati, the crowd went wild. Soon, slave songs like "Swing Low, Sweet Chariot," "Roll, Jordan, Roll," and "Go Down, Moses" were the main features of their program. Changing their name to the Fisk Jubilee Singers, the Fisk performers gained national visibility when Henry organized a concert for them in his Brooklyn church. Narrow-minded critics sneered at the singers as "Beecher's Nigger Minstrels," but the Fisk group was well on its way to success. After touring the East, the group traveled internationally.

The African-American intellectual and reformer W. E. B. Du Bois singled out the Fisk group as being chiefly responsible for bringing before the world "the Negro folk-song," which, he wrote, "stands today, not simply as the sole American music, but as the most beautiful expression of human experience born this side of the sea . . . the singular spiritual heritage of the nation and the greatest gift of the Negro people." Stowe wrote of the Fisk Jubilee Singers that "their history is the romance of our period."

The Fisk Jubilee Singers

She explained, "Starting poor, simple, unknown, with the disadvantage of color in their way, they first gained the ear and heart of the most refined circles in this country."

She was perceptive in recognizing the Fisks' achievement. In 2002 the Fisk Jubilee Singers were posthumously inducted into the Gospel Music Hall of Fame—a wonderful tribute, but one that does not come close to measuring their full significance. "The impact this music would have cannot be overstated," according to the music historians Tim Books and Richard Keith Spottswood. Vaudeville, blues, jazz, swing, rock, rap, hip-hop—these are some of the musical forms that have been influenced by the kind of music first popularized by the Fisk group.

Largely forgotten today is the Tom shows' key role in disseminating this music. Not long after the Fisk group and some imitators had appeared, Tom-show producers incorporated jubilee music into their programs. Many Tom troupes used black performers to sing this music. Since the companies traveled far and wide—stopping in the largest cities and the smallest hamlets, performing in all kinds of venues—they brought spirituals to countless people who otherwise would not have heard them. A deluge of black entertainers joined the Tom shows from around 1877 onward. Among the many groups that joined such shows were the New Orleans Jubilee Singers, the Tennessee Jubilee Singers, and the hundred-member Sawyer's Original Jubilee Singers. These black singers augmented what was called the "realistic" portrayal of *Uncle Tom's Cabin* onstage. One Tom troupe offered "morsels of Ethiopian fun and frolic, descriptive of the different phases of 'Slave Life on the Old Plantation.' "

Such plantation images, despite the incorporation of black singers, call attention to a conservative strand in certain Tom plays in which Stowe's narrative was distorted to become a vehicle for the values of the Old South. This process began not long after Stowe's novel was published. In the 1850s, there appeared minstrel skits like Frank Brower's *Happy Uncle Tom* and Rose Merrifield's *Topsy* that presented slaves as carefree and contented under their master's care. Although most of the early Tom plays were based on the strongly antislavery Aiken text, great liberties were sometimes taken with Stowe's plot by those who wanted to romanticize plantation life. A New Orleans theater manager presented a "modified" version of *Uncle Tom's Cabin* which was "made to suit the locality." A producer in Richmond made the play "entirely unobjectionable to a southern audience" when he "purged [it] of its objectionable features." Joyous slaves populated many of the Tom shows after the Civil War in a retrospective nostalgia. Uncle Tom himself generally became an older, more passive figure—partly because the original actors aged in their roles, and partly because the stereotypes of minstrelsy were amplified when theater managers wanted to highlight the gentleness of loyal slaves. Several sorrowful scenes in the play, even slave auctions and the episode on Legree's plantation, were bookended by slaves singing, dancing, and expressing thanks to their "good massa."

From the 1870s onward, the songs performed in most Tom shows were a mixture of African-American spirituals and minstrel tunes, sung by numerous black performers posing as slaves at work or play. The dancing typically consisted of the cakewalk (a high-step routine in which the actors pranced about in imitation of sophisticated whites), the buck-and-wing (foot stomps and arm-waving), and the breakdown, which featured rapid, sometimes frenzied movements. The songs and dances were accompanied by blacks playing a variety of instruments: banjos, fiddles, tambourines, bones (animal bones or wooden sticks used for percussion).

The music and frolic were designed to underscore the alleged happiness of plantation life. One ad for a Tom show promised the appearance of "THE JOLLY FOUR COONS," whose songs were said to show that "DAR'S A HEAP OF FUN in Dem Nigs, You Bet." Another offered a "WONDERFUL CONGREGATION OF HAPPY SLAVES." A third claimed to present "All the Magic Romance of the Storied South," with "Real Fields of Snowy Cotton," "Mammies Who Croon Soft Lullabies," and "Real Pickaninnies That Sing and Dance."

Such cheerful slave spectacles portrayed blacks stereotypically to reach the mass audience. There can be no doubt that some of the Tom plays accelerated not only the plantation legend but also the image of blacks as dim-witted entertainers. But recent commentators generally miss another strain in the Tom plays. Whenever the shows included spirituals sung by jubilee groups, which was often the case, the potential for authentic expression by African-Americans was always there. Even the apparently jubilant spirituals could carry a fierce longing for freedom and equality, as was noted by Frederick Douglass when he wrote that slaves expressed their buried bitterness in happy-sounding songs. Later W. E. B. Du Bois pointed out that the spirituals, for all their gleeful fervor, were "distinctly sorrowful," the "music of trouble and exile, of strife and hiding" laced with the hope "that sometime, somewhere, men will judge men by their souls and not by their skins."

Nor can the non-jubilee performances in the Tom shows be merely dismissed as running counter to the progress of African-Americans. The shows provided employment and visibility for an untold number of blacks, most of whom would have been otherwise relegated to menial jobs. As theater historian Michele Wallace points out, many blacks who started out in Tom shows went on to star in vaudeville, jazz, and other areas.

As for the racial stereotypes in the Tom shows, they were more complicated than they first appear. The fact that the widely respected Fisk Jubilee Singers and their many imitators sang minstrel songs along with spirituals—sometimes mixing the two genres in the lyrics of individual songs—points to the fact that even African-Americans proudest of their own cultural heritage could perform songs by Stephen Foster and other white composers. Read in this way, the Tom shows affirmed a new kind of democracy by showing both blacks and whites onstage singing songs from each other's cultures. This was the same kind of cultural democracy that informed Stowe's play *The Christian Slave,* where the African-American Mary Webb sang Foster's "Old Folks at Home," and that opened the way for the rich cross-racial borrowings that became an underpinning of twentieth-century mass entertainment.

The Tom show dances, also, cannot be dismissed as merely insulting to blacks. The cakewalk, sometimes seen as degrading to African-Americans, in fact allowed blacks to mimic, exaggerate, and, by implication, mock the refined manners of white gentlefolk. The buck-and-wing, which required

The cakewalk

great dexterity of feet and hands, prefigured the superb tap dancers, black and white, who appeared in many films of the early Hollywood era. The breakdown, often performed by Topsy along with other black characters, represented an explosive release of energy and passion, appealingly vibrant in contrast to the staidness of the Shelbys, the coldness of Aunt Ophelia, and the urbanity of St. Clare.

What seems like a distinctly conservative element in the Tom shows, the plantation myth, is thus not quite as conventional as it at first may seem. The same can be said of another prime ingredient of the plays: religion. Stowe's visionary gospel of love was an essential part of the great majority of the shows, which presented Tom and Eva reading the Bible, having a mutual vision of "spirits bright," and sharing the destiny of a sorrowful death followed by an ecstatic entrance into heaven. The shows would never have become as popular as they did without the religious element, which before the Civil War had turned theatergoing into a respectable pastime and after it made the far-traveling Tom shows acceptable almost everywhere they went. Today, the religious scenes seem sentimentally pious—even campy, as Ann Douglas describes Eva's tear-soaked departure to heaven. But in the nineteenth century, when many were still escaping the twin shadows of Calvinism and skepticism, the pious message of the Tom shows could seem both comforting and contemporary.

Stowe was hardly the only one caught up in spiritualism, which attracted some 11 million adherents worldwide and intrigued the philosopher William James so much that in 1886 he founded the American Institute for Psychic Research with the help of many of America's top scientists and philosophers. Stowe's young friend Elizabeth Stuart Phelps, who had studied with Calvin Stowe at Andover and was in the Stowe home often, wrote a best-selling trilogy about the afterlife—*The Gates Ajar* (1868), *Beyond the Gates* (1883), and *The Gates Between* (1887)—that revealed concrete details about heaven, where children, for example, enjoy gingersnaps and toys. *The Gates Ajar* spawned similar spiritualist novels, such as George Wood's *The Gates Wide Open; or, Scenes in Another World* (1870), which gave even more precise pictures of heaven, such as

Eva's flight to heaven

a personal meeting with Michelangelo and a description of Beethoven, Mozart, Haydn, and Handel teaming up and writing a new oratorio for God, in whose presence they were basking.

How fitting, then, for nineteenth-century theatergoers to be reminded again and again—in living color, right there on the stage—that heaven wasn't a distant realm but readily attainable, not just by a select few but by all, from innocent children to persecuted blacks. In the deaths of Eva and Tom, heaven became visible, tangible, and lovely. Spectacular tableaux— scenes in which the characters posed silently in front of painted or illumi- nated backdrops—brought heaven into the very presence of the audience, the most hardened of whom could not but feel inspired and often driven to tears. The tradition of heavenly tableaux began in the 1850s with the earliest Tom plays, including Stowe's *The Christian Slave,* which concludes with Eva flying upward on a large white dove and looking down benignly on the kneeling Tom and St. Clare. Stowe had so much faith in the nearness of the afterlife that she had "A VOICE FROM ABOVE" speak resonantly to Tom just before he died.

In most Tom shows, however, it was not a divine voice but a celestial choir that hailed the ascension of Eva and Tom. The sopranos in the chorus, accompanied by orchestral swells, hit their sweetest notes to suggest the consoling presence of angels. Eva died against a backdrop of billowing white clouds filled with winged spirits. Often she literally ascended, by way of piano wire or rope controlled by a pulley—or, hidden by sobbing mourners, she sneaked behind the curtain, donned papier-mâché wings, climbed a backstage ladder, and appeared as one of the angels in the clouds. In the playbills and acts, the scene was given various names: "Grand Transformation. Eva in Heaven," "A Glimpse of the New Jerusalem; OR, THE PORTALS OF THE GOLDEN CITY!!!" or, most commonly, using the phrase Elizabeth Stuart Phelps had popularized, "The Beautiful Gates Ajar." Eva's ascension was often a drawn-out affair that took her through several celestial phases; one production advertised "A Magnificent Transformation Scene of Fifteen Minutes' Duration" in which Eva went through the Bower of Roses to the Bower of Butterflies, past the Recording Angel, and on to the Cobweb Grotto, the Silver-lined Cloud Drop, and finally the Bower of Elysium. Her afterlife seemed especially glorious when illuminated by lightbulbs, invented by Thomas Edison in 1879 and first used the next year in a New York production of the play—a technological breakthrough in theatrical performance.

The Tom plays were aggrandized in other ways. Ever since the master showman Phineas T. Barnum had opened his museum of curiosities in New York in 1836, Americans had been obsessed by the -*est* factor, a fascination with the biggest, smallest, thinnest, oldest, and most outrageous, which reflected the bumptious confidence of the rapidly expanding nation. The first Uncle Tom play opened in the Troy Museum, which also exhibited "curiosities of every description, including . . . grand cosmoramas, fifty Burmese figures in their native costumes . . . and admirable paintings of the Great Sea Serpent." When Barnum put on the Conway version of *Uncle Tom's Cabin* at his museum, the public was invited to see midgets, a bearded lady, a Fiji mermaid, and hundreds of other exhibits "without extra charge." Another Barnum poster promoted "TOPSY / TOPSY / TOPSY" in *Uncle Tom's Cabin* while also plugging "THE WONDER OF WONDERS. A MAMMOTH FAT INFANT. 3 YRS OLD AND 196 POUNDS. A PERFECT MOUNTAIN OF FLESH."

As the century passed, unusually sized people or sensational effects continued to be offered as enticements to the Tom shows. In 1883 a dime museum ran *Uncle Tom's Cabin* in the main hall and in a nearby room exhibited "Hannah Battersby, the biggest and handsomest fat woman in the world, weighing 760 pounds, who is a wonderful curiosity and engaged at a salary of $200 a week." All of the major Tom companies preceded their evening showing of the play with a daytime street parade featuring the Tom characters in separate vehicles—the winged Eva with a silver wand, Legree snapping his whip, Topsy doing a breakdown on a wagon—along with brass bands, fife and drum corps, jubilee singers, pickaninny dancers, and, very often, unrelated curiosities, including at one parade "A CALIFORNIA GIANT COLORED BOY! HEIGHT EIGHT FEET! AND 17 YEARS OF AGE!"

The spectacular features of the street parade were amplified in the performances of the plays themselves. Among the many memorable scenes in the play, three were standouts of sensational spectacle: Eliza crossing the ice, the steamboat scene of Tom saving Eva, and the whipping of Uncle Tom. Also crucial were comic scenes involving Topsy and Marks. All of the scenes were infused with the -est factor. Eliza's escape vied for the most exciting, Tom's rescue of Eva the most heroic, Legree's lashing of Tom the cruelest, and Topsy's and Marks' clowning the funniest scenes on the nineteenth-century stage, with Eva's ascension always indisputably in first place as the most inspiring.

A competition developed between the scores of Tom companies to see who could create the greatest effects. The riverboat in which St. Clare buys Tom became a wonder of stage production. If Purdy at the National Theatre could boast that his tableau of the moonlit Mississippi was large enough to float the U.S. Navy, his biggest competitor, Barnum, offered in his Tom show a "SPLENDID MOVING PANORAMIC DIORAMA" of a steamboat moving along with puffs of smoke coming from the stack and the steamboat's wheels clearly heard.

The boat remained a prime setting through the long history of the Tom plays, but its increasingly realistic presentations proved insufficient for the thrill-seeking audiences. Starting in 1887, many of the plays included a race between two paddle wheelers, the *Natchez* and the *Robert E. Lee,* a dramatization of an actual boat race in 1870 won by the *Lee.* The stage race often ended in a collision in which the *Natchez* was smashed to smithereens—another gesture to the plantation mythos, awarding the Confederate general a symbolic victory. (In the excitement, theatergoers evidently didn't concern themselves with the anachronism of his name being used in a drama that takes place nine years before the war.)

Producers also decided that Eliza's escape across the ice floes—typically wooden boxes painted white—had to be made far more intense than in Stowe's novel, where the escape is reported, not seen, and where no dogs are in pursuit. In early stagings, actors offstage barked into a barrel as Eliza scampered across the Ohio. But beginning in the late 1870s, actual dogs were brought in to chase her and thus amplify the terror. Ordinary bloodhounds, who were used to trace human scent, were quickly found to be far too gentle-looking for the role, with their droopy ears and soft expressions. Instead, rare breeds of mean-looking hounds were imported from abroad, or larger breeds, especially Great Danes, substituted for the slave-chasing hounds. Tom companies came to be sneered at if they didn't include at least a few dogs. An 1885 Tom company came with "the only $5000 pack of man-eating Cuban bloodhounds, including the dog 'Emperor,' the largest Cuban bloodhound in America." One company's largest hound, Koloss, was seven feet from nose to tail and nearly four feet high, outdone by another troupe's giant dog, Tip, who was seven feet four inches long and weighed 246 pounds.

Eliza crossing the ice

Dogs, however, were not enough to entertain nineteenth-century audiences that feasted on traveling circuses. During the Civil War, the Old Bowery Theatre pioneered a multianimal craze with its "EQUESTRIAN MORAL DRAMA!" with "REAL HORSES, DOGS, AND MULES." In some productions, Eva rode onstage on a Shetland pony. Some shows included alligators, and at least one brought on an elephant. Although many of the animals were reserved for the preshow parade, at least some creatures were expected onstage—and sometimes drew more positive reviews than the actors, as in the case of a Minnesota journalist who, noticing that the hounds knew their cues better than Eliza, quipped, "The dogs were poorly supported."

Donkeys and burros were often taught tricks, such as turning in circles, bobbing their heads, or pawing the air with their hooves. Usually the donkeys or burros were associated with Lawyer Marks, who as the image of wily silliness became a comic figure far removed from the slave-hunting profiteer of Stowe's novel. Marks added a light touch to otherwise serious scenes. When he was hunting for slaves along with Haley and Loker, he was inevitably perched awkwardly on a burro, his feet nearly touching the

Lawyer Marks on his donkey and carrying his umbrella

ground. He wore a tall top hat and a tight-fitting dark suit. His signature was the umbrella he always carried, whether he was outside a house scheming to catch Eliza or at a slave auction, where he gave absurdly low bids. He always provoked guffaws with his greeting, "I'm a lawyer, and my name is Marks."

In some scenes he mixed it up with Topsy, who became a far more adventurous character than simply a prototypical pickaninny, as some have called her. Topsy sang, danced, somersaulted, and did odd things like eat flower petals, along with committing all the petty thefts that enrage Ophelia in the novel. Topsy became such a figure of wild fun that she flouted respectable behavior and sang songs with brash lines like "I tamed an alligator to move along de plow; / De first potater I turned up was our old brindle cow. / Oh, I can jump and I can hop, / And take a little snopsey; / Oh, I can sleep just like a top, / Bekase my name am Topsey."

After the belly dancer known as Little Egypt introduced the Hoochie-Coochie and other sensual dances to America at the 1893 Columbian Exposition in Chicago, the always-shimmying Topsy took on a surprising eroticism, reflected in songs like "Topsy's in Town," in which she is said to be so desirable that "She breaks hearts at will and has style fit to kill, / Look out for Topsy is in town." Adventurous and transgressive, Topsy also became a symbol of interracial love in her deep affection for Eva. In the twentieth century, this closeness would develop into a symbiotic interdependence in the popular play and film *Topsy and Eva*, starring the talented sisters Vivian and Rosetta Duncan. In direct contrast to the cultural milieu of Jim Crow, the Topsy-Eva pairing affirmed the possibility of wholehearted togetherness between the races.

In their emphasis on excess, it was only natural that the shows would multiply the characters. Not only did the singers, dancers, and musicians multiply, but so did the main characters. The rage for doubling began around 1880, when P. T. Barnum's circus merged with J. A. Bailey's. If Barnum and Bailey proved that two circuses were better than one, the Tom shows found that America's most beloved characters could be even more attractive as duos. Thus there were "2 Famous Topsys. 2 Marks, the Lawyer. 2 Educated Donkeys, Jack and Jill. 6 Mammoth Trained Siberian Bloodhounds." Sometimes *all* of the main characters were doubled, so that the play's climax had two Legrees whipping two Toms. "Everything double but the prices!" declared a typical poster. It was not long before the characters were tripled and even quadrupled.

One can only wonder what this multiplication of characters did to Stowe's Northern and Southern plots. They were diffuse already, pulling one's attention back and forth between the Harrises' flight north and Tom's multistage journey south to the hell of Legree's plantation. Few reviews of the doubled plays survive, and those that do just record the numbers in awe ("Two Evas—Two Uncle Toms—Count 'em") without specifying how the twinned roles work. A surviving double-Tom poster from a show staged by the Stetson Company in 1880 suggests that the pairings were intended to reveal different sides of a character. In the poster, one Uncle

Two Topsys

Tom seems like a fool—he is speaking with a chicken, which announces, "All coons look alike to me"—and in the other he is wearing glasses and reading a book, the very image of studiousness. But what new dimensions could be revealed by doubling fairly straightforward characters like Eva or Legree? It's difficult to say, but one thing is sure: for playgoers of the era, the more Tom characters, the better.

The Tom companies gave themselves grandiose names meant to match the size of their shows. They indulged in an orgy of one-upsmanship. There were C. H. Smith's Double Mammoth Troupe, Anthony & Ellis's World Famous Double Mammoth Uncle Tom's Cabin Company, and Joseph Frank's Great Touring Troupe of Double Numbers. One troupe boasted "The Best Uncle Tom! The Greatest Eva! The funniest Topsy & Marks on Earth!" Another reported, "The Verdict Is—BEST EVER SEEN." "LARGER IN PROPORTION AND GRANDER IN MAGNITUDE

THAN ALL OTHERS COMBINED," announced another. The Moyers Brothers Company promised "The most Colossal Production Ever Made of This All American Drama. The Barnum of them all!"

Tom companies, large and small, needed a constant infusion of actors and musicians. Thus arose the genus known as the Tommer: the actor who devoted his whole career to playing in *Uncle Tom's Cabin*. Tommer families were common, and almost always white. The youngest daughter in such a family could play Eva, her sister Topsy, her older brother George Harris, and her mother and father Ophelia and Tom, respectively. When the little girl grew up, she and her sister could assume adult female roles, and her brother could slip easily into Legree or Tom. Many troupes had individual actors who played different roles in the same play. The Eliza actress could reappear later in the evening as Ophelia and then as Cassy, or as one of the twin Topsys or Evas. Between acts she could be seen peddling candy or souvenirs to the audience. Eva could die, rise to heaven by

Two Uncle Toms, one talking with a chicken, the other reading a book

Broadside for a Tom show, with typical hyperbolic headlines and images of two banjo-playing Topsys, a street parade, and two Marks shaking hands. Also included are descriptions of dogs in the show, including "Colos, the largest Siberian Bloodhound in the United States," "Leo and Rose, the Prize Cuban Bloodhounds," and "the great Man-Killer, Major, whose pedigree is well known."

piano wire, scamper down a ladder, and then show up as one of her own mourners. More than one Tom died with only his boots showing from behind a curtain, and then eased himself out of his boots and reappeared as George Shelby, who has arrived to grieve over the deceased Tom. The boot trick also worked for many a Legree, who left only his boots showing and, after a quick costume change, came onstage as Marks, his own executioner! When actors ran thin, or if a performer aged in a role, adults often played Topsy or Eva—it was not unheard of for a man in his mid-thirties to become Eva by donning a dress and a blond wig.

Along with the proliferation of Tom plays came marked variations in quality. Some genuine talent was nurtured by the shows, whose managers, struggling to succeed in the increasingly crowded world of popular diversions, did what they could to find unusually skilled or promising performers. Among the African-Americans featured in the Tom shows, standouts included the famous banjoists Horace Weston and Warren Griffin and the celebrated pianist and orchestra leader Luke Pulley. For white actors the Tom shows proved a seedbed of the American entertainment industry. Mary Pickford, later known as the Woman Who Made Hollywood because of her memorable film roles and her cofounding of United Artists, had played Little Eva in a Tom show as a four-year-old in 1896 and five years later toured Canada as Eva with the large Cummings Company. Other future celebrities who played Eva included Jennie Yeamans, eventually a star of drama and vaudeville, who started playing Eva at six and alternated between that role and Topsy until her late teens; Pearl White, who also made her acting debut at six in a Tom show and went on to become known as the Stunt Queen in action films like *The Perils of Pauline* and *The Exploits of Elaine;* and the Broadway lead Effie Shannon, who never forgot gaping as a child at playbills where she saw herself announced as "Eva, La Petite Shannon." David Belasco, a distinguished actor who also brought naturalism to theater and film as a prolific producer and director, had grown up in Tom plays, having assumed roles as Marks, Legree, Topsy, George Harrris, Sambo, Tom Loker, and finally Uncle Tom. Male roles in Tom plays were also played by Guy Kibbee and Frank McHugh, who would appear in dozens of Warner Brothers films; by the silent-screen superstar Harry Carey; and by the great Spencer Tracy, who had played George Harris in a Grand Rapids, Michigan, production of *Uncle Tom's Cabin*.

Still, the sheer number of Tom companies guaranteed a certain amount of incompetence and self-parodying excess, which gave Tommers a bad name. Cordelia Howard, who had starred as Eva in the 1850s, lamented late in life that the Tom play had lost its "dignity and even grandeur" and it "gradually became so degraded, with its bloodhounds, donkeys, and double casts, that it has become really a burlesque and is the butt of all the critics' ridicule." The endless repetition of the Tom shows laid them open to severe criticism, as when a Lancaster, Pennsylvania, paper reported in 1880 that the tenth *Uncle Tom's Cabin* was coming to town "and no more are wanted." The next year a Detroit paper complained of being "tortured with an invasion of Uncle Toms!!!" An Ohio reviewer who saw an Uncle Tom play wrote in the *Dayton Courier-Press* that the actors deserved to be shot. He called the show "the essence of bumness, the ne plus ultra of rankness, and the acme of rottenness." A Tom company that got stranded in a blizzard got no pity from a Georgia reporter, who wrote, "An 'Uncle Tom's Cabin' show having been snowed in by a Western blizzard ate their donkeys to keep from starving, thus violating the principle which provides for the survival of the fittest."

Because of the number of Tom plays, producers who asked their newly hired actors to rehearse often found their efforts unnecessary, since the Tommers knew the play by heart, including every line uttered by each character. And where lines were forgotten, new ones were easily improvised to fit a scene. Many in the audience knew the lines as well as the actors, since they had seen the play over and over.

In this sense, the Tom plays accelerated the homogenization of culture through mass entertainment that later yielded formulaic movies, radio programs, and TV shows. The plays produced expected emotions among audiences, for whom the joy lay in the very predictability of the response.

The Legree of the evening would feel insulted if he didn't provoke a chorus of hisses. Eva and Tom could be assured that scores of handkerchiefs would flower in the audience as they approached death. Topsy and Marks would be outraged if they didn't hear shouts of laughter. Ads for Tom performances reinforced these standardized responses well into the twentieth century, as seen in the poster for a 1958 re-release of an earlier *Uncle Tom's Cabin* film that invited viewers to "Hate Simon Legree," "Laugh at Topsy," "Pity Uncle Tom," and "Love Little Eva." And for the first time, America witnessed the simultaneous playing of a show in different areas of the nation, since scores of Tom companies were on tour at the same time.

Along with the mass distribution of the Tom plays came a reflection of racial issues in America. Very real racial tensions sometimes lurked even in apparently comic aspects of the play. A prime example is the boxing performances featured in some of the productions between 1893 and 1910. Uncle Tom, between acts or just before dying, would momentarily trade his slave costume for boxing trunks and spar for three rounds with another actor before resuming his tragic role.

In 1893, the black Australian heavyweight champion Peter Jackson, who had moved to America to escape racial discrimination in his native country, took the stage as Uncle Tom in a troupe that toured nationally. Although Jackson played Tom as a frail old man, as was then customary, he brought an air of dignity and strength to the role that made his performance one of the most admired of the time. Even as he followed the story line to death at the hands of Legree, between acts he boxed for three rounds against a white fighter, Joe Choynski, who played George Shelby. But this "scientific" exhibition of boxing—a gentlemanly contest with no winner, since the boxers avoided hurting each other—was very frustrating for Jackson, whose real goal was to have a prizefight against the great white boxer James J. Corbett. Jackson, a hero among African-Americans, soon quit the Tom play to train for the fight with Corbett. But Corbett rejected Jackson's repeated requests for a bout, declaring that he would never fight against a black man. Disillusioned and bitter, Jackson fell out of shape and returned to Australia, where he died prematurely at the age of forty.

In a harsh historical irony, the next professional boxer to assume a major Tom-show role was John L. Sullivan, who played Legree in a well-publicized touring show in 1901–2. Like Corbett, Sullivan was a white supremacist who refused to meet black boxers in the ring. Sullivan appeared to pour racist fury into his enactment of Legree. There had always been a sadistic element in Legree's whipping of Tom, and, especially after the collapse of Reconstruction and the resurgence of institutionalized racism, the whipping scene tapped into the cruelest instincts of white audiences, who could supposedly sympathize with Tom even as they took pleasure in seeing a black man become the victim of the bloody lash—a version of the gloating spectatorship of mobs who regularly gathered to watch blacks being hanged, mutilated, or burned to death in the South during that era of mass lynching. Sullivan won praise for the "realism" of his portrayal of Legree. He whipped so hard and so relentlessly that he actually injured a number of Tom actors, even those who wore inch-thick padding under their shirts. The fact that he wore out many Tom actors made him a sensation. In one widely reported incident, he lashed an actor who writhed in pain, rose to his feet, and fought back, but Sullivan continued to apply the whip until the actor passed out and had to be carried to a nearby hotel to recover.

The racial conflicts that surrounded the Tom-show boxers were also played out in two other late nineteenth-century cultural phenomena related to *Uncle Tom's Cabin*: the World's Fair of 1893 and American literature. The battles over Stowe's novel in both of these major arenas presaged even more momentous conflicts that would come in the twentieth century.

Uncle Tom's Cabin played an important symbolic role in the World's Columbian Exposition held in Chicago in 1893. Many editions and translations of the novel were prominently displayed in a large case in the Women's Building that contained books, letters, and other materials

Uncle Tom at the whipping post, in a Christ-like position
Scene from a stage production of Uncle Tom's Cabin

related to *Uncle Tom's Cabin*. The aged Frederick Douglass emphasized his ongoing solidarity with Stowe by requesting to pose as Uncle Tom during a ceremony when Isabella Beecher Hooker unveiled a gleaming marble bust of the novelist.

Unfortunately, the kind of interracial message Douglass was trying to send was not heeded by the fair's managers, whose main aim was to proclaim the wonders of white civilization. In general, blacks were assigned a distinctly inferior position in the fair. It is telling that the most prominent black person at the fair was former slave Nancy Green, a rotund, genial housekeeper who impersonated Aunt Jemima, the symbol of the new pancake brand promoted at the fair by a firm later absorbed by Quaker Oats. Standing next to a huge flour barrel, Green served pancakes by the thousands to fairgoers, gleefully unaware that the handkerchief-headed character she played was destined to become viewed by many as a degrading mammy stereotype, a holdover from slavery days.

Meanwhile, Africa was very much marginalized at the fair. A tribe of

Frederick Douglass

Dahomey natives was restricted to a place among outer exhibits of so-called exotic cultures. The Africans appeared in their native costumes and habitats, beating drums and performing tribal rituals that the fair managers thought would have curiosity value while showing the "savagery" of Africans in contrast with the marvelously advanced "civilization" shown in the main American and European exhibits. A historian of the fair points out that the exposition grounded the racist views of the era in "ethnological bedrock." The guidebook of the fair said this of the Dahomeyans: "The habits of these people are repulsive; they eat like animals and have all the characteristics of the lowest order of the human family."

African-Americans felt demeaned by the fair managers, and understandably so. Frederick Douglass and Ida B. Wells distributed thousands of copies of a pamphlet that protested against the fair's failure to provide a permanent exhibit representing African-Americans. Blacks were granted just one day, August 25, 1893, on which they could present their achievements. Called Colored People's Day, it raised the hackles of Ida B. Wells and other blacks who dismissed it as an insulting example of tokenism— "Nigger Day," they called it.

Still, Frederick Douglass was ready to make the most of the day, and he appeared onstage prepared to denounce racial prejudice and promote African-American culture, which he associated with *Uncle Tom's Cabin*, spirituals, and the Beecher family. Accompanying him on the podium that day were Harriet's half-sister Isabella Beecher Hooker and the nieces of their brother James Beecher, who had led a black regiment during the Civil War. (The eighty-two-year-old Stowe, now frail and ailing, could not attend.) Douglass gave a militant speech calling for equal rights and stressing how blacks had been maltreated since the end of Reconstruction.

Then the ceremony was turned over to the skilled black composer and musician Will Marion Cook and a group of jubilee singers. Before a racially mixed crowd of 2,500, they performed part of a new opera Cook had composed based on *Uncle Tom's Cabin*—a testament to the interracial solidarity the novel symbolized for Cook, who could easily have drawn solely from the rich African-American musical heritage for his piece. His integrationist message was reinforced by the fact that the jubilee group also sang spirituals, the music Stowe and others associated with authentic African-American expression. Douglass saw Cook's Uncle Tom opera and the spirituals as the best way "to have represented at the fair some exhibition of the progress made by his race in music," as he had explained to President Benjamin Harrison prior to the fair.

The respect African-Americans expressed at the Columbian Exposition for Stowe and *Uncle Tom's Cabin* was echoed after her death in 1896. One black newspaper announced: "In the passing of Harriet Beecher Stowe, the Negro race loses one of its greatest benefactors. . . . 'Uncle Tom's Cabin' is the greatest production in American literature." She received equally fervent plaudits from an array of black organizations and leaders, including the John Brown League, Booker T. Washington, and

W. E. B. Du Bois. For James Weldon Johnson, a black journalist, lawyer, and educator whose 1912 novel *The Autobiography of an Ex-Colored Man* remained an underground classic until it was rediscovered during the Harlem Renaissance, *Uncle Tom's Cabin* had been a profoundly liberating work of his childhood. Stowe's novel, he wrote, "opened my eyes to who and what I was and what my country considered me; in fact, it gave me my being." In particular, it helped him speak candidly with his mother about racial questions about which she had been previously silent. This revelation of the African-American past was, he said, "one of the greatest benefits I derived from reading the book."

Two major novels by black writers, Frances Ellen Watkins Harper's *Iola Leroy* (1892) and Charles Chesnutt's *The Marrow of Tradition* (1898), show how Stowe's influence yielded fiction that made a powerful case for social equality. Both novels feature light-skinned mulatto protagonists who represent the ability of African-Americans to succeed in mainstream society. Harper was so stirred by *Uncle Tom's Cabin* that she wrote a poem, "Eliza Harris," that highlighted the maternal instincts and courage of Stowe's mulatta heroine—a portrait of the shared humanity that fed into Harper's devotion to what she called a "community of interests" by which blacks and whites, women and men should share equal rights. She promoted this view in her speech "Woman's Political Future" at the World's Fair in May 1893 and in her fictional portrait of Iola Leroy, a proud black woman capable of practical work as a nurse, accountant, and teacher, and who is an outspoken intellectual as well. Written in a bleak period for race relations, *Iola Leroy* struck a hopeful note, revealing the potential of blacks to advance through perseverance and intelligence while maintaining their dignity.

Chesnutt's *The Marrow of Tradition* also fosters hope, but its affirmations are tempered by a shattering recognition of the discriminatory forces that governed race relations in the late nineteenth century. Chesnutt builds his novel around the Wilmington, North Carolina, race riot of 1898, when a mob of whites went on a rampage that resulted in the murder of numerous blacks. Though fictionalized, Chesnutt's novel is so carefully textured to accord with actual people and events that it bears the obvious impress of literary realism, a movement that had held sway in America since the late 1860s and that was strongly influenced by *Uncle Tom's Cabin*.

In an 1868 article for *The Nation,* the novelist John W. De Forest, regarded as a pioneer of American literary realism, had coined the term "the Great American novel" to describe *Uncle Tom's Cabin.* Surveying all previous novelists, including Hawthorne, De Forest singled out Stowe for praise. He recognized flaws in her novel but insisted that no other work came close to its full-scale embrace of the details of American social reality. His praise was later echoed by the leader of the realist movement, William Dean Howells, who called *Uncle Tom's Cabin* "a very great novel," "a work of art" that "move[d] the whole world more than any other book has moved it." We've seen that Henry James admired the emotional force of Stowe's novel and claimed to have learned much about dramatic representation by attending Tom plays in his youth. It's not surprising, given such positive responses to Stowe, that a birthday party that had been held in her honor in 1882 was a literary lovefest in which many of the era's leading authors—Mark Twain, Oliver Wendell Holmes, Longfellow, Helen Hunt Jackson, and others—contributed glowing accolades to Stowe, both in person and by mail. (Helen Hunt Jackson was then writing her landmark novel of Indian reform, *Ramona* [1884], about which she said, "If I could write a story that would do for the Indian a thousandth part what *Uncle Tom's Cabin* did for the negro . . ." but "I do not dare to think I have written a second *Uncle Tom's Cabin.*")

Charles Chesnutt's tribute to Stowe was his marvelous, realistic novel that he acknowledged was inspired by *Uncle Tom's Cabin.* He said that he hoped *The Marrow of Tradition* would "become lodged in the popular mind as the legitimate successor to *Uncle Tom's Cabin.*" He added, "If I could write a book that would stir the waters in any appreciable degree like that famous book, I would feel that I had vindicated my right to live and the right of the whole race." Reviewers of Chesnutt's novel connected it immediately to Stowe's. "A New Uncle Tom's Cabin" was the title of an article that declared, "'The Marrow of Tradition' is to the Negro problem of today what 'Uncle Tom's Cabin' was to the Negro problem of antebellum days." Other reviews made the same point.

The Marrow of Tradition has few characters in common with Stowe's novel, yet one can see why the comparisons were made, since Chesnutt was responding as passionately to post-Reconstruction America as Stowe had to the horrors of slavery. Where the white scoundrel of *Uncle Tom's Cabin* was the whip-wielding Simon Legree, who exercises cruel power over the disobedient slave, the villain of *The Marrow of Tradition* is George McBane, the leader of a white supremacist group who uses persuasion and force to overturn a black-dominated government in a North Carolina town. Where Stowe's Uncle Tom is whipped to death for being disobedient, Chesnutt's black victim, Sandy Campbell, is framed for a murder committed by a white man. Where Stowe counts among her heroes two intelligent mulattoes, the Harrises, Chesnutt does so in his remarkable portrayal of the shrewd Dr. William Miller and his wife Janet. The difference is that Chesnutt gives us no Topsy to laugh at, no Tom or Eva to pity, nor an Ophelia, Marks, or St. Clare.

The stakes are just as high for Chesnutt's black characters as for Stowe's, since they have freedom and political power that the white characters grab from them by force. Based on the only coup d'état in American history, *The Marrow of Tradition* shows a group of unabashed racists taking over a black-dominated government and press in their city.

Even as late nineteenth-century black authors were bringing Stowe's reformist zeal to protest again the white-controlled South, other fiction writers of the period were nostalgically recalling the days when white control was assumed and blacks seemed to accept their inferior position without question.

Sometimes pro-Southern novelists of the 1880s and 1890s alluded to Stowe directly. For instance, Annie Jefferson Holland in her novel *The Refugees: A Sequel to "Uncle Tom's Cabin"* (1892) castigated the destructiveness of the Northern troops who, in her words, "had imbibed from Mrs. Stowe, from 'Uncle Tom's Cabin,' the idea we [Southerners] were all human monsters, and fire and brimstone our just portion." Holland had a character exclaim, "Harriet Beecher Stowe had as well lighted the torch and stuck it to our homes as to have flooded the country with such inflammatory literature as 'Uncle Tom's Cabin.' " And by helping to free American blacks, Holland continued, Stowe generated a spurious sense of equality between the races. An unblinking white supremacist, Holland writes that during the horrible Reconstruction period, "Caucasian blood, labeled pure and superior by the Creator, was to be forced in political equality with a coarse African race, incapable of self-government!"

More commonly, however, the new Southern authors appropriated Stowe instead of fighting her directly in order to appeal to Northerners. After all, since the Civil War Stowe had become a widely beloved figure. A number of the Tom theater posters showed Stowe's face alongside Lincoln's. An 1879 edition of Stowe's novel, with a preface (anonymously written by Stowe) presenting it as a literary classic on emancipation, sold well, as did several Houghton, Mifflin editions that appeared in the early 1890s, soon followed by popular mass-market versions issued by over a score of publishers.

Joel Chandler Harris, the writer of the popular Uncle Remus stories, maintained that Stowe had, ironically enough, written "a defense of the system that she intended to attack," explaining that "all the worthy and beautiful characters in her book—Uncle Tom, Little Eva, and the beloved Master—are the product of the system . . . the book is all this time condemning." He presented Uncle Remus's folksy fables about Bre'er Rabbit, Bre'er Fox, and other animals as a "sympathetic supplement to Mrs. Stowe's wonderful defense of slavery as it existed in the South."

Another Southerner who praised Stowe in order to conquer her was the Virginia author and statesman Thomas Nelson Page. Writing that "Mrs. Stowe did more to free the slave than all the politicians," and *Uncle Tom's Cabin* "contributed more than any other one thing to abolition,"

Broadside for a Tom play featuring pictures of
Stowe (upper left) and Lincoln

Page conceded that slavery had drawbacks but insisted that it was preferable to Reconstruction, which had given blacks a false and unnatural
preeminence. "As an argument against the evils inherent in slavery," he
wrote, Stowe's novel was "unanswerable." Nonetheless, freeing the slaves
had caused a chaotic race reversal and destroyed the glories of the Old
South. "Negroes," he wrote, "are inferior to other races. . . . Negroes fur-
nish the great body of rapists," and most "are ignorant and lack the first
element of morality." In his own fiction, such as *In Ole Virginia* (1887),
The Burial of the Guns (1894), and *Red Rock* (1898), Page conjured up an
edenic antebellum South in which intelligent, kindly whites care for and

protect inferior slaves, who remain loyal to their masters out of fidelity and love.

This nostalgia for plantation life suffuses *Lyddy: A Tale of New Orleans* (1898), by Eugenia J. Bacon, an Atlanta resident who had been raised in a palatial Southern home and tried to re-create its supposedly mild pleasures. Bacon reminds readers they must realize that "in face of the cruelties depicted in 'Uncle Tom's Cabin,' there were, on the other hand, many such characters as Lydia, with black skins but pure souls." Lyddy, Bacon tells us, is a slightly fictionalized portrait of the beloved Mammy figure of her childhood, who had lavished unfailing devotion on her "w'ite chilluns." Southern reviewers saw Bacon as an antidote to Stowe. A Delaware journalist wrote that *Lyddy* "is the antithesis of 'Uncle Tom's Cabin,' and shows how the black human chattels were not always treated like beasts, but led the lives of pleasure and healthful occupation." Similarly, Joel Chandler Harris in his review of the novel said, "In distinct contrast to 'Uncle Tom's Cabin' . . . 'Lyddy' faithfully mirrors the picture of contentment and happiness presented on most of the southern plantations before the war."

Bacon's novel was written in direct response to the popular Tom plays of the period. Although Stowe's novel continued to enjoy strong sales, the plays had replaced the novel as the touchstone of Stowe's popularity, since they reached so many people. As Bacon says in her preface to *Lyddy*, she attempted to depict the "faithfulness and devotion" of slaves because "the harrowing scenes depicted by Mrs. Harriet Beecher Stowe continue to attract throngs of men, women, and children to theatres and halls."

One would have thought that the Tom plays—with their bloatedness, blunders, animals, and clunky machinery—would have descended into self-parody by the turn of the century, or that since a portion of the plays featured "happy darkies" picking cotton and singing coon songs, while reducing Tom to a harmless old fogey, they would have fit comfortably into the plantation fable woven into the fiction idealizing the Old South. But they escaped this fate.

True, the Tom plays got increasingly snide reviews, and the endlessly repeated scenes and characters began to grow stale for audiences now diverted by professional circuses, Broadway shows, vaudeville, and the rising musical genres of ragtime and jazz. As for the pro-plantation theme in some of the plays, that appealed to the same impulse toward national reconciliation among white Americans which, as historian David Blight shows, also yielded many Blue-Gray reunions in which veterans and others convened to bury the Civil War hatchet in the closing decades of the century.

Still, *Uncle Tom's Cabin* was, after all, a story that focused squarely on race relations, which were ever worsening in the aftermath of *Plessy v. Ferguson*, the 1896 Supreme Court ruling that gave federal sanction to segregation. In the South, many blacks were disenfranchised and economically marginalized. Lynching was dramatically on the rise. For whites who looked back longingly to the pre–Civil War days of supposed stability and racial harmony, *Uncle Tom's Cabin* remained a highly threatening tale—so much so that in the early twentieth century some Southern states banned performances of the Tom plays.

Even before the legal crackdown, Southern protests against the play were common, as when bills about an Uncle Tom play were distributed in Athens, Georgia, saying, "The vile slander on the manhood and honor of our fathers will show to-night. Let all true Southerners stay away." A newspaper warned a Tom troupe headed for Atlanta: "Instead of carrying its own bloodhounds, two Topsys, two Uncle Toms, and a large assortment of Lawyer Marks, the Uncle Tom's Cabin Company that has ventured into Georgia had better invest its surplus cash in armor plate."

Kentucky in 1906 passed a bill, known as the Uncle Tom's Cabin Law, that banned performances of the Tom plays, which were said to promote disharmony between the races. The Daughters of the Confederacy, who originated the bill, had issued a declaration saying that "the incidents of 'Uncle Tom's Cabin' are not typical of slave life in the South" and that the Tom shows presented "a false idea of the history" and were "disrespectful to Southerners and their families." Similar bans were passed in Arkansas and Georgia, while high fees were charged for putting on Tom shows in parts of Texas, Florida, and Mississippi. The Tom plays were a cultural time bomb ready to explode.

When a rabidly racist Virginia author saw one of the plays and wrote an anti-Tom novel that inspired a Hollywood genius to produce an extraordinary, hateful film, an explosion did go off, and it shook the nation and changed the course of history.

⊶ 6 ⊷

TOM IN MODERN TIMES

IN 1901, THIRTY-SEVEN-YEAR-OLD Thomas Dixon Jr., a peripatetic Southern author, preacher, and reformer, attended a performance of an *Uncle Tom's Cabin* play while he was on a lecture tour in the Midwest. Like others in the audience, he wept. But his tears were not signs of sympathy for Stowe's characters. They were tears of outrage over what he saw as Stowe's gross misrepresentation of Southern life.

Born in King's Mountain, North Carolina, in 1864, Dixon was a dyed-in-the-wool Southern conservative. His grandfather on his mother's side had owned slaves, and his uncle, who had fought for the Confederacy, was active in the Ku Klux Klan after the Civil War. During Reconstruction, Dixon witnessed with revulsion scalawags (Southerners who supported the North's policies) and carpetbaggers (Northerners who went south to enforce these policies or make money). After graduating from Wake Forest in 1883, Dixon attended Johns Hopkins, where he befriended Woodrow Wilson, before going to New York to try his hand at acting. Soon he was back in North Carolina. He became, successively, a state politician, a lawyer, and a Baptist minister. He took his ministry to Boston and then New York, all the while publishing religious nonfiction. He was so successful as a preacher that in the late 1890s he was able to move to a large farm by the Chesapeake Bay in the Old Tidewater region of Virginia, where he lived in a colonial mansion with thirty-six rooms. He left the ministry in 1899 and toured the nation as an orator, addressing over five million people in four years. A tall, lanky man with dark hair and luminous eyes, he gave rousing lectures on social corruption, the evils of drinking, and the "infidelity" of the famous agnostic Robert Ingersoll.

He attended the Tom play at a time when Stowe's work was under savage attack. Earlier in 1901, another prominent Southerner, F. Hopkinson Smith, had launched a well-publicized crusade against *Uncle Tom's Cabin*. A sixty-two-year-old Virginian whose gray hair and long handlebar mustache gave him a dignified look, Smith was the grandson of a signer of the Declaration of Independence and the scion of slaveholders. After the Civil War, he became an artist, engineer, best-selling novelist, and popular lecturer. His watercolors earned him recognition as one of America's finest painters. He was especially well known as the designer of lighthouses along America's Eastern Seaboard. Among his major projects was his design for the foundation of the Statue of Liberty. A Boston journalist noted, "Today he occupies a unique place in the world of art and letters."

When Smith spoke, people listened. In a speech he gave in Newton, Massachusetts, on January 9 of that same year, he branded *Uncle Tom's Cabin* as "the most vicious book that ever appeared." He called it "an appalling, awful, and criminal mistake." He increased his invective against the novel over the next twelve years. He stated directly, "The book precipitated the [Civil] war and made the North believe nothing but the worst about the South. . . . It was an outrage to raise the North against the South." And the war, he continued, far from improving the condition of blacks, had greatly worsened it. To support his belief that Stowe's book had "done more harm to the world than any other book ever written," Smith claimed that it "was, in a measure, responsible for the insatiable brutality of the Reconstruction period," which was a "monstrous disgrace" because it reversed the power of the races.

Smith's attacks on Stowe were reprinted in newspapers nationwide, provoking many responses, pro and con. Smith later expanded his charge,

Francis Hopkinson Smith

saying that *Uncle Tom's Cabin* (along with John Brown's raid) continued to divide the nation right up to modern times. And he considered the Tom plays to be as loathsome as Stowe's novel. Smith's supporters agreed. The arch-segregationist John Temple Graves, editor of the *Atlanta Journal*, who believed that blacks should be removed from the South, announced, "Hopkinson Smith is exactly right." Graves singled out the plays for special criticism: "I think that the evil influence of the book itself is subordinate to the wholesale prejudice disseminated by the dozen or more companies presenting the dramatized version, which is the infernal instrument of sectional bitterness." He denounced this "malific [*sic*] drama which sprinkles sectional bitterness like a pestilence"—an attitude similar to the one that led to crackdowns on the play in Kentucky, with its 1906 Uncle Tom's Cabin Law (permitting the censorship of racially inflammatory entertainment), and in other states throughout the South where such heavy fees were imposed on Tom-show producers that the touring companies dwindled in the early decades of the century.

Thomas Dixon, equally disgusted by Stowe, decided to provide a historical sequel to Stowe's narrative from a Southern perspective. Putting a new spin on the genre of anti-Tom novels, he revised her characters and projected them into the post–Civil War period. After his painful experience of watching the Tom play, he vowed to tell "the true story" of what happened to the South over time as a result of Stowe's influence. He was determined to show the world how nightmarish America had become as a result of the racial reversal she had caused and how dire the future of America would be if the ascendancy of blacks continued.

Dixon's disdain for blacks reflected the ethnological pseudoscience of the day. Endorsed by books like Daniel G. Brinton's *Races and People: Lectures on the Science of Ethnography* (1890) as well as the exhibits of the 1893 World's Fair, ethnology reached apocalyptic expression in James Carroll's 1900 book *The Negro a Beast*. Carroll argued that blacks were animals with uncontrollable passions and little intellect. They posed a special threat to white women, as the book's illustration of a woman assaulted by a black vagrant showed. It was captioned "Natural Results: The screams of the ravished daughters of the 'Sunny South' have placed the Negro in the lowest rank of the Beast Kingdom."

Dixon incorporated such virulent racism into his novel *The Leopard's Spots* (1902), which became a best-seller and was followed by two others that spread the pro-Southern gospel, *The Clansman* (1903) and *The Traitor* (1909). Dixon's fiction, in turn, inspired D. W. Griffith's landmark film *The Birth of a Nation*.

In *The Leopard's Spots,* Dixon states unambiguously his belief that *Uncle Tom's Cabin* had brought on the Civil War. Of Stowe's portrait of Simon Legree, Dixon writes, "The picture of that brute with a whip in his hand beating a Negro caused the most terrible war in the history of the world. Three millions of men flew at each other's throats and for four years fought like demons. A million men and six billions of dollars' worth of property were destroyed."

Dixon was so obsessed with Legree that he made him the main villain of *The Leopard's Spots,* whose working title was *The Rise of Simon Legree.* In the novel, Legree—in an extreme reversal—having spent the war in the Upper South disguised as a female maid so he wouldn't have to fight, returns after the war to North Carolina, where he uses venal tactics and arm-twisting to push the Northern agenda of Reconstruction. He helps freedmen like Tim Shelby (another name borrowed from Stowe), an ex-slave who leads a takeover of state politics by blacks and their white Republican cohorts, who not only mismanage government but also pass terrifying bills like one encouraging interracial marriage.

Besides retooling Stowe's Legree and Shelby, Dixon presented Eliza Harris's son—called Harry in Stowe's novel, here renamed George—as an intelligent, light-skinned mulatto who graduated from Harvard and is now a welcome visitor to the home of the liberal Boston congressman Everett Lowell. Stowe's main character, Tom, is revised significantly in Dixon's portrait of Tom Camp, an aging white Southerner who was wounded while fighting for the Confederacy.

Dixon scattered these and other Stowe-based names (including St. Clare and Haley) through a novel that reversed Stowe's message about race relations in America. Stowe had portrayed the mulatto characters George and Eliza Harris sympathetically to expose the ironic fact that many of those held in slavery were the children of slaveowners and had much Caucasian blood in their veins. This image of the tragic mulatto, as noted before, had informed Frances Harper's *Iola Leroy* and Charles Chesnutt's *The Marrow of Tradition* and been used to extend sympathy for characters caught between the worlds of the two races. Dixon shows no such regard for the mulatto. In his view, a small amount of African blood taints a person irreparably—hence his novel's title, meant to show that blackness in a person is as ineradicable as spots on a leopard. When Harris falls in love with Everett Lowell's daughter and asks for her hand in marriage, Lowell, despite his alleged sympathy for blacks, explodes with rage. The idea of "a mixture of Negro blood in my family," he declares, is "nauseating" and "repulsive beyond the power of words to express it," insisting that such a marriage would put his family back by three thousand years. George Harris descends to gambling and crime, and then drifts about the nation depositing flowers on the ashes of black people who have been burned to death by whites—grisly remnants of the widespread lynching Dixon sees as white supremacists' stern but necessary policing of a nation threatened by the rising power of blacks.

Dixon's twin fears of political equality and interracial intimacy reaches a culmination in his portrait of the severe punishment of two African-Americans suspected of being sexual predators. When the black politician Tim Shelby makes a pass at the daughter of the ex-Confederate Tom Camp, Tom takes revenge by leading a Ku Klux Klan attack in which the white-hooded vigilantes seize Shelby and hang him from the balcony of a courthouse, where he is found the next morning bearing a grim message. As Dixon writes, "His thick lips had been split with a sharp knife, and from his teeth hung this placard: '*The answer of the Anglo-Saxon race to Negro lips that dare pollute with words the womanhood of the South. K. K. K.*' " Dixon expects us to recognize the justice of the Klan's deed. Later in the novel, a white mob takes vindictive action when Tom Camp's other daughter, the blue-eyed, blond Flora—modeled, as critic Sandra Gunning notes, on Stowe's Eva—is raped and murdered. The mob captures the main suspect in the case, a black man named Dick, and burns him alive.

For Dixon, such retaliatory violence by whites is understandable and justifiable in light of the terrible danger for American democracy he thought was posed by the ascendancy of African-Americans in the wake of the Civil War. The threat of miscegenation was terrible to Dixon. *Any* mixture of African with Caucasian blood was ruinous. As he writes, "One drop of Negro blood makes a Negro. It kinks the hair, flattens the nose, thickens the lip, puts out the light of intellect, and lights the fires of brutal passions." What Dixon especially feared was that America would eventually become a mulatto nation through intermarriage. In his words, "The beginning of Negro equality as a vital fact is the beginning of the end of this nation's life. There is enough Negro blood here to make mulatto the whole Republic."

"At last has appeared the 'Uncle Tom's Cabin' of the South!" announced one enthusiastic reviewer of *The Leopard's Spots*. An Atlanta journalist agreed, adding that Dixon's characters were in fact more true to life than Stowe's. That was tragically the case in many parts of the nation, especially the South, during the closing decades of the nineteenth century and continuing well into the twentieth century, when racially motivated lynchings were common and segregation was federally sanctioned.

The Leopard's Spots became a huge best-seller, as did Dixon's next novel, *The Clansman*, which also features a public lynching, this time involving a black man who, after he rapes a young girl in the presence of her mother, is captured by the Klan and burned alive. The girl is so humiliated by being violated by a black man that she leaps off a cliff hand in hand with her equally distraught mother. *The Clansman* describes the typical black person as "half child, half animal, the sport of impulse, whim, and conceit . . . a being who, left to his will, roams at night and sleeps in the day, whose speech knows no word of love, whose passions, once aroused, are as the fury of the tiger." Dixon maintains that race reversal has created nauseous smells—"perspiring African odour," "onion-laden breath," "the reek of vile cigars and stale whiskey, mingled with the odour of perspiring negroes"—that have "become the symbol of American Democracy." *The Clansman* was turned into a popular play and was followed by another best-selling novel, *The Traitor*, in which Dixon lamented the collapse of the KKK in the early 1870s as a result of federal prosecution under the congressional Force Acts.

As famous as he was in his own time, Dixon might have fallen into the historical dustbin if his novels had not attracted the interest of director D. W. Griffith.

Born and raised in Kentucky, David Wark Griffith inherited typically Southern racial attitudes from his father, Jacob, who earned his nickname

Roaring Jake as a colonel in the Confederate Army. Jacob died when David was seven, leaving the family struggling to stay above the poverty level. Griffith developed an interest in acting and toured with traveling troupes before taking on roles in silent films. Soon he found his true calling as a filmmaker. He directed many films for the Biograph Company before forming his own studio with fellow director Harry E. Aitken and screenwriter Frank E. Woods. Woods had previously written a screenplay based on Dixon's *The Clansman,* which went into production with the Kinemacolor studio, but that firm folded before the project was done. D. W. Griffith was acquainted with Thomas Dixon, having once played the lead role in the latter's play *The One Woman.* Thrilled at the prospect of making a film of *The Clansman,* Griffith met with Dixon, who at first demanded a then-astounding $25,000 for screen rights but, after much haggling, settled for $2,000 up front plus 25 percent of the eventual gross profits of Griffith's movie—a deal that turned out spectacularly for Dixon because of the film's huge earnings. The movie was originally called *The Clansman,* but that title was changed, at Dixon's suggestion, to the more epic and benign *The Birth of a Nation.* Dixon participated actively in the film, contributing his services as a consultant, writer, and producer. Griffith, drawing from all three of Dixon's Reconstruction novels—and reaching back to the pre–Civil War period and the war years as well—greatly expanded Dixon's historical scope and delivered the novelist's anti-Stowe message to millions of moviegoers. In doing so, he indelibly shaped America's vision of its past.

Not only did *The Birth of a Nation* (1915) establish D. W. Griffith as a film innovator, but it coincided with, and helped promote, the so-called Dunning school of American historiography. This group of historians, which formed around the Columbia professors William Archibald Dunning and John W. Burgess, interpreted Reconstruction as a tragic time when Northerners and opportunists created havoc in the South, largely by encouraging newly emancipated blacks to assume political power. The Dunning historians believed that black men, awarded a social position they did not deserve, proved to be incompetent leaders and, worse, a constant threat to white women because of their uncontrollable lust. Dunning wrote of "the hideous crime against white womanhood which now assumed new meaning in the annals of outrage." Or, as the historian Claude G. Bowers put it, "Rape is the foul daughter of Reconstruction."

The Birth of a Nation brought this view of history alive by integrating the story of the black sexual predator into a full-scale imagining of the Civil War era. Griffith determinedly used Stowe-like devices to humanize and personalize the Dixon-Dunning message.

The film focuses on two families: the slaveowning Camerons of Piedmont, South Carolina, and a Pennsylvania family headed by Austin Stoneman, the film's name for the antislavery Republican leader Thaddeus Stevens. Before the war, the Camerons are at peace in their Southern home, with slaves happily picking cotton or serving the family as domestics. Meanwhile, up north, abolitionists like Stoneman are agitating against slavery. This geographical contrast followed the plotlines that had been established in the anti-Tom novels of Stowe's time.

In the film, the Civil War proves ruinous to both the North and the South. Griffith titles a battlefield scene "The war claims its *bitter, useless sacrifice.*" Two Stoneman boys and one Cameron son die in battle. Sherman's march to the sea is portrayed as a chaotic overrun of the South by pillaging Union troops.

After peace is declared, President Lincoln is determined to treat the South with clemency, but he is strongly opposed by Austin Stoneman and his fellow Radical Republicans, who argue that the Southern states should be treated as conquered provinces. Lincoln firmly objects to the plan, announcing, "I shall deal with them as though they had never been away." But then comes the fateful evening of April 14, 1865, when Lincoln is assassinated in Ford's Theatre. Griffith re-creates the scene in detail, and then indicates the South's reverence for Lincoln by flashing the words "Our best friend is gone. What is to become of us now?" In the original version of the film, masses of black people are shown going aboard ships heading for Africa, a scene—titled "Lincoln's solution," in reference to the president's earlier colonization scheme—that Griffith cut, along with some other controversial scenes, as a sop to the NAACP and other black groups that launched angry protests during early showings of the movie.

But since colonization did not occur, Griffith indicates, blacks and their traitorous white cohorts caused mayhem in the South during Reconstruction. Blacks are shown taking over the state legislature in Columbia, South Carolina, where they create chaos: drinking whiskey, eating chicken, and leering at white women sitting in the balcony, while forcing through dangerous laws like one endorsing miscegenation.

African-Americans cause tragedy in the once-happy Cameron family. A brutish black man, Gus, chases the young Flora Cameron, known as Little Sister, who leaps from a cliff to avoid being raped by a black man. Flora's father, Ben Cameron, leads a Ku Klux Klan group that chases down Gus, kills him, and deposits his body at the door of Silas Lynch, a mulatto politician who, in keeping with the black man's impulse of unbridled lust, has made a pass at the daughter of Austin Stoneman. Later, the women and the older men in the Cameron family become trapped inside a small cabin that is under attack by savage blacks. As the blacks burst through the door and windows of the cabin, the Cameron men hold guns to the heads of the women on the then-accepted principle that for a white woman death is preferable to being raped by a black man. But the imperiled whites are spared their grim fate when Ben Cameron and his fellow clansmen, in their hoods and robes, gallop to the rescue on white horses, dispersing the black mob and later restoring political and social order by keeping black people away from polling booths.

Griffith creates the most powerful anti-Tom work in history by appropriating several of Stowe's images and reversing them, as Dixon did in his books. As in Stowe, home is the haven of bliss and innocence, but here it is threatened by the liberation of blacks, not by their enslavement. Chastity remains a primary virtue, but in Griffith it is the purity of white women that is under assault by black men, not that of black women by white slaveowners. Stowe's Little Eva, who dies so that blacks can be freed, is answered by Griffith's Little Sister, who dies so that they can be lynched or returned to virtual slavery through terror and disenfranchise-

The Birth of a Nation *(1915)—Ku Klux Klan lynch mob seizes Gus*

ment. Stowe begins her work with a cabin that houses a happy black family cruelly ripped asunder by the white institution of slavery; Griffith's work reaches a climax in which a distressed white family in a cabin faces great peril at the hands of black fiends who are defeated by white saviors. Both Griffith and Stowe alternate between resonant domestic scenes and sensational, adventurous ones. Stowe has her dramatic ice-crossing, rocky-pass shoot-out, and slave-whipping; Griffith his violent Civil War battles, the blacks' attack on the cabin, and, above all, the KKK's furious ride to the rescue. Griffith even borrows Stowe's main religious device—a vision of the spiritual world—in the film's remarkable closing image of the appearance of Jesus Christ, intended to bestow a divine blessing on the white characters' defense of racial purity and national harmony through the violent suppression of blacks—the exact opposite of the divine visions in Stowe's novel, which announce the possibility of interracial respect and affection.

The Birth of a Nation was now squared off against *Uncle Tom's Cabin* in a titanic struggle over versions of the American past. The reactionary (or, in David Blight's term, white supremacist) view, dramatized by Griffith's film—a visual representation of Dixon's fiction, buttressed by the Dunning historians and later popularized by Margaret Mitchell's *Gone with the Wind*—saw the Civil War as an exercise in futility, spurred by vicious abolitionists like Stowe and John Brown, who had allegedly disrupted the stable, idyllic society of the Old South. After the war, according to this outlook, Radical Republicans of the North had committed the darkest crime in American history by awarding political and social rights to blacks. What resulted was pandemonium. Inferior and bestial by nature, blacks ushered in corruption, political incompetency, and brutality. Only the forceful restoration of white supremacy would bring national reconciliation and a semblance of order to the South.

In contrast, from the progressive, pro-Stowe, emancipationist vantage point, carried forward by reform-minded blacks such as those in the NAACP, slaveholders were history's true villains. As Stowe had pointed out, there had been kindly masters and moments of joy for slaves, but slavery involved so much cruelty and sexual exploitation that any mitigating elements could be quickly destroyed by white men's savagery or lust, as evidenced by the sad histories of Tom, Cassy, Prue, and other enslaved blacks. From this perspective, the Civil War was a necessary and majestic war of liberation.

Both the reactionaries and the progressives highlighted Lincoln—a beloved national hero—to burnish their own argument. The Southern apologists reclaimed Lincoln, pointing to his charitable attitude toward the South and especially his notion, which he publicly advocated during his first term in office, that blacks should be deported to Liberia, Central America, or elsewhere because they couldn't live equally with whites in America. From the emancipationist perspective, however, Lincoln was especially worthy of veneration because he was the one president who had stood up strongly against slavery and led what became a war for the liberation of enslaved blacks.

The Birth of a Nation established itself immediately as a strong contender in the mammoth contest over versions of American history. Not only did it make the white supremacist point more powerfully than any other work of the era, but it changed movies through its techniques, including its masterly use of camera angle, perspective, lighting, and narrative development. Griffith "achieved what no other known man has ever achieved," rhapsodized James Agee, who compared watching his work to "being witness to the beginning of melody, or the first conscious use of the lever or the wheel"—an opinion echoed by the film historian David Cook, who called Griffith's achievement "unprecedented in the history of Western art, much less Western film" (although he added that Griffith was "a muddleheaded racial bigot").

The film won over the public. It became one of the highest-grossing movies of the silent era, earning more than $10 million in its first year and $50 million by 1949. President Woodrow Wilson, who had been Thomas Dixon's college chum and shared his racial views, saw the film in a private viewing at the White House and is said to have remarked, "It is like writing history with lightning. And my only regret is that it is all so terribly true."

For many who were unaware of academic historians like Dunning, the film drove home their view of Reconstruction as a tragic era when blacks threatened to usurp whites in America. As historian and biographer David Levering Lewis notes, the film "was uniquely responsible for encoding the white South's view of Reconstruction on the DNA of several generations of Americans." *The Birth of a Nation* helped galvanize the resurgence of the Ku Klux Klan, which by the 1920s was a nationwide organization that terrorized blacks, Jews, and others. The Dixon/Griffith view of history was consolidated in Don Carlos Seitz's *The Dreadful Decade* (1926), Claude G. Bowers' best-seller *The Tragic Era* (1929), George Fort Milton's *The Age of Hate* (1930), E. Merton Coulter's *The South During Reconstruction* (1947), and other books that for a time were standard classroom texts. In 1979, the distinguished African-American historian John Hope Franklin wrote that *The Birth of a Nation* "remains the single most important source of the current attitude toward Reconstruction." Franklin, expanding on anti-Dunning works like Du Bois's *Black Reconstruction* and Gunnar Myrdal's *An American Dilemma,* exposed the utter falsity of most of the film's historical claims, as have several subsequent historians.

If, as Franklin pointed out, Griffith's *The Birth of a Nation* was actually "pure Dixon, all Dixon!" we should add that *Uncle Tom's Cabin* had motivated Dixon to write his anti-Stowe novels, which in turn yielded Griffith's film.

But Dixon and Griffith were not the only forces in the chain reaction caused by *Uncle Tom's Cabin* in the twentieth century. An opposing force was a marked upsurge of action on behalf of equal rights for African-Americans. As had been true with fragmented antislavery groups before the Civil War, many African-Americans of varying opinions agreed upon their respect for Harriet Beecher Stowe. In 1882, Frederick Douglass had declared, "To no one person had it been given to move so many minds and hearts in behalf of the lately enslaved as Mrs. Stowe. Hers was the word of the hour, and it was given with skill, force, and effect." Nearly two decades later, the black poet Paul Laurence Dunbar chimed in with a poetic paean that contained the lines: "Prophet and priestess! At one stroke she gave / A race to freedom, and herself to fame." For Charles Chesnutt, *Uncle Tom's Cabin* was "the wonderful book" that "set the world on fire over the wrongs of the slave." Booker T. Washington credited Stowe with opening the way to the emancipation of blacks.

African-Americans' enthusiasm for Stowe fused with a fierce reaction against Dixon to help nurture two leading black organizations: the Niagara Movement, formed in 1905, and its successor, the NAACP, created four years later. Two African-American promoters of the movements, the Southern preacher-novelist Sutton E. Griggs and the Atlanta University professor W. E. B. Du Bois, both believed that blacks must take action in order to restore Stowe's emancipatory message and challenge Dixon's segregationist one. Griggs wrote that *Uncle Tom's Cabin* had "lifted a despised and helpless race into living sympathy with the white race," whereas Dixon's influence threatened "to cut these chords [*sic*] of sympathy and re-establish the old order of repulsion, based on the primitive feeling of race hatred." In answer to white supremacists, Griggs penned five powerful pro-black novels. One of them, *The Hindered Hand* (1905), included vehement attacks on Dixon as well as an appalling lynching scene in which a black husband and wife are, for no reason, tied to separate trees by a white mob and slowly mutilated for three hours—their fingers chopped off, their breasts sliced open, and flesh ripped from their bodies—before they are burned alive.

W. E. B. Du Bois, like Griggs, combined a deep respect for Stowe with alarm over the growing intensity of white supremacist sentiment. Of Stowe, Du Bois wrote, "Thus to a frail overburdened Yankee woman with a steadfast moral purpose we Americans, black and white, owe gratitude for the freedom and union that exist today in the United States of America." Dixon's anti-Stowe fiction was a chief motivation behind Du Bois's promotion of African-American culture as well as his prominent role in the NAACP's protests against racial discrimination. The publication of Dixon's *The Leopard's Spots* fed the urgency with which Du Bois wrote his seminal book *The Souls of Black Folk* (1903), which describes African-Americans' contributions to culture and society so powerfully that another black activist-author, James Weldon Johnson, later declared that it "has had a greater effect upon and within the Negro race than any other single book published in this country since *Uncle Tom's Cabin*." When Dixon's novel *The Clansman* appeared, Du Bois denounced it as "a sordid and lurid melodrama" and enlisted in the NAACP's vigorous efforts to have *The Birth of a Nation* suppressed. Eventually these efforts contributed to the banning of the film in five states and nineteen cities.

These protests against Griffith's film also helped consolidate African-American activism while offering a reasoned view of race in American history. Du Bois challenged the Dunning historians, who, he wrote, "twisted the emancipation and enfranchisement of the slave in a great effort toward universal democracy, into an orgy of theft and degradation and wide rape of white women." In his 1935 book *Black Reconstruction in America, 1860–1880*, Du Bois became one of the first to correct such popular misrepresentations of the Civil War and its aftermath. Dixon, meanwhile, made Du Bois the "Black Villain" of his novel *The Flaming Sword* and dismissed the professor as a *"Race Imbecile!"* who wanted to foment "Negro Insurrection," promote interracial sexual intercourse, and "array race against race in another war of hate."

And so, in the same kind of bounce-back rippling that in the 1850s had gone from Stowe through the proslavery author George Fitzhugh to Lincoln and his fellow Republicans, *Uncle Tom's Cabin* opened the twentieth century by setting off a chain reaction that led to Dixon, Griffith, and the revitalized Ku Klux Klan, on the one hand, and to self-assertion and protest on the part of Du Bois and other African-Americans.

This rising black activism was paralleled by the emancipationist message of the nine silent films based on Stowe's novel that appeared between 1903 and 1927. So much emphasis has been placed on the reactionary impact of *The Birth of a Nation* that historians have largely overlooked the progressive contributions to film history and the cultural dialogue over race made by the Uncle Tom films. Those who have discussed these Stowe-based films—from Donald Bogle and Daniel Leab through Patricia Turner and others—have emphasized the stereotypes they allegedly perpetuated. Actually, though, these movies not only made technical breakthroughs but offered depictions of race that were strikingly unconventional for the era.

On a purely cinematic level, none of the films measure up to Griffith's achievement in *The Birth of a Nation*. But taken together, the Uncle Tom films made breakthroughs. The 1903 *Uncle Toms* [*sic*] *Cabin; or, Slavery Days,* produced by Edwin S. Porter for Thomas Edison's company, was one of the most expensive and, at fifteen minutes, one of the longest films made to that date. Today, the film seems choppy and artificial, since it consists of a prologue and fourteen scenes in which actors perform on what appear to be stage sets borrowed from a Tom troupe. Still, it and Porter's *The Great Train Robbery* (also 1903) were the first motion pictures that told a continuous narrative, and they've been called the first feature films. *Uncle Toms Cabin; or, Slavery Days* was the first movie that used interpolated titles to tell a story. The titles of the scenes—"Eliza Pleads with Tom to Run Away," "The Escape of Eliza," "The Death of Eva," and so on—provide little continuity to the plot, but in 1903 most Americans already had the plot down cold. Indeed, many had seen the play many times. They could thus fill in the details Porter omitted. Among the film's other innovations were special effects that were cinematic improvements on the Tom plays, such as an angel swooping down and lifting up Eva, Tom's vision of an angel as he dies, superimposed images of historical figures from the Civil War, and a race between two miniature steamboats shot up close to make them appear larger.

Later Uncle Tom films brought more advances. A definite progression can be noted from the stage-like settings of Porter's 1903 film, also used that year in a shorter Uncle Tom film by Sigmund Lubin, through the increasingly realistic and stylistically adventurous versions that appeared over the next fourteen years. J. Stuart Blackton's *Uncle Tom's Cabin* (1910) was unusually long for its day, consisting of three 1,000-foot reels of forty-two minutes apiece. Advertised as "The Most Magnificent, Sumptuous, and Realistic Production" of Stowe's novel, this film promised "the real thing in every respect—real ice, real bloodhounds, real Negroes, real actors, real scenes from the real life as it was in antebellum days." Otis Turner's "four-reel-super-super special" (1913) contained actual "vistas of cotton country, stretches of far Southern rivers, kinetic glimpses of old side-wheel steamboats, freighted with passengers of the period."

All such efforts in verisimilitude were dwarfed by Harry A. Pollard's *Uncle Tom's Cabin*, released in 1927 by Carl Laemmle's Universal Pictures. The Pollard-Leammle version cost nearly $2 million to produce, making it the third most expensive film of the silent era; *The Birth of a Nation*, by contrast, cost $100,000. Laemmle gave Pollard virtually a blank check on a film that was expected to be a gold mine for Universal. A stickler for detail, the actor-turned-director Pollard, who had played Uncle Tom in the 1913 Universal film, used sixty-five sets (eight times the average) and traveled 26,000 miles around the nation to reproduce Stowe's settings as faithfully as possible. For outdoor scenes to frame Eliza's escape, he followed the Saranac River in upstate New York for four months in search of ice floes, though the final shoot of her perilous crossing involved diverting the Los Angeles River to a three-acre plot near Laemmle's Universal Studios, where a month was devoted to filming the scene. The company spent $70,000 to construct a replica of St. Clare's home, $62,000 for Shelby's, and $40,000 for Legree's. For snow, Pollard used 400 tons of gypsum and twelve carloads of breakfast cereal. For dogs, he paid $20,000 for purebred Ledburn bloodhounds imported from England. He created a number of expensive special effects, notably Eva's ascension to an angel-filled heaven and Tom's phantom, which haunts the tormented Legree.

It's fitting that *Uncle Tom's Cabin*, which had fed into the literary techniques of realistic writers like John W. De Forest, William Dean Howells, and Henry James, also made such contributions to scenic realism in film. At the same time, the Tom films carried forward the compelling mix of sensational adventure, comedy, and piety that made both the novel and the plays such huge hits.

Still, whatever cinematic advances the Tom films contributed were not as significant as their dramatization of Stowe's progressive themes regarding race and the meaning of American history. We saw that the conservative Dixon/Griffith position on these topics was grounded in a belief in the inferiority of African-Americans, who were portrayed as brutish, corrupt, or ignorant. The Tom films presented a very different picture of blacks. Recent commentators have generally downplayed the progressive portrayal of blacks in the early Tom movies. For instance, Donald Bogle describes the Uncle Tom of the Pollard-Laemmle film, played by the black actor James B. Lowe, as "a genial darky," representative of blacks in the other Uncle Tom films, who "ne'er tun against their massas" and remain "submissive, stoic, generous, selfless, and oh-so-very-kind." Actually, though, Lowe's Uncle Tom represented a dramatic departure from Griffith's depiction of blacks, as reviewers of the time recognized. Indeed, one African-American journalist considered the Pollard-Laemmle *Uncle Tom's Cabin* the ideal antidote to Griffith's racial poison: "Those Negroes who hated David Wark Griffith for his *Birth of a Nation* should flock to see Carl Laemmle's version of the famous Harriet Beecher Stowe story, and I feel sure they would agree with me that Mr. Laemmle seems to have tried to take just the opposite view of the Negro that Griffith took. . . . All through the story the Negro is shown to splendid advantage."

The same can be said about several of the earlier Tom films. The 1903 version by Edwin S. Porter had featured the first black character in the lead role of a film drama. As was then customary, the character was played by a white man (Porter himself) in blackface, but that fact did not diminish the sympathy with which Stowe's victimized hero was presented—a far cry from other treatments of blacks in some other Edison films, such as the silly scamps who raid a chicken coop in *Chicken Thieves* (1897), or the caricatured fruit-devourer in *The Watermelon-Eating Contest* (1896), or the happy-go-lucky jig dancers of *The Pickaninnies* (1908). Porter not only emphasizes the goodness and nobility of Stowe's character but makes it clear that Tom will be joining Eva, and some of history's heroes too, in heaven. As Tom dies, embraced by George Shelby, a glowing angel appears and is followed by successive historical pictures: John Brown on his way to the gallows, dead white Civil War soldiers, Grant and Lee shaking hands at Appomattox, and Abraham Lincoln.

This scene set a pattern for the other Tom films, which portrayed slavery as a heinous institution and the Civil War as a glorious struggle for freedom, essential for establishing human rights in America. The Tom films made a point of highlighting abolitionists' heroism, slaveholders' cruelty, and Lincoln as the Great Emancipator—despite his presidency coming a decade after Stowe's novel. The 1910 film by Blackton begins with a picture of Lincoln and has an African-American actress play Chloe.

A standout among the early Tom films for its radical position on slavery and race was William Robert Daly's version of 1914, released by the World Film Corporation. In this pioneering film, Uncle Tom was played by an African-American—the first black ever to assume a lead film role. The actor was none other than Sam Lucas, who had previously broken ground by playing Tom onstage in 1878. Now a world-famous star of vaudeville and Broadway, the seventy-two-year-old Lucas was known as the Grand Old Man of the Stage and the Dean of the Theatrical World. In the movie, Lucas plays Tom with gentleness, dignity, and boldness. Patricia Turner holds that Daly's film is primarily important for popularizing the stereotype of what she calls the "docile" Uncle Tom. To the contrary, Sam Lucas's Tom shows real backbone, as when he firmly refuses Legree's command to flog a young black man who has angered Legree. For his disobedience, Tom is tied to a whipping post with his arms spread in a position symbolizing Christ on the cross.

Not only did the film retain Stowe's spirit by demonstrating Tom's firmness, it also depicted extraordinary militancy among other black characters. In the rocky pass scene, George Harris and his fellow fugitive slave have a lively shoot-out with the slave-chasers, one of whom they kill and the rest of whom they drive away with their gunfire. Later, Cassy, Legree's bitter mistress, holds a revolver to her master's head as he lies in bed, passed out from drink. Although Cassy decides not to pull the trigger, soon thereafter the young black man whom Tom had refused to flog takes a pistol and shoots Legree, who tumbles off his horse, dead. Legree comes off in the film as a thoroughly depraved lout, all booze, sadism, and lechery. We cheer Cassy when she raises her gun at him, and we feel joy when she and Emmeline later escape his hounds. We look right down the barrel of the black man's pistol as he aims it at the despicable Legree. The director uses effective camera angles to make us share the perspective of the pistol-wielding black man. For a moment, we *are* the angry black man avenging the terrible treatment the white man has inflicted on innocent blacks. This scene of armed black revolt, sympathetically portrayed, was unparalleled in that day, when many unoffending blacks were lynched by violent white supremacists.

The Pollard-Laemmle film also created a dramatic moment of rebellion on the part of blacks, but it was more cleverly integrated into Stowe's original plot than in the Daly film. Pollard and Laemmle reimagined Stowe's characters in a historical context slightly later than hers, beginning in 1856, the year John Brown waged war against proslavery forces in

Uncle Tom's Cabin *(1914 film)—enslaved black man shoots Legree*

Kansas. The 1856 start date introduces a film that takes us through *Dred Scott*, Fort Sumter, and the Emancipation Proclamation, all leading to a triumphantly rendered Sherman as he leads his troops through Georgia. This altering of Stowe's timeline intensifies the already vigorous anti-slavery force of Stowe's narrative.

The historical revision is accompanied by a dramatic deepening of the radical elements of Stowe's plot. The film does away with the Northern liberation narrative by preventing Eliza and George from escaping to freedom in Canada. All the exciting features of the escape plot are there—the ice, the dogs, the slave-catchers—but the film makes a complete turn-around by having Eliza, George, and little Harry caught and sold into the Deep South, just as Tom is. More than this, the Harris family is violently separated during the Southern journey, with Harry kidnapped by a plantation owner, George becoming a roving fugitive, and Eliza sold into sexual slavery when she is purchased by Legree.

Like Stowe, Pollard makes use of the tragic mulatto figure. If Stowe utilized the ironic situation of people with very little black blood experiencing racial oppression, Pollard not only uses white actors for the Harris family—including his wife Margarita Fischer in the Eliza role—but uses little if any makeup to darken their skin. Reviewers were stunned by the Harrises' whiteness, including one who commented that Fischer looked "either pure Nordic or a mixture of Nordic and Gallic or Slavic or Mediterranean," and that the same could be said of Arthur Edmund Carewe as George. The Harrises appear so light that they drive home Stowe's point about people being enslaved and exploited even though there is often little distinction between them and their masters in skin color, mental ability, or manners. They also accent her theme of interracial bonding, since, while appearing white, they are close to their fellow slaves, who are played by African-Americans. Moreover, Eliza seems like part of the Shelby family. We witness a joyful wedding arranged for George and Eliza by Mrs. Shelby, who says, "Eliza was as well educated as one of my daughters."

This is not to say that the film is an unequivocal pro-Northern work. Pollard was from the South, and, like Stowe, he makes charitable concessions to the Southern view of slavery. He noted, for instance, that some of the cruelest slaveholders were transplanted New Englanders. Still, Pollard had a deep respect for African-American culture—he once called slave spirituals "the only genuine and definite folk music of which Americans can boast"—and he added some important anti-Southern elements to *Uncle Tom's Cabin*. Startlingly, the film opens by flashing antislavery words uttered before the Civil War by none other than Robert E. Lee. This reshaping of Stowe's story continues through the film and is especially visible in the portrait of Legree, who comes across as extra-devilish in this rendering. Pollard reportedly experimented with eighteen variations of makeup before arriving at the fierce, debauched appearance Legree has in the film. George Siegmann's Legree shocked moviegoers of the day. One reviewer complained, "There is an overbalance of 'realism' in the Legree of George Siegmann. The brutality of the character is overstressed."

Overstressed? That was hard to do, given all the harsh Legrees who had populated the Tom shows for decades. But Legree's savagery is not the only sensational cruelty portrayed in the film. "Those with sadistic tendencies will revel in the too frequent use of the blacksnake whip with which the blacks are lashed indiscriminately," remarked a reviewer. Not only does Legree have his henchmen Sambo and Quimbo lash Tom, but his mistress, Cassy, takes up the whip in a jealous rage against his reluctant new paramour, Eliza.

But Cassy is only feigning jealousy. Her whipping of Eliza is a charade, for it occurs in a room, locked off from Legree, in which Cassy announces that she is Eliza's long-lost mother. This confession heralds the solidarity among enslaved blacks that leads to the film's striking climax. Cassy and Eliza hide in Legree's cobweb-filled attic, manipulating his well-known fear of ghosts. This is close to Stowe's novel, but the film transforms the episode into a forceful assertion of the power of African-American women over oppressive white males. Legree turns out to be cowardly and weak. Afraid, he has Sambo and Quimbo lead the way into the attic, where he finds Cassy and Eliza ready to fight him to the death. A violent confrontation between him and the women occurs in which they often gain the upper hand: they batter him with chairs and other objects, and at one point Cassy comes close to stabbing him with a knife.

Just as remarkable is the appearance of Tom in the scene. Pollard chose the forty-year-old black actor James B. Lowe to play Tom after his first choice, Charles Gilpin (a veteran who had played in Eugene O'Neill's *Emperor Jones* and other sophisticated plays), refused to take the role on the ground that the character was too sheepish. But there was nothing sheepish about the way Lowe played Tom. As in Stowe's novel, Tom in the film is a loving family man who is kind to the Shelbys and the St. Clares; but he is as strong in character as he is physically. Pollard said he wanted to be true to Stowe by portraying Uncle Tom as having "the humility of Christ" without being "a lackey and a coward." Indeed, Tom, when ordered by Legree to whip Cassy, stands erect and firmly refuses. He dies after having a vision of Jesus.

This all is straight from Stowe, but then come Pollard's radical additions. After Tom's death, Legree sees the spirit of Tom, who points at him accusingly and then beckons him to follow the stairs to the attic where Cassy and Eliza are hiding. Pollard plays the spirit-sighting to the hilt

Uncle Tom's Cabin *(1927 film)—Cassy (with knife) and Eliza rebel against Legree*

to draw out the full pro-black militancy of the scene. Tom's spirit smiles sarcastically at Legree, beckoning him to his violent encounter with the brave women. Tom saves the women by luring Legree away. He backs down the stairs away from the attic as Legree chases him, flailing his whip futilely. Meanwhile, Sambo and Quimbo have run outdoors to tell the arriving Union troops about the enslaved black women. Then Tom's ghost stands in the staircase window, through which the enraged Legree leaps, plunging to his death.

What we've witnessed is as close to a group rebellion on the part of blacks as could possibly be portrayed in a mainstream film of that era. The women fight intrepidly and skillfully against their white oppressor, while Sambo and Quimbo end up running to the Northern troops for help. Tom becomes a vindictive rebel, even after his death. In effect, he kills the white man who has killed him. And history is depicted as being on the side of the surviving black insurrectionists, who are saved by the Union soldiers. Having Sherman's troops arrive by horse to rescue the endangered blacks is Pollard's answer to Griffith's galloping clansmen coming to save trapped whites from threatening blacks.

Pollard's film presented a formidable challenge to the Dixon/Griffith view of race relations—so much so that, though briefly popular, it stirred up controversy. Many theaters refused to show it, especially in the South, where its racial themes seemed particularly threatening. Kentucky banned the film, leading one black newspaper to predict that soon "the picture . . . may be kept out of southern territory entirely." When Atlanta and other cities passed similar bans, another African-American paper noted sarcastically that the South "can revel in such a picture as 'The Birth of a Nation' " but "hasn't enough guts to view the story of Harriet Beecher Stowe." Three decades later, in 1958, when the civil rights movement was emerging, the movie was reissued to counteract repeated revivals of *The Birth of a Nation*. This re-release strengthened Pollard's emancipationist message by deleting some of the film's lighter scenes—Topsy's more clownish moments, for instance—and adding a running narration by Raymond Massey, whose previous film roles as Lincoln and John Brown gave him a strong antislavery aura.

Besides offering a progressive statement on race, Pollard's film made an international celebrity of Lowe, who used his sudden fame to make a case for African-American rights. He had grown up in the South and had once watched in horror as a black man was burned alive. He told of the racism then prevalent in Hollywood, where blacks were relegated to undesirable roles or excluded altogether. But Lowe's moment in the limelight faded quickly. He never received another film role. By 1931, he was working as a tailor in Paris.

Meanwhile, efforts to suppress the Tom plays took their toll. By 1931, the death knell of the Uncle Tom shows rang throughout the nation. That year it was widely reported that for the first time in many decades, no Tom play appeared anywhere in America. The critic Elizabeth Corbett announced in *Theatre Guild Magazine:* "This play, which boasts the longest continuous run in theatrical history, incorporated in itself a whole history of American drama and acting." The play's seventy-seven-year run, she pointed out, was "half as long as American history itself" and

> was as wide as it was long. It was not confined to New York, nor to half a dozen big cities, nor even to the road as we knew it twenty years ago. *Uncle Tom's Cabin* played in theatres wherever there was a theatre to be played in. But it also played in town halls, in empty rooms over warehouses, and under canvas. The troupe traveled by wagon in the early days, and later by special car. There were dozens of *Uncle Tom's Cabin* companies and they came back year after year to every hamlet and village in the nation.

But it turned out that the Tom plays were *not* dead. Articles on their demise prompted letters from around the nation reporting local performances of the plays in several areas. Indeed, Uncle Tom plays appeared with regularity through the mid-1950s, and versions of the play—some straightforward, some modernized—have been put on right into the twenty-first century.

There were also sporadic efforts to make new film versions of Stowe's novel. In 1944, MGM announced that another *Uncle Tom's Cabin*, to star Paul Robeson and Lena Horne, was in the works, but the plan never came to fruition. In 1955, Alistair Cooke's *Omnibus* series ran a sober made-for-TV version that tried to avoid controversy by leaving out Stowe's strongest antislavery scenes, such as Eliza's escape and the whipping of Tom, and focusing instead on St. Clare's cogitations. This mild approach angered some progressives, who were looking for a strong statement on race in the wake of *Brown v. Board of Education,* and yet it failed to appease the ever-vigilant Daughters of the Confederacy, who tried to prevent the airing of the teleplay by insisting that *Uncle Tom's Cabin* "slanders the South." A later TV rendition came in 1987 with Stan Lathan's workman-like *Uncle Tom's Cabin,* starring Avery Brooks as Uncle Tom, Bruce Dern as St. Clare, and Phylicia Rashad as Eliza. Between these TV efforts came the 1965 film *Uncle Tom's Cabin* by the Hungarian director Géza von

Radványi, which exaggerated Stowe's erotic and violent themes, making a hash of her plot in the process.

Meanwhile, from around World War I through the early 1950s, a new phenomenon emerged. In different mediums—tie-in products, ads, stage shows, songs, films, and cartoons—images of *Uncle Tom's Cabin* were fragmented, chopped up, and cast in many directions. What I am calling the "post-Tom mode" refers to characters or images from *Uncle Tom's Cabin* that appeared in contexts outside of the narrative Stowe had created.

Stowe's characters had such appeal that they were used to promote a welter of products. Toward the end of the nineteenth century, there appeared ads for Uncle Tom's Smoking Tobacco; in one, Eva asks Tom why he smokes that brand, and he replies, "Dis yer tobacco am de best." An ad for Topsy Tobacco shows the impish girl holding a box of tobacco and exclaiming merrily, "I is so wicked! . . . 'Spect Massa make it lively if he done cotch dis chile." Overt racism sometimes entered such ads, as in one for a thread company in which Topsy, told to come in out of the rain to avoid getting soaked, declares, "Oh! it won't hurt me, Missy. I'm like COAT'S BLACK THREAD. De Color won't come off by wettin." The first two decades of the twentieth century brought Uncle Tom's Salted Peanuts, Uncle Tom's Fine Granulated Sugar, Uncle Tom's Health Food, Uncle Tom's Root Beer, and a Cream of Wheat ad featuring Tom in his garden. In the ads for these products, Tom was pictured as a benign, gray-haired man—a kind of male Aunt Jemima. In 1925, a Pennsylvania broom company included among its "De Luxe Brands" an Uncle Tom broom and a Topsy broom. Then there came a Topsy Thermometer, a Topsy Honey Dairy Drink, and six desserts by Elizabeth Woody divided into three light-colored ones called "Evas" and three dark ones, "Topsies." In the mid-1940s, the Inkograph Co., Inc. ran a full-page magazine ad for a fountain pen showing a dignified, studious-looking Tom holding a pen and writing slate while Eva clings to him and looks on.

In 1934, America's most important advertising agency, the J. Walter Thompson Company of New York, proudly revealed in an ad in *Fortune* magazine that it used the same techniques that had made *Uncle Tom's*

Ink-o-Graph Pen ad (c. 1945) with caption
"Uncle Tom & Little Eva awritin' "

Cabin uniquely successful. Stowe's novel, the ad went, was "the shrewd-est piece of selling ever" and proved that "great masses of people can be influenced through their emotions." The novel had made the Civil War and the fall of slavery "inevitable" and had sufficient power "to have ended the organized oppression of peoples for all time." Why? Because it connected a specific message to basic human emotions. This was the surefire technique for selling any product. The ad offered this sweeping generalization: "The power of advertising to influence great numbers of people depends on the extent to which the methods of *Uncle Tom's Cabin* can be used." Evidently the Thompson Company followed its own advice, for it continued to expand and now, as JWT, remains one of the world's largest ad agencies.

Other prime examples of the post-Tom mode were vaudeville routines and popular songs, which drew unexpected comic energy from Stowe's themes and characters. A 1916 "Burlesque Review" written by George M. Cohan delivered what *The Washington Post* called "a deliciously funny travesty on 'Uncle Tom's Cabin,' written and spoken in the rag-time chatter." The black comedian Bert Williams in 1918 performed a skit for the Ziegfeld Follies in which he brought the house down by enacting both Uncle Tom and Simon Legree. The prolific playwright Walter Ben Hare in 1921 came out with a "song monologue" called *"Uncle Tom's Cabin" at the Op'ry House* that lampooned a small-town production of a Tom play, in which Eliza kicks aside a bloodhound stuffed with hay, Marks gets in funny fistfights, Tom is sold to a "red-nosed critter named Sime Legree," and "little Evey" is pulled to heaven, "But the dog-gawn rope it had to break. / She fell with a flop clean off the platform, / Lit in the middle of the big bass drum." The Jazz Age spoofs continued with the popular song "Oh! Eva (Ain't You Comin' Out Tonight?)" (1924), in which Uncle Tom is, amazingly enough, a randy cad who has an affair with a newly married white woman, Eva, whose husband finds out, and "BIP BOP! BIP BOP! There was an awful fight, / That guy hit him with so much vim, / That Uncle Tom turned white"—whiteness wins here, but not until the song has made its extraordinary excursion into interracial sex. Another song of the 1920s has Legree introducing Tom to the latest dance craze: "He took his whip and said to Uncle Tom—'C'mon, Charleston!'"

In films, there was a transitional phase in which Tom plays were, as we might term it now, deconstructed. The ups and downs of the touring Tom troupes—their mishaps, triumphs, and impact on audiences—provided fodder for many movies. While European modernists were devising self-referential techniques, as in Luigi Pirandello's *Six Characters in Search of an Author* (1921), which was very much *about* making theater, numerous American films featured dramas about Tom companies. In *The Troubles of a Stranded Actor* (1909), the country audience of a Tom show is so infuriated by an actor's maladroit performance that it drives him from the stage with rotten tomatoes. *The Death of Simon LaGree* [*sic*] (1915) portrays a love triangle involving a Tom actor, a country girl, and her jealous boyfriend; the film ends with a stagehand getting caught on the rope used to lift Eva and being hauled onstage, as the audience laughs uproariously. Such parody is featured as well in *Little Eva Ascends* (1922), in which a teenage boy who has long played Eva gets so disgusted with the role that one night he tears off his blond wig and stomps off the stage, knocking down the backdrop as he leaves.

In time, such post-Tom comedy infiltrated movies featuring recognizable actors. The Our Gang/Little Rascals films *Uncle Tom's Uncle* (1926) and its sound-era remake, *Spanky* (1932), included all kinds of sight gags and funny accidents associated with the wee gang's efforts to put on a Tom show. *The Wonder Bar* (1934) has a blackfaced Al Jolson, wearing wings and mounted on a flying mule, visiting an all-black heaven where he spots "Uncle Tom" and his "cabin show," with a parade wagon that advertises "Uncle Tom To-night." Judy Garland, a year before her star-making turn in *The Wizard of Oz,* appeared in blackface as Topsy in *Everybody Sing* (1938), in which she delivered a jazzy medley of "Swing Low, Sweet Chariot" and "Dixie" containing the words "Uncle Tom's got a new routine; Eliza crossed the ice in a limousine, while Simon Legree shakes a mean tambourine." Betty Grable and June Haver played twin Topsys in the 1945 musical film *The Dolly Sisters.*

Snippets of Stowe's novel appeared in other films as well. In a Tom scene in the Bud Abbott and Lou Costello movie *The Naughty Nineties* (1945), Costello, playing the winged Eva, tumbles to the ground when the rope hauling him heavenward snaps. In Walter Lang's Oscar-winning film *The King and I* (1956), based on the Rodgers and Hammerstein musical, the King of Siam (Yul Brynner) is given a copy of *Uncle Tom's Cabin*. The king entertains his European guests by having his servants' theater troupe put on a tragicomic ballet, "Small House of Uncle Thomas." The play's villain, King Simon of Legree, chases Eliza and her baby with his hounds across the ice until Buddha intervenes and melts the ice, so that Legree drowns.

The post-Tom craze represented a radical departure from Stowe's novel, and, as such, to some extent it diminished the book's stature. At the same time, though, it opened the way for the lighthearted treatment of pressing social issues that later defined mainstream American comedy. On some level, it pointed to the refreshing notion that the painful conflicts that had long surrounded *Uncle Tom's Cabin,* and continued in the cultural wars over race and history, had either been incorporated into American popular culture enough to play as a point of reference or used in a new way to comment on racial relations.

It also offered new possibilities for white performers to draw from the African-American experience. Later on, Elvis Presley made musical history through what has been called cultural mixing; by assimilating black and white music, he was, in historian Tim Parrish's words, "achieving on a cultural level what *Brown v. Board of Education* decreed on a legal one." One can go back in time, to the post-Tom performances, to find early versions of this kind of mixing. Al Jolson or Judy Garland in blackface may seem offensive today, but for the 1930s this cross-racial impersonation permitted talented white singers to open up in new ways. Especially impressive is Garland as Topsy delivering her wonderfully fluid, soulful mix of "Swing Low" and "Dixie" in a jazzy blend that prefigures rhythm and blues, one made all the more startling because it empowers Eliza by imagining her in a limousine and strips Legree of his whip, handing him a tambourine.

Early cartoons brought zany imaginativeness to the post-Tom mode. Like numerous Hollywood stars, many iconic cartoon characters— Felix the Cat, Mickey Mouse, Mighty Mouse, Bugs Bunny, to name a few—took on Tom roles. Particularly notable is Walt Disney's *Mickey's Mellerdrammer* (1933), in which Mickey, Minnie, Clarabelle Cow, and Horace Horsecollar put on a Tom show that lapses into comic mayhem. There were also other popular animated features, including the Jingle Jinks cartoon *Uncle Tom and Little Eva* (1932) and the Tex Avery films *Uncle Tom's Bungalow* (1937) and *Uncle Tom's Cabaña* (1947).

With all its fun and frolic, the post-Tom mode was thematically rich. It was marbled with erotic undertones, straight and gay, that signaled— and may have sped—a relaxation in cultural attitudes toward sexuality. Henry Louis Gates Jr. rightly wonders how *Mickey's Mellerdrammer* got

Minnie Mouse as Eva dancing with Mickey Mouse in blackface
as Topsy in Mickey's Mellerdrammer *(1933)*

past the censors, since it features Mickey as Tom and Minnie as Eva, and, in Gates's words, the two mice are, "as they say, an item, and unmistakably so." We might add that yet another dimension opens when we see Mickey cross-dress as he takes on the role of Topsy, too. A gender-bending moment also comes in Tex Avery's *Uncle Tom's Bungalow* when the voice-over narrator asks a blond girl what her name is and gets the shouted reply, in a rough male voice, "Little Eva, you dope!" The masculine identity of Eva, reflecting Tom troupes' common use of men or boys in the Eva role, adds further interest to a suggestive scene in which Eva raises her dress and exposes her underwear. Avery floods his later film *Uncle Tom's Cabaña* with sexual images. Simon Legree, depicted as an evil urban landlord, goes to Uncle Tom's nightclub with the intention of killing Tom but is diverted by the fetching stage performance of Eva, a sexy blonde who delivers "Carry Me Back to Ole Virginny" as a suggestive promise to "do anything for massa." Overcome with desire, Legree becomes a figure of bristling phallicism, with his eyes, his stomach, and his whole body popping forward excitedly. Legree rushes onstage, grabs Eva, and carries her away but is stopped by Tom, who rips open his shirt and shows a huge *S* on his chest; he is Supertom, who survives everything Legree assaults him with—bullets, a PT boat, a railroad train, and a buzz saw—until Tom hurls the Umpire [*sic*] State Building, with Legree inside, over the moon so that it falls into the ocean and kills Legree.

Tom's prodigious power here points to surprisingly progressive racial undertones in several post-Tom works. The first half of the twentieth century is usually viewed as a bleak period for the treatment of race in film. Segregation, the argument goes, was a settled fact of American life, and its attitudes were projected in countless film roles in which blacks were associated with various demeaning stereotypes—toms, coons, mammies, and bucks, as film historian Donald Bogle calls them, or, in Daniel Leab's account, blacks were presented as "subhuman, simpleminded, superstitious, and submissive."

But the post-Tom mode showed that such stereotypes could actually be manipulated to deliver progressive messages about both race and gender. Avery's Supertom, for instance, first appears in the film as a caricatured lazy, cigar-smoking fogey who tells stories to wide-eyed children. But in the course of the film, Tom is invested with such phenomenal strength

Uncle Tom as Supertom, invincible against Legree's bullets, in Tex Avery's cartoon Uncle Tom's Cabaña *(1947)*

that he easily defeats the malevolent Legree. This trope of the apparently feeble but actually strong black person ran through the cartoons, in which Legree is usually killed off or made to look foolish. In Jingle Jinks's *Uncle Tom and Little Eva,* the athletic Eliza outruns Legree across the broken ice, even though he has the advantage of a superfast boat; then Uncle Tom comes to the rescue, throwing his ball and chain at Legree's boat, which tumbles over a waterfall. In *Mickey's Mellerdrammer,* the blackfaced, gray-bearded Mickey, as Uncle Tom, hobbles obediently onstage to receive a lashing, but Legree, unable to use his whip when it entangles the offstage Goofy, is soon buried under a pile of debris hurled at him by the theater crowd. In *Southern Fried Rabbit,* Bugs Bunny appears as a doddering old black man but then he puts Legree (played by Yosemite Sam) through his paces by scampering about in several disguises, including the commanding Abraham Lincoln, a Confederate army officer, and finally a beguiling Southern belle.

The use of racial stereotypes to cloak a progressive message is particularly visible in one of the major post-Tom works, *Topsy and Eva,* a popular vaudeville act starring the San Francisco sisters Vivian and Rosetta Duncan that was made by United Artists into a feature film (1927). Having first hit the vaudeville boards in 1914, when they were in their early teenage years, the Duncan sisters, a white song-and-dance team, toured widely before taking on the musical comedy *Topsy and Eva,* written by popular playwright Catherine Chisholm Cushing. The Duncan sisters opened in *Topsy and Eva* in July 1923 in San Francisco, with Rosetta appearing in blackface as Topsy and Vivian in the Eva role. The show was an immediate hit, and the sisters performed it over the next three years, grossing over $900,000 and appearing in twenty-three major cities, wowing audiences and critics everywhere. In 1927 came *The Duncan Sisters in Topsy and Eva,* a movie directed by Del Lord. The public's fascination with *Topsy and Eva* was unflagging. After the movie had a successful run, the Duncan sisters continued with their stage musical right up to the early 1950s, even as they appeared in other shows and films as well.

Topsy and Eva has been roughly handled by historians of theater and film, largely for what appears today to be its use of degrading racial stereotypes. Barbara Tepa Lupack sums up the common view: "Considered by many film historians to be the worst Tom adaptation or spinoff ever, it brimmed with overt racist stereotypes and demonstrated the Hollywood studios' ignorance of—and insensitivity to—black criticism."

But *Topsy and Eva* did *not* provoke such criticism by blacks or whites in its time. To the contrary, the show and the film can best be seen as another context in which *Uncle Tom's Cabin* became a vehicle for the empowerment of African-Americans and women. Black journalists joined the general chorus of praise for *Topsy and Eva*. For one thing, the show gave fifty black actors the chance to appear in a highly popular touring show, what one African-American newspaper called "the largest all-colored musical comedy since [Bert] Williams' and [George] Walker's time." Also, the fact that the Duncan sisters incorporated spirituals into the show was meaningful to black journalists, one of whom wrote that "they still stir in us memories of wrongs we have suffered."

In the film version, several characters are played by African-Americans, most notably Noble Johnson as Uncle Tom. An experienced actor, Johnson was also a film director who had formerly run a movie studio devoted to promoting African-American culture in film. Although Noble's Tom has a diminished role in the film, Johnson plays him with strength, dignity, gentleness, and humor. Like Eva, he remains alive at the end of the film, avoiding the grim fate Stowe had assigned to him. Throughout the film, Johnson's Tom, who is vigorous and handsome, serves as a bridge between the white characters and the rebellious Topsy, maintaining even-handed compassion and self-respect.

The film is progressive in its treatment of race in other senses as well. Rosetta Duncan in blackface as Topsy at first seems to embody the stereotype of the ignorant, thievish, and superstitious black person. Born on April Fools' Day, when a black stork dumps her in a trash can, she appears through much of the film in a dirty, ragged dress, with her kinky hair tied in white-ribboned knots that sprout from her head in all directions. Not only has she "neber been born," but she's never had a bath, until a white maid gives her one.

Topsy's subversive streak is revealed in her unflagging resistance to white characters who are either uptight, like Ophelia, or cruel, like Legree. In Stowe's novel, Topsy never even meets Legree. Here, she reluctantly becomes his slave and fights him tooth and nail—quite literally, for she scratches him, bites him, trips him, butts him like a goat, and leaps on his back. And she ends up defeating him during a winter-set scene. The whip-wielding Legree chases her. She confronts him, grapples with him, and then sends him over a snowy cliff into an icy river, presumably killing him. Far from being a racist portrayal, Rosetta's Topsy suggests that both races can learn much from the kind of black person she impersonates: one who is self-reliant, ever flexing her muscles, and ready to fight for herself.

Topsy learns how to love from Eva, played with mystic splendor by the golden-haired Vivian Duncan. Scholar Michele Wallace perceives that the film features what can be best described as a love affair between Topsy and Eva. Indeed, the two girls often caress each other, proclaim their love for each other, and end up in the same bed, when the tuckered-out Topsy, having magically revived the apparently dying Eva, falls asleep next to the blond beauty. In an era of so-called Boston marriages (living-together arrangements between women, some nonsexual), there was a certain fluidity in sexual roles that made same-sex intimacy commonly accepted and not necessarily trangressive. And the fact that the Duncans were very famous as *sisters* put their onscreen love under the safe umbrella of family affection.

That said, Rosetta Duncan's Topsy has a striking physicality and sometimes a sensuousness that bends her performance toward the erotic. In her short dress, she squats on the ground near Eva, almost exposing her crotch. When showing Eva a dance, she swings her hips suggestively, and at moments she strokes Eva's hair. Eva, for her part, falls deathly ill as a direct result of Topsy's forced departure from her home. "I love you! I love you! I love you!" Eva cries to Topsy, who later returns the sentiment,

The Duncan Sisters in Topsy and Eva *(1927)*

telling others, "I lubs her." Indeed, Eva's health depends on Topsy's love. As Eva says, "Now I'll never die, because I love you, Topsy."

Whereas in Stowe's novel Eva dies so that Topsy and others can be spiritually saved, in this movie Eva lives because Topsy loves her, and Eva wants to continue the relationship. Whatever the erotic messages are here—and we must avoid imposing today's views too easily on the film—the bonding between the white Eva and the black Topsy is an even stronger proclamation of interracial togetherness than in Stowe's novel. Produced in a decade of rampant racial discrimination, when the Ku Klux Klan had made a huge comeback due in part to the Dixon/Griffith collaboration, *Topsy and Eva* made boldly defiant racial statements. Since Griffith himself is said to have helped edit the film, it may be that he was in part vindicating himself in the face of obloquy from blacks that was directed at him in the wake of *The Birth of a Nation*—an idea that seems to be confirmed by the fact that Griffith later directed a film on Lincoln (1930) in which Old Abe's antislavery views were compassionately presented.

To some reviewers, *Topsy and Eva* was such a departure from Stowe that it seemed to leave *Uncle Tom's Cabin* behind altogether. It appeared to be part of a larger movement by which Stowe's narrative had become so maltreated that its death was again being considered. As the writer Amy Leslie noted in a Chicago newspaper:

> For fifty-odd years we have been submitting Mrs. Stowe's melodramatic classic to orgies of mutilation. "Uncle Tom's Cabin" was imperishable and it was done finally with double Evas and pairs of Topsys and bunches of Marks and droves of mules and dogs, to say nothing of husky platoons of Simon Legrees and blacksnake whips, and all the inquisitoria [*sic*] of drama dying hard. But it took Catherine Chisholm Cushing to give it a dig in the ribs which may lay its ghost.

But still Stowe's narrative had not given up the ghost. In the 1930s came the arrival of the child superstar Shirley Temple.

Topsy and Eva can be said to have set the stage for Temple's naughty-nice roles. Vivian Duncan's Eva represented a notable departure not only from Stowe but also from Eva as she appeared in Tom shows. As one journalist commented, she was "a healthy, happy, somewhat mischievous girl, not trying to 'save' Topsy, but to become like her." Shirley Temple combined the saucy sweetness of Vivian Duncan's Eva with the mischievous self-assertiveness of Rosetta's Topsy. Temple actually played Eva in an *Uncle Tom's Cabin* scene in the film *Dimples,* and in *The Little Colonel* she parroted Topsy by declaring, "I'm so wicked. Isn't I awful?" And if the Duncan sisters had an African-American friend in Uncle Tom as portrayed by Noble Johnson, Shirley Temple had her own kindly Tom figure, the tap dancer Bill "Bojangles" Robinson.

Born in Richmond, Virginia, in 1878, Robinson started performing publicly at six and went on to become a star in vaudeville and on Broadway before going to Hollywood. Like many black actors in the 1930s, he was generally confined to servant roles. Despite this, his phenomenal dancing skills and composed screen presence allowed him to shine. As a tap dancer, he updated the buck-and-wing style, long popular in Tom shows and on vaudeville, by minimizing the wing—that is, by reducing arm-flailing and upper-body gyrations. He brought understated grace and lightness to tap, concentrating on the toes and subtle modulations of sound, combined with impeccable rhythm.

Robinson first appeared with Shirley Temple in *The Little Colonel* (1935), when she was seven. By that time, she had already developed strong dance skills, but he honed them as her coach, at the request of film directors. She loved being taught by Robinson, whom she called Uncle Billy. If the Tom-Eva-Topsy relationship had been one of shared affection in the Duncan sisters' show, the Temple-Robinson pairing was an affirmation of zestful performance shared by a black man and a white child. "Your little child is your only true democrat," Stowe had written of Eva. In her films with Robinson, Temple created a visual democracy in which she and her post-Tom partner danced expertly in happy unison. The famous stair dance in *The Little Colonel* exemplified the uncanny parallelism of sound, foot placement, and body position that brought the two together in dazzling harmony. The pair continued their wonderfully meshed performances in *The Littlest Rebel* (1935), *Just Around the Corner* (1938), and *Rebecca of Sunnybrook Farm* (1938). *Dimples* (1936) has a particular connection to Stowe's novel, despite not including Robinson. Set in the 1850s, it includes an episode about the supposed first stage version of *Uncle Tom's Cabin*, with Temple as Eva. Although Bill Robinson didn't appear in the film, he choreographed the scenes in which Temple dances for pennies in the streets.

Robinson's collaboration with Shirley Temple has sometimes been seen as an example of Hollywood's racism, since Robinson played subservient roles in Temple's movies. But as is true about so much of African-American performance in post-Tom contexts, Robinson and his fellow black actors in the Temple films represented empowerment for African-Americans, at least in some circles. One black journalist called Robin-

*Shirley Temple and Bill "Bojangles" Robinson performing the
stair dance in* The Little Colonel *(1935)*

son's relationship with Temple "Hollywood's Friendship Number One"
and declared that Robinson was a "truly great American" who had done
as much to "promote a general good feeling among the races as any other
living human," largely through his film appearances with her. Another
declared that everyone must see *Dimples*, whose "dance numbers were
staged by the incomparable . . . BILL (Bojangles) ROBINSON." The writer
took note of a dance Temple did with two black men "that knocks you
right from under your seat," adding that her rendition of the spiritual
"Get on Board, Lil Chillun" was sung "like one born to the 'brush harbor'
churches of the 'Ante-Bellum' era of slavery."

The same reviewer noted that featured in *Dimples*, along with Shirley
Temple, was "that laugh-producing wizard Stepin Fetchit." The fact that
a black journalist sang praise to Lincoln Perry, whose stage name Stepin
Fetchit became a byword for obsequious blacks because of the demeaning

roles he often played, again complicates the picture of black performance in film. To be sure, the part that made Perry famous—the lazy, befuddled fool—was no compliment to people of color. But as Perry's biographer, Mel Watkins, points out, he was "an amazingly complex man" whose shiftless persona was in fact a new guise for the African-American trickster figure, playing the old con from slavery days that, in Watkins' words, "was called 'putting on old massa—break the tools, break the hoe, do anything to postpone the work that was to be done.' "

Another complex figure that showed up in the Temple films was the mammy, a stock character that Patricia Turner suggests is rooted in Stowe's Chloe. When the most famous black actress of the day, Hattie McDaniel, who appeared in over fifty films during the 1930s, played the mammy figure Mom Beck in *The Little Colonel,* some black reviewers criticized her for playing a contented slave. But others saw real achievement in the skill with which she played the role. A reviewer for a black Pittsburgh newspaper commented, "Twelve million Negroes will be pleased by *The Little Colonel,*" mainly because of McDaniel's moving, funny performance.

The conflict between racial stereotyping and empowering black performance became especially heated in the controversy over the era's most popular film, *Gone with the Wind* (1939). The novel by the Atlanta journalist Margaret Mitchell on which the film was based was, like many Southern novels, written largely in reply to Stowe, with Mitchell making direct stabs at *Uncle Tom's Cabin*. Mitchell writes, "Accepting *Uncle Tom's Cabin* as revelation, second only to the Bible, the Yankee women all wanted to know about the bloodhounds which every Southerner kept to track down runaway slaves . . . the dreadful branding irons . . . and the cat-o'-nine-tails with which they beat them to death, and they evidenced what Scarlett felt was a very nasty and ill-bred interest in slave concubinage."

When the anti-Stowe novelist Thomas Dixon wrote Mitchell congratulating her on the novel, she replied with an effusive letter in which she told him that his books had been among her favorites in childhood. When a German reader sent her a fan letter, she replied, "I am happy to learn that *Gone with the Wind* is helping to dispel the myth of the South that *Uncle Tom's Cabin* created." As a book, *Gone with the Wind* was a massive best-seller, and it won the Pulitzer Prize. David O. Selznick's film version won ten Oscars and stands as America's highest-grossing film ever, adjusted for inflation.

The Old South had never appeared as beguilingly romantic as in *Gone with the Wind*. But there was another element at work here: the debate over the film's portrayal of African-Americans. Like most films of the period, *Gone with the Wind* put blacks in subservient roles. But the black actors in the film—especially Hattie McDaniel as Mammy, Oscar Polk as Pork, and Butterfly McQueen as Prissy—enacted these roles expertly, as many reviewers of the time noted. McDaniel brought her strongest mammy performance to the film, and in doing so she achieved a landmark in the history of African-Americans: winning the Academy Award for Best Supporting Actress. For McDaniel herself, the honor was a triumph for black people. She declared, "I realize that this is another hurdle that has gone down before the Negro and his art, and I consider this recognition a step further for the race, rather than personal progress." Several black journalists agreed. One commented that although black film stars like McDaniel, Bill Robinson, and Louise Beavers usually appeared in inferior roles, they used these roles to promote the talent and humanity that African-Americans possessed and that would otherwise be unappreciated by whites. "By the arrival of Hattie McDaniel," the writer noted, "the Negro had awakened to the fact of reality and the odium has largely passed and so instead of heckling Miss McDaniel, the Negro hails her."

Not all blacks of the time, however, had this positive response, especially the so-called New Negroes who considered roles like McDaniel's mammies or Robinson's servants as despicable sellouts to the white establishment. A black journalist in Chicago branded *Gone with the Wind* "an insult to the race," charging that the film had put the progress of blacks back by many years. The writer insisted that McDaniel and the other black actors in the film "forgot about self-respect, pride, and duty to their race," adding, "Our disgust is that Hollywood should waste the talents of three performers like McDaniel, [Oscar] Polk, and Miss [Butterfly] McQueen on a picture that insults millions of folk who support theatres throughout the land." Many other black journalists joined the protest against the film. And so, as in the case of Dixon/Griffith, *Gone with the Wind* was sharply condemned by the NAACP and other black groups that considered the film racist.

The fact is, the black actors of the era *were* assigned degrading roles. They *did* encounter severe racial prejudice in their private lives, even when they were widely beloved among white audiences. (For example, when Bill Robinson was in Palm Springs filming a movie with Shirley Temple, he was quartered in a chauffeur's room above a garage, while she was given a cottage at the Desert Inn—a fact that appalled the young actress, who later called this her introduction to racism.) Some effective vehicle was needed to alert the nation to the problem of unremitting prejudice. African-Americans, caught in the malicious atmosphere of Jim Crow, needed a weapon that would help them to establish pride, self-reliance, and a healthy race consciousness. They found that weapon in a powerful revisioning of Uncle Tom.

It's the height of irony that Stowe's novel, which had long been hailed by blacks as a chief means of liberation for their race, should yield the damning epithet that was applied to sycophants who compromised integrity and ethics by kowtowing to whites. In the nineteenth century, Uncle Tom was rarely used in this negative way. In fact, a group of ex-slaves to whom author Albion Tourgee read Stowe's novel in 1896 said they found Stowe's Uncle Tom unrealistic because of his unbending refusal to obey his master's commands; few enslaved blacks, they said, would have dared to be so rebellious.

The first use of Uncle Tom as a symbol of weakness that I've found is when Frederick Douglass, praising the North's African-American soldiers in 1865, said that "it was formerly thought that the negro would not fight; that he possessed only the most sheepish attributes of humanity; was a perfect 'Uncle Tom,' disposed to take off his coat whenever required, fold his hands, and be whipped by anyone who wanted to whip him," whereas the black soldier has proven to be as brave as any white one.

How could Douglass, a strong admirer of *Uncle Tom's Cabin*—so much so that, as we saw, he asked to pose as Uncle Tom in the Stowe exhibit at the 1893 Columbian Exposition—use the Uncle Tom phrase contemptuously? Actually, he was the first of many African-Americans who recognized the power of Stowe's novel and yet, in order to goad fellow blacks toward pride and self-assertion, used the Uncle Tom phrase as a convenient symbol of obsequiousness—the image that was being popularized in some of the Tom plays.

W. E. B. Du Bois joined Douglass in extolling Stowe even as he made use of the Uncle Tom epithet. On the one hand, Du Bois thought that no author was more responsible for ending slavery than Stowe. On the other, when he attacked Booker T. Washington's program of vocational education for blacks as accommodationist, Du Bois, as one writer summarizes, "mercilessly ridiculed Washington as the first Uncle Tom, who passively tolerated maltreatment from whites, in exchange for a pat on the head and the hypocritical embrace of their paternalistic benevolence."

Du Bois, in turn, was called an Uncle Tom by the black separatist Marcus Garvey, who, perceiving the intransigence of white racism, called for the voluntary emigration of American blacks to Africa in order, he said, to build "a nation of our own." Du Bois's notion of a "talented tenth" of blacks who would spearhead the advance of African-Americans angered Garvey, who classed Du Bois among the "white men's niggers" who "are allowing themselves to be used even as Uncle Tom and his bunch were used for hundreds of years." Still, Garvey was not above using Stowe for his own purposes, as when his back-to-Africa book was promoted in ads as "A Second Uncle Tom's Cabin." And Garvey himself received the Uncle Tom label when in the 1920s he approached the Ku Klux Klan for help in devising a plan for shipping blacks out of America. A former supporter of Garvey was so infuriated by his complicity with the segregationist group that he described Garvey "running like a good old uncle Tom to do as much bowing and scraping in the plantation style" to "the

Southern ruling class," leaving "no boots unlicked in the effort to make himself a 'white man's nigger.' "

Uncle Tom became such a controversial trademark that many blacks tried to distance themselves from Stowe's character. Alain Locke, known as the Father of the Harlem Renaissance, said in 1925, "The days of 'aunties,' 'uncles,' and 'mammies' is . . . gone. Uncle Tom and Sambo have passed on." Similarly, Richard Wright's story collection *Uncle Tom's Children* (1938), commonly considered the first example of black protest fiction, had as its epigraph "Uncle Tom is dead!" Wright, who had experienced segregation firsthand while growing up in Mississippi, was rejecting what he saw as Stowe's wimpy Uncle Tom—whom he described as "the cringing type who knows his place among white folk"—even as he appropriated words from Stowe's title in order to bring attention to the fact that he was providing an updated, angry version of the kind of protest literature she had pioneered. He enforced this idea through his naturalistic portraits of African-Americans suffering at the hands of whites in both his autobiography *Black Boy* and his novel *Native Son,* in which Stowe's kindly hero, Uncle Tom, is reconceived as the surly antihero Bigger Thomas, a Chicago tenement dweller driven by white racism to commit murder.

Because Uncle Tom was no longer the character portrayed in Stowe's novel and was now considered spineless, any significant effort to revive him met with vehement protest. In 1944 the NAACP led the effort to squelch MGM's plans for a grandiose Technicolor remake of *Uncle Tom's Cabin,* for which Lena Horne had been invited to play Eliza and Paul Robeson to appear as Uncle Tom. The film's producer, Simon Hornblow, held that *Uncle Tom's Cabin* was historically important and had contributed more than any other work to freedom for blacks. But the African-American press disagreed. One newspaper said of the film, "We tire of seeing ourselves depicted as bootblacks, porters, maids, and now—of all things—as slaves." African-American protests against the proposed film led Horne and Robeson to refuse the roles. Even Vice President Henry Wallace, who heard of the planned film, objected to the movie, saying that the time was not right to bring back Uncle Tom. The International Film and Radio Guild launched a major campaign for improving the kinds of roles blacks were given in the mass media. In June 1944, five hundred members of the Entertainment Emergency Committee called for a cessation of media images of blacks as "happy-go-lucky, lazy illiterates, clowns, cowards, superstitious, ghost-ridden, liquor-drinking, chicken-stealing, watermelon-eating, jazz-crazed Aunt Jemimas or Uncle Toms." The protest had its wanted effect: MGM halted its plans for the movie. "'Uncle Tom's Cabin' Film Now 'Gone with the Wind' " was the witty headline of an article about the film's demise.

To terminate the Uncle Tom film was one thing. To diminish the importance of Stowe's novel was quite another. But that's what was happening. Sales of Stowe's novel declined in these years. Fewer than ten new editions were issued between 1930 and 1959, a far smaller number than in the periods just before and just after this one. Some of these editions featured prefaces by writers who described Stowe as old-fashioned and didactic, like Raymond Weaver, who compared her unfavorably to the more ambiguous Melville, and Charles Angoff, who noted the "blemishes of craftsmanship," "preachments," and "bathos" in *Uncle Tom's Cabin*.

Such claims reflected the New Criticism, which arose in the 1930s and basically ruled university literature departments until at least the 1960s. Many of the early New Critics were conservative Southern agrarians who disparaged socially relevant, message-oriented fiction, especially when written by women or from a Northern perspective. One leading New Critic, Allen Tate, who admired antebellum fire-eaters like John C. Calhoun and George Fitzhugh, called slavery, despite its evils, "a necessary element in a stable society," since "the master and slave were forever bound by ties of association and affection that exceeded all considerations of interest." Another New Critic, John Crowe Ransom, born in Pulaski, Tennessee (recognized as the birthplace and early command center of the original Ku Klux Klan of the late 1860s), said that slavery had often been "humane in practice" and that its abolition did not effect "any great revolution in society." Small wonder, given this conservative critical climate, that the first detailed study of pre–Civil War American literature, F. O. Matthiessen's *American Renaissance* (1941), excluded sustained discussion of Stowe's novel, concentrating instead on Emerson, Thoreau, Whitman, Melville, and Hawthorne, whose works fit the priorities of thematic suggestiveness and complex artistry as defined by the New Critics.

This alleged lack of complexity in *Uncle Tom's Cabin* also struck a writer far removed from the New Critics, the novelist James Baldwin, whose 1949 article "Everybody's Protest Novel" was seemingly aimed at killing the novel once and for all. *Uncle Tom's Cabin*, Baldwin wrote, is "a very bad book," because it tried to promote a political cause and showed no "devotion to the human being, his . . . freedom which cannot be legislated, fulfillment which cannot be charted." Baldwin took the opportunity to attack as well Richard Wright's novel *Native Son*, calling it an equally misled attempt to use fiction as political propaganda. Literary art, Baldwin emphasized, was not about social protest. Its aim was to say something about "the human being . . . his beauty, dread, power."

This blinkered critique neglected the fact that *Uncle Tom's Cabin* had indeed invested blacks with beauty and power to a degree that no other pre–Civil War novel began to approach. Baldwin's piece prompted a harsh reply from Langston Hughes, who praised Stowe's novel as "a moral battle cry" that sparked the Civil War and "also happened to be a good story, exciting in incident, sharp in characterization, and threaded with humor." Hughes noted that Baldwin, who objected to using fiction for social protest, was himself a writer of the "strongest protest literature" who, ironically, adopted Stowe's technique of making political points through fiction in some of his own writings on race. "The weight of the Negro problem," Hughes wrote, "has caused him to out-Tom 'Uncle Tom's Cabin.' "

Meanwhile, the epithet "Uncle Tom" continued to be available as a weapon used by some blacks who accused others of not being sufficiently militant. Among those over the years branded as Uncle Toms were Jesse Owens, Nat King Cole, Jackie Robinson, Louis Armstrong, Willie Mays, Harry Belafonte, Floyd Patterson, and Sammy Davis Jr., to name a few.

The civil rights movement saw an endless use of the epithet. The pioneering civil rights leader Ralph Bunche, who became the first black person to win the Nobel Peace Prize, declared in 1954 that the movement's "main struggle would be with the Uncle Toms, who prefer segregation over integration." But with the rise of the Black Power movement, it was the integrationists who lay themselves open to charges of Uncle Tomism. The Black Nationalist Malcolm X, like other black leaders before him, recognized the unique power of *Uncle Tom's Cabin* and yet freely used the Uncle Tom slur. He declared that he had learned about "slavery's total horror" by reading history books and *Uncle Tom's Cabin,* which he called "the only novel I have ever read since I started serious reading." Still, he and a fellow black nationalist, the poet Leroi Jones, often labeled moderates Uncle Toms. The most common objects of their attacks were those who called for peaceful protest, including Martin Luther King Jr., NAACP leader Roy Wilkins, the pacifist Bayard Rustin, and A. Philip Randolph, a leader of the 1963 March on Washington for Jobs and Freedom. A militant speaker at a Black Power conference in Newark in 1967 declared, "A black man today is either a radical or an Uncle Tom." Some radicals also called white liberals Uncle Toms, "for they have assumed subservient Uncle Tom roles, a 'yas massa' status almost identical to that which Negro leaders scorn in their own race."

The phrase became truly feared. A number of lawsuits were filed by those who were called Uncle Toms. By 1964, it was announced that "'Uncle Tom' [was] outstripping 'N—r' as a hated term" among blacks. At times it seemed that the epithet would tear apart the whole movement for black rights. *Life* reported, "It has become increasingly difficult for a Negro leader of any recognizable stature to avoid being called an Uncle Tom." Even Malcolm X, who, as Alex Haley wrote, "'Uncle Tommed' practically every Negro leader in the nation," received the label from the Nation of Islam when he discussed with white reporters the marital infidelities of one of the Nation's leaders.

When we survey all the uses and abuses of the phrase during the civil rights period, we see that the true Uncle Tom—Stowe's Uncle Tom— in a sense won the day. Time proved that the era's most effective force for social change was the firm-principled nonviolence of protesters like Rosa Parks and Martin Luther King Jr.—that is, those who were closest in spirit to Uncle Tom as Stowe had portrayed him. Rosa Parks didn't mind the Uncle Tom label, since she believed that great change could be brought about through nonviolent moral protest. "It does not take loud talking, and lots of noise, to be free," she said. "Even the Uncle Toms who had no choice, they all helped." King, although often branded as an Uncle Tom, stuck to nonviolent protest. In doing so he created a revived respect for Stowe's character. Howard Mumford Jones in 1962 described Uncle Tom as a "splendid black Prometheus . . . whose attitude toward injustice anticipates . . . the Christianity of Dr. Martin Luther King, Jr." Another commentator wrote that Tom was "a model of character of Christian virtue" and was newly incarnated in King, whose "non-violent resistance movement against segregation in the south demonstrates the spirit of Uncle Tom." When Martin Luther King Jr. took an assassin's bullet while standing on the balcony of the Lorraine Motel in Memphis on April 4, 1968, Uncle Tom died again. And again he had opened the way to freedom.

A quiet woman who refused to give up her bus seat in Montgomery, a pacifist minister who told America about his dream of a more egalitarian nation: these are among the recognized heroes of recent history. Their form of protest was just as active as Tom's, and just as firm.

New cultural offshoots of Stowe's novel had a role in exposing historical injustice against blacks. The films *Uncle Tom's Cabin* (1965) by Géza von Radványi and *Goodbye Uncle Tom* (1972) by Gualtiero Jacopetti and Franco Prosperi dwelt on the erotic, ruthless, and perverse aspects of slavery.

Géza von Radványi's *Uncle Tom's Cabin* modernized the subversive themes of Stowe's novel to reflect the anger of black militants of the time. A Hungarian director, von Radványi had an eye on the international scene and utilized Stowe's narrative to highlight the corruption of slaveholding whites while offering sympathy for African-Americans. In the film, von Radványi follows Stowe by presenting Legree as a depraved lecher but departs from her by having St. Clare engage in a dalliance with a blond houseguest, as witnessed by Little Eva, whose death is sped by her shock over her father's transgression. Besides highlighting the unethical nature of slaveholding whites, von Radványi portrays blacks as both victims and rebels. The devilish Legree eventually shoots St. Clare and pins the murder on a black bartender, who is lynched by a white mob. Then Legree tries to kill the rebellious Cassy by unleashing a horse stampede that instead crushes the heroic Uncle Tom, who is trying to save her. Legree gets his due when enslaved blacks battle his men with guns and destroy his plantation by opening levees that flood it. A poster for the movie (retitled *Cassy* in one American release) played up von Radványi's rebellious themes by showing Legree embracing the scantily clad Cassy, flanked by angry-looking black men, with the caption: "BLACKS FOUGHT BACK WITH GUNS IN MANDINGO COUNTRY"—a message amplified in an American release of the film that added a remarkable scene in which a mob of retaliatory blacks lynch three white men.

The Italians Jacopetti and Prosperi, who had previously shocked moviegoers with their brutal film on indigenous cultures, *Mondo Cane,* in *Goodbye Uncle Tom* took Stowe's notion of the slave as the victim of sexual violation and physical torture to an extreme. Harriet Beecher Stowe appears briefly as a character in the movie, voicing her disapproval of slavery and saying, "I heard God's voice—he told me to write *Uncle Tom's Cabin.*" But the movie completely leaves out the brighter side of Stowe's vision. It uses all the devices of "mondo films" and "shockumentaries" to explore American slavery. Jacopetti and Prosperi used hundreds of Haitian extras, many of them naked, to show slaves in the 1850s being caged, force-fed, hung upside down, having their anuses stuffed with corks, and exploited sexually with callous nonchalance. The film ends in modern times with an Afro-haired black man on a Florida beach having a Nat Turner–like fantasy of butchering middle-class whites. *Goodbye Uncle Tom* accentuates the white racism that fueled the rage of twentieth-century black militants. Jacopetti and Prosperi claimed to have a serious intention of exposing the most disturbing elements of slavery, but it's hard to disagree with Pauline Kael's assessment of the directors as "perhaps the most devious filmmakers who have ever lived," and their film as "the most specific and rabid incitement of the race war."

Whatever their intention, these films, with their B-movie sensationalism, did nothing to heal the social wounds left over from the turbulent sixties and in fact appear to have been foreign efforts to smear America and its history. Mainstream America needed something to bring it together in the wake of that decade's assassinations, race riots, and sharply divergent views of race. A work equivalent in impact to *Uncle Tom's Cabin* was needed to bring home the pain, frustrations, dreams, rage, and religious hopes of American blacks. That work came in the form of Alex Haley's best-selling novel *Roots* and the TV miniseries based on it.

Alex Haley was born in 1921 in Ithaca, New York, where his father was a graduate student in agriculture at Cornell University. At six months old, Haley was taken with his mother to Henning, Tennessee, to live with his grandparents, Will and Cynthia Palmer. His father stayed at Cornell to complete graduate school before joining the family in Henning and operating the family lumber business there. During Alex's early years in Henning, his grandmother Cynthia told him stories about the family's ancestry, which reached back seven generations to West Africa. In 1929, Alex relocated with his parents and siblings when his father became a roving college professor of agriculture. But Haley often stayed summers with his grandparents in Henning. He attended a North Carolina teachers college briefly before dropping out in 1939 and joining the Coast Guard, in which he honed his writing skills by serving as a journalist and by ghostwriting love letters for fellow sailors. After retiring from the Coast Guard in 1959, Haley penned pieces for *Reader's Digest, Playboy,* and *The New York Times Magazine.* Like Harriet Beecher Stowe, he was a sensitive observer of popular culture and contemporary debates over race. For *Playboy,* he interviewed both Martin Luther King Jr. and Malcolm X.

Through his interview he came to author the searing *Autobiography of Malcolm X: As Told to Alex Haley* (1965), which sold over 6 million copies within a decade.

Obsessed with his grandmother's stories, Haley traced his genealogy. After a dozen years of research and writing, he produced *Roots: The Saga of an American Family*, which became an immediate sensation when it appeared in 1976. It sold over a million copies in its first year and earned Haley more than two hundred awards, including the National Book Award and the Pulitzer Prize. Its publisher proudly announced that *Roots* "galvanized the nation, and created an extraordinary political, racial, social, and cultural dialogue that hadn't been seen since the publication of *Uncle Tom's Cabin*." Just as far more people saw Tom plays or films than read Stowe's novel, so millions saw the eight-part, twelve-hour miniseries *Roots: The Triumph of an American Family*, which aired on ABC in 1977. Over 130 million Americans—an astonishing 85 percent of all television households—watched all or part of this moving, suspenseful series, which won nine Emmy Awards and was followed by another miniseries, *Roots: The Next Generation* (1979) and by a Christmas special, *Roots: The Gift* (1988).

Haley's reputation was somewhat tarnished when he was charged with plagiarism. In 1978, the folklorist and novelist Harold Courlander filed a suit against Haley for having borrowed from his 1967 book *The African*. Haley settled the suit by paying Courlander $650,000 and admitting publicly that some material from *The African* had made its way into *Roots*. He also revealed that he relied partly on Shirley Graham's *The Story of Phillis Wheatley* and a seventeenth-century travelogue of West Africa, *The Travels of Mungo Park*. A group of scrupulous genealogists discovered that the family history Haley had presented in *Roots* did not always square with historical records.

All of which is to say that *Roots*—despite being labeled as nonfiction— like *Uncle Tom's Cabin* before it, transformed all kinds of factual and imaginative elements into a compelling narrative that had a powerful impact on America's understanding of race. Vernon Jordan, executive director of the National Urban League, called *Roots* "the single most spectacular educational experience in race relations in America." The historian John Hope Franklin declared, "People may find areas in *Roots* that they can criticize, but it seems to me the importance of *Roots* is as a symbol of the historical development of the spirit of a family and of a race."

Indeed, *Roots* was the first popular work to dramatize the full scope of American history from a black perspective. It was the post–civil rights era's answer to conservative versions of history. Its irresistible power and drama came from its use of devices similar to those that had made *Uncle Tom's Cabin* uniquely influential.

Haley knew *Uncle Tom's Cabin* well—not just the novel but the story of its afterlife in plays and its use as a reference point in the civil rights movement. He defended Stowe's novel and its hero in a 1964 article for *The New York Times Magazine,* "Uncle Tom for Today." He pointed out that the Uncle Tom epithet that was hurled about freely by black activists was in fact a misrepresentation of Stowe's character, who, he insisted, was not a weak, yielding sellout but rather a person of dignity and quiet strength. Haley saw "deep irony" in the fact that even though *Uncle Tom's Cabin* had "helped to end the institution of slavery," now, a century after its publication, "the very name of Mrs. Stowe's hero is the worst insult the slaves' descendants can hurl at one another out of their frustrations in seeking what all other Americans take for granted."

In *Roots,* Haley used Stowe's technique of humanizing and personalizing the experience of slavery by giving us sharply rendered characters we pity, admire, and with whom we laugh and cry. First among Haley's engaging black characters is Kunta Kinte, the fiercely proud Mandinka tribesman born in Gambia, West Africa, in 1750, captured at seventeen by white slave-traders, shipped on the nightmarish Middle Passage, and sold into slavery in America. In Virginia, Kunta befriends a musically gifted slave known as the Fiddler and is married to a spirited cook, Bell. Then come other intriguing members along the family line: Kunta and Bell's daughter Kizzy, who develops into an intelligent, literate woman; Kizzy's ambitious, lively son Chicken George, an expert gamecock trainer;

and George's son Tom Murray, the enterprising blacksmith who carries forward the family spirit of pride and determination into the Reconstruction period.

Like Stowe, Haley channels even the most militant positions on racial politics into middle-class values associated with domesticity. In effect, he retakes the home, which had long been occupied by the conservative Dixon/Griffith forces, and fills it with successive generations of an appealing black family. As Stowe uses domesticity to demonstrate that blacks are people, not things, Haley renders in great detail the familial relations of his ur-hero, Kunta Kinte. Here is where *Roots* differs most notably from writings such as Courlander's *The African* or films like *Goodbye Uncle Tom* or the hit movie *Mandingo*. In those works, the home and family are mentioned only in passing or, in the case of the films, described as an arena of depravity and racist exploitation. In *Roots,* as in *Uncle Tom's Cabin,* the home remains a constant haven of virtue that forwards a progressive political point. Haley devotes no less than thirty-two chapters to describing the young Kunta's respectful, loving relationships with his family in Gambia. Haley showed that African culture, contrary to the popular view of it as savage and primitive, was religious, mannerly, and ceremoniously formal.

By creating an aura of domestic virtue around Kunta, Haley is free to make radical pronouncements on race and religion without alienating middle-class readers. Malcolm X had told Haley in the *Playboy* interview that white people were murderous devils who deserved to die and whose Christian faith was the despicable foe of the only true religion, Islam. Given the long history of cruelty inflicted on blacks by whites, Malcolm added, American blacks must form a separate civilization of their own. Martin Luther King Jr., in his interview with Haley, had presented the opposite perspective. Dismissing Malcolm X and his violent Muslim cohorts, the Reverend King told Haley that violence would do no good for American blacks, who must use nonviolent, Christian tactics to gain equal rights in America.

Through his portrait of Kunta Kinte, Haley is able to voice the anti-

Christian, anti-white, black-separatist fury of Malcolm X while ending up with a Christian, integrationist vision similar to that of Martin Luther King Jr. As a fully realized character devoted to his family heritage, Kunta can express all the rebelliousness and violence of black Muslims while still seeming heroic to the American reader. Haley gains artistic latitude as well, since he can describe all the gruesomeness of slavery without tumbling into the kind of gratuitous sensationalism that compromises the antislavery message of *Goodbye Uncle Tom*. Kunta, snatched by venal whites from his African world of domesticity and ritual, is thrust into the chaotic, suffocating hold of an American-bound slave ship, where he is chained in darkness with scores of other naked Africans amidst rats, lice, disease, vomit, sweat, and excrement. The blacks chant about killing whites, and they launch a futile slave revolt. Kunta's loathing of whites continues through the early period of his enslavement in Virginia, when he attempts to escape four times. Slave-chasers with dogs catch him each time and finally chop off part of his foot. At this point, his identity is as the Mandinkan warrior who prays to Allah and doesn't forget his roots.

But eventually Kunta reconciles himself to his lot. He becomes more and more like Stowe's Uncle Tom. Kunta at first views his Christian wife, Bell, as an infidel, but he accedes to her request that their daughter Kizzy be baptized at a camp meeting. No longer bitter and rebellious, Kunta gives up thoughts of escape and becomes, like Tom, the trusted carriage-driver for a good master. Also like Tom, Kunta is known for his sobriety and his dignified presence. He even has an integrationist epiphany. At a holiday celebration attended by both slaves and their masters, he reflects that "in some strong, strange, and very deep way, the blacks and the tou-bob [whites] had some *need* for each other." He witnesses integration in action when Kizzy bonds with Missy Anne, the daughter of a nearby plantation owner. Flaxen-haired, cheerful, and pious, Missy Anne is the Little Eva of *Roots*. Like Stowe's character, she represents a child's radically democratic capacity to form a tender relationship with people of a different race.

The marriage of the Muslim Kunta and the Christian Bell and the friendship between the black Kizzy and the white Missy Anne are the first in a long series of events in *Roots* that carry the family narrative through the Civil War and beyond. Since all of Kunta's descendants are under the halo of domesticity and family loyalty, they too remain figures of virtue and dignity even in the most humiliating circumstances. Kizzy, for example, is used as a sex slave by her master, Tom Moore. But far from enjoying "pleasuring" her master as do the enslaved women in *Goodbye Uncle Tom,* she stoically endures her master's repeated assaults, while remaining deeply devoted to her family heritage and, later, to her son George.

Over time, the family learns to live with whites and, in some cases, love them. During the Civil War, Tom Murray gives food to a starving white vagrant, George Johnson, who is so grateful that he becomes close to the black family and eventually lives in their community along with his wife Martha. The family reaches a kind of integrationist haven in Henning, Tennessee, where eventually a group of white businessmen award the presidency of a large lumber company to another of Kunta's descendants, Will Palmer, destined to be the grandfather of Alex Haley. The family remains devoutly Christian and in fact helps build the New Hope Colored Methodist Episcopal Church in Henning.

Although Haley's novel is close in spirit to *Uncle Tom's Cabin,* with which it comes to share an integrationist, Christian perspective, the *Roots* miniseries is closer yet. As pronounced as the domestic theme is in Haley's novel, it is even more so in the film. Homes are central in virtually every scene in the miniseries: Kunta's childhood home in Gambia; the hut his father builds him after he passes the manhood ritual; the cabin in which Kunta and Bell live and raise Kizzy; and the many other homes inhabited by the successive generations. Home is portrayed as the place where blacks share pain, love, and dreams. As in Stowe, these homes are repeatedly violated by white people. The most striking instance of this is when Kizzy's lascivious master, Tom Moore, enters her cabin the night before her planned wedding to a black man and rapes her.

Haley's novel, with its distinctly black perspective, did not focus long

Domesticity in Africa—Kunta Kinte with his mother and baby brother in
Roots *(1977 ABC miniseries)*

on wicked white characters. The miniseries took a different tack. Besides showing a range of sympathetic black characters—their attractiveness bolstered by their being played by well-known black actors like Cicely Tyson, Leslie Uggams, Ben Vereen, and Louis Gossett Jr.—the film followed Stowe in its portrayal of whites. Just as she included a range of white characters, from the kindly Shelbys to the violent Legree, so the miniseries featured some well-intentioned whites, such as a conscience-stricken slave-ship captain and a kindly plantation owner, along with a gallery of unrepentant racists, several of them sadists. Among the white actors who played proslavery roles in the miniseries were Chuck Connors of *The Rifleman* fame; Lloyd Bridges, the iconic hero of *Sea Hunt;* Lorne Greene, who had played the patriarch of a Western family in *Bonanza;* Ed Asner, of the comedy series *The Mary Tyler Moore Show;* Robert Reed, the father in *The Brady Bunch;* Burl Ives, the affable folk singer; and George Hamilton, the eternally tanned, grinning Hollywood star.

In previous roles, these performers had been prominent vehicles of pop-culture fun, adventure, or romance—and, by implication, political complacency. By taking on parts in *Roots* that were often racist and cruel, they became part of a massive mea culpa for the American entertainment industry, which in effect was using *Roots* to apologize for the politically irresponsible pabulum it had been serving the American public for decades. In its effort to chastise whites for their past injustices, the miniseries, unlike the novel, portrays the harsh side of Reconstruction. In his novel, Haley had sent Tom Murray's family on its trek to Tennessee to pursue the American Dream not long after the Civil War. In the miniseries, the family remains in place long enough to face persecution by the Ku Klux Klan, who, in a nighttime raid, destroy the village where Tom and other blacks are living. The Klan later returns, ties Tom to a tree, and whips him savagely.

This scene suggests that producers of the miniseries couldn't resist replying to Griffith's memorable paean to the Klan. Indeed, *Roots* can be said to have made a resounding challenge to the distorted image of history that had begun in earnest with *The Birth of a Nation* (derived from Dixon's anti-Stowe fiction) and had gained impetus with *Gone with the Wind* and the Dunning historians. Several contemporary reviewers of *Roots* predicted that the miniseries would bring about a sea change in opinions on race and the American past. *The Washington Post* called *Roots* "a stunning passage in the mass culture of America. . . . It trampled the old mythology into the dust, relentlessly tore it up." A number of commentators described *Roots* as the *Uncle Tom's Cabin* of modern times. Just as "Tom mania" had swept the nation after the publication of Stowe's novel, so *Roots* set off nationwide discussions of race. As one African-American paper reported, "A galloping, enveloping and compelling longing for and discussion of Alex Haley's extraordinary 'Roots' has come about as a result of the recent 12-hour serialization. Families that have not communicated in the past . . . were talking to each other again. In short, from coast to coast a 'Rootsmania' or fixation engulfed the American people."

Roots not only sparked a genealogy craze that has lasted to this day but also opened the way for new adaptations of *Uncle Tom's Cabin* in which blacks and others are portrayed with sympathy and candor. The

1987 made-for-TV Showtime version of *Uncle Tom's Cabin,* as Patricia Turner points out, removes Tom from racial stereotypes while sending an integrationist message by tailoring him for the white audience. Bill T. Jones' dance-theater piece *Last Supper at Uncle Tom's Cabin/The Promised Land* (1990) draws from both Stowe's novel and Aiken's play to explore African-American history and Jones' life as a gay, black artist. Robert Alexander's often-performed Afrocentric play *I Ain't Yo' Uncle: The New Jack Revisionist Uncle Tom's Cabin* (1991) makes resonant connections between Stowe's narrative and contemporary black experience while rejecting some stereotypes the Tom plays had spread. Alexander also makes a Haley-like distinction between nonviolence and aggressive protest, linking Tom with the former and George Harris with the latter. Topsy comes alive as a street-savvy yet desperate urban woman who chants about her wickedness to a rap beat. Like Haley's Kunta Kinte with his children, Alexander's Uncle Tom lectures Topsy on her African roots.

Another trenchant reworking of Stowe's characters came in *Uncle Tom's Cabin; or, The Preservation of Favoured Races in the Struggle for Life* by Floraine Kay and Randolph Curtis Rand, first staged by The Drama Department in New York in 1997 and revived over the years in other cities. Incorporating images from African tribal ritual, Japanese Noh drama, minstrel shows, slave narratives, and melodrama, this talky but provocative play also connects Tom directly to Martin Luther King Jr. and includes words from prominent figures such as George Sand, W. E. B. Du Bois and Henry Louis Gates Jr. A revised version of this play, performed at the Cleveland Theatre in 2004, had its five main characters appear in black, Mao-like costumes and showed Uncle Tom crossing a picket line, yielding a pun about "Uncle Tom scabbin'." The contributions of Stowe's novel to the early twentieth-century Communist revolution in China was celebrated in 2007 at the Beijing International Theater Festival by a revival of Zeng Xiaogu's revolutionary 1907 play *Heinu yutian lu* (*Black Slave's Cry to Heaven*), based on Stowe's novel.

Roots was also followed by a number of films featuring sympathetic, realistic depictions of blacks in nurturing roles. There arose a phenomenon that has been called "Tomming," whereby white characters receive comfort, counsel, friendship, or healing from blacks, sometimes accompanied by imagery from Stowe's novel. Several films—among them *Driving Miss Daisy* (1989), *The Shawshank Redemption* (1994), *The Green Mile* (1999), *The Legend of Bagger Vance* (2000), *Save the Last Dance* (2001), and *Far from Heaven* (2002)—feature such strong, supportive black characters. These characters are not stereotypical Uncle Toms but have gifts or depths of humanity that in fact make them valuable assets for their white friends.

The frankness and often compassion characterizing the portrayal of blacks in the media has been accompanied by a remarkable resuscitation of Stowe's novel. The civil rights movement and the rise of cultural studies have made *Uncle Tom's Cabin* one of the must-reads of American literature. A forty-year slowdown in reprintings of the novel ended in 1960; at least half a dozen new editions per decade appeared in English between 1960 and 2000, and more than a score of new editions have greeted the new millennium. The number of foreign translations is also impressive. That number reached sixty-eight by 1995, ranging from Arabic and Armenian through Persian and Polish to Vietnamese; as of this writing, more translations are appearing every year—and, in numerous cases, there are many different translations in the same language.

While regaining stature globally, *Uncle Tom's Cabin* and its author are breeding ever-intensifying interest and discussion. If the New Critics found the novel lacking in the qualities they valued—paradox, ambiguity, organic unity—more recent readers, tapping interdisciplinary approaches that have burgeoned over the past several decades, have shown that the novel is uniquely rich in its treatment of socially charged themes like gender, sex, race, religion, and ethics.

The derogatory Uncle Tom epithet survives but now rings hollow, because Stowe's actual, original Uncle Tom is being understood even as African-American contributions to society are increasingly recognized. Many blacks once labeled Uncle Toms, such as Jackie Robinson, Willie Mays, and Louis Armstrong, are today widely viewed as pioneers who broke racial barriers. We may hope for a time when America is, in President Barack Obama's phrase, "beyond race," when we can erase the negative usage of Uncle Tom because it is inapplicable to social reality.

On the night before he was murdered, Martin Luther King Jr. declared that he envisioned a Promised Land of racial equality for the nation. That dream can come true only if Americans imbibe the spirit of interracial sympathy and true democratic justice that Reverend King died for—the very spirit that Harriet Beecher Stowe's two great fictional martyrs, the black Uncle Tom and the white Eva, had ushered into the world.

Abbreviations

B Birdoff, Harry. *The Worlds's Greatest Hit: "Uncle Tom's Cabin."* New York: S. F. Vanni, 1947.

BAR Reynolds, David S. *Beneath the American Renaissance: The Subversive Imagination in the Age of Emerson and Melville.* New York: Alfred A. Knopf, 1988.

Ch Stowe, Charles Edward. *Life of Harriet Beecher Stowe Compiled from Her Letters and Journal.* Boston, Mass.: Houghton, Mifflin, 1889.

F Fields, Annie. *Life and Letters of Harriet Beecher Stowe.* Boston, Mass.: Houghton, Mifflin, 1897.

FiF Reynolds, David S. *Faith in Fiction: The Emergence of Religious Literature in America.* Cambridge, Mass.: Harvard University Press, 1981.

G Gossett, Thomas F. *Uncle Tom's Cabin and American Culture.* Dallas, Tex.: Southern Methodist University Press, 1985.

H Hedrick, Joan D. *Harriet Beecher Stowe: A Life.* New York: Oxford University Press, 1994.

HBS Harriet Beecher Stowe.

HWB Beecher, William Constantine, Samuel Scoville, and Mrs. Henry Ward Beecher. *A Biography of Rev. Henry Ward Beecher.* New York: Charles L. Webster, 1888.

K E. Bruce Kirkham Collection at the Harriet Beecher Stowe Center Library, Hartford, Conn.

Key Stowe, Harriet Beecher. *The Key to Uncle Tom's Cabin; Presenting the Original Facts and Documents Upon Which the Story is Founded. Together with Corroborative Statements Verifying the Truth of the Work.* London: Clarke, Beeton, 1853.

LB *Autobiography, Correspondence, etc., of Lyman Beecher, D.D.* Edited by Charles Beecher. Vol. 1: 1863; repr., New York: Harper & Brothers, 1864; vol. 2: 1863; repr., New York: Harper & Brothers, 1865.

M Stowe, Harriet Beecher. *Men of Our Times; or, Leading Patriots of the Day.* Hartford, Conn.: Hartford Publishing Co., 1868.

MW Stowe, Harriet Beecher. *The Minister's Wooing*. 1859; repr., Boston, Mass.: Houghton, Mifflin, 1881.

NAL *The Norton Anthology of American Literature*. 7th ed. Edited by Nina Baym et al. Vols. A and B. New York: W. W. Norton, 2007.

OF Stowe, Harriet Beecher. *Oldtown Folks*. Boston, Mass.: Houghton, Mifflin, 1869.

SD *The Stowe Debate: Rhetorical Strategies in Uncle Tom's Cabin*. Edited by Mason I. Lowance Jr., Ellen E. Westbrook, and R. C. Prospo. Amherst: University of Massachusetts Press, 1994.

TS *Transatlantic Stowe: Harriet Beecher Stowe and European Culture*. Edited by Denise Kohn, Sarah Meer, and Emily B. Todd. Iowa City: University of Iowa Press, 2006.

UTC Stowe, Harriet Beecher. *Uncle Tom's Cabin; or, Life Among the Lowly*. Edited by Elizabeth Ammons. 1852; repr., New York: W. W. Norton, 1994. Unless otherwise noted, page citations in the notes are from this Norton Critical Edition of Stowe's novel.

UVA *Uncle Tom's Cabin & American Culture: A Multi-Media Archive*. Directed by Stephen Railton, Department of English, University of Virginia. At http://utc.iath .virginia.edu/.

W Wilson, Forrest. *Crusader in Crinoline: The Life of Harriet Beecher Stowe*. Philadelphia, Pa.: J. B. Lippincott, 1941.

NOTES

INTRODUCTION

ix On January 1, 1863 ... graying curls: For descriptions of the Music Hall concert, see *The Liberator,* January 9, 1863; H, 306; and W, 487.

ix "Everybody I meet": K, letter from HBS to Charles Sumner, December 13, 1862.

x "Is this the little woman": Lincoln's remark, which he reportedly made when Stowe met with him on December 2, 1862, was first mentioned in 1896, the year of her death, in an article by her friend Annie Fields ("Days with Mrs. Stowe," *Atlantic Monthly: A Magazine of Literature, Science, Art, and Politics* 78 [August 1896]: 148, where Lincoln is quoted as having used the words "the great war"). The next year, Fields reprinted the greeting—changing the president's words to "this great war"—in her biography *Life and Letters of Harriet Beecher Stowe* (F, 269). Twenty-two years later, Charles Edward Stowe, in a revised version of his 1889 biography of his mother, wrote that Lincoln's words were "So you're the little woman who wrote the book that made this great war!" (Charles Edward Stowe and Lyman Beecher Stowe, *Harriet Beecher Stowe: The Story of Her Life* [Boston, Mass.: Houghton, Mifflin, 1911], 199). Daniel R. Vollaro discusses the alleged remark at length in "Lincoln, Stowe, and the 'Little Woman/Great War' Story: The Making, and Breaking, of a Great American Anecdote," *Journal of the Abraham Lincoln Association* (Winter 2009); at http://www.historycooperative.org/journals/jala/30.1/vollaro.html #FOOT54.

x "its political effect": This assessment by Thomas Gossett is in G, 182.

x "sentiment limited": Richard Yarborough, "Strategies of Black Characterization in *Uncle Tom's Cabin* and the Early Afro-American Novel," in *New Essays on Uncle Tom's Cabin,* edited by Eric J. Sundquist (New York: Cambridge University Press, 1986), 63.

x "In what sense": John William Ward, afterword to Stowe's *Uncle Tom's Cabin* (New York: Signet, 1966), 480. Similarly, the historian Dwight L. Dumond dismisses as "absurd" the idea that the novel brought on the war (Dumond, foreword to Stowe's *Uncle Tom's Cabin* [New York: Collier, 1962], 10). See Claire Parfait, *The Publishing History of* Uncle Tom's Cabin, *1852–2002* (Hampshire, UK: Ashgate, 2007), 186. For an opposing view, see David Grant, "*Uncle Tom's Cabin* and the Triumph of Republican Rhetoric," *New England Quarterly* 71 (Sept. 1998): 429–48, and Vivian Gornick's piece on an Oxford University Press reissue of *Uncle Tom's Cabin* in the *Los Angeles Times,* December 15, 2002.

x public opinion ... which Tocqueville regarded as: See Leo Damrosch, *Tocqueville's Discovery of America* (New York: Farrar, Straus & Giroux, 2010), 106–7.

x "Our government": A. Lincoln, speech at a Republican banquet, Chicago, Illinois, December 10, 1856, in *Collected Works of Abraham Lincoln*, edited by Roy P. Basler (New Brunswick, N.J.: Rutgers University Press, 1953), 2:385.

x "Public sentiment": Abraham Lincoln, The First Joint Debate at Ottawa, August 21, 1858, in *The Lincoln-Douglas Debates: The First Complete, Unexpurgated Text*, edited by Harold Holzer (New York: Fordham University Press, 2004), 75.

xi "more an event": *National Era*, February 25, 1853.

xi "for an immense number of people": H. James, *A Small Boy and Others* (New York: Charles Scribner's Sons, 1913), 159.

xi Recent decades have witnessed: A good number of recent secondary works on Stowe's novel are discussed throughout this book, especially in the notes. The major recent biography is Joan Hedrick's *Harriet Beecher Stowe: A Life*. For rare primary materials, see especially the UVA website.

xii Other writers of the day ... ambiguous symbols: See my discussion of these and other writers in *BAR* and *Walt Whitman's America: A Cultural Biography* (New York: Alfred A. Knopf, 1995).

xii "had given birth": Joseph Hodgson, *The Cradle of the Confederacy; or, The Times of Troup, Quitman, and Yancey* (Mobile, Ala.: n.p., 1876), 341.

xiii "A little Yankee woman": T. Dixon Jr., *The Leopard's Spots: A Romance of the White Man's Burden, 1865–1900* (1902; repr., New York: A. Wessels, 1908), 264.

xiii "In the four quarters": *The Edinburgh Review*, January 1820.

xiii "Dear soul": G, 96.

1. The Gospel According to Stowe

3 "Oh, I'm sorry": *LB*, 1:529. The quotation in the next sentence is on p. 118.

3 "had more influence in moulding": F, 12.

3 "no devout Catholic": Joseph Howard Jr., *Life of Henry Ward Beecher* (Philadelphia, Pa.: Hubbard Brothers, 1887), 33.

5 "Harriet is a great genius": Letter from Lyman Beecher to George Foote, January 24, 1819, quoted in H, 29–30. Biographical sections of the current chapter are informed especially by Joan Hedrick's excellent life of Stowe.

5 "What wonderful stories those!": Ch, 10.

5 "The heroic element": Ch, 11.

5 "heroic element" ... "true Puritan seed": HBS, *Poganuc People: Their Lives and Loves* (New York: Fords, Howard, & Hulbert, 1878), 199; and *MW*, 343.

6 Her stance invites us ... promise of America: This argument is most extensively advanced by Sacvan Bercovitch in his books *The Puritan Origins of the American Self* (New Haven, Conn.: Yale University Press, 1974), *The American Jeremiad* (Madison: University of Wisconsin Press, 1978), and *The Rites of Assent: Transformation in the Symbol Construction of America* (New York: Routledge, 1993).

6 Actually, Puritanism in the North ... social ills: I discuss the relation between Puritanism and social reform at length in *John Brown, Abolitionist: The Man Who Killed Slavery*,

Sparked the Civil War, and Seeded Civil Rights (New York: Alfred A. Knopf, 2005); see especially chap. 2.

6 "fertile forms of antinomianism": Ralph Waldo Emerson, *Essays and Lectures* (New York: Library of America, 1983), 592.

6 "Puritanism and nothing else": *New Englander and Yale Review* 4 (July 1846): 308.

7 "I have been steeped": *LB*, 2:389.

7 "The wrath of God": *NAL*, A:427.

7 "When the theology": *LB*, 2:389.

8 "There were days and weeks": *HWB*, 604.

8 "On one memorable day": *HWB*, 605.

9 Henry became . . . optimistic preaching: Debby Applegate, *The Most Famous Man in America: The Biography of Henry Ward Beecher* (New York: Doubleday, 2006).

9 "shrieks and wailings": *MW,* 337. The quotation in the next paragraph is on pp. 87–88.

9 "There is a ladder": *MW,* 66.

9 "Behold, I call you": F, 50. The next two quotations are on pp. 52 and 53, respectively.

10 "Harriet, do you feel": Quoted in Ch, 36.

10 "Do not think of God": K, letter from HBS to Elizabeth Phoenix, December 23, 1828.

10 "My whole life": F, 53.

11 "rationalistic methods": *OF,* 263.

11 In an 1830 letter: *LB,* 2:238.

11 "involuntary fear": K, letter from HBS to Thomas Kinnicut Beecher, June 2, 1845.

11 "colorless, all-color": Herman Melville, *Moby-Dick; or, The Whale* (1851; repr., New York: W. W. Norton, 1967), 169.

11 "Who knows anything" . . . "no more Eva": *UTC,* 262. The next quotation in this paragraph is on p. 418.

12 "pretty much made up his mind": *The English Notebooks,* in *The Centenary Edition of the Works of Nathaniel Hawthorne,* edited by William Charvat et al. (Columbus: Ohio State University Press, 1962), 2:163.

12 "In America feelings": Ch, 78–79.

13 Walt Whitman noted . . . union and love: W. Whitman, *Prose Works, 1892,* edited by Floyd Stovall (New York: New York University Press, 1964), 2:514.

13 "I was made": Quoted in H, 64.

13 Her father and brothers . . . American sermons: See David S. Reynolds, "From Doctrine to Narrative: The Rise of Pulpit Storytelling in America," *American Quarterly* 32 (Winter 1980): 479–98.

13 In Brooklyn's Plymouth Church . . . common life: See John Henry Barrows, *Henry Ward Beecher: The Shakespeare of the Pulpit* (New York: Funk & Wagnalls, 1893), 503.

14 "secret, innate horror": Ch, 17.

14 "outrageous style": Ch, 69. The quotation in the next sentence is also on p. 69.

15 "generally employed": *Western Monthly Magazine* 1 (March 1833): 121.

15 "a little introductory breeze": *Western Monthly Magazine* 3 (April 1834): 169.

16 The angelic and heavenly images . . . overlooked: My discussion of popular religious literature in the following pages derives in part from my research into such writings

for *FiF* and *BAR,* chap. 1. For discussions of Stowe and Calvinism, see especially Charles H. Foster, *The Rungless Ladder* (Durham, N.C.: Duke University Press, 1954); Lawrence Buell, "Calvinism Romanticized: Harriet Beecher Stowe, Samuel Hopkins, and *The Minister's Wooing," ESQ: A Journal of the American Renaissance* 24 (1978): 119–32; and Peter J. Theusen, "Geneva's Crystalline Clarity: Harriet Beecher Stowe and Max Weber on Calvinism and the American Character," in *John Calvin's American Heritage,* edited by Peter J. Davis (New York: Oxford University Press, 2010), 219–38. Thomas J. Davis explores anti-Calvinism in Catharine Sedgwick, Lydia Maria Child, and Sylvester Judd in "Rhetorical War and Reflex: Calvinism in Nineteenth-Century Popular Literature," *Calvin Theological Journal* 33 (1998): 443–56.

16 "all imaginary sights"... "the pretended": From *A Treatise Concerning Religious Affections* (1746), edited by Russell B. Nye and Norman S. Grabo (Boston, Mass.: Houghton Mifflin, 1965), 1:413, 414.

16 If Calvinism ... vistas of heaven: *FiF,* chaps. 1 and 2.

17 "visionary ladder"... "language of": E. Hitchcock, *Memoirs of the Bloomsgrove Family* (Boston, Mass.: Thomas and Andrews, 1790), 1:74–75.

17 Other novelists ... visions of friends: *FiF,* 46–47.

17 "an angel on earth"... "You need not hide": C. M. Sedgwick, *A New-England Tale* (1822; repr., New York: George P. Putnam, 1852), 102, 138.

17 "an angelic influence": L. M. Child, *The Rebels; or, Boston Before the Revolution* (1825; repr., Boston, Mass.: Phillips, Sampson, 1850), 254.

17 "mythic and allegorical being"... "some bright angel": *UTC,* 126, 245.

18 In an autobiographical ... air around him: For a detailed account of Calvin's visions, see Ch, 423–38.

19 "I always lived": HBS, *Oldtime Fireside Stories* (Boston, Mass.: James R. Osgood, 1871), 191.

19 she became interested in spiritualism ... Kate Fox: See her discussion of Fox and spiritualism in K, letter from HBS to Mary Ann Evans Lewes (George Eliot), February 8, 1872.

19 "mountebank tricks": F, 309.

19 "friends here": Charles Beecher presents HBS's conversation with Brontë's spirit in *Spiritual Manifestations* (Boston, Mass.: Lee and Shepard, 1879), 25–26.

19 "I fell in love": Quoted in W, 120.

21 "I am but a mere drudge": Letter from HBS to Georgiana May, June 21, 1838, in Ch, 92.

21 "a dark, sloppy, rainy": K, letter from HBS to Calvin Ellis Stowe, June 16, 1845. The quotation in the next sentence is in K, letter from HBS to Georgiana (May) Sykes, January 1849.

21 "How lovely": K, letter from HBS to Sarah Buckingham Beecher, before April 15, 1843.

21 "Holy, holy, holy": *New-York Evangelist* 14 (June 8, 1843): 1.

21 The Beecher family ... religious perfection: H, 150–51.

22 "The sudden death": K, letter from HBS to Thomas Kinnicut Beecher, June 2, 1845.

22 "Even now he is": K, letter from HBS to Henry Ward, Charles, and James Beecher,

July 4, 1843. The quotation in the next sentence is in K, letter from HBS to Catharine Beecher and Sarah Buckingham Beecher, July 6, 1843.

22 "haunted and pursued" . . . "some vision": K, letter from HBS to Thomas Kinnicut Beecher, June 2, 1845. The quotation in the next paragraph is also from this letter.

23 "always living on the borders" and subsequent quotations in this paragraph: HBS, "Old Testament Pictures—No. 1," *New-York Evangelist* 15 (November 14, 1844): 1.

23 "Through the light that dazzles": HBS, "Love and Fear," *New-York Evangelist* 15 (December 5, 1844): 196.

23 By the late 1840s . . . their relatives: See, for example, her essay "On the Ministration of Departed Spirits in the World," *New-York Evangelist* 20 (January 25, 1849): 1.

23 "I cannot think that Henry": Ch, 350–51.

23 Actually, Calvin's problem . . . into his life: See K, letter from HBS to Calvin Ellis Stowe, before May 24, 1844.

24 "I am depressed": K, letter from HBS to Calvin Ellis Stowe, May 23–27, 1844.

26 "the monstrous doctrine": *Christian Examiner and Theological Review* 5 (May–June 1828): 229.

26 "stale yeast": Quoted in Marie Caskey, *Chariot of Fire: Religion and the Beecher Family* (New Haven, Conn.: Yale University Press, 1978), 379; H. W. Beecher, "The Study of Human Nature," in *American Protestant Thought in the Liberal Era,* edited by William R. Hutchison (Lanham, Md.: University Press of America, 1968), 42–43.

26 Perfectionism, the belief . . . Christian Science: See Douglas M. Strong, *Perfectionist Politics: Abolitionism and the Religious Tensions of American Democracy* (Syracuse, N.Y.: Syracuse University Press, 1999), chap. 1.

26 Postmillennialism posited . . . harmony and justice: For useful discussions of HBS's postmillennial views, see Helen Petter, "Confronting Antichrist," and Mason I. Lowance Jr., "Biblical Typology and the Allegorical Mode," in *SD,* 141–84.

27 Harriet desperately . . . Oberlin paper: HBS, "The Interior Life; or, Primitive Christian Experience," *New-York Evangelist* 16 (June 19, 1845): 1.

27 "Well, we have five": K, letter from HBS to Calvin Ellis Stowe, July 19, 1844.

28 "as a sign of him who" . . . "Wouldst thou know": *New-York Evangelist* 17 (January 15, 1846): 1.

28 "I am happier now": *The Youth's Companion* 17 (November 28, 1843): 103.

28 "My Charley": K, letter from HBS to Calvin Ellis Stowe, July 26, 1849.

29 "one more great lesson" . . . "Poor Charley's dying cries": K, letter from HBS to Delia Bacon, after July 29, 1849.

29 "The Bible as Comforter" . . . Jesus was poor too: *New-York Evangelist* 16 (September 9, 1842): 70.

29 The Bible . . . read it often: *New-York Evangelist* 15 (November 14, 1844): 1.

29 What was needed . . . more vivid: HBS, preface to Charles Beecher, *The Incarnation; or, Pictures of the Virgin and Her Son* (New York: Harper, 1849), iii.

30 "Should I be well pleased": *Episcopal Recorder* 23 (September 27, 1845): 109.

30 "It is my blood": *New-York Evangelist* 19 (December 28, 1848): 1.

30 "old faiths": C. M. Sedgwick, *Redwood: A Tale* (1824; repr., New York: George P. Putnam, 1850), xv.

31 "Papal Rome is an enchantress!": F, 230.

31 She later followed . . . Protestant could be: John Gatta illuminates this topic in "The
    Anglican Aspect of Harriet Beecher Stowe," *New England Quarterly* 73 (September
    2000): 412–23.

31 "I wish to my heart": *OF,* 816.

31 In *Uncle Tom's Cabin* . . . an aestheticism that reflected Catholic ritual: For sacramental
    religious images in *UTC,* see especially Michael T. Gilmore, "*Uncle Tom's Cabin* and the
    American Renaissance: The Sacramental Aesthetic of Harriet Beecher Stowe," in *The
    Cambridge Companion to Harriet Beecher Stowe,* edited by Cindy Weinstein (New York:
    Cambridge University Press, 2004), chap. 3.

31 "as the Italian sailor": *UTC,* 224. The subsequent quotations in this paragraph are on
    pp. 247 (two) and 195, respectively.

32 "The Pope having read": *Boston Traveller,* quoted in *The New York Times,* January 13,
    1859; UVA. Some of the articles in *TS* touch on Stowe's relation to Catholicism.

32 "insidious, all-pervading": *New-York Evangelist* 17 (February 5, 1846): 1.

32 "They believe that [the pope]": Quoted in Tracy Fessenden, *Culture and Redemption:
    Religion, the Secular, and American Literature* (Princeton, N.J.: Princeton University
    Press, 2007), 121.

33 "a sort of patriarch": *UTC,* 26.

33 "American Republicanism": Quoted in Fessenden, *Culture and Redemption,* 128.

33 "a stab at the freedom": Charles Beecher, *The Duty of Disobedience to Wicked Laws: A
    Sermon on the Fugitive Slave Law* (Newark N.J.: J. McIlvaine, 1851), 13.

33 "blown into her mind": Ch, 149. The quotation in the next paragraph is also on the
    same page.

33 "It all came before me": G, 96.

35 Even more relevant to Harriet: For a discussion of religious seers of the era, see David S.
    Reynolds, *Waking Giant: America in the Age of Jackson* (New York: HarperCollins, 2008),
    chap. 4.

35 Although Walt Whitman . . . probably did not: The idea that Whitman's poetry was
    rooted in a mystical awakening, supposedly described in section 5 of "Song of Myself,"
    was first proposed by Richard Maurice in his book *Cosmic Consciousness* (1901); see the
    discussion of Whitman and visionary experiences in Reynolds, *Walt Whitman's America,*
    262–68, and Jerome Loving, *Walt Whitman: Song of Himself* (Berkeley: University of
    California Press, 1999), 175.

36 "spirits bright": *UTC,* 227. The subsequent quotations in this paragraph are on pp. 255
    and 257, respectively.

36 "the mind back": *UTC,* 141. The subsequent quotation in this paragraph is also on p.
    141.

37 "a vision rose before him": *UTC,* 339.

37 The Christ connection . . . cross-shaped post: Jo-Ann Morgan provides a useful analy-
    sis of religious pictures in illustrated editions in *Uncle Tom's Cabin as Visual Culture*
    (Columbia: University of Missouri Press, 2007). For an example of Tom's arms tied in
    a cross-like position, see the photographs of William A. Brady's 1901 "revival" of the
    "Tom Show" in UVA.

37 "clar 'cross Jordan": *UTC,* 62. The quotation in the next sentence is also on p. 62. The quotations at the end of the paragraph are on p. 25.

38 "The sweeter graces": A. Kinmont, *Twelve Lectures on the Natural History of Man* (Cincinnati, Ohio: U. P. James, 1839), 218. The next quotation in this paragraph is on p. 192. Josephine Donovan points out that Kinmont, a Swedenborgian, espoused religious and racial views that influenced Stowe; see J. Donovan, "A Source for Stowe's Ideas on Race in *Uncle Tom's Cabin,*" *NWSA Journal* 7 (1995): 24–34.

38 "the hard and dominant": *UTC,* xiii. Among the critical discussions of Stowe's racial views, an especially useful one is Samuel Otter, "Stowe and Race," in *The Cambridge Companion to Harriet Beecher Stowe,* chap. 1.

38 "hymns and expressions": *UTC,* 25. The subsequent quotations in this paragraph are on pp. 455 and 141, respectively.

38 "the highest form": *UTC,* 155–56.

39 "the brain of the Negro": Quoted in Louis Menand, *The Metaphysical Club* (New York: Farrar, Straus & Giroux, 2001), 109.

39 "We can make nothing": Quoted in David S. Smiley, *Lion of White Hall: The Life of Cassius M. Clay* (Madison: University of Wisconsin Press, 1962), 56.

39 "I am not nor ever have been": *The Lincoln–Douglas Debates,* edited by Harold Holzer, 189.

39 "The nigger": Horace Traubel, *With Walt Whitman in Camden* (1907; repr., New York: Rowman and Littlefield, 1961), 2:283.

39 Recent critics . . . "feminized": See especially Ann Douglas, *The Feminization of American Culture* (New York: Alfred A. Knopf, 1977).

39 "degrading man": Quoted in Elizabeth P. Peabody, *Reminiscences of Rev. William Ellery Channing* (Boston, Mass.: Roberts Bros., 1880), 30, 195.

39 Another prominent liberal . . . strong and self-reliant: *American Unitarian Biography* (Boston, Mass.: J. Munroe, 1851), 1:77.

39 "that crawling": *Proverbs from Plymouth Pulpit* (New York: D. Appleton, 1887), 125.

40 "flesh and nerve impregnable": *UTC,* 45.

40 "I can understand why Jesus": *UTC,* 240.

40 "a large, broad-chested": *UTC,* 18. The subsequent quotations in this paragraph are on pp. 351 and 355, respectively.

41 "About half of them": HBS, *Dred; A Tale of the Great Dismal Swamp* (Boston, Mass.: Phillips, Sampson, 1856), 2:211.

42 "Mr. Garrison, are you a Christian?": Quoted in G, 292–93.

42 "progressive element" . . . shared emotions: K, letter from HBS to William Lloyd Garrison, before November 30, 1853.

42 "spread the gospel": *Brooklyn Circular,* April 20, 1853.

2. TAMING CULTURAL BEASTS

43 He had long been tormented . . . Stowe's novel: Heine wrote, "I now find myself on the same stand-point where poor Uncle Tom stands,—on the Bible. . . . With all my science I have come no farther than the poor ignorant negro who has scarce learned how

to spell." Quoted in Harriet Beecher Stowe's introduction to the 1878 edition of *UTC* (Boston, Mass.: Houghton, Mifflin, 1878), lvii.

43 The novel . . . Sunday school text: For the effect of *UTC* on Bible sales, see Florine Thayer McCray, *The Life-work of the Author of "Uncle Tom's Cabin"* (New York: Funk & Wagnall's, 1889), 111. For Sunday school use of the novel, see "*Uncle Tom's Cabin* as a Sabbath School Book," in *The Pittsburgh Dispatch*, reprinted in *The Liberator*, March 18, 1853.

43 One appreciative father . . . children's book: The father wrote of his daughter's response to *UTC*: "The charming Christian characters there drawn, of 'Uncle Tom' and 'little Eva,' were like beckoning angels to her. Her young heart went strongly after them; and soon, I doubt not, she joined them in their celestial mansions" (see *Frederick Douglass' Paper*, March 25, 1853). Among children's books based on Stowe's novel are: *Pictures and Stories from Uncle Tom's Cabin* (Boston, Mass.: John P. Jewett, 1853); *A Peep into Uncle Tom's Cabin* (London: Sampson Low & Son, 1853); *Cassy; or, Early Trials* (Boston, Mass.: John P. Jewett, 1855); *Topsy* (New York: McLoughlin Bros., 1890); H. E. Marshall, "*Uncle Tom's Cabin" Told to Children* (New York: E. P. Dutton, c. 1904); *Uncle Tom's Cabin: Young Folk's Edition* (Chicago, Ill., and New York: M. A. Donohue, c. 1905); Helen Ring Robinson, *Uncle Tom's Cabin for Children* (Philadelphia, Pa.: Penn Publishing Co., 1908); and *Uncle Tom's Cabin; or, Life Among the Lowly: Abridged for Use in Schools with Sixty Illustrations* (Cleveland, Ohio: World Publishing Co., n.d. [c. 1920]). For other children's titles, see UVA.

44 "Mrs. Stowe throws an ultra Christian hue" . . . "scenes of license": *Southern Literary Messenger* 19 (June 1853): 321–29.

44 The novel was variously branded: "Revolting and unjust," *The Literary World*, April 24, 1852; "obscene reflections," *The New Orleans Daily Picayune*, October 8, 1852; "vivid descriptions of sensuality," review in *The Boston Post*, reprinted in *The Liberator*, January 21, 1853; "shamelessly profligate," *New-York Evangelist* 24 (March 31, 1853): 52; "deficient in the delicacy . . . no modest woman could conceive of," comment by a Southern woman in *The New Orleans Daily Picayune*, reprinted in *The Liberator*, March 4, 1853.

44 "Mrs. Stowe belongs to the school": *Southern Literary Messenger* 18 (October 1852): 630.

44 "termagant virago" . . . "deliberately step[ped]": *Southern Literary Messenger* 18 (December 1852): 721.

44 "the man Harriet" . . . "unsexed herself": *The New Orleans Daily Picayune*, February 11, 1853.

44 "a perfect female Hercules": *Southern Literary Messenger* 19 (May 1853): 5.

45 "the timid exploits": Douglas, *The Feminization of American Culture*, 1.

45 On women's issues: The body of scholarly literature over the past several decades on *UTC* and the themes of gender, domesticity, and sentimental popular culture is substantial. Highlights include Jane P. Tompkins, "Sentimental Power" (1978), reprinted in "Modern Critical Views of *Uncle Tom's Cabin*," in the Norton Critical Edition of *UTC*, 501–22; David Schuyler, "Inventing a Feminine Past," *New England Quarterly* 51 (September 1978): 291–308; David S. Reynolds, "The Feminization Controversy: Sexual Stereotypes and the Paradoxes of Piety in Nineteeth-Century America," *New*

England Quarterly 53 (March 1980): 96–106; Josephine Donovan, "Harriet Beecher Stowe's Feminism," *American Transcendental Quarterly* 48–49 (Summer 1982): 141–57; Karen Haltunnen, *Confidence Men and Painted Women: A Study of Middle-class Culture in America, 1830–1870* (New Haven, Conn.: Yale University Press, 1982), 125–52; Philip Fisher, *Hard Facts: Setting and Form in the American Novel* (New York: Oxford University Press, 1985), 104–10; Jean Fagan Yellin, "Doing It Herself: *Uncle Tom's Cabin* and Woman's Role in the Slavery Crisis," in *New Essays on Uncle Tom's Cabin,* edited by E. J. Sundquist, 85–105; Mary Kelley, Anne Throne Margolis, and Jeanne Boydston, *The Limits of Sisterhood: The Beecher Sisters on Women's Rights and Woman's Sphere* (Chapel Hill: University of North Carolina Press, 1988); H. Gregg Camfield, "The Moral Aesthetics of Sentimentality: A Missing Key to *Uncle Tom's Cabin,*" *Nineteenth-Century Literature* 43 (1988): 319–45; Lora Romero, "Bio-Political Resistance in Domestic Ideology and *Uncle Tom's Cabin,*" *American Literary History* 1 (1989): 715–34, and L. Romero, *Home Fronts: Domesticity and Its Critics in the Antebellum United States* (Durham, N.C.: Duke University Press, 1997); *The Cultural of Sentiment: Race, Gender, and Sentimentality in 19th-Century America,* edited by Shirley Samuels (New York: Oxford University Press, 1992); Gillian Brown, *Domestic Individualism: Imagining Self in Nineteenth-Century America* (Berkeley: University of California Press, 1990), and G. Brown, "Getting in the Kitchen with Dinah: Domestic Politics in *Uncle Tom's Cabin,*" *American Quarterly* 36 (1984): 503–23; Nancy Bentley, "White Slaves: The Mulatto Hero in Antebellum Fiction," *American Literature* 65 (1993): 501–22; Nancy Armstrong, "Why Daughters Die: The Racial Logic of American Sentimentalism," *The Yale Journal of Criticism* 7 (1994): 1–24; Cynthia Griffin Wolff, "Masculinity in *Uncle Tom's Cabin,*" *Amercan Quarterly* 47 (December 1995): 595–618; Lori Merish, "Sentimental Consumption: Harriet Beecher Stowe and the Aesthetics of Middle-Class Ownership," *American Literature History* 8 (1996): 1–33; Amy Kaplan, "Manifest Domesticity," *American Literature* 70 (1998): 581–606; Joan D. Hedrick, *The Oxford Harriet Beecher Stowe Reader* (New York: Oxford University Press, 1999), as well as Hedrick's biography of Stowe (1994); Jim O'Loughlin, "Articulating *Uncle Tom's Cabin,*" *New Literary History* 31 (2000): 573–97; Marianne Noble, *The Masochistic Pleasures of Reading Sentimental Literature* (Princeton, N.J.: Princeton University Press, 2000), 141–43; Susan M. Ryan, "Charity Begins at Home: Stowe's Antislavery Novels and the Forms of Benevolent Citizenship," *American Literature* 71 (December 2000): 751–82; Myra Jehlen, *Readings at the Edge of Literature* (Chicago, Ill.: University of Chicago Press, 2002); Kenneth W. Warren, "The Afterlife of *Uncle Tom's Cabin,*" in *The Cambridge Companion to Harriet Beecher Stowe,* edited by Cindy Weinstein (Cambridge, UK: Cambridge University Press, 2004); 219–34; Barbara Hochman, "*Uncle Tom's Cabin* in the *National Era*: An Essay in Generic Norms and the Contexts of Reading," *Book History* 7 (2004): 143–69; Noelle Gallagher, "The Bagging Factory and the Breakfast Factory: Industrial Labor and Sentimentality in Harriet Beecher Stowe's *Uncle Tom's Cabin,*" *Nineteenth Century Contexts* 27 (June 2005): 167–87; Dawn Coleman, "The Unsentimental Woman Preacher of *Uncle Tom's Cabin,*" *American Literature* 80 (2008): 265–92.

45 "to raise woman": S. J. Hale, *The Lecturess; or, Woman's Sphere* (Boston, Mass.: Whipple and Damrell, 1839), 24–25.

46 One alarmed father . . . gave lectures: *The Valley Farmer,* April 1854.

46 "a clear, energetic": *UTC,* 220, 29.

46 Also, she tells Uncle Tom ... special praise: Typical reviews of *The Christian Slave* include those in *The Illustrated London News,* August 1856, and *The Liberator,* December 14, 1855; the latter piece also includes excerpts of reviews from *The New York Times* and *New-York Tribune.*

47 "every word issues glistening": *Blackwood's Magazine,* quoted in *The Independent,* October 20, 1853.

47 "that refinement of taste": *The Independent,* February 16, 1854.

47 the adventure feminist ... the sensual woman: See *BAR,* chap. 12.

49 The postmillennial dream ... lurid and sensational: *BAR,* chap. 2.

49 In the 1830s the moral reformer: "infamous bawdy," in *Morning Courier and New York Enquirer,* October 5, 1833; "the most foul," in *New York Commercial Advertiser,* August 8, 1836.

49 Some temperance lecturers: *Autobiography and Personal Recollections of John B. Gough* (Toronto: A. H. Hovey, 1870), 199–200.

49 In popular fiction: *BAR,* 68–69.

50 "poison ... deliriums and death" ... "Upon the opening": Melville, *Moby-Dick,* 21, 401.

50 "the most immoral" ... "more read": Lippard, *The Quaker City; or The Monks of Monk Hall,* edited by David S. Reynolds (1845; repr., Amherst: University of Massachusetts Press, 1995), 1, 2.

51 "founded on the principle": "George Lippard," *Nassau Literary Magazine* 8 (April 1849): 189.

51 "works of imagination": Catharine E. Beecher, preface to HBS, *The Mayflower; or, Sketches of Scenes and Characters among the Descendants of the Pilgrims* (New York: Harper & Bros., 1843), xii.

52 "denunciation, recriminations": C. E. Beecher, "An Essay on Slavery Abolitionism Addressed to Miss A. E. Grimke," in *Against Slavery: An Abolitionist Reader,* edited by Mason Lowance (New York: Penguin, 2000), 208, 215.

52 "monster-galleries": H. W. Beecher, *Lectures to Young Men on Various Important Subjects* (1843; repr., Philadelphia, Pa.: Henry Altemus, 1895), 215. The quotation from "The Strange Woman" is on p. 202.

54 Stowe's sensitivity ... sufficiently recognized: There are, however, exceptions, such as Ronald G. Walters, "Harriet Beecher Stowe and the American Reform Tradition," in *The Cambridge Companion to Harriet Beecher Stowe,* edited by C. Weinstein, 167–88, and Lisa Watt MacFarlane, "'If Ever I Get to Where I Can': The Competing Rhetorics of Social Reform in *Uncle Tom's Cabin,*" *American Transcendental Quarterly* 4 (1990): 135–47.

54 The amount of absolute alcohol ... U.S. government: Alice Felt Tyler, *Freedom's Ferment: Phases of American Social History from the Colonial Period to the Outbreak of the Civil War* (1944; repr., New York: Harper & Row, 1962), 318.

54 "Everybody asked everybody": T. L. Nichols, *Forty Years of American Life* (1864; New York: Negro University Press, 1968), 1:87.

54 "like the Egyptian": A. Lincoln, *Speeches and Writings: 1832–1858* (New York: Library of America, 1989), 88.

55 "the strong flavor": HBS, "Literary Epidemics—No. 2," *New-York Evangelist* 14 (July 13, 1843): 1.

55 In her 1842 tale . . . total abstinence: HBS, "The Coral Ring: The Temperance Pledge," *Rural Repository* 19 (November 15, 1842): 82. This tale also appeared in *Godey's Magazine and Lady's Book, Ladies' Garland and Family Wreath, Youth's Companion, The Huntress,* and the *Boston Recorder.*

55 "This tiresome temperance": HBS, "The Drunkard Reclaimed," *New-York Evangelist* 10 (November 30, 1839): 1.

56 "Woman, Behold Thy Son!": HBS, *The May Flower and Miscellaneous Writings* (Boston, Mass.: Phillips, Sampson, 1855), 364–74.

56 In the former tale . . . sad family: HBS, "Somebody's Father," *The Independent* 3 (February 27, 1851): 36.

56 "plenty of the *real stuff*": *UTC,* 55. The subsequent quotations in this paragraph are on pp. 57 and 168, respectively. For an interesting discussion of temperance themes in the novel and in fiction by its opponents, see Ryan C. Cordell, "'Enslaving You, Body and Soul': The Uses of Temperance in *Uncle Tom's Cabin* and 'Anti-Tom' Fiction," *Studies in American Fiction* 36 (2008): 3–26. See also Melissa Erwin Croghan, "Alcohol and Art in Nineteenth Century American Fiction: Studies of Poe and Stowe" (PhD diss., University of Pennsylvania, 1992).

57 "I hated it, too": *UTC,* 326.

57 "He drank and swore": *UTC,* 323. The next two quotations in this paragraph are on pp. 323 and 326, respectively.

57 "I never drink": *UTC,* 131. The subsequent quotations in this paragraph are on pp. 177 and 178 (three), respectively.

58 "morally offensive": *New-York Evangelist* 21 (July 25, 1850): 120.

58 an Edinburgh book publisher . . . solely to temperance: *The National Era,* June 9, 1853.

58 In July 1854: *The Liberator,* August 4, 1854.

59 "with constant horror": G, 16.

59 "I feel as Aunt Mary": K, letter from HBS to Calvin Ellis Stowe, after December 27, 1850.

59 "if the whole country": *UTC,* 194.

59 "very handsome mulatto girl": K, letter from HBS to Eliza Lee Follen, December 16, 1852.

60 "I consider a woman": Quoted in Eddie Donoghue, *Black Breeding Machines: The Breeding of Negro Slaves in the Diaspora* (Bloomington, Ind.: AuthorHouse, 2008), 360.

60 A historian of the African . . . because of breeding: Donoghue, *Black Breeding Machines,* 362.

60 Light-skinned enslaved women . . . Charleston: Deborah Gray White, *Ar'n't I a Woman?: Female Slaves in the Plantation South* (New York: W. W. Norton, 1985), 37. See also Michael Tadman, *Speculators and Slaves: Masters, Traders, and Slaves in the Old South* (Madison: University of Wisconsin Press, 1989), 126.

60 "Girls, the children": T. Parker, *Letter to the People of the United States, Touching the Matter of Slavery* (Boston, Mass.: James Munroe, 1841), 121. Parker's emphasis.

60 "monsters who have": *The Liberator,* January 21, 1848.

60 "Of the grown females": D. Nelson, "Slavery a System of Licentiousness," *The Anti-Slavery Record* 2 (October 1836): 6.

60 "one vast brothel": *American Protestant Vindicator,* December 1, 1841.

60 Although the statistics: For an example of the statistical debate over sex and slavery, see Herbert G. Gutman, *Slavery and the Numbers Game: A Critique of Time on the Cross* (Urbana: University of Illinois Press, 1975).

60 "always maintained a delicacy and reserve": K, letter from HBS to Eliza Lee Follen, December 16, 1852.

61 The sensational cheap: See *BAR,* 260–62.

61 "frightful list": K, letter from HBS to Calvin Ellis Stowe, July 19, 1844. The remaining quotations in this paragraph are also from this letter.

61 "I try to be spiritually-minded": Quoted in Marianne K. Noble, "Masochistic Eroticism in *Uncle Tom's Cabin*: Feminist and Reader-Response Approaches," in *Approaches to Teaching Stowe's* Uncle Tom's Cabin, edited by Elizabeth Ammons and Susan Belasco (New York: Modern Language Association, 2000), 152. In her article, Noble suggests that Stowe's prudish posture was in fact a willed stance of passionlessness that conformed with the ideal of true womanhood, achieved through vigorous mental repression.

62 Sensational novels and newspapers: *BAR,* 86–87.

62 "dangerous" . . . "lively relish": H. W. Beecher, *Lectures to Young Men on Various Important Subjects,* 184–85.

62 "They are powerful": K, letter from HBS to Calvin Ellis Stowe, July 19, 1844.

62 Among the others were some: HBS, "Literary Epidemics—No. 1," *New-York Evangelist* 13 (July 28, 1842): 120.

63 The 1840s also saw the rise: For a thorough overview of flash newspapers and other racy literature of the period, see Donna Dennis, *Licentious Gotham: Erotic Publishing and Its Prosecution in Nineteenth-Century New York* (Cambridge, Mass.: Harvard University Press, 2009).

63 "Any one who has kept the run": HBS, "Literary Epidemics—No. 2."

63 She made these pronouncements . . . partial dishabille: For a discussion of the era's erotic fiction, see *BAR,* chap. 7.

63 "her youthful bosom": Lippard, *The Quaker City,* 83–84. See BAR, chap. 7.

63 Leslie Fiedler calls: L. Fiedler, "The Male Novel," *Partisan Review* 37 (1970): 74–89.

65 "dress of the neatest": *UTC,* 4. The subsequent quotations in this paragraph are on pp. 288 and 316, respectively. As Marianne K. Noble plausibly argues, the novel's undertone of eroticized violence and titillation played a role in its popularity (see Noble, "Masochistic Eroticism in *Uncle Tom's Cabin,*" 157).

65 "The gross misrepresentation": Review in *The Boston Post,* reprinted in *The Liberator,* January 21, 1853.

65 "has found it easier": *Southern Quarterly Review,* January 1854.

65 "the swarming issues": *The New York Times,* April 25, 1853; UVA.

66 "a pious, good girl": *UTC,* 96.

66 "The negro, in fact": *Southern Quarterly Review,* July 1853.

66 "are more ardent after their female": T. Jefferson quoted in P. Finkelman, *Defending*

Slavery: Proslavery Thought in the Old South: A Brief History with Documents (Boston, Mass.: Bedford/St. Martin's, 2003), 51. The statement by T. Parker quoted in the next sentence is on p. 154.

67 "the fiery and insatiate": G. Thompson, *City Crimes; or, Life in New York and Boston* (New York: William Berry, 1849), 49.

67 "The literary taste of our day": *Southern Quarterly Review,* January 1853.

67 "Mrs. Stowe has been so successful": *Southern Quarterly Review,* January 1854.

67 There were two main types ... extreme situations: *BAR,* 183–98.

68 "one of those collections": *UTC,* 348. Karen Haltunnen explores *UTC*'s connection to the Gothic tradition in "Gothic Imagination and Social Reform: The Haunted Houses of Lyman Beecher, Henry Ward Beecher, and Harriet Beecher Stowe," in *New Essays on Uncle Tom's Cabin,* edited by E. J. Sundquist, 107–34.

68 "down, down, down": *UTC,* 327.

69 When she moved to Cincinnati ... classes and backgrounds: W, 99.

69 "social ranks are intermingled": Alexis de Tocqueville, quoted in Damrosch, *Tocqueville's Discovery of America,* 136–37.

69 "the whole class of the oppressed": HBS, "Literary Epidemics—No. 2."

69 "The Bible as Comforter": HBS, "Narrative. The Bible a Comforter," *New-York Evangelist* 16 (September 9, 1842): 70.

69 The seamstress ... who buy them: HBS, "The Seamstress," *Godey's Magazine and Lady's Book,* December 1848.

69 Charity to the poor ... "friend of the poor": "The Tea-Rose," in HBS, *The Mayflower* (1843), 80–90; "So Many Calls," in HBS, *The Mayflower* (1843), 272–74; "Christmas; or, The Good Fairy," *The National Era* 4 (December 26, 1850): 205.

70 "all the moral and Christian virtues": *UTC,* 129. The quotations in the next sentence are also on p. 129.

70 "universally despised" ... "But who, sir": *UTC,* 115.

71 Some reviewers unfairly attacked ... European cities: See, for example, the reviews in *Southern Literary Messenger* 18 (October 1852): 630, and *Graham's American Monthly Magazine* 42 (February 1853): 209; UVA. See also William J. Grayson's poem "The Hireling and the Slave" (1854), in Finkelman, *Defending Slavery,* 175–79. Many anti-Tom novels of the period make the same point.

71 "The cause of Hungary": "Kossuth," *The National Era* 42 (October 16, 1851): 166.

71 "there is a mustering": *UTC,* 202. For an interpretation of HBS's relationship to working-class reform, see Gallagher, "The Bagging Factory and the Breakfast Factory," 167–87. See also Josephine Donovan, *Uncle Tom's Cabin: Evil, Affliction, and Redemptive Love* (Boston, Mass.: Twayne, 1991), 3.

71 But it's worth noting ... widely distributed: See Samuel Moore, preface to the English edition of K. Marx and F. Engels, *The Communist Manifesto,* translated by S. Moore (1888; repr., New York: Penguin, 1967), 201.

72 "the working people, one and all": *New-York Tribune,* November 12, 1851, p. 6.

72 "*when the boilers* [*will*] *burst*": *UTC,* 234.

72 "formed an essential part": *New-York Tribune,* November 6, 1851, p. 6.

72 "Religion!": *UTC,* 159.

73 "the eruption of the vast volcano": *The Circular* 2 (May 7, 1853): 99.

73 "produce a very distinct and decided": Review of *UTC* in the *Richmond Examiner*, reprinted in *The National Era*, May 12, 1853.

73 "My mother used to tell me": *UTC*, 202.

74 The Brotherhood . . . in newspapers: See *New-York Tribune*, December 23, 1850, p. 7, and *New-York Tribune*, September 5, 1850, p. 7.

74 "protect the men who work": *New-York Tribune*, September 5, 1850, p. 7.

75 "white and black slavery": From an 1848 lecture by G. Lippard, printed in the weekly *Quaker City* (September 30, 1848), reprinted in *George Lippard, Prophet of Protest: Writings of an American Radical, 1822–1854*, edited by David S. Reynolds (New York: P. Lang, 1986), 111.

75 "for the regeneration": *New-York Tribune*, September 5, 1850, p. 7.

75 "that abominable, contemptible Hayti": *UTC*, 234. The next quotation in this paragraph is on p. 374.

75 "George was, by his father's side": *UTC*, 94. The quotation in the next paragraph and the block quotation that follows it are both on p. 172.

77 Those interested in tracing . . . in the 1840s: For a discussion of minstrelsy in antebellum Cincinnati, see Wendy Jean Katz, *Regionalism and Reform: Art and Class Formation in Antebellum Cincinnati* (Columbus: Ohio State University Press, 2002), 62–69.

77 Born in New York in 1829: The biographical information on Levison here comes from an article in the *American Phrenological Journal*, September 1856.

78 "my feller citizens": *UTC*, 66.

78 "pint wich ebber way": *The Country Gentleman*, May 4, 1854 (reprinted from an earlier edition of the *New York Picayune*).

79 "contained a great deal of a particular species": *UTC*, 38.

79 "electioneering politician": *UTC*, 65.

79 "bumbling, giggling": Yarborough, "Strategies of Characterization in *Uncle Tom's Cabin* and the Early Afro-American Novel," in *New Essays on Uncle Tom's Cabin*, edited by E. J. Sundquist, 47. James Benses contests this reading in "Myths and Rhetoric of the Slavery Debate and Stowe's Comic Vision of Slavery," in *SD*, 187–204.

79 But some have recently . . . characters: Among the most thoughtful recent studies of Stowe and the contexts of minstrelsy are Sarah Meer, *Uncle Tom Mania: Slavery, Minstrelsy, and Transatlantic Culture in the 1850s* (Athens: University of Georgia Press, 2005), 352; Eric Lott, *Love and Theft: Blackface Minstrelsy and the American Working Class* (New York: Oxford University Press, 1993); William J. Mahar, *Behind the Burnt Cork Mask: Early Blackface Minstrelsy and Antebellum American Popular Culture* (Urbana: University of Illinois Press, 1999); and W. T. Lhamon Jr., *Raising Cain: Blackface Performance from Jim Crow to Hip Hop* (Cambridge, Mass.: Harvard University Press, 1998).

79 Levison has Hannibal note . . . Barnum's Museum: Julius Caesar Hannibal [W. H. Levison], *Black Diamonds; or, Humor, Satire, and Sentiment, Treated Scientifically . . . A Series of Burlesque Lectures, Darkly Colored. Originally Published in the New York Picayune* (1855; repr., New York: A. Ranney, 1857), 14. The subsequent quotations in this paragraph are on p. 142.

80 His master, Shelby . . . slave-trader Haley: *UTC,* 3. The quotations in the next sentence are on the same page.

80 "a noted character": *UTC,* 215.

81 When Topsy announces . . . identity of his father: *UTC,* 209–10. Both of the subsequent quotations in this paragraph are on p. 217.

81 " 'I'se so wicked!' ": *UTC,* 217.

81 "sinfulness and vileness": J. Edwards, "Personal Narrative," in *NAL,* A:395.

82 "Old Uncle Ned": E. Lott, introduction to *Inside the Minstrel Mask: Readings in Nineteenth-Century Blackface Minstrelsy,* edited by Annemarie Bean, James Vernon Hatch, and Brooks McNamara (Hanover, N.H.: University Press of New England, 1996), 22.

82 "O Sambo was a gentleman": Dan Emmett, "The Fine Old Color'd Gentleman" (Boston, Mass., 1843); UVA.

83 "When Old Ned die": S. C. Foster, "Old Uncle Ned" (New York: Millet's Music Salon, 1848); UVA.

84 "Way down upon de Swanee ribber": S. C. Foster, "Old Folks at Home, Ethiopian Melody" (New York: Firth, Pond, 1851); UVA.

84 "Heaven is better": *UTC,* 362.

84 "De sun shines bright" . . . "By'm by Hard Times" . . . "Oh good night": S. C. Foster, "Poor Uncle Tom, Good Night" (1852), handwritten manuscript in Foster Hall Collection, Center for American Music, University of Pittsburgh Library System; UVA.

85 It may be that Foster . . . paean to Kentucky: See Ken Emerson, *Doo-Dah!: Stephen Foster and the Rise of American Popular Culture* (New York: Simon & Schuster, 1998), 193–95.

85 "Weep no more, my lady": S. C. Foster, "My Old Kentucky Home, Good Night!" (New York: Firth, Pond, 1853); UVA.

3. Antislavery Passion

88 "We have never read": *The National Era,* April 15, 1852.

88 "He who can read this thrilling": *Ohio Star,* quoted in the *New-York Evangelist* 23 (May 27, 1852): 87.

88 The seasoned antislavery editor: Charles Nichols, "The Origins of *Uncle Tom's Cabin,*" *The Phylon Quarterly* 19 (1958): 333.

88 "It was at *his* dying bed": K, letter from HBS to Eliza Lee (Cabot) Follen, December 16, 1852.

88 "Oh, mother that reads this": *UTC,* 75.

89 "This work, more, perhaps": *Key,* 1.

89 He was a member of the American Colonization Society: For the origins and influence of the American Colonization Society, see Reynolds, *Waking Giant,* 27–29.

90 By the mid-1830s . . . political parties: For Garrison's attack on Beecher, see Henry Mayer, *All on Fire: William Lloyd Garrison and the Abolition of Slavery* (New York: W. W. Norton, 1998), 226–27.

90 "No union with slaveholders!": Wendell Phillips Garrison and Francis Jackson Gar-

rison, *William Lloyd Garrison, 1805–1879: The Story of His Life Told by His Children* (New York: Century, 1889), 100. The quotation in the next sentence is on p. 88.

90 "Oh, Garrison, you can't reason": Quoted in Lyman Beecher Stowe, *Saints, Sinners and Beechers* (Indianapolis, Ind.: Bobbs-Merrill, 1934), 60.

91 "the abolitionists as a body": *LB,* 2:345.

91 Catharine sharply censured . . . Garrison's statements: She characterized Garrison's style as "offensive, inflammatory, and exasperating"; C. E. Beecher, "An Essay on Slavery," in *Against Slavery: An Abolitionist Reader,* edited by M. Lowance, 209.

91 "conciliation, good-natured": *HWB,* 268.

91 "there was a class of professed": G, 63.

93 "she kept that book": Sarah Weld, unpublished manuscript of reminiscences by her mother Angelina Grimke Weld, quoted in Gilbert Hobbs Barnes, *The Antislavery Impulse, 1830–1844* (New York: D. Appleton-Century, 1933), 231.

93 "With all credit": K, letter from HBS to Wendell Phillips, February 28, 1853.

93 Promising a "mild" . . . center of an uproar: *The Philanthropist* 1 (January 22, 1836): 2.

94 "I can easily see how such proceedings": Ch, 84.

94 "there would actually be war": Ch, 86. The subsequent quotations in this paragraph are on p. 84.

95 After Lovejoy's death: For Garrisonian attacks on Lovejoy, see *The Liberator,* December 8, 1837, and December 22, 1837. For more positive responses to the Alton martyr, see the clippings reprinted in *The Philanthropist* 2 (December 12, 1837): 2.

95 "died in the defense" . . . "Though dead": E. Beecher, *Riots at Alton in Connection with the Death of Rev. Elijah P. Lovejoy* (Alton, Ill.: George Holton, 1838), 108.

96 "the most important single event": *Uncollected Letters of Abraham Lincoln,* edited by Gilbert A. Tracy (Boston, Mass.: Houghton, Mifflin, 1917), xx.

96 "the heroes of Bunker Hill": E. Beecher, *Riots at Alton,* 137. For comparisons between George Harris and the freedom fighters of the American Revolution, see *UTC,* 172.

96 "sometimes talks quite *Abolitiony*": Quoted in H, 93. The next quotation in this paragraph (Calvin's statement about abolitionism) is in H, 100.

96 "about half abolitionists": Ch, 87. The next two quotations in this paragraph are in Ch, 88.

97 Weld and his cohorts . . . stay in the city: See G, 32, and Lyman Abbott and Samuel Byram Halliday, *Henry Ward Beecher: A Sketch of His Career* (Hartford, Conn.: American Publishing Co., 1887), 156.

97 "If you want to teach": *LB,* 2:325.

97 "the smartest black woman": Quoted in *LB,* 1:127.

98 "always called [her master] her husband": K, letter from HBS to Eliza Lee Follen, December 16, 1852. The next quotation in this paragraph is also from this letter to Follen.

98 "not the biography": K, letter from HBS to *The Indianapolis Times,* July 27, 1882, and K, letter from HBS to Madam, May 19, 1875. The next two quotations in the paragraph are from the letter to Madam.

98 "honest, bluff": K, letter from HBS to Eliza Lee Follen, December 16, 1852.

99 "performed for the fugitive": *Key,* 36.

99 "The Rev. John Rankin": Quoted in William Birney, *James G. Birney and His Times* (New York: D. Appleton, 1890), 168.

99 This abolitionist family . . . February 1838: My account here of this woman's escape across the ice is informed by Fergus M. Bordewich, *Bound for Canaan: The Underground Railroad and the War for the Soul of America* (New York: Amistad, 2005), and by Ann Hagedorn, *Beyond the River: The Untold Story of the Heroes of the Underground Railroad* (New York: Simon & Schuster, 2002), 300.

100 The Coffins named . . . Lake Erie to Canada: *Reminiscences of Levi Coffin, the Reputed President of the Underground Railroad* (Cincinnati, Ohio: Robert Clarke, 1876), 147–50.

100 Three years later . . . send them all to Canada: Tricia Martineau Wagner, *It Happened on the Underground Railroad* (Guilford, Conn.: Globe Pequot Press, 2007), 51–56.

100 Bird's real-life counterpart: Harriet related the Upham story in a note to Catharine; see K, letter from HBS to Catharine E. Beecher, after September 18, 1850.

101 "a beautiful quadroon": *Key,* 34. The remaining quotations in this paragraph are also on p. 34.

102 "scene after scene": Ch, 72.

102 "My vocation is simply": K, letter from HBS to Gamaliel Bailey, March 9, 1851.

102 "little house": W. Whitman, *Notebooks and Unpublished Prose Manuscripts,* edited by Edward F. Grier (New York: New York University Press, 1984), 4:1524, and *Leaves of Grass: Comprehensive Reader's Edition,* edited by Harold Blodgett and Sculley Bradley (New York: New York University Press, 1965), 642.

103 Few issues remain . . . and these works: Modern critical opinion on this topic ranges from Eric J. Sundquist's claim that Stowe's debt to these autobiographical works is "open to question" to Joan Hedrick's assertion, "It is well known that for her plot Stowe drew on the narratives of escaped slaves, particularly those of Josiah Henson and Henry Bibb." See Sundquist, Introduction to *New Essays on Uncle Tom's Cabin,* 16–17, and H, 211.

103 Shortly after *Uncle Tom's Cabin* . . . book's proceeds: *Frederick Douglass' Paper,* April 29, 1853.

103 Henson promoted . . . specific characters: He insisted that he was Uncle Tom; his wife Charlotte was Tom's wife Chloe; a young man named George Ripley was George Shelby; Eliza Harris was the woman who escaped across the icy river in 1838; George Harris was Lewis Clarke; a willfully disobedient girl, Dinah, became Topsy; Cassy was a cook named Polly, owned by the cruel Bryce Litton, who was the source for Legree; Stowe's Eva was actually a girl named Susan, the daughter of a real St. Clair Young— Henson said he once saved her when she fell into a river; see *An Autobiography of the Rev. Josiah Henson (Mrs. Harriet Beecher Stowe's "Uncle Tom"),* edited by John Lobb (London: Christian Age, 1878), chap. 25.

103 "None of the characters": K, letter from HBS to editor of *Brooklyn Magazine,* April 2, 1885.

104 There are elements . . . real source of the novel: Ishmael Reed, for instance, argues that *UTC* is completely Henson's story; see I. Reed, *Flight to Canada* (New York: Random House, 1976), 7–11. Charles Nichols, on the other hand, claims Hildreth's *Archy Moore* was the novel's main source: Nichols, "The Origins of *Uncle Tom's Cabin.*"

104 "I am of the opinion": *Frederick Douglass' Paper,* April 29, 1853.

104 "had received more confirmations": *Key,* 37.

104 Stowe reported . . . laudatory preface: K, letter from HBS to Susan Mitchell (Mrs. Charles Edward) Stowe, March 8, 1882. She writes: "After I had begun the story I got, at the anti-slavery rooms in Boston, the autobiography of Josiah Henson, and introduced some of its most striking incidents into my story." For HBS's preface to Henson's narrative, see Josiah Henson, *Truth Stranger Than Fiction: Father Henson's Story of His Own Life, With an Introduction by Harriet Beecher Stowe* (Boston, Mass.: John P. Jewett and Co., 1858). In the preface, HBS writes, "Among all the singular and interesting records to which the institution of American slavery has given rise, we know of none more striking, more characteristic and instructive, than that of Josiah Henson" (iii).

104 "I have been called 'Uncle Tom' ": *Autobiography of the Rev. Josiah Henson,* 158.

105 "glad tidings of the Gospel": *Autobiography of the Rev. Josiah Henson,* 12.

106 "my own strength of character": *Autobiography of the Rev. Josiah Henson,* 25.

106 "his Christian principle": *Key,* 42.

106 This Christian forbearance . . . *Memoirs of Archy Moore*: Nichols, "The Origins of *Uncle Tom's Cabin,*" 328.

107 "he never tasted whiskey": R. Hildreth, *The Slave; or, Memoirs of Archy Moore* (Boston, Mass.: John H. Eastburn, 1836), 2:72. The subsequent quotations in this paragraph are on the same page.

107 A more tantalizing . . . "DEATH OF THE ORIGINAL UNCLE TOM": *The Saturday Evening Post,* March 7, 1857; UVA. The information on Magruder in this paragraph is compiled from several sources: Jacob Piatt Dunn, "Indiana's Part in Making the Story of *Uncle Tom's Cabin,*" *Indiana Quarterly Magazine of History* 5 (March 1909): 112–18; J. P. Dunn, *Greater Indianapolis: The History, the Industries, the Institutions, and the People of a City of Homes* (Chicago, Ill.: Lewis Publishing Co., 1910), 243–44; and Ronald L. Baker, *Homeless, Friendless, and Penniless: The WPA Interviews with Former Slaves Living in Indiana* (Bloomington: Indiana University Press, 2108), 177.

108 "If there ever was a Christian": Dunn, *Greater Indianapolis,* 244.

108 Also intriguing is the fact . . . nicknamed Topsy: Baker, *Homeless, Friendless, and Penniless,* 178.

108 "Mother, tell master": *Narratives of the Sufferings of Lewis and Milton Clarke, Sons of a Soldier of the Revolution, During a Captivity of More Than Twenty Years Among The Slaveholders of Kentucky* (Boston, Mass.: Bela Marsh, 1846), 28.

109 "Soon after [Clarke's] escape": *Key,* 18.

109 "If [Stowe] had not": *The Washington Post,* May 12, 1890. However, Stowe, in old age, when her mind was going, twice denied having known of Clarke before writing the novel. See K, letter from HBS to Mr. Robb, March 27, 1893, where she writes of Clarke, "I never saw the man and don't remember to have ever heard of him. . . . The man was not in my mind at the time of writing *Uncle Tom's Cabin.* Neither he or any other man stood for the character of George Harris, who was a creation of my own brain: a probable but not living character." Similarly, in K, letter from HBS to an unknown recipient, December 8, 1895, she notes, "Again as I said in the columns of the *New York Morning Journal* the character of Uncle Tom and George Harris had no living prototypes but were created by me."

110 "was so unfortunate": *Narratives of the Sufferings of Lewis and Milton Clarke,* 102. The quotation in the next sentence is on p. 75.

110 There's a legend . . . the Shelby place in *Uncle Tom's Cabin:* See *The Washington Post,* July 12, 1896, and Gerald R. Tudor, "Fiction, Fact, and Embellishment: The Kennedys and Uncle Tom's Cabin" (1999), at http://freepages.genealogy.rootsweb.ancestry.com /~josephkennedy/Source%20Materials/Kennedy/fiction_fact_and_embellishment .htm.

110 When Clarke later in life . . . center stage: *The Chicago Daily Tribune,* August 30, 1880.

111 "are nearly *all* hard drinkers": *Narratives of the Sufferings of Lewis and Milton Clarke,* 123.

111 Another was Frederick Douglass . . . learning to read: In the *Key* (p. 23), Stowe writes, "With regard to the intelligence of George, and his teaching himself to read and write, there is a most interesting and affecting parallel to it in the 'Life of Frederick Douglass.' "

111 Especially pertinent is William Wells Brown's narrative: *Narrative of William W. Brown, a Fugitive Slave* (Boston, Mass.: Anti-Slavery Society, 1847), 4, 66.

111 "I got that from knockin' ": Quoted in W, 218.

111 Of the three . . . black lackeys: For the debate over Meredith Calhoun as a possible source of Legree, see *The Washington Post,* July 19, 1896, and August 31, 1896.

112 Litton is a better . . . assault Henson: *Autobiography of the Rev. Josiah Henson,* 5.

112 "His chief delight": D. B. Corley, *A Visit to Uncle Tom's Cabin* (Chicago, Ill.: Laird Lee, 1893), 12.

112 When McAlpin died: LeeAnna Keith, *The Colfax Massacre: The Untold Story of Black Power, White Terror, and the Death of Reconstruction* (New York: Oxford University Press, 2008), 27.

112 Henry Bibb's autobiography . . . down his throat: *Narrative of the Life and Adventures of Henry Bibb, an American Slave, Written by Himself. With an Introduction by Lucius C. Matlack* (New York: n.p., 1849), 1:88.

112 "a regular Yankee": *Narrative of William W. Brown,* 21. The quotation in the next sentence is on p. 24.

113 "although slavery has been abolished": *Key,* 52.

113 "Race prejudice seems stronger": Alexis de Tocqueville, *Democracy in America,* edited by J. P. Mayer (1835; repr., New York: Anchor, 1969), 343.

113 "prejudice at the North" . . . "The prejudices of the North": *The Black Abolitionist Papers,* edited by C. Peter Ripley (Chapel Hill: University of North Carolina Press, 1991) 4:202; and W. L. Garrison, "Address to the Colonization Society" (at the Park Street Church, Boston, Mass., July 4, 1829), American Antiquarian Society.

113 "I have often noticed": *UTC,* 154.

114 "her warm red blood" . . . "brutal assault": *Narrative of the Life of Frederick Douglass,* in *NAL,* B:2075; and *The Life of Josiah Henson, Formerly a Slave* (Boston, Mass.: Arthur D. Phelps, 1849), 1.

115 "poet of slaves": The quoted words here are in an early manuscript notebook that can be viewed at the website of the Walt Whitman Archive, created by Kenneth M. Price and Ed Folsom at http://whitmanarchive.org/.

115   "Husbands and wives": *Autobiography of the Rev. Josiah Henson,* 27.
115   "Generally, there is but little": *Narratives of the Sufferings of Lewis and Milton Clarke,* 106.
115   "what a poor slave mother": K, letter from HBS to Eliza Lee (Cabot) Follen, December 16, 1852.

4. IGNITING THE WAR

118   "We doubt if abler": *Frederick Douglass' Paper,* April 1, 1852.
118   "the tears which [*Uncle Tom's Cabin*] has drawn": *New Englander* 10 (November 1852): 590.
118   "this new missionary": *Southern Literary Messenger* 18 (December 1852): 721.
118   "all the enemies": *Democratic Review* 33 (June 1854): 301.
118   "So fallen!": *The Complete Poetical Works of Whittier* (Boston, Mass.: Houghton, Mifflin, 1892), 186.
118   "Fallen, fallen, fallen": In Allan Nevins, *The Ordeal of the Union* (New York: Charles Scribner's Sons, 1947), 2:292.
118   "no forms, neither constitutions": "The Fugitive Slave Law," in *The Essential Writings of Ralph Waldo Emerson* (New York: Modern Library, 2119), 787.
119   "moved over to the side": *M,* 227. The subsequent quotations in this paragraph are also on this page.
119   Before her novel appeared . . . law with godliness: Charles Beecher, *The Duty of Disobedience to Wicked Laws. A Sermon on the Fugitive Slave Law* (Newark, N.J.: J. McIlvaine, 1851).
119   In the spring of 1843: Information about the Van Zandt case in this and the following paragraphs is collated from *M,* 259–63; John Niven, *Salmon P. Chase: A Biography* (New York: Oxford University Press, 1995), 77–83; *The Western Law Journal* 2 (March 1845): 245; *The Western Law Journal* 4 (September 1847): 529; and *New-York Daily Tribune,* March 10, 1847.
120   "No legislature": S. P. Chase, *Reclamation of Fugitives from Service. An Argument for the Defendant, Submitted to the Supreme Court of the United States, at the December Term, 1846, in the Case of Wharton Jones vs. John Vanzandt* (Cincinnati, Ohio: R. P. Donogh, 1847), 93. The quotation in the next sentence is on the same page.
120   "which partake largely": *M,* 108.
121   "stand by the Constitution": *The National Era,* April 8, 1847.
121   "he died broken-hearted": *M,* 262.
121   "Van Zandt's best monument": In Frederick W. Seward, *Seward at Washington as Senator and Secretary of State* (New York: Derby & Miller, 1891), 40.
122   "may be enlightened": HBS, "Immediate Emancipation," *Cincinnati Weekly Philanthropist* 9 (February 5, 1842): 2.
122   In the former . . . sold at auction: HBS, "The American Altar of 1850," *The Independent,* July 10, 1851.
122   In "The Freeman's Dream" . . . "Of late, there seem to be many": HBS, "The Freeman's Dream," *The National Era;* reprinted in the *New-York Evangelist* 21 (August 15, 1850): 1.

122 "witnesses the good-humored": *UTC,* 8. The quotation in the next sentence is also on p. 8. For a discussion of higher-law images in *UTC* in the context of figures like Emerson and Douglass, see Gregg D. Crane, *Race, Citizenship, and Law in American Literature* (New York: Cambridge University Press, 2002), esp. chap 2.

123 "a shameful, wicked": *UTC,* 69. The two quotations at the end of this paragraph are both on p. 170.

123 All these higher ideals . . . halo-like round hat: See Jo-Ann Morgan, "Illustrating *Uncle Tom's Cabin,*" at http://utc.iath.virginia.edu/interpret/exhibits/morgan/morgan.html.

124 "American legislators . . . our great men": *UTC,* 115. The next quotation in this paragraph is on the same page.

124 "the vital force of the institution": *Key,* 279, 291.

124 "at this very moment": *UTC,* 384.

124 A historian of the domestic: Steven Deyle, *Carry Me Back: The Domestic Slave Trade in American Life* (New York: Oxford University Press, 2005), 4.

125 "something unutterably horrible" . . . "If he had only been instructed": *UTC,* 113.

125 "a full and public retraction": W, 286. For a detailed account of the Parker affair, see H, 225–30.

125 "What are the evils": *The Discussion between Rev. Joel Parker, and Rev. A. Rood, on the Question "What Are the Evils Inseparable from Slavery"* (New York: S. W. Benedict, 1852), 32–33.

126 Interest in the novel grew . . . came out serially: Among the most informative accounts of the early publication history of *UTC* are E. Bruce Kirkham, *The Building of Uncle Tom's Cabin* (Knoxville: University of Tennessee Press, 1977), 61–149; Susan Belasco Smith, "Serialization and the Nature of *Uncle Tom's Cabin,*" in *Periodical Literature in Nineteenth-Century America,* edited by Susan Belasco Smith and Kenneth Price (Charlottesville: University Press of Virginia, 1995), 69–89; Michael Winship, "The Greatest Book of Its Kind: A Publishing History of *Uncle Tom's Cabin,*" *Proceedings of the American Antiquarian Society* 109, part 2 (1999): 309–32; and Barbara Hochman, "*Uncle Tom's Cabin* in the *National Era.*"

126 On March 20, 1852 . . . version at $2.00: *The National Era,* March 20, 1852. Among the most careful analyses of the early editions of *UTC* are Susan Geary, "Harriet Beecher Stowe, John P. Jewett, and Author-Publisher Relations in 1853," in *Studies in the American Renaissance,* edited by Joel Myerson (Boston, Mass.: Twayne, 1977), 345–67, and Michael Winship, "*Uncle Tom's Cabin*: History of the Book in the 19th-Century United States" (2007); UVA.

126 Within a month . . . train or steamboat: *The Literary World,* May 22, 1852.

126 The number of printed copies: *New-York Evangelist* 23 (May 26, 1852): 75.

127 "What could have been done": *The Independent,* May 13, 1852.

127 "Such a phenomenon": *Putnam's Monthly Magazine* 1 (January 1853): 98.

128 Within a year of its publication: Charles D. Cleveland, *A Compendium of American Literature, Chronologically Arranged* (New York: A. S. Barnes, 1859), 663. See also C. Parfait, *The Publishing History of* Uncle Tom's Cabin, *1852–2002,* and Margaret Holbrook Hildreth, *Harriet Beecher Stowe: A Bibliography* (Hamden, Conn.: Archon, 1976).

128 "Uncle Tom has probably ten": *The Literary World,* December 4, 1852.

128 "victorious Uncle Tom": *The Liberator,* April 29, 1853.

128 "a new era in cheap literature": Quoted in W, 327.

128 "with horror!": Quoted in Clair Parfait, *The Publishing History of* Uncle Tom's Cabin, *1852–2002*, 106.

129 Still, $30,000 was a healthy sum: In 1860, the average annual income for unskilled American workers was $363; for skilled artisans, mechanics, and craftsmen, it was from $400 to $800. Less than one percent of Americans—considered the "rich"—earned more than $5,000 annually. See Bruce A. Kimball, *The "True Professional Ideal" in America: A History* (Lanham, Md.: Rowman & Littlefield, 1995), 169.

129 Three decades later: Parfait explains that Stowe's royalties from *UTC*, after declining during the Civil War and Reconstruction, were $2,300 per year from 1881 to 1885 and $2,500 per year from 1886 to 1891; see *The Publishing History of* Uncle Tom's Cabin, *1852–2002*, 136.

129 "The touching, but too truthful": *Frederick Douglass' Paper*, April 29, 1853.

130 "the value of *Uncle Tom's Cabin*": Quoted in G, 362.

130 "The effects of the book so far": K, letter from HBS to George William Frederick Howard, Seventh Earl of Carlisle, about January 6, 1853.

130 "We confess to the frequent": *The Liberator*, March 26, 1852. Not that he and his followers didn't have quibbles. Garrison extolled Stowe's portrayal of the long-suffering Tom, who, he wrote, "triumphantly exemplifies . . . CHRISTIAN NON-RESISTANCE," but he wondered whether "Mrs. Stowe is a believer in the duty of non-resistance for the white man . . . as well as for the black man."

130 "prodigious, and therefore eminently": *The Liberator*, March 26, 1852.

130 "In the recent work of HARRIET BEECHER STOWE": This statement, in a resolution presented at the society's annual meeting in New York on May 11, 1852, was reprinted in *The National Era*, May 13, 1852. Some abolitionists were bothered by the passages in *Uncle Tom's Cabin* that endorsed colonization. But Stowe's defenders noted that her stance on the issue was not as coercive as that of the American Colonization Society. Besides, in a time when many mainstream politicians, including Lincoln and Henry Clay, endorsed colonization, Stowe's passages on it were widely accepted. Moreover, some committed promoters of colonization felt she had lent validity to their views. Edward W. Blyden, a native of the U.S. Virgin Islands who had emigrated to Liberia, wrote that he was "very agreeably surprised at noting that Mrs. Harriet B. Stowe, at the close of her inimitable *Uncle Tom's Cabin*, represents an intelligent colored man in America, educated abroad, as expressing a desire for an 'African nationality,' and as intending to migrate to Liberia" (*The African Repository*, August 1854).

131 "The fact that the wildest": Ch, 169.

131 "many factions" . . . "sending to England": K; Letter from HBS to the Earl of Carlisle, the Earl of Shaftesbury, and Joseph Sturge, before February 12, 1856.

132 "decidedly reject": K, letter from HBS to Charles Sumner, December 25–31, 1852.

132 "Even our diplomacy stands": *The Liberator*, March 4, 1853.

132 Sweeping the force along: *The New York Times*, March 1, 1853. Interesting information about the Tomitudes can be found on the UVA site, which includes pictures of many tie-ins as well as Louise L. Stevenson's useful article "Virtue Displayed: The Tie-ins of *Uncle Tom's Cabin*" (2007); UVA. See also Stephen A. Hirsch, "Uncle Tomitudes: The

Popular Reaction to *Uncle Tom's Cabin*," in *Studies in the American Renaissance,* edited by Joel Myerson (Boston, Mass.: Twayne, 1978), 303–30.

132 "artists of all grades now find": *The Liberator,* December 23, 1852.

133 "engravings of various degrees": *The Liberator,* December 23, 1852.

133 More dramatically, dioramas: One, by a Professor Foster of Michigan, drew "unbounded applause" from audiences that crowded to see it. Another, a huge *Uncle Tom* panorama by the Indiana artist Barton S. Hays, made a sensation when it was exhibited in the East in 1853 (*Frederick Douglass' Paper,* June 3, 1853). Yet another diorama, by a Mr. Leslie of Cincinnati, enjoyed "great success" in Western cities before being shown in the Northeast, where he was praised for presenting "in a true light the leading characters of Mrs. Stowe's celebrated work" (*Frederick Douglass' Paper,* July 15, 1853).

133 One, played like Go Fish: *The Independent,* December 23, 1852.

133 Europe saw an explosion: For images and descriptions of these and other Tomitudes, see UVA, at http://utc.iath.virginia.edu/tomituds/tohp.html

133 A European dice game . . . "another soul owner": The Harriet Beecher Stowe Center Collection, catalogue no. 69.104; at http://utc.iath.virginia.edu/tomituds/game2f.html.

136 One mantelpiece screen: "Decorative Screen," Clifton Waller Barrett Collection, University of Virginia; UVA, at http://utc.iath.virginia.edu/tomituds/screenf.html.

136 One very popular doll: "Topsy/Eva Doll"; UVA, at http://utc.iath.virginia.edu/tomituds/topsyevadoll.html.

136 In London . . . were named "Uncle Tom's Cabin": W, 144.

136 In Paris: *The Liberator,* March 4, 1853.

137 "I was the first": Quoted in B, 49.

139 "wholly impracticable": Quoted in B, 52. Much of the information presented over the next few paragraphs about Aiken, the Howards, and performances of the Aiken play is gleaned from B as well as from reviews and headnotes on the UVA site.

139 Attracted by Aiken's . . . "The Moral Temple of New-York": *The New York Times,* February 28, 1854.

140 Aiken's script shows why: All of the quotations from the Aiken play are from George L. Aiken, *Uncle Tom's Cabin: A Domestic Drama in Six Acts* (1852; New York: Samuel French, 1858); UVA. See http://utc.iath.virginia.edu/onstage/scripts/aikenhp.html.

140 "Every music publisher": *Dwight's Journal of Music,* July 31, 1852.

140 "The Youthful Wonder": Poster for Aiken's *Uncle Tom's Cabin,* National Theatre, July 26, 1853; UVA.

142 "to rig out more than half": Quoted in B, 103.

143 Conway added minstrel characters . . . "Plantation Jig": Playbill for H. J. Conway, *Uncle Tom's Cabin,* Boston Museum, December 13, 1852; UVA. The subsequent quotations in this paragraph are also from this playbill.

143 "a mere burlesque": *New-York Tribune,* November 15, 1853.

143 Still, it contained enough . . . proslavery ones: See the UVA's headnote to the playbill for the performance of Conway's play at the Boston Museum, December 13, 1852, at http://utc.iath.virginia.edu/onstage/scripts/conwayhp.html.

143 "Yes, niggers, lay down": All of the quotations from Conway in this paragraph and

the succeeding ones are from H. J. Conway, *Uncle Tom's Cabin: A Drama in Five Acts* (1852; from the manuscript); UVA. See http://utc.iath.virginia.edu/onstage/scripts/conwayhp.html.

144 "Ain't I a woman?": S. Truth's speech is reprinted in *Why Freedom Matters: The Spirit of the Declaration of Independence in Prose, Poetry, and Song, 1776 to the Present,* edited by Daniel R. Katz (New York: Workman, 2003), 126–27.

145 "Now, the Theatre is openly": *The Liberator,* December 24, 1852.

146 "Walt Whitman the b'hoy" . . . "the 'representative man' " . . . "the 'Bowery Bhoy' ": *New York Daily News,* February 27, 1856; *Washington Daily National Intelligencer,* February 18, 1856; and *New York Examiner,* January 19, 1882. Although Whitman left no record of having attended Uncle Tom plays, it's tempting to think that the working-class persona of "Song of Myself" was created by a poet who was able to give deeply sympathetic vignettes of fugitive slaves and human portraits of African-Americans in part because he was shaped by the b'hoy culture that had enthusiastically embraced these plays.

146 "If the shrewdest abolitionist": *The Liberator,* September 8, 1853. The *Tribune* reported of a New York performance: "The 'b'hoys' were on the side of the fugitives. The pro-slavery feeling had departed from among them. . . . They believed in the higher law" (*New-York Tribune,* reprinted in the *National Anti-Slavery Standard* [August 1853]). *The New York Times* ran an article titled "Uncle Tom Among the Bowery Boys," and another one expressing delight that "the great ideas of Brotherhood, Equality, and religious responsibility were preached to the Bowery Boys from the stage" (*The New York Times,* August 6, 1853, and October 25, 1853).

146 "One may infer a hopeful change": *Philadelphia Sunday Dispatch,* September 11, 1853.

147 "the lower classes in New York": N. W. Senior, *American Slavery: A Reprint of an Article on "Uncle Tom's Cabin"* (London: Longman, Brown, Green, Longmans, and Roberts, 1856), 29. The next Senior quotation in this paragraph and the one in the following paragraph are also on p. 29.

147 And so, Senior pointed out: See Albert J. Von Frank, *The Trials of Anthony Burns* (Cambridge, Mass.: Harvard University Press, 1994), 197–219.

147 "Perhaps a slaveholder might": *The National Era,* September 8, 1854.

147 "persons seldom seen": *The National Era,* August 25, 1853. The next quotation in this paragraph is also from this article.

148 "Men, women, and children": *National Anti-Slavery Standard,* August 1853.

148 "The immense issues": *The Thirteenth Annual Report of the American and Foreign Anti-Slavery Society* (New York: Lewis J. Bates, 1853), 131; UVA. Much of the information in this paragraph is from this source and from *The National Era,* July 14, 1853. That Harriet Jacobs' moving narrative did not get published at this time is Stowe's fault; Jacobs approached Stowe, who was so preoccupied with the *Key* that she wanted Jacobs' story for that volume and took no further steps to aid Jacobs, who in 1861 published her autobiography with the aid of Lydia Maria Child.

148 Forty thousand copies: See *Frederick Douglass' Paper,* April 1, 1853, and *The New York Times,* December 20, 1854.

149 The 1850s also brought . . . 20,000 over a few months: John David Smith, Introduction to F. Douglass, *My Bondage and My Freedom* (New York: Penguin, 2003), xlv.

149 Besides establishing . . . Hale: For examples of her closeness to politicians, see the fol-

lowing letters, all in K: letter from HBS to Charles Sumner, November 7, 1852; letter from HBS to Charles Sumner, December 25–31, 1852; letter from HBS to the Ladies' Anti-Slavery Society of Glasgow, November 18, 1853; letter from HBS to Edward Everett Hale, February 15, 1854; letter from HBS to Charles Sumner, February 23, 1854; letter from HBS to Edward Everett Hale, February 28, 1853; and letter from HBS to Edward Everett Hale, March 13, 1854.

150 "Individuals composing the old": *The National Era,* March 17, 1853.

150 "many votes cast": Henry Wilson, *History of the Rise and Fall of the Slave Power in America* (Boston, Mass.: Osgood, 1876), 2:519.

150 In an address to the House . . . commended the novel: *New-York Evangelist* 23 (May 27, 1852): 87.

150 "A lady with her pen": "Speech of Hon. Joshua R. Giddings of Ohio, in the House of Representatives, December 14, 1852," in *Frederick Douglass' Paper,* December 31, 1852.

150 George W. Julian: "Speech of Hon. Geo. W. Julian, at the Free Democratic State Convention. Held at Indianapolis, May 25, 1853," *Frederick Douglass' Paper,* July 29, 1853.

150 Most Southern states . . . criminalized it: "When 'Uncle Tom's Cabin' first made its appearance," a newspaper reported, "it could not have been offered for sale any where south of the Potomac, without exposing the vendor and the purchases to the terrors of Lynch-law" (*The Independent* 7 [March 22, 1855]: 92).

150 "The wide dissemination": *The Richmond Daily Dispatch,* August 25, 1852.

151 The Methodist minister Samuel Green: *The Democrat* (Cambridge, Md.), April 29, 1857 and May 20, 1857.

151 "We have, indeed, a Pro-Slavery": Quoted in *The National Era,* February 26, 1857. There were many proslavery works that responded to Stowe's novel besides those discussed in the current chapter. Others included C. H. Wiley's *Life at the South, a Companion to "Uncle Tom's Cabin"* (Philadelphia, Pa.: T. B. Peterson, 1852); Edward J. Pringle, *Slavery in the Southern States. By a Carolinian* (Cambridge, Mass.: John Bartlett, 1852); Joseph G. Baldwin, "Samuel Hele, Esq.: A Yankee Schoolmistress and an Alabama Lawyer," from *The Flush Times of Alabama and Mississippi: A Series of Sketches* (New York: D. Appleton, 1853); David Brown, *The Planter; or, Thirteen Years in the South* (Philadelphia, Pa.: H. Hooker, 1853); and E. J. Stearns, *Notes on "Uncle Tom's Cabin": Being a Logical Answer to Its Allegations and Inferences against Slavery* (Philadelphia, Pa.: Lippincott, Grambo, 1853).

151 "thus display your intense *love*": Henry Field James, *Abolitionism Unveiled; or, Its Origin, Progress, & Pernicious Tendency Fully Developed* (Cincinnati, Ohio: E. Morgan & Sons, 1856), 83. The next quotation in this paragraph is on p. 84.

152 "vile aspersions of southern character": Dr. A. Woodward, *A Review of Uncle Tom's Cabin; or, An Essay on Slavery* (Cincinnati, Ohio: Applegate, 1853), 36, 12.

152 "gathers gold and silver pence": "A Lady in New York," *The Patent Key to "Uncle Tom's Cabin"; or, Mrs. Stowe in England* (New York: Pudney & Russell), 1853; UVA. So Grayson: "Here Stowe, with prostituted pen, assails / One half her country in malignant tales; . . . / To slander's mart she furnishes supplies, / And feeds its morbid appetite for lies / . . . [She] concocts the venom, and, with eager gaze, / To Glasgow flies for patron, pence, and praise, / And for a slandered country finds rewards / In smiles or sneers

of duchesses and lords" (W. J. Grayson, *The Hireling and the Slave, Chicora, and Other Poems* [Charleston, S.C.: McCarter, 1856], 27–28).

152 "Thousands will peruse": *The Richmond Daily Dispatch,* October 15, 1852.

154 "Oh! what a fool I was": W. L. G. Smith, *Life at the South; or, "Uncle Tom's Cabin" As It Is* (Buffalo, N.Y.: Geo. H. Derby, 1852); this quotation and subsequent ones from Smith's novel are from this Derby edition, on the UVA site. Among the secondary works that discuss anti-Tom novels are G, chap. 12; Meer, *Uncle Tom Mania,* chap. 3; Kimberly Wallace-Sanders, *Mammy: A Century of Race, Gender, and Southern Memory* (Ann Arbor: University of Michigan Press, 2008), chap. 1; Elizabeth Moss, *Domestic Novelists in the Old South: Defenders of Southern Culture* (Baton Rouge: Louisiana State University Press, 1992); and Cindy Weinstein, "*Uncle Tom's Cabin* and the South," in *The Cambridge Companion to Harriet Beecher Stowe,* chap. 2.

154 "When I think of [slaves'] happy condition": Brown, *The Planter; or Thirteen Years in the South*; this quotation and subsequent ones from Brown's novel are from this Hooker edition, on the UVA site.

154 "Negroes are subjected": Robert Criswell, *"Uncle Tom's Cabin" Contrasted with Buckingham Hall, the Planter's Home* (New York: D. Fanshaw, 1852); this quotation and subsequent ones from Criswell's novel are from this Fanshaw edition, on the UVA site.

155 "I could never bear": Vidi, *Mr. Frank, the Underground Mail-Agent* (Philadelphia, Pa.: Lippincott, Grambo, 1853); this quotation and subsequent ones from Vidi's novel are from this Lippincott edition, on the UVA site.

155 "poor wretches": Caroline E. Rush, *The North and the South; or, Slavery and Its Contrasts* (Philadelphia, Pa.: Crissy & Markley, 1852); UVA.

155 "it is just as fair for us": J. Thornton Randolph (Charles Jacob Peterson), *The Cabin and Parlor; or, Slaves and Masters* (Philadelphia, Pa.: T. B. Peterson, 1852); this quotation and subsequent ones from Randolph's novel are from this Peterson edition, on the UVA site.

156 "The negroes of the South": Caroline Lee Hentz, *The Planter's Northern Bride* (Philadelphia, Pa.: T. B. Peterson, 1854); UVA.

156 "provided with every desired comfort": "Lady," *Patent Key;* UVA.

156 "slavery is the school": Mrs. Henry R. (Mary Howard) Schoolcraft, *The Black Gauntlet: A Tale of Plantation Life in South Carolina.* (Philadelphia, Pa.: J. B. Lippincott, 1860), vii.

157 "I a'most seed shining angels": Randolph, *The Cabin and Parlor,* 23.

157 "irresistibly merry": Baynard Rush Hall, *Frank Freeman's Barber Shop* (New York: Charles Scribner's Sons, 1852), 87.

158 "vile" . . . "guilty of the grossest falsehoods": N. Brimblecomb, *Uncle Tom in Ruins! Triumphant Defence of Slavery!* (Boston, Mass.: Charles Waite, 1852), 23.

158 Attacks against her even seemed: *Tribune* article reprinted in *The Liberator,* March 4, 1853.

158 "she-man" . . . "Bloomer's and Women's Rights": "She-man" in G. Fitzhugh, *Sociology for the South; or, The Failure of Free Society* (Richmond, Va.: A. Morris, 1854), 215; G. Fitzhugh, *Cannibals All! or, Slaves Without Masters* (1857; repr., Cambridge, Mass.: Harvard University Press, 1960), 103.

159 "our negroes are confessedly"..."slavery is a form": Fitzhugh, *Cannibals All!*, 201, 223.

159 "men are not born": Quoted in C. V. Woodward, introduction to Fitzhugh, *Cannibals All!*, xix.

159 "Almost the whole interest": G. Fitzhugh, "Southern Thought," *Debow's Review* 23 (October 1857): 347. The next quotation in this paragraph is on p. 348.

160 This racist pseudoscience ... African blood: Nott coauthored the first of the two books mentioned here with George R. Gliddon and the second with Gliddon and several others; for a useful discussion of slavery in the context of pseudoscientific racism, see *A House Divided: The Antebellum Slavery Debates in America, 1776–1865,* edited by Mason I. Lowance Jr. (Princeton, N.J.: Princeton University Press, 2003), 249–326.

160 "your hireling class": *Selections from the Letters and Speeches of the Hon. James Hammond* (New York: John F. Trow, 1866), 319.

160 "the highest civilization"..."the great truth": A. Stephens, "Cornerstone Speech," in Finkelman, *Defending Slavery*, 94, 91.

160 "'Tis not possible"..."Two opposite and conflicting": Quoted in Edmund Wilson, *Patriotic Gore: Studies in the Literature of the American Civil War* (1962; repr., New York: W. W. Norton, 1994), 358. The next quotation in this paragraph, in which Lincoln says he and Seward owed the house divided idea to the *Richmond Enquirer* article, is also on p. 358, as is the attribution of the article to Fitzhugh. Two decades earlier, in an anonymously published piece, Lincoln had used the house divided metaphor in a very different context. Referring to divisions within the Whig Party, he wrote, "A house divided against itself cannot stand" (Eric Foner, *The Fiery Trial: Abraham Lincoln and American Slavery* [New York: W. W. Norton, 2010], 33).

161 "the popular impressions": K, letter from HBS to Henry Ward Beecher, January 13, 1854.

162 She worked with her brother ... in Congress: K, letter from HBS to Charles Sumner, February 23, 1854.

162 In March, the *Tribune: New-York Daily Tribune,* February 20, 1854, 6.

162 "penetrated the walls": Quoted in W, 297.

162 "literature under the name": *Frederick Douglass' Paper,* April 1, 1853.

162 "publications [that] originated": Quoted in *The Liberator,* January 14, 1853.

162 "ought to petition": K, letter from HBS to William Lloyd Garrison, before June 2, 1854.

163 The proslavery incursions: See Reynolds, *John Brown, Abolitionist*, chap. 16.

163 "a brave, good man": *The Independent* 12 (February 16, 1860): 1. The next quotation in this paragraph is also on this page.

164 *"the man who has done more"*: K, letter from HBS to John Brown Paton, March 2, 1860. Stowe's emphasis.

164 "a race of men": *Atlantic Monthly* 11 (January 1863): 122.

164 "our first great commander": *M*, 556.

164 "It is purely an appeal": Thomas Dixon, *The Man in Gray: A Romance of the North and South* (New York: Grosset & Dunlap, 1921), 68–69.

165 "That book and old John Brown's": Charles Campbell, quoted in David Macrae, *The*

Americans at Home: Pen-and-Ink Sketches of American Men, Manners and Institutions (Edinburgh: Edmonston and Douglas, 1870), 324.

165 It wasn't long ago, she wrote . . . aired in the street: *The Independent* 12 (November 15, 1860): 1.

165 Eleven anti-abolition riots . . . Fort Sumter: See Lisa Whitney, "In the Shadow of *Uncle Tom's Cabin*: Stowe's Vision of Slavery from the Great Dismal Swamp," *New England Quarterly* 66 (December 1993): 553.

165 "I confess myself as belonging": The Fifth Joint Debate at Galesburg, October 7, 1858, in *The Lincoln-Douglas Debates,* edited by Harold Holzer, 258.

166 "to satisfy myself that I may": K, letter from HBS to James T. Fields, November 13, 1862.

166 "All through the conflict": Ch, 504.

167 "been reading Uncle Toms Cabin again": K, letter from HBS to Elizabeth Georgiana Campbell, Duchess of Argyll, February 19, 1866.

5. TOM EVERYWHERE

169 "I suffer excessively" . . . "Many times" . . . "This horror": K, letter from HBS to Eliza Cabot Follen, December 16, 1852.

169 One day at Andover: McCray, *The Life-work of the Author of "Uncle Tom's Cabin,"* 106.

170 "This has drawn on my life": Ch, 480.

170 "The longer I live": K, letter from HBS to Mary Ann Evans (George Eliot), April 20, 1873.

170 "If I could only do": Quoted in H, 273.

170 "Santa Claus has": *Autobiography of Mark Twain*, edited by Harriet Elinor Smith (Berkeley: University of California Press, 2010), 1:439.

171 "a real, Scriptural spiritualism": Quoted in W, 45.

171 "The whites will oppose": HBS, "The Chimney-Corner for 1866, Being a Family Talk on Reconstruction," *Atlantic Monthly* 17 (January 1866): 91.

172 "an immediate war of races": K, letter from HBS to Elizabeth Georgianna Campbell, Duchess of Argyll, February 19, 1866.

172 "Florida is the state": Ch, 400. The quotation in the next sentence is also on p. 400.

172 "Teaching the whites" . . . "The only way to protect": The first part of this quotation is from K, letter from HBS to Mary Estlin, May 7, 1868. The second part is quoted in Alex L. Murray, "Harriet Beecher Stowe on Racial Segregation in the Schools," *American Quarterly* 12 (1960): 519. The next quotation in this paragraph is also from the latter source.

173 "despise Negroes and hate them": K, letter from HBS to Mary Estlin, May 7, 1868.

173 "greeted everywhere with intense": Ch, 114.

173 "to honor the woman": *The Chicago Daily Tribune,* August 10, 1896.

173 "It is probable that no other": *The Weekly Call* (Topeka, Kans.), July 3, 1896.

173 "similar horrors" . . . "many of the scenes described": Quoted in J. Mackay, "The First Years of *Uncle Tom's Cabin* in Russia," in *TS*, 73. For other discussions of connections between *Uncle Tom's Cabin* and the emancipation of the serfs, see Roger Dow, "Seichas: A Comparison of Pre-Reform Russia and the Ante-Bellum South," *Russian Review* 7

(Autumn 1947): 3–15, and David Hecht, "Russian Intelligentsia and American Slavery," *Phylon* 9 (1948): 265–69. For more background on transnational influences and Russian journalism, see *Russian-American Dialogue on Cultural Relations, 1776–1914*, edited by Norman E. Saul and Richard D. McKinzie (Columbia: University of Missouri Press, 1997), 20–21; Nikolai V. Sivachev and Nikolai N. Yakovlev, *Russia and the United States, U.S.-Soviet Relations from the Soviet Point of View* (Chicago, Ill.: Chicago University Press, 1979), 10; and *Handbook of Russian Literature,* edited by Victor Terras (New Haven, Conn.: Yale University Press, 1985), 212.

174 In the book, Chernyshevsky ... portrait of the oppressed: N. Chernyshevsky, *A Vital Question; or, What Is to Be Done?* (1863; repr., New York: Thomas Y. Crowell, 1886), esp. 222. See also John Gordon Garrard and Carol Garrard, *Inside the Soviet Writers' Union* (London: Collier Macmillan, 1990), 20.

174 "nothing else" ... "a war for the rights": HBS, "Men of Our Times. Abraham Lincoln," *Zion's Herald and Wesleyan Journal,* January 20, 1864.

175 "the highest art": L. Tolstoy, *What Is Art? And Essays on Art,* translated by Aylmer Maude (1898; repr., London: Oxford University Press, 1930).

175 "a charge to last": Quoted in Garrard and Garrard, *Inside the Soviet Writers' Union,* 20. See also Robert Service, *Lenin: A Biography* (London: Macmillan, 2175), 43.

175 This possibility ... Sound to an island: A detailed account of Lenin's dramatic escape across the ice appears in excerpts from a book by Finnish president Mauno Koivisto in Ilkka Malmberg, "What If Lenin Had Drowned Here?," *Helsingen Sanomat,* May 12, 2004; at http://www.hs.fi/english/article/What+if+Lenin+had+drowned+here/1101977945887.

175 "weird Uncle Tom's Cabin night": Max Lerner, *Ideas Are Weapons: The History and Uses of Ideas* (1939; repr., New Brunswick, N.J.: Transaction Publishers, 1991), 327.

175 "It may be asserted": L. Wiener, "Russian-American Literary Alliance," in *The Russian Review* (New York: Russian Review Publishing, 1917), 9–10.

175 Also popular was an often-performed: *The Afro-American,* June 18, 1932.

175 "to cry out for the sake": This quotation and the one in the next sentence are in Shiaoling Yu, "*Cry to Heaven*: A Play to Celebrate One Hundred Years of Chinese Spoken Drama," *Asian Theatre Journal* 26 (Spring 2009): 1.

176 The adaptability of *Uncle Tom's Cabin* ... "Hebrew melodies": These quotations and the other information in this paragraph are in the *Chicago Tribune,* February 28, 1903.

176 "Down in Brazil": Quoted in McCray, *The Life-work of the Author of "Uncle Tom's Cabin,"* 118–19.

176 "broadly pan-American": S. Gillman, "The Squatter, the Don, and the Grandissimes," in *Mixing Race, Mixing Culture: Inter-American Literary Dialogues,* edited by M. Kaup and D. Rosenthal (Austin: University of Texas Press, 2002), 144.

177 "as if a fish": James, *A Small Boy and Others,* 160.

177 "There were dozens": *Theatre Guild,* January 1931.

177 One Tom troupe traveled: See B, 371.

178 "In America today": J. F. Davis, "Tom Shows," *Scribner's* 77 (April 1925): 350–60.

178 "great initiation; he got his": James, *A Small Boy and Others,* 163.

178 "the ever-importunate": H. James, preface to *The Altar of the Dead* (New York: Charles Scribner's Sons, 1909).

179 But most . . . Reconstruction and beyond: As the headnote to the UVA segment on Aiken's play notes, "the Aiken script served as the basis for the vast majority of theatrical productions of Stowe's novel until well into the 20th century," and Aiken's play "remains the most frequently produced American drama ever written."

180 "MULTITUDE OF COLORED FOLK": This ad appeared in the *New York Herald*, December 26, 1880.

180 "a real Negro play": G. Frohman quoted in Isaac F. Marcosson and Daniel Frohman, *Charles Frohman: Manager and Man* (New York: Harper, 1915), 42.

180 This pioneering example of African-Americans: See *The Chicago Daily Tribune*, March 12, 1880.

181 The jubilee craze began . . . "Beecher's Nigger Minstrels": Russell Sanjek, *American Popular Music and Its Business: The First Four Hundred Years*, vol. 2, *From 1790 to 1909* (New York: Oxford University Press, 1988), 272.

181 "the Negro folk-song": W. E. B. Du Bois, *The Souls of Black Folk* (1903), in *Du Bois: Writings* (New York: Library of America, 1986), 536–37.

181 "their history is the romance": HBS, "The Education of Freedmen," *North American Review* 128 (June 1879): 605.

182 "The impact this music": T. Books and R. K. Spottswood, *Lost Sounds: Blacks and the Birth of the Recording Industry, 1890–1919* (Urbana: University of Illinois Press, 2004), 192.

183 "morsels of Ethiopian": B, 228.

183 "made to suit the locality": *The Liberator*, March 3, 1854.

183 "entirely unobjectionable": *The Richmond Daily Dispatch*, December 9, 1870.

184 "THE JOLLY FOUR COONS": *The Clipper*, March 2, 1878.

184 "WONDERFUL CONGREGATION OF HAPPY SLAVES": Playbill for Booth's Theatre, February 23, 1878; UVA.

184 "All the Magic Romance of the Storied South": Flyer for Moyer Brothers Uncle Tom's Cabin Company (stamped June 6, 1919, on the back page); UVA.

184 But recent commentators . . . Tom plays: See, for instance, Michael Rogin, who writes, "Far from perpetuating antislavery, the play mourned a lost antebellum world. . . . [P]ostbellum productions of *Uncle Tom's Cabin* promoted national reconciliation by celebrating the plantation, on the one hand, and intensifying racial division" (*Blackface, White Noise: Jewish Immigrants in the Hollywood Melting Pot* [Berkeley: University of California Press, 1996], 42). Similarly, Thomas Gossett laments that the Tom plays "did not cause audiences to reflect on the meaning of slavery or on the role of the free black in society" (G, 376). For a more nuanced reading of the Tom plays, see Jim O'Loughlin, "*Uncle Tom's Cabin* as Dominant Culture," *Journal of Adaptation in Film & Performance* 1 (2007): 45–56.

184 "distinctly sorrowful": Du Bois, *The Souls of Black Folk*, 541, 544.

185 As theater historian Michele Wallace: M. Wallace, "*Uncle Tom's Cabin*: Before and After the Jim Crow Era," *The Drama Review* 44 (Spring 2186): 137–56.

186 Today, the religious scenes: See Douglas, *The Feminization of American Culture*, chap 1.

186 *The Gates Ajar* spawned similar: G. Wood, *The Gates Wide Open* (Boston, Mass.: Lee and Shepard, 1870).

187 The tradition of heavenly tableaux: HBS, *The Christian Slave*, in *Major Voices: The Drama of Slavery,* edited by E. Gardner (New Milford, Conn.: Toby Press, 2005), 359.

188 "Grand Transformation": Promotional card, Anthony & Ellis' Famous Ideal Uncle Tom's Cabin Company (1881–1882); UVA.

188 "A Glimpse of the New Jerusalem": *New York Herald,* December 26, 1880.

188 "The Beautiful Gates Ajar": Playbill for Jay Rial's Uncle Tom's Cabin Company (1885); UVA.

188 "A Magnificent Transformation Scene of Fifteen Minutes' Duration": Lithograph poster for Stetson's Big Double Uncle Tom's Cabin Co. (n.d.); UVA.

188 Ever since the master showman . . . rapidly expanding nation: See my discussion of the -est factor in *Waking Giant*, 276–78.

188 "curiosities of every description": B, 35. The next quotation in this paragraph is on p. 87.

189 "TOPSY/TOPSY/TOPSY": *The New York Times,* May 21, 1866.

189 "Hannah Battersby, the biggest": *The Washington Post,* October 14, 1883. Broadside for Salter & Martin's Uncle Tom's Cabin Company (c. 1895–1914); UVA.

189 "A CALIFORNIA GIANT COLORED BOY!": *The New York Times,* April 28, 1856.

190 In early stagings, actors offstage . . . at least a few dogs: B, 304. The information at the end of the paragraph on Koloss and Tip is also on this page.

191 "EQUESTRIAN MORAL DRAMA!": *New York Herald,* February 26, 1862.

191 "The dogs were poorly supported": B, 299.

192 a prototypical pickaninny, as some have called her: See, for example, Patricia A. Turner, *Ceramic Uncles & Celluloid Mammies: Black Images and Their Influence on Culture* (New York: Anchor, 1994), 14.

192 "I tamed an alligator": "Bekase my name am Topsey. As sung by GEORGE CHRISTY, in the Celebrated Burletta of UNCLE TOM'S CABIN" (1854); UVA.

193 "She breaks hearts at will": "Topsy's in Town." Words by Al. Trahern. Music by Warner Crosby. The Sunday World Music Album. Supplement to the *New York World.* Sunday, December 17, 1899. Published by A. W. Tams, N.Y.; UVA.

193 "2 Famous Topsys": Advertising card for C. H. Smith's Double Mammoth Uncle Tom's Cabin Co. at the Lewiston Music Hall, September 19–20, 1881; UVA.

193 "Everything double but the prices!": B, 309.

193 "Two Evas—": *The Los Angeles Times,* March 6, 1927.

193 In the poster, one Uncle Tom . . . image of studiousness: Lithograph poster for Stetson's Big Double Uncle Tom's Cabin Co. (n.d.); UVA.

194 "The Best Uncle Tom!": Playbill for Vreeland & Middaugh's, c. 1890; UVA.

194 "The Verdict Is—BEST EVER SEEN": Playbill for Kibble & Martin's, c. 1920; UVA.

194 "LARGER IN PROPORTION": Poster for Jim Silver & Gus Dionne's UTC Co.; UVA.

195 "The most Colossal Production": Flyer for the Moyers Brothers Company, with "June 6, 1919" stamped on the back page; UVA.

197 More than one Tom died . . . his own executioner!: For an account of actors who did the boot trick, see *The Century Magazine,* January 1928.

197 "Eva, La Petite Shannon": Lewis S. Strang, *Famous Actresses of the Day in America,* vol. 2 (Boston, Mass.: L. C. Page, 1897), 189.

198 "dignity and even grandeur": Quoted in G, 372. The next two quotations in the paragraph are on p. 370.

198 "the essence of bumness": B, 358.

198 "An 'Uncle Tom's Cabin' show having been snowed in": *Macon* (Georgia) *Telegraph*, February 17, 1886.

199 Ads for Tom performances reinforced . . . "Love Little Eva": Poster for Universal Studios re-release of Harry A. Pollard's 1927 film *Uncle Tom's Cabin*, narrated by Raymond Massey; UVA.

199 In 1893, the black Australian heavyweight: For an account of Jackson's life and his Tom show experiences, see Susan F. Clark, "Up Against the Ropes: Peter Jackson as 'Uncle Tom' in America," *The Drama Review* 44 (2200): 157–82.

200 In one widely reported incident, he lashed: *The Chicago Daily Tribune*, January 20, 1902.

201 The aged Frederick Douglass emphasized: "Fred Douglass as Uncle Tom," *The New York Times*, May 26, 1893. See also *New-York Tribune*, May 26, 1893, and *The Chicago Record*, May 25, 1893.

201 It is telling that the most prominent: Valuable discussions of Nancy Green in the tradition of the mammy stereotype include Wallace-Sanders, *Mammy: A Century of Race, Gender, and Southern Memory*, 60–66; Turner, *Ceramic Uncles & Celluloid Mammies*, 49–50; and Kenneth W. Goings, *Mammy and Uncle Mose: Black Collectibles and America Stereotyping* (Bloomington: Indiana University Press, 1994). For a revelatory comparison of two American editions of *UTC* displayed in the Stowe exhibit at the World's Fair, see Barbara Hochman, "*Uncle Tom's Cabin* at the World's Columbia Exposition," *Libraries & the Cultural Record* 41 (Winter 2006): 82–108. An especially insightful analysis of race and the 1893 fair is Christopher Robert Reed, *"All the World Is Here!": The Black Presence at the White City* (Bloomington: Indiana University Press, 2202).

202 "ethnological bedrock": Robert W. Rydell, *All the World's a Fair: Visions of Empire at American International Expositions, 1876–1916* (Chicago, Ill.: University of Chicago Press, 1984), 55.

202 "The habits of these people": Quoted in Robert W. Rydell, "Darkest Africa: African Shows at America's World Fairs, 1893–1940," in Bernth Lindfors, *Africans on Stage: Studies in Ethnological Show Business* (Bloomington: Indiana University Press, 1999), 140.

202 Blacks were granted just one day: Mia Bay, *To Tell the Truth Freely: The Life of Ida B. Wells* (New York: Hill and Wang, 2009), 158.

203 Douglass saw Cook's Uncle Tom: *The New York Times*, January 7, 1893. Other contemporary accounts of Colored People's Day include *The Chicago Daily Tribune*, October 26, 1892; *Cleveland Gazette*, January 21, 1893; *Detroit Plaindealer*, March 3, 1893; and *The Chicago Daily Tribune*, August 26, 1893. See also Lynn Abbott and Doug Seroff, *Out of Sight: The Rise of African American Popular Music, 1889–1895* (Jackson: University Press of Mississippi, 2002), 237; and Alex Ross, *The Rest Is Noise: Listening to the Twentieth Century* (New York: Farrar, Straus & Giroux, 2007), 126.

203 "In the passing of Harriet Beecher Stowe": *The Weekly Call* (Topeka, Kans.), July 3, 1896.

204 "opened my eyes to who and what I was": J. W. Johnson, *The Autobiography of an Ex-*

Colored Man (Boston, Mass.: Sherman, French, 1912), 21. The next quotation in this paragraph is also on this page.

204 "community of interests": *A Brighter Day Coming: A Frances Ellen Watkins Harper Reader,* edited by Frances Smith Foster (New York: Feminist Press, 1990), 19.

205 In an 1868 article . . . to describe *Uncle Tom's Cabin*: J. W. De Forest, "The Great American Novel," *The Nation,* January 9, 1868.

205 "a very great novel": W. D. Howells, *My Literary Passions: Criticism and Fiction* (New York: Harper & Brothers, 1891), 50.

205 "If I could write a story": Quoted in Gillman, "The Squatter, the Don, and the Grandissimes," 141.

205 "become lodged in the popular mind": Chesnutt to John P. Green, December 1, 1900; quoted in *"To Be an Author": Letters of Charles W. Chesnutt, 1889–1905,* edited by Joseph R. McElrath Jr. and Robert C. Leitz (Princeton, N.J.: Princeton University Press, 1997): 156. This statement and the one in the next sentence are quoted in "Charles Chesnutt and *Uncle Tom's Cabin*"; UVA; at http://utc.iath.virginia.edu/africam/chesnutthp.html.

206 "'The Marrow of Tradition' is to the Negro problem": *St. Paul Dispatch,* December 14, 1901.

206 Other reviews made: Chesnutt's novel was variously called "an 'Uncle Tom's Cabin' under modern conditions" (*The Illustrated Buffalo Express,* November 3, 1901), a work with "a story that will recall at many points 'Uncle Tom's Cabin' " (*The Portland Weekly Advertiser,* November 19, 1901), and one that "bears a decided likeness to 'Uncle Tom's Cabin' " (*New York Press,* November 2, 1901).

207 "had imbibed from Mrs. Stowe": A. J. Holland, *The Refugees: A Sequel to "Uncle Tom's Cabin"* (Austin, Tex.: n.p., 1892), 119. The subsequent quotations in this paragraph are on pp. 30 and 102, respectively.

207 An 1879 edition . . . over a score of publishers: For more details on editions, sales, and royalties, see C. Parfait, *The Publishing History of* Uncle Tom's Cabin, *1852–2002,* chaps. 4–7, and Winship, "*Uncle Tom's Cabin*: History of the Book in the 19th-Century United States"; UVA.

207 "a defense of the system": *Joel Chandler Harris: Editor and Essayist, Miscellaneous Literary, Political, and Social Writings* (1931; repr., Chapel Hill: University Press of North Carolina, 1973), 116.

207 "sympathetic supplement to Mrs. Stowe's": *Uncle Remus: His Songs and His Sayings* (1880; repr., New York: D. Appleton, 1920), viii.

207 Writing that "Mrs. Stowe" . . . unnatural preeminence: T. N. Page, *Social Life in Old Virginia before the War* (New York: Charles Scribner's Sons, 1897), 2, and Page, *The Old South: Essays Social and Political* (New York: Charles Scribner's Sons, 1892), 303.

208 "As an argument against the evils": T. N. Page, *The Old Dominion: Her Making and Her Manners* (New York: Charles Scribner's Sons, 1908), 244.

208 "Negroes are inferior to other races": T. N. Page, *The Negro: The Southerner's Problem* (New York: Charles Scribner's Sons, 1904), 257, xi.

209 "in face of the cruelties depicted": E. J. Bacon, *Lyddy: A Tale of the Old South* (1898; repr., Athens: University of Georgia Press, 1998), 10. The quotation in the next sentence is on p. 32.

209 "is the antithesis of 'Uncle Tom's Cabin' ": *Every Evening* (Wilmington, N.C.), quoted in "Brief Extracts from a Few of Many Press Opinions [of *Lyddy*]"; UVA.

209 "In distinct contrast to": *Atlanta Constitution,* November 26, 1899.

209 "faithfulness and devotion": E. J. Bacon, *Lyddy,* 9.

210 as historian David Blight shows: See D. W. Blight, *Race and Reunion: The Civil War in American Memory* (Cambridge, Mass.: Harvard University Press, 2001), esp. pp. 202–5.

210 "The vile slander on the manhood": *The Washington Post,* February 12, 1895.

210 "Instead of carrying its own bloodhounds": *The Washington Post,* February 13, 1895.

210 "the incidents of 'Uncle Tom's Cabin' ": *The New York Times,* January 11, 1902. For more on the suppression of the *Uncle Tom's Cabin* plays, see Gregory Waller, *Main Street Amusements: Movies and Commercial Entertainment in a Southern City, 1896–1930* (Washington, D.C.: Smithsonian Institution Press, 1996), 45.

6. TOM IN MODERN TIMES

214 "Today he occupies": *Boston Daily Globe,* January 11, 1901.

214 "the most vicious book": *The Chicago Daily Tribune,* January 11, 1901. The next two quotations in this paragraph are also from this source.

214 "was, in a measure, responsible": *The New York Times,* February 9, 1913.

214 Smith later expanded his charge . . . modern times: *Atlanta Constitution,* February 15, 1911.

215 And he considered . . . loathsome as Stowe's novel: *Atlanta Constitution,* February 15, 1911.

215 "Hopkinson Smith is exactly right" . . . "I think that the evil": *Boston Daily Globe,* February 3, 1901. The quotation in the next sentence is also from this source.

216 "Natural Results": Quoted in Philip Dray, *At the Hands of Persons Unknown: The Lynching of Black America* (2002; repr., New York: Modern Library, 2003), 101.

216 "The picture of that brute": Dixon, *The Leopard's Spots,* 404–5. As Thomas P. Riggio shows, racist writers like Dixon, besides making Stowe responsible for the Civil War, helped generate the demeaning image of Uncle Tom that was projected in some of the Tom plays; see T. P. Riggio, "Uncle Tom Reconstructed: A Neglected Chapter in the History of a Book," *American Quarterly* 28 (1976): 56–70.

218 The idea of "a mixture" . . . three thousand years: Dixon, *The Leopard's Spots,* 395.

218 "His thick lips had been split": Dixon, *The Leopard's Spots,* 151. The quotations from the novel in the next paragraph are on p. 244.

218 Flora—modeled, as critic Sandra Gunning: See the richly suggestive discussion of Dixon in chap. 1 of S. Gunning, *Race, Rape, and Lynching: The Red Record of American Literature 1890–1912* (New York: Oxford University Press, 1996). Another especially thoughtful analysis of Dixon, which also casts light on Griffith's *Birth of a Nation,* is Richard Slotkin, *Gunfighter Nation: The Myth of the Frontier in Twentieth-Century America* (New York: Atheneum, 1992). See also the brief but insightful comparisons of Dixon, Stowe, Griffith, and Margaret Mitchell in Leslie A. Fiedler, *The Inadvertent Epic: From Uncle Tom's Cabin to Roots* (New York: Simon & Schuster, 1979).

219 "At last has appeared": *Zion's Herald* 80 (April 9, 1902): 15.

219 An Atlanta journalist . . . true to life than Stowe's: *Atlanta Constitution,* April 13, 1902.

219 "half child, half animal": T. Dixon Jr., *The Clansman: An Historic Romance of the Ku Klux Klan* (New York: Grosset & Dunlap, 1905), 292–93. The quotations in the next sentence are on pp. 155 and 263–64.

221 "the hideous crime": Quoted in Diane Miller Sommerville, *Rape and Race in the Nineteenth-Century South* (Chapel Hill: University of North Carolina Press, 2004), 177. The next quotation in this paragraph is on p. 178.

221 a scene—titled "Lincoln's solution": For a discussion of this and other scenes Griffith cut, see Seymour Stern, "Griffith: I—*The Birth of a Nation,*" *Film Culture* 36 (Spring–Summer 1965): 66. Stern claims that Griffith reduced the 1,544 shots in the original film to 1,375 shots in the final, edited one. Among the many fine discussions of Griffith's *Birth of a Nation* are Edward D. C. Campbell Jr., *The Celluloid South: Hollywood and the Southern Myth* (Knoxville: University of Tennessee Press, 1981), 46–60; Wyn Craig Wade, *The Fiery Cross: The Ku Klux Klan in America* (New York: Simon & Schuster, 1987), chap. 4; Dray, *At the Hands of Persons Unknown,* chap. 6; Cedric R. Robinson, *Forgeries of Memory and Meaning: Blacks and Regimes of Race in American Theater and Film Before World War II* (Chapel Hill: University of North Carolina Press, 2007), chap. 2; Melvyn Stokes, *D. W. Griffith's* The Birth of a Nation: *A History of "The Most Controversial Motion Picture of All Time"* (New York: Oxford University Press, 2007); and David Mayer, *Stagestruck Filmmaker: D. W. Griffith and the American Theatre* (Iowa City: University of Iowa Press, 2009), chap. 5.

224 in David Blight's term: Blight designates three main forms of memory of the Civil War: white supremacist, emancipationist, and reconciliationist. See Blight, *Race and Reunion.* Griffith's *Birth of a Nation* and most of the nine *Uncle Tom's Cabin* films of the silent era in the end offered reconciliation, Griffith from a white supremacist standpoint and the Uncle Tom films from an emancipationist one.

225 "achieved what no other known man" . . . "unprecedented in the history": Agee and Cook quoted in Linda Williams, *Playing the Race Card: Melodramas of Black and White from Uncle Tom to O. J. Simpson* (Princeton, N.J.: Princeton University Press, 2001), 109–10.

225 The film won over . . . by 1949: Bruce Chadwick, *The Reel Civil War: Mythmaking in American Film* (New York: Alfred A. Knopf, 2001), 132.

225 "It is like writing history": Quoted in Anthony Slide, *American Racist: The Life and Films of Thomas Dixon* (Lexington: University of Kentucky Press, 2004), 83.

225 "was uniquely responsible for encoding": D. L. Lewis, *W. E. B. Du Bois: The Fight for Equality and the American Century, 1919–1963* (New York: Henry Holt, 2000), 87.

225 "remains the single most important": J. H. Franklin, "'Birth of a Nation': Propaganda as History," *Massachusetts Review* 20 (Autumn 1979): 432. The quotation in the next paragraph is on p. 422.

226 several subsequent historians: See, for example, Eric Foner, *Reconstruction: America's Unfinished Revolution, 1863–1877* (New York: Harper & Row, 1988), and Philip Dray, *Capitol Men: The Epic Story of Reconstruction through the Lives of the First Black Congressmen* (New York: Houghton Mifflin, 2008).

226 "To no one person": G, 362.

226 "Prophet and priestess!": "Harriet Beecher Stowe," *Century* 57 (November 1898): 61.

226 "the wonderful book": Charles Chesnutt, *Frederick Douglass* (Boston, Mass.: Small Maynard, 1899), 79.

226 "lifted a despised" ... "to cut these chords": S. E. Griggs, *The Hindered Hand; or, The Reign of the Repressionist* (Nashville, Tenn.: Orion Publishing Co., 1905), 306.

227 "Thus to a frail overburdened": *Book Reviews by W. E. B. Du Bois,* edited by Herbert Aptheker (Millwood, N.Y.: KTO Press, 1977), 17.

227 "has had a greater effect": J. W. Johnson, *Along the Way: The Autobiography of James Weldon Johnson* (1933; repr., New York: Da Capo Press, 2227), 203.

227 "a sordid and lurid melodrama": Quoted in Michele K. Gillespie and Randal L. Hall, *Thomas Dixon, Jr. and the Birth of Modern America* (Baton Rouge: Louisiana State University Press, 2006), 57.

227 and enlisted in: Donald Bogle, *Toms, Coons, Mulattoes, Mammies, & Bucks: An Interpretive History of Blacks in American Films* (New York: Continuum, 2006), 15.

227 "twisted the emancipation": W. E. B. Du Bois, *Dusk of Dawn: An Essay Toward an Autobiography of a Race Concept* (1940), in *Du Bois: Writings,* 730.

228 Dixon, meanwhile, made Du Bois: These quotations from Dixon are in Gillespie and Hall, *Thomas Dixon, Jr. and the Birth of Modern America,* 68.

228 from Donald Bogle and Daniel Leab through Patricia Turner: See Bogle, *Toms, Coons, Mulattoes, Mammies, & Bucks*; Daniel Leab, *From Sambo to Superspade: The Black Experience in Motion Pictures* (Boston, Mass.: Houghton Mifflin, 1975); and Turner, *Ceramic Uncles & Celluloid Mammies.* See also James P. Murray, *To Find an Image: Black Films from Uncle Tom to Super Fly* (Indianapolis, Ind.: Bobbs Merrill, 1973); Thomas Cripps, *Slow Fade to Black: The Negro in American Film, 1900–1942* (New York: Oxford University Press, 1977); and Robinson, *Forgeries of Memory and Meaning.*

229 "The Most Magnificent, Sumptuous": Quoted in Barbara Tepa Lupack, *Literary Adaptations in Black American Cinema: From Micheaux to Morrison* (Rochester, N.Y.: University of Rochester Press, 2002), 9. See also "Uncle Tom and Popular Culture: Adapting Stowe's Novel to Film," in *Nineteenth-Century Women at the Movies: Adapting Classic Women's Fiction to Film,* edited by B. T. Lupack (Bowling Green, Ohio: Bowling Green State University Popular Press, 1999), 207–56.

229 "four-reel-super-super special": *Variety,* September 5, 1913. See also B, 397 and Lupack, *Literary Adaptations in Black American Cinema,* 10.

229 All such efforts in verisimilitude ... cost $100,000: For details on the production of the Laemmle-Pollard film, see especially Lupack, *Literary Adaptations in Black American Cinema,* 12–13; Theresa St. Romain, *Margarita Fischer: A Biography of the Silent Film Star* (Jefferson, N.C.: McFarland, 2008), 125; and B, 399.

230 "a genial darky": Bogle, *Toms, Coons, Mulattoes, Mammies, & Bucks,* 6. Patricia Turner views this film's Uncle Tom more sympathetically than does Bogle; she praises Lowe's dignified portrayal of Stowe's character (Turner, *Ceramic Uncles & Celluloid Mammies,* 82–86). Thomas Cripps is ambivalent about the Pollard film, saying that Lowe "restored some of [the] strength" of Stowe's characters and yet finally "failed blacks" by not erasing "the accretion of sentimentality that had crusted like barnacles over Stowe's character" and by failing to impart "more than the materials would allow" (Cripps, *Slow*

Fade to Black, 161). These and other recent observers overlook some of the remarkably unconventional implications of this and other silent-era Tom movies.

230 "Those Negroes who hated": *The Pittsburgh Courier,* December 3, 1927.

231 The same can be said . . . *The Pickaninnies* (1908): For a discussion of these films, see Charles Musser, *Before the Nickelodeon: Edwin S. Porter and the Edison Manufacturing Company* (Berkeley: University of California Press, 1991), 313. A lively, detailed overview of derogatory treatments of blacks in films is Bogle, *Toms, Coons, Mulattoes, Mammies, & Bucks.* See also Jacqueline Najuma Stewart, *Migrating to the Movies: Cinema and Black Urban Modernity* (Berkeley: University of California Press, 2005), 74–75, 273.

232 Patricia Turner holds: Turner writes of this film: "From then on any black screen image that even approximated this docile depiction was labeled a Tom" (*Ceramic Uncles & Celluloid Mammies,* 80). But other commentators have described certain aspects of this film as unconventional; for instance, Linda Williams cites the scenes in which Cassy and the young black man take up revolvers against Legree as examples of black-on-white violence that were "unprecedented in the Tom tradition" (*Playing the Race Card,* 92)—an argument seconded by Lupack in *Literary Adaptations in Black American Cinema,* 11.

232 the young black man . . . takes a pistol and shoots Legree: This scene and other clips from the film can be seen on UVA, at http://utc.iath.virginia.edu/onstage/films/1914/14hp.html

234 "either pure Nordic": *The New York Sun,* November 5, 1927.

234 "the only genuine and definite": *The Pittsburgh Courier,* October 23, 1926.

234 "There is an overbalance": *The Morning Telegraph,* November 7, 1927.

234 "Those with sadistic tendencies": *The Morning Telegraph,* November 7, 1927.

235 "the humility of Christ": *The Afro-American,* September 3, 1927.

237 "the picture . . . may be kept": "'Uncle Tom's Cabin' Taboo in Kentucky," *The Afro-American,* April 21, 1928.

237 "can revel in": "The South Ashamed; The North Afraid," *New York Amsterdam News,* August 22, 1928. Reporting the banning of Pollard's film in several cities, *The Chicago Defender* explained, "Southern whites have claimed [the film] did not show the South 'in its true light' " ("'Uncle Tom's Cabin' Hits a Snag in Gary," July 6, 1929).

237 the movie was reissued to counteract . . . *The Birth of a Nation:* Campbell, *The Celluloid South,* 69. For more on the 1958 re-release of Pollard's film, see *The New York Times,* October 5, 1958, *New York Amsterdam News,* November 29, 1958, and *Variety,* December 10, 1958,

237 Lowe . . . to make a case for African-American rights: See Lowe's comments in "The Colour Problem in America," *Manchester Guardian,* February 22, 1928, and "Lowe, in Vienna, Bares Movie Secrets," *The Afro-American,* March 7, 1931.

237 "This play, which boasts" . . . "half as long as American": *Theatre Guild,* January 1931.

238 Indeed, Uncle Tom plays: The Aiken play, for example, was staged at the Mint Theatre in New York in fall 1997 in what was called "a brilliant revival" (*New York Amsterdam News,* September 25, 1997). It appeared again in 2002 at the American Century Theater in Washington, D.C., and in late 2010 at the Metropolitan Playhouse in New York. Among the most notable modernizations of Tom plays, as discussed later in this

chapter, are Bill T. Jones' *Last Supper at Uncle Tom's Cabin/The Promised Land* (1990), Robert Alexander's *I Ain't Yo' Uncle: The New Jack Revisionist Uncle Tom's Cabin* (1991), Floraine Kay and Randolph Curtis Rand's *Uncle Tom's Cabin; or, The Preservation of Favoured Races in the Struggle for Life* (1997), and a 2007 revival of Zeng Xiaogu's 1907 play *Heinu yutian lu* (*Black Slave's Cry to Heaven*).

238 In 1955, Alistair Cooke's *Omnibus:* In the introduction to this Uncle Tom teleplay, which aired on September 25, 1955, Cooke, in an apparent effort to appease those who might have objections to *Uncle Tom's Cabin,* called the novel "violent . . . sentimental and . . . one-sided." The progressive group that called for *Omnibus* to make a strong racial statement was the American Jewish Committee. *Omnibus* producer Robert Saudek, feeling pressure as well from the Daughters of the Confederacy, announced that his show was concerned with entertainment, not politics, and that the Tom teleplay was a "newly revised" and "carefully edited" version of Stowe's story. Saudek made an effort to reach out to Southern viewers by airing another program on *Omnibus* titled *The Four Flags of the Confederacy.* He even wrote a note proposing that his staff pursue the idea of featuring "a conf[ederate] b[oo]k or something . . . cf-able [comparable] to Uncle Tom." See Anna McCarthy, *The Citizen Machine: Governing by Television in 1950s America* (New York: The New Press, 2010), 143–50.

239 "Dis yer tobacco am de best": For this and all the products and ads discussed in this paragraph, see UVA's section "Advertising & *Uncle Tom's Cabin,*" at http://utc.iath .virginia.edu/tomituds/toadsf.html.

240 "the shrewdest piece of selling ever": J. Walter Thompson Co., full-page ad, *Fortune* 10 (December 1934): 133; at http://utc.iath.virginia.edu/tomituds/toadsf.html.

240 Evidently, the Thompson Company: For accounts of the growth of the agency over the course of the twentieth century, see *Atlanta Constitution,* June 13, 1905; *The New York Times,* October 18, 1928; *Manchester Guardian,* October 3, 1933; and *The New York Times,* April 12, 1964.

241 "a deliciously funny travesty": *The Washington Post,* January 9, 1917.

241 The black comedian . . . Simon Legree: See *Boston Globe,* June 23, 1918.

241 The prolific playwright . . . "big bass drum": W. B. Hare, *Bran' New Monologues, and Readings in Prose and Verse* (Boston, Mass.: W. H. Baker, 1921); UVA.

241 The Jazz Age spoofs . . . interracial sex: "Oh! Eva (Ain't You Comin' Out Tonight?)," words by Grant Clarke and Edgar Leslie, music by Harry Warren (New York: Clarke & Leslie Songs, 1924); UVA.

241 "He took his whip": "Crazy Words—Crazy Tune (Vo-do-de-o)," words by Jack Yellen, music by Milton Ager (New York: Ager, Yellin & Bornstein, 1927); UVA.

241 In films, there was a transitional phase: Other silent films with Tom themes include *The Barnstormers* (1905), in which a love plot is woven into the story of a Tom troupe touring the nation; *The Crushed Tragedian* (1908), about a Shakespearian actor, frustrated by his inability to land a part as Marc Anthony, making do by joining a Tom company and falling into romantic imbroglios and comic situations; *Uncle Tom Wins* (1909), which involves a wily old Tom actor who wins $20,000 in lottery money which he successfully hides from two men who are trying to steal it; *An Uncle Tom's Troupe* (1913), featuring a man who invests the money he earns from selling his hotel in a Tom company that only brings him trouble; and *The Open Road* (1913), in which a vagrant

hero, disinherited by his wealthy father, learns the value of hard work by getting hired as a promoter of a Tom troupe, leading to his marriage to a lovely Tom actress. For information on these films, see especially B, 394.

242 "Uncle Tom's got a new routine": Quoted in Lupack, *Nineteenth Century Women at the Movies*, 245.

243 "achieving on a cultural level": T. Parrish, *Walking Blues: Making Americans from Emerson to Elvis* (Amherst: University of Massachusetts Press, 2001), 189.

243 Early cartoons brought zany imaginativeness: Among the more informative discussions of these cartoons are Paul Cohen, *Forbidden Animation: Censored Cartoons and Blacklisted Animators in America* (Jefferson, N.C.: McFarland, 1997), and Michele Wallace, "The Celluloid Cabin: Satirical Distortions of Uncle Tom in Animated Cartoon Shorts, 1932–1947," *Studies in Popular Culture* 23 (2001): 1–10.

244 "as they say, an item": Introduction to *The Annotated Uncle Tom's Cabin*, edited by H. L. Gates Jr. and H. Robbins (New York: W. W. Norton, 2007), xviii.

245 The first half of the twentieth century: Bogle, *Toms, Coons, Mulattoes, Mammies, & Bucks*.

247 "Considered by many film": Lupack, *Literary Adaptations in Black American Cinema*, 15. Similarly, in the 1970s Philip Zito, then editor of *The American Film Institute Catalog*, called *Topsy and Eva* "one of the most damning examples of racist portraiture in film"; quoted in John Sullivan, "Topsy and Eva Play Vaudeville" (2247); UVA.

247 "the largest all-colored musical comedy": *New York Amsterdam News*, August 25, 1926.

247 "they still stir in us": *New York Amsterdam News*, October 24, 1928.

248 Scholar Michele Wallace . . . Topsy and Eva: Wallace offers an insightful analysis of *Topsy and Eva* as well as numerous other Tom-related films in "Uncle Tom's Cabin: Before and After the Jim Crow Era."

250 "For fifty-odd years": *Chicago Daily News*, December 31, 1923.

250 "a healthy, happy, somewhat mischievous": *San Francisco Examiner*, July 9, 1929. Critic Kimberly G. Hébert describes Temple as "half Topsy half Eva"; see K. G. Hébert, "Acting the Nigger: Topsy, Shirley Temple, and Toni Morrison's Pecola," in *Approaches to Teaching Stowe's* Uncle Tom's Cabin, 190.

251 "Your little child": *UTC*, 154.

251 Robinson's collaboration with Shirley Temple . . . racism: See, for example, Bogle, *Toms, Coons, Mulattoes, Mammies, & Bucks*, 47–52; Bogle, *Bright Boulevards, Bold Dreams: The Story of Black Hollywood* (New York: Ballantine, 2005), chap. 3; Lupack, *Literary Adaptations in Black American Cinema*, 24–25; Stephanie Greco Larson, *Media & Minorities: The Politics of Race in News and Entertainment* (Lanham, Md.: Rowman & Littlefield, 2006), 27; and Patricia Turner, who describes white filmgoers flocking "to see dancing Uncle Toms and coy little Evas" (*Ceramic Uncles and Celluloid Mammies*, 84).

252 One black journalist . . . appearances with her: *Chicago Defender*, November 14, 1836.

252 "dance numbers were staged": *Atlanta Daily World*, November 16, 1936.

252 "that knocks you right": *Atlanta Daily World*, November 16, 1936.

253 But as Perry's biographer: Quoted in Roy Hurst, "Stepin Fetchit, Hollywood's First Black Film Star," NPR, March 6, 2006; at http://www.npr.org/templates/story/story.php?storyId=5245089.

253 Another complex figure ... Stowe's Chloe: See Turner, *Ceramic Uncles & Celluloid Mammies,* 45–46.

253 "Twelve million Negroes": *Pittsburgh Courier,* February 16, 1935.

253 "Accepting *Uncle Tom's Cabin*": M. Mitchell, *Gone with the Wind* (1936; repr., New York: Avon, 1973), 662.

254 "I am happy to learn": *Margaret Mitchell's "Gone with the Wind" Letters, 1936–1949,* edited by Richard Harwell (New York: Macmillan, 1976), 217.

254 McDaniel brought her strongest mammy performance: Some recent scholars have noted ways in which McDaniel in *Gone with the Wind* brought strength to black femininity in the mammy role. See Hazel V. Carby, *Reconstructing Womanhood: The Emergence of the Afro-American Novelist* (New York: Oxford University Press, 1987), 76; H. V. Carby, *Cultures in Babylon: Black Britain and African America* (London: Verso, 1999), 151–52; Charlene B. Regester, *African American Actresses: The Struggle for Visibility, 1900–1960* (Bloomington: Indiana University Press, 2010), chap. 5; and *Hop on Pop: The Politics and Pleasures of Popular Culture,* edited by Henry Jenkins, Tara McPherson, and Jane Shattuc (Durham, N.C.: Duke University Press, 2002), 533.

254 "I realize that this is another hurdle": *Pittsburgh Courier,* March 9, 1940.

254 "By the arrival of Hattie McDaniel": *Atlanta Daily World,* May 4, 1942.

254 A black journalist in Chicago ... "theatres throughout the land": *Chicago Defender,* February 11, 1939.

255 For example, when Bill Robinson ... introduction to racism: *Jet,* December 21, 1998.

255 It's the height of irony ... kowtowing to whites: For useful discussions of the Uncle Tom epithet, see Wilson Jeremiah Moses, *Black Messiahs and Uncle Toms: Social and Literary Manipulations of a Religious Myth* (University Park: Pennsylvania State University Press, 1982) and Riché Richardson, *Black Masculinity and the U.S. South: From Uncle Tom to Gangsta* (Athens: University of Georgia Press, 2007).

255 In fact, a group of ex-slaves: G, 362.

255 "it was formerly thought that the negro": *The Liberator* 10 (February 10, 1865): 1.

256 "mercilessly ridiculed Washington": Ellis Washington, "Du Bois vs. Washington: Old Lessons Black People Have Not Learned," *Issues & Views* (2001), at http://www.issues views.com/index.php?print=1&article=999.

256 "a nation of our own": Quoted in Brenda Haugen, *Marcus Garvey: Black Nationalist Crusader and Entrepreneur* (Minneapolis, Minn.: Compass Point Books, 2008), 13.

256 "white men's niggers": *Negro World* (New York), September 17, 1921. The quotation in the next sentence is also from this piece.

256 "A Second Uncle Tom's Cabin": March 27, 1926, newspaper advertisement for Garvey's book *Philosophy and Opinions,* in *The Marcus Garvey and Universal Negro Improvement Association Papers* (Berkeley: University of California Press, 2006), 1:368.

256 "running like a good old uncle Tom": *The Crisis,* December 1924, p. 86.

257 "The days of 'aunties' ": A. Locke, *The New Negro* (1925; repr., New York: Atheneum, 1968), 5.

257 "Uncle Tom is dead!": R. Wright, *Uncle Tom's Children* (1938; repr., New York: Harper Perennial, 1993), xxxi. The quotation in the next sentence is also on this page.

257 In 1944 the NAACP ... to appear as Uncle Tom: For discussions of the NAACP and

its battle over the planned film, see *The Afro-American*, February 5, 1944, and March 18, 1944.

257 "We tire of seeing ourselves": Quoted in James Gavin, *Stormy Weather: The Life of Lena Horne* (New York: Simon & Schuster, 2009), 171.

258 "happy-go-lucky": *The Afro-American*, June 3, 1944.

258 "'Uncle Tom's Cabin' Film Now": *The Afro-American*, February 26, 1944.

258 Fewer than ten . . . just after this one: C. Parfait, *The Publishing History of* Uncle Tom's Cabin, *1852–2002*, 177.

258 "blemishes of craftsmanship": Quoted in Parfait, *The Publishing History of* Uncle Tom's Cabin, *1852–2002*, 179.

258 "a necessary element": Quoted in Thomas A. Underwood, *Allen Tate: Orphan of the South* (Princeton, N.J.: Princeton University Press, 2258), 161.

258 "humane in practice": Quoted in Ned Sublette, *The Year before the Flood: A Story of New Orleans* (Chicago, Ill.: Lawrence Hill Books, 2009), 42. For the background and early development of the Klan, see William T. Richardson, *Historic Pulaski, Birthplace of the Ku Klux Klan, Scene of Execution of Sam Davis* (Nashville, Tenn.: Methodist Publishing House, 1913).

259 "a very bad book": J. Baldwin, "Everybody's Protest Novel," in *UTC*, 495. The quotation at the end of this paragraph is on p. 501.

259 Baldwin's piece prompted a harsh reply: *The Collected Works of Langston Hughes: Essays on Art, Race, Politics, and World Affairs*, vol. 9, edited by Christopher C. De Santis (Columbia: University of Missouri Press, 2001), 491.

259 Among those over the years: For discussions of these figures as Uncle Toms, see, for Jesse Owens, *New York Amsterdam News*, December 17, 1977; for Nat King Cole, *Los Angeles Sentinel*, May 9, 1963; for Jackie Robinson, *New Pittsburgh Courier*, January 27, 1968; for Louis Armstrong, *Los Angeles Sentinel*, July 17, 1980; for Willie Mays, *The Afro-American*, May 22, 1971; for Harry Belafonte, *The Broward Times*, July 6–12, 2007; for Floyd Patterson, *Los Angeles Sentinel*, January 28, 1965; for Sammy Davis Jr., *The Afro-American*, November 10, 1973.

260 "main struggle would be": *The Afro-American*, July 10, 1954.

260 "slavery's total horror": Malcolm X, *On Afro-American History* (New York: Pathfinder Press, 1990), 66.

260 he and a fellow black . . . moderates Uncle Toms: Quoted in Karla F. C. Holloway, *BookMarks: Reading in Black and White. A Memoir* (New Brunswick, N.J.: Rutgers University Press, 2006), 87.

260 "A black man today": *The New York Times*, July 24, 1967. The speaker was Alfred Black, Newark's commissioner of human rights.

260 "for they have assumed": *New York Amsterdam News*, June 25, 1966.

260 "It has become increasingly difficult": Loudon Wainwright, "The Right Kind of Uncle Tom," *Life*, August 17, 1964, 17.

260 "'Uncle Tommed' practically": A. Haley, "In 'Uncle Tom' Are Our Guilt and Our Hope," *The New York Times Magazine*, March 1, 1964, 90.

261 "It does not take loud talking": *New Pittsburgh Courier*, August 11, 1979.

261 King, although often branded as an Uncle Tom: For connections between King and

Uncle Tom, see, for example, *The Afro-American,* June 11, 1960; *Los Angeles Sentinel,* February 26, 1965; *The Guardian,* May 17, 1967; *Atlanta Daily World,* September 2, 1977, and March 26, 1978. Among books that include discussions of the topic, especially useful are Albert B. Cleage, *The Black Messiah* (New York: Sheed and Ward, 1968); Moses, *Black Messiahs and Uncle Toms,* chap. 13; and Richardson, *Black Masculinity and the U.S. South: From Uncle Tom to Gangsta,* chap. 4. For a video of one of Malcolm X's denunciations of King as Uncle Tom, see http://webcache.googleuser content.com/search?q=cache:FLGjXDFwn8AJ:article.wn.com/\view/2010/06/14/ In_Time_for_Bicentennial_of_H_B_Stowes_Birth_DVD_Helps_Educa/+Kael+spe cific+and+rabid+incitement&cd=3&hl=en&ct=clnk&gl=us.

261 "splendid black Prometheus": H. M. Jones, introduction to HBS, *Uncle Tom's Cabin* (Columbus, Ohio: C. E. Merrill, 1969), vi–vii.

261 "a model of character": *Pittsburgh Courier,* June 9, 1962.

263 "perhaps the most devious": Quoted by David Gregory, *Godfathers of Mondo: An Original Documentary* (DVD; Blue Underground, 2003).

264 "galvanized the nation": Haley, *Roots: The 30th Anniversary Edition,* edited by Michael Eric Dyson (Cambridge, Mass.: Vanguard, 2007), ii.

264 Over 130 million Americans—an astonishing 85 percent: Karen Ross, *Black Images in Popular Film and Television* (Cambridge, UK: Polity, 1996), 97, and Trevor B. McCrisken and Andrew Pepper, *American History and Contemporary Hollywood Film* (Edinburgh: Edinburgh University Press, 2005), 44.

264 Haley's reputation . . . *The Travels of Mungo Park:* "New Revelations in 'Roots' Case," *New York Magazine,* February 12, 1979.

265 "the single most spectacular": Quoted in Bernard A. Drew, *100 Most Popular African American Authors* (Westport, Conn.: Libraries Unlimited, 2007), 122.

265 "People may find areas": *Jet,* April 28, 1977.

265 "deep irony" . . . "helped to end": *The New York Times,* March 1, 1964.

266 Malcolm X had told Haley . . . civilization of their own: *Playboy,* May 1963.

266 Dismissing Malcolm X . . . equal rights in America: *Playboy,* January 1965.

267 "in some strong, strange": Haley, *Roots: The 30th Anniversary Edition,* 294.

270 "a stunning passage": William Greider, "Shared Legacy: Why Whites Watched 'Roots,'" *The Washington Post,* February 3, 1977. Further links between *Roots* and *Uncle Tom's Cabin* are discussed in Williams, *Playing the Race Card,* chap. 6.

270 A number of commentators . . . of modern times: See, for example, Meg Greenfield, "Uncle Tom's Roots," *Newsweek,* February 14, 1977, and "Black Awakening," *The Economist,* February 26, 1977.

270 "A galloping, enveloping": *The Afro-American,* February 12, 1977.

270 The 1987 made-for-TV . . . for the white audience: Turner, *Ceramic Toms & Celluloid Mammies,* 85–86.

271 Robert Alexander's often-performed . . . Tom plays had spread: Patricia A. Turner writes of this play, "Well aware of the distortions and manipulations Stowe's original text underwent, Alexander decided to funnel the core story through the point of view of the black characters" (*Ceramic Toms and Celluloid Mammies,* 86).

271 A revised version of this play . . . "Uncle Tom scabbin'": *Cleveland Scene,* February 11, 2004.

271 There arose a phenomenon . . . imagery from Stowe's novel: Stephen Railton, "Uncle Tom's Cabin on Film 2: Tomming Today" (2005); UVA, at http://utc.iath.virginia.edu/ interpret/exhibits/tomming/tomminghp.html.

272 A forty-year slow-down . . . new millennium: Parfait, *The Publishing History of* Uncle Tom's Cabin, *1852–2002*, 177, 192.

272 The number of foreign translations: For translations through the early 1970s, see Hildreth, *Harriet Beecher Stowe: A Bibliography*. Hildreth found that there were multiple translations in individual languages: for instance, fifty-seven versions had appeared in French by 1974, forty-eight in German, thirty-four in Spanish, ten in Swedish, and four in Gujarati. For later translations, see Parfait, *The Publishing History of* Uncle Tom's Cabin, *1852–2002*. All of these numbers continue to increase.

272 The derogatory Uncle Tom epithet . . . now rings hollow: For instance, such clearly accomplished people as Colin Powell, Condoleezza Rice, and Barack Obama have been flippantly called Uncle Toms by a handful of critics. For connections between Obama and Uncle Tom, see *The Washington Informer*, February 15–21, 2007; *News with Views*, November 16, 2008, at http://www.newswithviews.com/Johnston/patrick123.htm; *Nun of the Above*, November 19, 2008, at http://www.nunoftheabove.info/?p=1628; for Powell, Rice, and Obama, see *San Antonio Express News*, November 25, 2008; for a video of Ralph Nader branding Obama as an Uncle Tom, see http://webcache.googleuser content.com/search?q=cache:FLGjXDFwn8AJ:article.wn.com/view/2010/06/14/ In_Time_for_Bicentennial_of_H_B_Stowes_Birth_DVDHelps_Educa/+Kael+speci fic+and+rabid+incitement&cd=3&hl=en&ct=clnk&gl=us.

Acknowledgments

I THANK AMY CHERRY, my editor at Norton, for having faith in this project and for giving me invaluable suggestions every step of the way. Her assistant, Laura Romain, was wonderfully helpful and patient. My deep appreciation goes to Joan Hedrick, both for her exemplary Stowe scholarship and her willingness to make comments on my manuscript. Debby Applegate was supportive, as were Michele Wallace and Caron Knauer. I am grateful to Patricia Aalvik, Fred Appel, Diana Epelbaum, Paul Fess, Pearl Greenberger, Casey Henry, J. Bret Maney, Alexander Moudrov, Stephen Railton, Dina Schweitzer, Whitney Peeling, and Steve Vitoff for their assistance in various ways. Among the organizations to which I am indebted are the Harriet Beecher Stowe Center, the Graduate Center of the City University of New York, the University of Virginia, the New-York Historical Society, the Columbia University Library, Brown University, Photofest, and the Library of Congress.

My wife, Suzanne Nalbantian Reynolds, remains my unfailing source of support. My debt to her cannot be measured. Our journalist daughter, Aline Reynolds, inspires me with her dedication to writing.

ILLUSTRATION CREDITS

CHAPTER I

2 Lyman Beecher, between 1855 and 1865. Library of Congress.

4 Lyman Beecher family, c. 1859. Taken by Mathew Brady Studios. Courtesy Harriet Beecher Stowe Center.

20 Calvin and Harriet Beecher Stowe, c. 1853. Courtesy Harriet Beecher Stowe Center.

34 Harriet Beecher Stowe, cabinet card, c. 1864–66. Courtesy Harriet Beecher Stowe Center.

CHAPTER 2

51 Title page of George Lippard's novel *The Quaker City; or, The Monks of Monk Hall* (1845). Courtesy American Antiquarian Society.

53 Henry Ward Beecher, between 1855 and 1865. Library of Congress.

64 Illustration in George Thompson's novel *Venus in Boston* (1849). Courtesy Boston Public Library.

74 George Lippard. Library of Congress.

CHAPTER 3

91 William Lloyd Garrison. Library of Congress.

105 Josiah Henson. Courtesy Franklin Trask Library, Andover Newton Theological School.

109 Lewis Garrard Clarke, frontispiece of *Narratives of the Sufferings of Lewis and Milton Clarke, Sons of a Soldier of the Revolution, During a Captivity of More Than Twenty Years Among The Slaveholders of Kentucky* (Boston, Mass.: Bela Marsh, 1846). Courtesy New-York Historical Society.

CHAPTER 4

121 Salmon P. Chase. Library of Congress.

121 William Henry Seward. Library of Congress.

127 Title page of *Uncle Tom's Cabin* by Harriet Beecher Stowe, published by John P. Jewett. Courtesy Harriet Beecher Stowe Center.

CHAPTER 5

CHAPTER 6

236 *Uncle Tom's Cabin* (1927 film)—Cassy and Eliza rebel against Legree. Universal Pictures. Courtesy Photofest.

240 Ink-o-Graph Pen ad. Caption: "Uncle Tom & Little Eva awritin'." The Inkograph Co., New York, c. 1945. Courtesy the Clifton Waller Barrett Collection, Special Collections, University of Virginia.

244 Minnie Mouse and Mickey Mouse dancing. *Mickey's Mellerdrammer* (1933). Walt Disney Studios. Courtesy Photofest.

245 Tex Avery's cartoon *Uncle Tom's Cabaña* (1947)—Uncle Tom as Supertom. Metro-Goldwyn-Mayer. Courtesy Photofest.

249 The Duncan Sisters in *Topsy and Eva* (1927 film). United Artists. Courtesy Photofest.

252 Shirley Temple and Bill Robinson performing the stair dance in *The Little Colonel* (1935 film). Twentieth Century Fox. Courtesy Photofest.

269 Domesticity in Africa—Kunta Kinte with his mother and baby brother in *Roots* (1977 ABC miniseries). Courtesy Photofest.

INDEX

Page numbers in *italics* refer to illustrations.
Page numbers beginning with 277 refer to endnotes.